SEASON FINALE

SEASON FINALE

THE UNEXPECTED RISE AND FALL OF THE WB AND UPN

Susanne Daniels and Cynthia Littleton

HARPER

An Imprint of HarperCollins*Publishers*
www.harpercollins.com

HarperCollins books may be purchased for educational, business,
or sales promotional use. For information, please write: Special
Markets Department, HarperCollins Publishers, 10 East 53rd
Street, New York, NY 10022.

FIRST EDITION

Designed by William Ruoto

Library of Congress Cataloging-in-Publication Data is available
upon request.

ISBN: 978-0-06-134099-4
ISBN-10: 0-06-134099-5

07 08 09 10 11   DIX/RRD   10 9 8 7 6 5 4 3 2 1

For Greg
For Tom and Daisy. Zygone.

ACKNOWLEDGMENTS

The authors would like to thank everyone who gave of their time, their scrapbooks and their insights to help us document this dynamic chapter in broadcasting history. The research for this book began on the morning of the WB-UPN merger announcement, January 24, 2006, and involved more than 70 interviews with executives, producers, writers, actors, agents, TV station owners, publicists, and fans of the shows that defined the networks.

Special thanks is owed to those who took the time to help us get it right: J. J. Abrams, Ed Adler, Garth Ancier, Barry Baker, Gail Berman, Bob Bibb, Kevin Brockman, Barbara Brogliatti, Bob Daly, Jonathan Dolgen, Chris Ender, Dennis FitzSimons, Lee Gabler, Steve Goldman, Lew Goldstein, Marna Grantham, Len Grossi, Sandy Grushow, Chris Harbert, David Janollari, Jamie Kellner, Kathleen Letterie, Jordan Levin, Kerry McCluggage, Paul McGuire, Linda McMahon, Barry Meyer, Rusty Mintz, Bonnie Moffet, Leslie Moonves, Gary Newman, Tom Nunan, Dawn Ostroff, Jed Petrick, Hal Protter, Peter Roth, Bruce Rosenblum, Scott Rowe, Lucie Salhany, Amy Sherman-Palladino, Michael Sullivan, Kevin Tannehill, Sarah Timberman, Brad Turell, Dean Valentine, Dana Walden, John Wentworth, Kevin Williamson, and Jim Yeager.

Our deepest gratitude is extended to our editors at HarperCollins, Matt Harper and Cal Morgan, and to Judith Regan for believing that there was a good story to be told in this tale of two networks. Our lawyer, Erik Brown, was also unwavering in his support and scrutiny of our contract's fine print.

For Susanne Daniels, the first person to get thanked is Cynthia Littleton. Her dedication to pursuing this story and her talent in telling it means the world to me.

An extra special thanks goes to Jamie Kellner and Garth Ancier. You are televisionaries, and I am honored to have worked for you. Thank you to Lorne Michaels, Christina McGinniss, and Eric Ellenbogen for starting my career at *Saturday Night Live* and Broadway Video. Thank you Ted Harbert, Gary Levine, and John Hamlin for introducing me to network television at ABC, and thank you to Peter Chernin and Tom Nunan for including me at Fox during a fascinating time in its history.

The biggest thank you of all goes to my incredible family. Haley, Owen, and Charlotte, thank you for always being happy to see me when I get home from work. You all make me unbelievably proud. Judy and Stan Lieberstein (aka Mom and Dad) thank you for your over-abundance of insight, love, and support. You convinced me that I could do anything; having amazing parents is my secret weapon. Paul, Warren, and Angela, there would be no sanity breaks without your precious gifts of time. Judy, Aaron, and Alex, your enthusiasm and optimism help keep me going. And Greg, thank you for listening, endlessly. Thank you for knowing when to make fun and when to let me cry. You write brilliant comedy, but you've given me the greatest love story of all.

For Cynthia Littleton, this book would not have been possible without the love, support, and eternal patience of my husband, Tom Troccoli, and our beautiful daughter, Daisy. My parents, Scott and Mary Ann Littleton, started it all by instilling in me and my sister Leslie a genuine love of reading and writing long before we reached kindergarten.

On a professional level, heartfelt thanks are owed to Howard Burns, Robert J. Dowling, and Nellie Andreeva for allowing me the time and space to report and write these pages. Others who helped make my life easier while working on this book include "Boss" Linda Kaufman, Karl Gibson, Darlene Basch, Kathy Brandon, Emma

Brandon, Jean Desmond, Christine Cathern, Ray Richmond, Claire Hambrick, Peter Bart, Michael Speier, and Kathy Lyford.

Special thanks to Susanne Daniels for casting me as your coauthor in this most ambitious development project.

Finally, I owe a debt of gratitude to Valerie Kuklenski, for teaching a green UPI stringer how to be a good reporter.

CONTENTS

CAST OF CHARACTERS

J. J. Abrams—The film and TV producer whose drama *Felicity* helped make the WB a critical darling.

Garth Ancier—The WB's entertainment president from 1994 to 1998; Ancier had filled the same role for Jamie Kellner a decade earlier at Fox.

Bob Bibb and Lewis Goldstein—The revered heads of marketing for the WB whose evocative and innovative advertising and promotional campaigns were a crucial factor in the network's success.

Bob Daly—The long-serving cochairman and CEO of Warner Bros. who saw that the studio needed its own broadcast network for its TV production operations to survive.

Susanne Daniels—A fledgling number of the WB's creative team, Daniels was a Fox recruit who headed the WB's program development before succeeding Ancier as the network's entertainment president.

Jonathan Dolgen—The chairman and CEO of Viacom Entertainment and Kerry McCluggage's boss.

Dennis FitzSimons—The seasoned station operator and Tribune Broadcasting head who pushed the Chicago-based media conglomerate to align its stations with the WB.

Brenda Hampton—The comedy writer tapped to oversee what would become the WB's longest-running series, family drama *7th Heaven*.

Jamie Kellner—Founder, chairman, and CEO of the WB Network. A linchpin of the team that launched Fox in the 1980s,

Kellner saw an opening for a fifth network and was driven to prove he could do it again with the WB.

Jordan Levin—The right-hand man to Ancier and Daniels whose youthful sensibilities greatly informed the WB's most successful shows. Levin would rise to succeed Daniels as head of programming and serve briefly as the WB's CEO.

John Maatta—The WB's first employee, a lawyer and business strategist who helped establish the network's infrastructure and remained with the WB through its last night on the air.

Kerry McCluggage—Paramount's top-ranking television executive from 1991 to 2001 who pushed the studio to launch UPN and played a critical role during the network's formative years.

Barry Meyer—Daly's veteran lieutenant and ultimate successor at Warner Bros., whose long friendship with Jamie Kellner paved the way for the WB venture.

Leslie Moonves—The charismatic TV executive who led the turnaround of CBS in the mid-1990s and later assumed oversight of UPN from McCluggage.

Tom Nunan—UPN's entertainment chief under Dean Valentine from 1997 to 2001.

Dawn Ostroff—The smart, ambitious programming executive who ran UPN under the direction of CBS's Leslie Moonves for the last four and a half years of UPN's existence.

Jed Petrick—The WB's New York-based head of advertising sales from 1994 to 2001 who effectively marketed the WB's youthful niche to Madison Avenue.

Robert Pittman—The AOL Time Warner copresident whose post-merger reorganization plans had a detrimental effect on the WB.

Sumner Redstone—The chairman of Viacom who inherited the plan to launch UPN when his company bought Paramount Pictures in 1994.

Bruce Rosenblum—Warner Bros.' business whiz who crafted the WB's original business plan with Kellner and supervised the studio's interest in the network for Daly and Meyer.

Peter Roth—The former 20th Century Fox Television executive, who became the Warner Bros.' Television president and brought harmony to the WB's relations with its sister studio.

Lucie Salhany—The firebrand and trailblazer who was recruited as UPN's founding president and CEO.

Amy Sherman-Palladino—The creator and executive producer of the WB's critically praised mother-daughter dramedy *Gilmore Girls*.

William Siegel—The son of Chris-Craft chairman Herbert Siegel who oversaw Chris-Craft's investment in UPN.

Aaron Spelling—The legendary producer whose work involvement with the WB early on gave the network respectability in Hollywood and its first hit, *Savannah*.

Michael Sullivan—The producer and former ABC executive recruited as UPN's first head of programming.

Kevin Tannehill—UPN's head of distribution from 1994 to 1999, he was a syndication sales veteran who did battle with his WB counterparts in the never-ending chase for the strongest TV station affiliates.

Evan Thompson—The Chris-Craft/United TV head who worked closely with Kerry McCluggage in the launch of UPN.

Brad Turell—Head of communications for the WB and a loyal soldier to Jamie Kellner from the Fox era, he expertly manipulated the media spin in the WB-versus-UPN wars and played star-maker to the young actors who populated the network's top shows.

Ted Turner—The major Time Warner shareholder who tried to convince the company's board of directors to shut down the WB and use resources devoted to it for buying an established network or investing in better programming for Turner's TNT and TBS channels.

Dean Valentine—Former Disney and NBC executive and UPN's CEO from 1997 to 2001, after Lucie Salhany stepped down in 1997.

Joss Whedon—The creator of *Buffy the Vampire Slayer*, the dis-

tinctive drama that pointed the WB toward the young audience
that would become its trademark.

Kevin Williamson—The budding screenwriter whose autobiographical coming-of-age drama *Dawson's Creek* fueled the
WB's ascent in the late 1990s.

SEASON
FINALE

ONE FROGGY EVENING

Finally, it was show time: Wednesday, January 11, 1995. The first of two new broadcast television networks, both backed by Hollywood film studios and both slated to launch that month, was less than an hour away from stumbling on the air with a show so bad it made executives cringe.

It was pouring rain in Los Angeles that evening as I and a few dozen other staffers of the fledgling WB Television Network gathered for the network's premiere party at Chasen's, the famed West Hollywood restaurant that was a hangout to moguls and movie stars. The affair was deliberately low-key, as envisioned by Jamie Kellner, the WB's coolly charismatic founder and chief executive officer. Kellner reasoned that the WB was still very much a work in progress; it needed time to experiment a little before putting the hard sell on the American public. This he knew instinctively from his many years in network television and program sales.

As Kellner sat in one of Chasen's red-leather upholstered booths that night, celebrating with young WB staffers and respected senior executives from Warner Bros. and the Tribune Company—the two media giants backing his latest venture, he was ready to celebrate the prospect of ushering in the start of the "fifth network" era in American television. But I was extremely anxious. I had been fortunate enough to play a role in this story as the WB's head of program development.

Six months earlier, I had been plucked from the middle-executive ranks at Fox to work shoulder to shoulder on the construction of the network with Kellner and his hand-picked head of entertainment,

Garth Ancier. Kellner and Ancier had been cornerstones of the executive team that prevailed against all odds and launched the Fox network for Barry Diller and Rupert Murdoch a decade before. Now, here I was squeezing into a booth with my energetic new WB colleagues to toast the arrival of Jamie Kellner's next network. I was 29 years old, and while I'd already had my share of breaks in show business—like landing a job as an assistant to *Saturday Night Live* creator Lorne Michaels fresh out of college—this scene was something new altogether.

The surreal feeling of the WB's premiere night was underscored for all of us by the sight of a man wearing a giant frog suit, top hat, and cane. He was greeting partygoers as they walked into Chasen's. The suit was a poor representation of the WB's crooning cartoon mascot, Michigan J. Frog, who was chosen as a nod to the studio's Looney Tunes legacy. As guests filtered into Chasen's wood-paneled main dining room, they were met by a clutch of bleary-eyed executives who were excited but exhausted from running at full throttle for more than six months in preparation for this night. We watched in admiration as Kellner enthusiastically shook hands and took in a stream of congratulations and attaboys for defying the naysayers and "actually getting on the air," as more than one person put it.

Kellner and Co. had spent the morning of WB's launch night taking part in a photo-op event staged on Warner Bros.' famed studio lot in Burbank. On a cold and rainy January morning, an outdoor media event turned out to be less than a home run. Jim Yeager, the WB's first head of publicity, had the idea to make a "rare" adjustment to the studio's landmark 135-foot water tower. It's a beacon of filmdom visible from most places in Burbank and from the freeway that runs near one edge of the 110-acre lot. Knowing the network's association with its parent studio was an important selling point for the start-up venture, Yeager arranged to have a giant stand-up cutout of Michigan J. Frog affixed to the top of the water tower next to the mighty Warner Bros.' shield logo, recognized as a trademark of quality since the days of *42nd Street* and *Casablanca*.

The stunt drew a respectable number of cameras and reporters that morning, and standing there at the base of the water tower, the crowd watched as studio grounds workers tried to pull back the drape that was hiding the revamped icon. The ceremony, however, did not go quite as planned. The cloth covering the Michigan J. Frog figure got stuck, and by the time they were able to pull it down, the cutout frog was off-kilter. It wasn't the image we wanted to project. A group of us wound up shivering outside in a light drizzle, trying to act cheerful and unconcerned about the gaffe that unfolded in front of the cameras. Yeager got an earful from Ancier later in private, one of many such encounters that spurred his departure before the end of the WB's first year on the air.

That evening, the rain was steady and heavy—the kind of soaking that turns Los Angeles' streets into gridlocked flood zones. The WB's partygoers were soggy and flustered by the time they gathered amid Chasen's green awnings and 1950s-era interior for the launch party. The choice of Chasen's for the party seemed an odd juxtaposition—a fading old-Hollywood haunt meets a new-paradigm television network. Thanks to the weather, the restaurant smelled of dampness; it would close for good six months later.

Time Warner's Chairman and CEO, Gerald Levin, made a special trip from New York to attend the premiere party. Warner Bros.' Cochairmen Bob Daly and Terry Semel were there to show their support. Also in attendance were the two executives responsible for pushing the studio into the broadcasting business, chief operating officer Barry Meyer and television strategy whiz Bruce Rosenblum. Leslie Moonves, the charismatic head of the Warner Bros.' Television production division, also made a point of attending. At that moment, the career of Moonves was riding high; he had just unleashed two huge hits—*ER* and *Friends*—on NBC a few months earlier.

Moonves was striving to be a team player by showing up for the launch party. He'd been upset by the way the WB came together in secret among Barry Meyer, Jamie Kellner, and a few other Warner Bros.' executives during the summer of 1993. He felt undeservedly snubbed by having been kept out of the loop, and he was not happy that neither Kellner nor the network reported to him within the Warner Bros.' hierarchy. Moonves figured that if his division was expected to supply the bulk of the network's shows, he ought to be able to at least have a say in how the network was run. But Kellner was not about to let Moonves into the tent. During his time with Fox, Kellner had earned his credentials as a network builder. This time around, Kellner intended to be an owner, not an employee, of his new venture. He would report to Meyer, not Moonves.

Inside Chasen's that night, there was plenty of exulting and cheerleading from a team that had slogged through months of planning and tedious labor on contracts, personnel issues, leases for everything from copier machines to satellite time for beaming the network's shows out to its affiliate stations. A handful of people in the room, including Kellner, Warner Bros.' Bruce Rosenblum, and the WB's General Counsel, John Maatta, had been working nonstop on the network for a grueling year and a half.

Although it wasn't stated so plainly in the toasts that evening, everyone in the room knew that the WB would succeed or fail based on the strength of its programming. Distribution to strong television stations around the country was vital, but it ultimately wouldn't matter unless the WB offered something that a distinct audience, even a narrowly defined audience, wanted to watch. The network couldn't afford to mount a major national marketing campaign to promote its launch, so it had to slip quietly onto the air, entering as a work-in-progress with hastily thrown together programs and an experimental, see-which-way-the-wind-blows attitude. Nobody understood the importance of the WB being quick and nimble in finding its niche on the prime-time landscape better than Jamie Kellner.

Kellner beamed and even choked up for a moment late in the afternoon of the launch, as he and others watched the feed of the WB Eastern time-zone premiere in the network's conference room. A few hours later, the drinks were flowing at Chasen's as the big moment arrived on the West Coast. Any keen-eyed observer would have seen the trepidation—and the occasional wince—on some faces in the room as the first program unspooled. Nobody showed it more than me and Jordan Levin, our 27-year-old executive in charge of comedy program development, with whom I'd formed a fast friendship during the whirlwind of the past four months.

WB set sail at 8 p.m. with *The Wayans Bros.*, a half-hour comedy series starring Shawn and Marlon Wayans, younger members of the acting Wayans clan. A year before, a similar "Wayans Show" had been rejected by NBC. During the late summer of 1994, the WB wound up resuscitating it in our desperate scramble to find original shows in time for the January 11 launch date. Under those circumstances, we had to make do with the best material we could find in a short amount of time. And though they were raw, it was clear to anyone who understood comedy that brothers Shawn and Marlon were destined for long careers.

Applause broke out as the first flicker of the network feed on Tribune-owned KTLA-TV Los Angeles popped up on the TV sets scattered throughout Chasen's. The opening was a mix of live action and animation, featuring Bugs Bunny and Daffy Duck on a soundstage arguing over who should be the new network's on-air mascot. That scene cut to a shot of legendary animator Chuck Jones sitting at an easel drawing his high-spirited creation, Michigan J. Frog, who leaps from the easel as Jones finishes his sketch. Michigan J. then flicks a cartoon-size switch to launch the network and segue into *The Wayans Bros.* The episode was entitled "Goop, Hair It Is." It built to a climax, when guest star Gary Coleman's hair caught fire.

"I remember looking at Bob Daly's and Terry Semel's faces," Jordan Levin says. "And it was like someone had opened up an awful, smelly piece of cheese. It just looked like it was over before it began."

The party broke up about an hour after the network signed off at 10 p.m. Semel made a point of seeking out Kellner on his way out the door. Semel's show business roots were on the film side of the business, unlike his cochairman partner at Warner Bros., Bob Daly, who spent 25 years at CBS before he joined Warner Bros.

Semel gave Kellner a quizzical look as the two shook hands. "Very nice . . . very nice," Semel told Kellner. "I don't think I understand the television business."

• • •

There was no such low-key launch strategy for UPN. The opening night of the United Paramount Network on Monday, January 16, five nights after the WB's debut, was heralded with klieg lights and red carpets at simultaneous launch parties in New York and Los Angeles. UPN's calling card was its promise to deliver a new *Star Trek* series at a time when the 1960s space-opera franchise Gene Roddenberry had created for NBC was enjoying a renaissance. Paramount Pictures, UPN's studio backer, had expertly capitalized on the success of its *Star Trek* feature films from the 1980s by launching the TV series *Star Trek: The Next Generation* in 1987 and *Star Trek: Deep Space Nine* in 1993. The next incarnation of the show would become the centerpiece of Paramount's broadcast network.

The lure of a new *Star Trek* edition, this one with a female captain at the helm of the ship, generated a torrent of free media for the new network, far more than the WB had garnered when it bowed onto the scene. This press attention contributed to the swagger that UPN had at the outset, a stance that also reflected the nature of its founding president and CEO, Lucie Salhany, another former Fox executive.

Salhany's team at UPN had gone through the same chaotic prelaunch phase as their WB counterparts, but they were cocky in a way that WB executives could not be. On the big night, UPN's two-person public relations team spearheaded simultaneous events in New York City and Hollywood. The New York party packed a few hundred advertisers, station executives, and other media and business types into the Roundabout Theater to screen the two-hour *Star Trek: Voyager* premiere. The bash on the Paramount studio lot in Hollywood had all the trimmings of a Hollywood blockbuster premiere, except that it was something more momentous for the studio, something Paramount had flirted with on and off for years: the launch of its own broadcast network.

Of course, the bolder the effort, the greater the chance that the fledgling enterprise might fall flat on its face. For the New York event, the plan was to run the *Voyager* premiere around 6 p.m., in advance of the network's formal sign-on on WWOR-TV in New York at 8 p.m. Eastern time. That meant a high-quality videotape dub of the premiere episode had to be sent to New York in advance.

Around midday West Coast time on January 16, as network staffers and event planners were scrambling to finish preparations for the party on the lot that night, one of the event staffers went looking for the envelope with the dubs of the two-hour *Voyager* premiere episode that was supposed to screen during the Hollywood party. When the envelope was found, there were two sets of *Voyager* tapes inside. UPN's energetic young head of publicity, Kevin Brockman, thought he was going to be ill when he realized what had happened. One of the *Voyager* dubs was supposed to be at the Roundabout Theater for the screening at the New York party. Brockman sprinted from the soundstage where the party was to be held, across the lot, and back to his office.

"I thought I was going to throw up because, here you have the launch of a network and no way of showing the program at its New York premiere," Brockman recalls.

By this time, most UPN staffers were running on fumes, caffeine, and the fear of disappointing Salhany, who was a notoriously demanding boss. In the weeks leading up to the launch, most of them worked nonstop—literally—for days on end. One new mother in the group had her husband bring her infant son to the studio every night so she could kiss him goodnight.

As he gathered his wits, Brockman and others consulted with the studio technicians, who rigged a solution that amounted to the broadcasting equivalent of scotch tape and paper clips. Shortly after 4 p.m. in New York, they determined that Paramount could beam via satellite the two-hour *Voyager* episode in 20-minute increments to a satellite reception facility at Manhattan's Empire State Building. Those feeds were then dubbed onto videotapes and hand-delivered to the Roundabout. The satellite station was still receiving *Voyager* feeds from the West Coast when partygoers began filing into the New York event.

Kevin Tannehill, the network's head of distribution, had been chosen to serve as master of ceremonies and to represent the network at the New York party; Salhany and other senior executives involved with UPN had stayed in Hollywood. So it was Tannehill who got a nervous tap on his shoulder from one of the New York event organizers just as guests started to arrive in large numbers. When Tannehill turned around, the frantic-looking event producer was asking him to kill time so they could make sure the last increment of the *Voyager* episode had arrived before starting the screening—just in case.

Until that moment, Tannehill's only worry had been not tripping on his tongue at the microphone when he introduced the special guests, including Herbert Siegel, the chairman of Chris-Craft Industries, which was bankrolling the network in partnership with Paramount, and Sumner Redstone, chairman of Viacom, which acquired Paramount in early 1994. Now Tannehill was being told to stall for 20 minutes. He had to work hard to contain his sense of panic. "I'm not Jerry Seinfeld," he says.

Tannehill wound up giving the crowd the pitch for the network anchored by *Star Trek: Voyager,* the same spiel he'd been delivering ad nauseum to TV station owners around the country for the past 10 months. After what seemed like an eternity, he got the all-clear signal from the stage manager. Fifteen minutes later, as the episode was under way, Tannehill felt another urgent poke at his back. The episode was running longer than they'd projected, and it would not end before UPN's 8 p.m. sign-on on Chris-Craft's WWOR-TV New York, which was also carried on the JumboTron screen in Times Square that night.

By this time, Tannehill was exasperated enough to make what he recalls as "a command decision": they would stop the film 10 minutes before 8 p.m. and wheel out a giant button to count down to the on-air launch.

"In the episode they are having this gigantic, intergalactic battle. Spaceships are blowing up, photon torpedoes are flying, and the special effects are going off. And all of a sudden, EEERRRGGG—it stops. Lights come up, everyone's going, 'What's wrong? What happened?' " Tannehill says.

On cue, a big red button was wheeled onto the stage. To Tannehill, it looked like a portable refrigerator draped in red plastic sheeting. He initiated a countdown, and then Redstone, Siegel, Tannehill, and a handful of others were all smiles as they leaned clumsily against the button. UPN and WWOR logos flashed on the giant screen exactly at 8 p.m. After the applause died down, the episode picked up where it had left off, without much comment from the crowd.

Later that night as the party cleared out, Tannehill was standing in the rear of the auditorium, taking in the scene and still catching his breath from dodging a bullet on opening night. Redstone and Siegel, who were both in their early 70s at the time, sauntered by as they were leaving.

"I think that went rather well, don't you?" Redstone said to Siegel.

Television is an unpredictable business, as I and my former colleagues at the WB and UPN can attest.

The morning after UPN's big launch party, when the spectacular ratings for the *Star Trek: Voyager* premiere were staring us in the face, the WB team was despondent. Our premiere-night numbers had barely registered on the national radar. UPN's premiere had been impressive by any network's standards. Publicly, we kept up a brave face and were encouraged by Jamie Kellner's unflagging faith that we would build the WB into a big success. But privately, a bunch of us at the WB looked at the glitzy premiere-party photos of UPN's New York and Hollywood launch events and compared them with the faded red-leather booths and the big-headed Michigan J. Frog guy at Chasen's. We had a hard time suppressing our doubts.

Nevertheless, within five years the WB would field a string of hits and come to dwarf UPN in ratings, advertising revenue, and the intangible asset of pop-culture buzz. Kellner steered his young, hungry management team like the captain of a swift schooner, and for six heady go-go years, the WB caught the wind. Kellner's success with the WB brought him his fondest wishes as an executive: recognition and riches; both, he felt, had been denied him during his Fox tenure. He was a patriarchal, enigmatic figure among the WB's tight-knit staff.

By the time we had our roster of successful signature drama series, from *Buffy the Vampire Slayer* to *7th Heaven*, and *Dawson's Creek* to *Smallville*, I thought we'd made it. I thought we could legitimately call ourselves the fifth network. We were the alternative to the big boys. We were hip and cool and seeding the industry with hot young stars, from showrunner auteurs like Joss Whedon and J. J. Abrams to starlets the caliber of Sarah Michelle Gellar, Katie Holmes, Keri Russell, and Michelle Williams. We were television's future.

UPN, on the other hand, was nearly done in by management dysfunction between Paramount and its partner, television station group owner Chris-Craft Industries, that began even before the network went on the air. Despite their stronger opening night, there was precious little trust between the partners. As the WB took flight, UPN's performance descended from bad to worse.

And yet, the old cliché about network television being a cyclical business happens to be true. Just a few years after the WB's peak, on the morning of Tuesday, January 24, 2006, the corporate heads of the network dropped a bombshell: UPN, our rival, the outfit we had been battling for more than a decade, would merge with the WB to form a single new network, the CW. The announcement, which came as a shock to most employees at both networks, signaled many things to the entertainment industry, but perhaps most dramatically, it heralded the end of an era in broadcast television. Since the inception of commercial television in the 1940s, broadcast networks had been the dominant form of TV in the marketplace. Yet with the rapid growth of cable during the 1980s and 1990s and the swift expansion of the Internet, suddenly the notion of the traditional broadcast model was becoming quaint and outdated. By the time we hit critical mass at the WB, the race to be the fifth network was irrelevant to our target demographic: viewers born MTV A.D., i.e., after 1981, who grew up with 30–40 channels on every cable box instead of merely three or four big broadcast networks.

UPN and the WB arrived the same year that Netscape ignited the era of the Internet and "irrational exuberance" over its market-dazzling IPO. This exuberance would continue for the first half of UPN and the WB's existence, and both would benefit from the insulation provided to their parent companies by the stock market boom of the late 1990s. During their 12-year lifespans, both networks would be buffeted by megamergers in the media and entertainment sector. As everyone tried to discern what role the Internet would play in conventional media's future, questions began to emerge about traditional television and whether its business model makes sense in the digital age. In hindsight, Warner Bros. and Paramount placed big bets on broadcast TV just as media began to move, in fits and starts, to broadband. With the dawn of the CW, it seems clear that the WB and UPN comprise the last chapter in the storied history of broadcast television.

For the entertainment industry, the rise and fall of the WB and UPN provide an important case study for examining a transformative period in the behind-the-scenes business of television. It is a story of the interconnected, sometimes incestuous, nature of the entertainment industry, and the risks that exist in a world where government regulation, politics, entertainment, celebrity, and egos all combine to become the driving force behind success and failure. It is a story of the limits of foresight that occur at the intersection of entertainment and technology, and the risks that these limits hold for media corporations in the present and future.

With the perspective that only comes from a little time and distance, it's apparent the WB and UPN were both the symptom and the byproduct of an industry in transition as well as a broader business environment gone bananas in the 1990s. Still, when the news broke on that Tuesday morning that the WB and UPN would merge, it was heartbreaking for me and many other WB alumni. Intellectually, we knew it made perfect sense for both networks, and by then things were so dire for the WB that it was the only way to preserve any part of what we had given so much of ourselves to build. But emotionally, it was hard, almost baffling news to absorb. I couldn't stop thinking about the heights we'd attained.

"It's a tragedy," a former colleague insisted to me during a phone conversation shortly after the news broke. By then, thoughts of my WB days had summoned memories that ran the gamut from hilarious to hysterical, painful to embarrassing.

The more I thought about it, the more I realized that the great tragedy that killed the WB had actually taken place nearly five years earlier. "When we let our baby go to UPN," I replied with a mixture of anger and sadness, "it was as if we'd surrendered right then." The news that came on January 24, 2006, was merely the formal announcement.

CHAPTER ONE

VOYAGERS

During the summer of 1993, nobody who worked in the main executive office building on the sprawling Warner Bros.' studio lot in Burbank, California, could figure out why Jamie Kellner was spending so much time in Barry Meyer's office. Kellner was barely six months removed from his resignation as president and chief operating officer of Fox Broadcasting Company. Meyer was the chief operating officer of one of Hollywood's largest studios and the executive responsible for overseeing Warner Bros.' vast television production operation. The two had become close friends a few years earlier by prospering together in a programming deal between Fox and Warner Bros.

Kellner had turned to Meyer for help when he wanted to push forward with what had become a pet project during his final years at Fox. He wanted to see the network expand its Fox-branded footprint into morning and afternoon time periods with children's programming. Kellner proposed to Meyer a wide-ranging production deal that called for Warner Bros. to draw on its trove of cartoon characters to produce several new series in the classic Looney Tunes zany, gag-driven style.

Fueled by shows like *Tiny Toon Adventures* and *Taz-Mania,* the Fox Children's Network debuted in 1990 with morning and afternoon program blocks that quickly became a cash cow for the network and its affiliates. Warner Bros. made a profit on producing the shows for Fox, and it made still more money—much more, in some instances—from selling T-shirts, lunchboxes, calendars, and all sorts of other licensing and merchandising. It was found money derived from intellectual property assets that had been gathering dust in the studio's vault for decades.

Kellner and Meyer also hit it off on a personal level despite their different temperaments. Jamie is a born salesman and bold entrepreneur; Barry is a lawyer and a gentleman who is respected as a highly effective manager. The two moved in the same business circles, and they enjoyed conversing about the entertainment business and debating about where it was all headed next. Given their friendship, Meyer was not particularly surprised to get a call from Kellner one day in early June 1993. When Meyer picked up, it was clear from the crackle of the connection that Kellner was calling from a car phone. Their exchange was brief, but it piqued Meyer's interest.

Kellner asked Meyer if he would be interested in meeting to talk over a new network venture he was considering. Meyer didn't hesitate in his reply. He respected his friend enough to know that he needed to take the meeting. At that moment Kellner was on his way to catch a flight to New York to visit his brother, Tom, on Long Island. He was pleased that Meyer hadn't paused when he'd said "network." The launch of a broadcast network was not for the faint of heart, as Kellner knew from experience. He would spend the next few days sitting on a beach with a yellow legal pad propped up on his knees, sketching out his "fifth network" presentation to Warner Bros.

A man of medium height, sandy brown hair, cut short and preppy, and penetrating blue eyes, Kellner sported a boyish grin just beneath his otherwise steely exterior. He had a nervous habit of twirling a quarter in his fingers when he was deep in thought. Early on in the summer of 1993, he kept the quarters spinning as he and Meyer had long talks about the state of the television business and the monumental changes that were then looming. The entertainment industry was being forced to come to grips with a deregulatory juggernaut in Washington, D.C., that would span the decade, the growth of cable as a mainstream competitive force, and the audience fragmentation it spurred. With more channel choices than ever pouring into the average American living room, ABC, CBS, and NBC couldn't help but lose audience share to Fox and myriad cable upstarts.

It was the confluence of these forces that spurred Kellner to pick up the phone to call Meyer when he did. But according to the WB's founder, there was no more powerful motivator than the visit he paid to his former coworkers at Fox in May 1993, as the 1992–93 television season drew to a close. About five months had passed since his resignation, and Kellner, by his own account, was dismayed by what he found. Most of his closest former coworkers at Fox were either unhappy, insecure in their jobs, burned out, or all three. After laying low at his home in bucolic Montecito, California, Kellner had forgotten, at least a little bit, how cutthroat the environment at the network could be.

Kellner pulled out of his VIP visitor's parking spot and out of the 20th Century Fox studio gate in West Los Angeles that day feeling sad. The people who had slaved in the early days to build Fox, against all odds and a Greek chorus of naysayers, were not getting the chance to enjoy the fruits of their labor. Many of them, himself included, had left on less than happy terms. As much as he tried to take it easy in the months after his resignation, Kellner couldn't turn off his entrepreneurial gene. He couldn't stop thinking about the potential opportunity for a start-up broadcast network aimed at a younger audience—like Fox in its early days.

"I began to wonder if I could create a network where we could have fun, an environment where the people who built it could then enjoy it," Kellner says. "That sounds a bit idealistic, but that's what I had in my head."

When Kellner decided to act on his impulse, Warner Bros. was his first choice for a partner. On top of his close relationship with Meyer, Kellner knew Warner Bros.' chieftain Bob Daly from their respective tenures at CBS in the early 1970s, when Daly was rising through the senior management ranks and Kellner was emerging as a business and marketing whiz. Kellner respected Daly and Meyer, and he believed they would trust him to run the network his way. Warner Bros. had a well-established reputation for nurturing mavericks, whether they were directors, actors, musicians, or executives.

Kellner wasn't surprised at how receptive Meyer seemed to be to the idea of Warner Bros. backing a new broadcast television network. It was no secret to industry insiders at the time that Warner Bros. was concerned about its long-term future in television production. The changes coming out of Washington's regulatory agencies and the federal courts were ominous for Hollywood's old guard as it became clear that a massive shift in public policy and regulation regarding media was underway. During the 1980s and early 1990s, Daly led the public policy and public opinion fight for the major studios, which were trying to combat the major TV networks' efforts to kill a set of Federal Communications Commission rules that ABC, CBS, and NBC viewed as onerous. But by 1993, it was quickly becoming apparent that Daly had a losing battle on his hands.

After the formative discussions about the network in Barry Meyer's office, Jamie Kellner holed up in a tiny conference room under a staircase in the executive building, where he worked closely with a rising-star business affairs executive, Bruce Rosenblum. They tucked themselves away as discreetly as possible for a reason. Meyer wanted to keep the project under the radar, even among studio insiders, while Kellner and Rosenblum did their due diligence.

Kellner and Rosenblum spent weeks researching and analyzing reams of ratings data, advertising figures, and television schedules in local markets around the country. It was clear to their curious colleagues that the two were crunching the numbers on a new venture. Because of Kellner's background, Warner Bros.' insiders figured it involved some kind of network. Rosenblum's role in the creation of the WB was one of the achievements that moved him up the senior management ranks at Warner Bros. in the 1990s. A bookish Southern California native, Rosenblum impressed Meyer and Daly with his approach to working with Kellner that summer on developing the complex business plan. Not that he had much choice. He was handed the high-priority assignment just as his boss was heading out of the country on a European vacation.

"Jamie wants to start a fifth network," Meyer instructed Rosenblum. "Sit with him for two weeks; work on a business model, and present it to me and Bob when I get back."

And so they did. Meyer was encouraged by what Kellner and Rosenblum presented him upon his return. It struck him as something that was at once a bold strategic move for a new era and a throwback. The cutting edge of the entertainment industry at that time was cable. Cable channels had the benefit of generating revenue from advertising sales and from fees paid by cable operators to carry their channels. Broadcast TV was seen as old-fashioned technology.

"There was a feeling that this was something that was kind of low-tech. This wasn't the latest kind of television network model that everyone was talking about," Meyer says. "But we saw that broadcast TV was still the only way we could reach a mass of viewers to support the kind of (high-end) programming that we were accustomed to making."

Bob Daly was a tougher sell than Time Warner chairman Gerald Levin, Meyer recalls, because Daly knew so much about the broadcasting business from his years at CBS.

"Bob knew how tough it was going to be to put together," Meyer says. "To Jerry, it sounded great—something new and interesting. He was all for it."

When Daly and Levin were on board, it seemed that the network actually had a chance to get off the ground. A month after Daly and Levin gave their OKs, another well-regarded Warner Bros.' Television executive, John Maatta, joined Kellner and Rosenblum and their assistants in their cramped quarters on the first floor of the executive building. Together, the small group worked on the finer points of the business plan.

As the summer drew to a close, Daly and Terry Semel, Meyer, and Kellner convened a meeting of high-level studio executives to discuss the network venture. The idea was met with more than a little skepticism from the assembled managers, but Daly and Meyer were steadfast: Warner Bros. needed to launch its own broadcast network for the sake of its long-term future in television production. Daly was convinced that Jamie Kellner was the guy they needed to get a network off the ground. The Warner Bros.' boss believed in Kellner so much he agreed to grant Kellner an 11 percent ownership stake in the network, a portion of which Kellner would later share with a handful of key lieutenants.

"I gave Jamie a piece of the WB because that's the only way I could get him," Daly says. "I also felt that we'd own 89 percent, and he'd kill for the 11 percent, and therefore we would become very successful."

Long before Kellner proved him right, the conviction Daly showed in a sun-drenched conference room was enough to reassure the executives. Daly knew what it would take to make a go of a network, the executives reasoned.

"Bob was very matter-of-fact about it: it was, 'OK, we're going to put together this network,' " recalls one participant.

With Kellner now in the Warner Bros.' fold, the plan of attack appeared to be so cut-and-dried. It would prove to be anything but.

Warner Bros.' top brass felt the urgency to birth their own network because they believed it was nothing less than a strategic imperative, vital to ensuring a bright future for its industry-leading television production division. The Warner Bros.' parent company, Time Warner, employed enough lobbyists in Washington for the studio managers in Burbank to know by early 1993 that the rules of engagement in Hollywood were about to change. Big time.

By the end of 1992, it was clear that a set of federal regulations that had strictly governed business dealings between Hollywood's major studios and ABC, CBS, and NBC since the early 1970s were about to be repealed for good. Since the early 1970s, the Federal Communications Commission's so-called financial interest and syndication rule had barred the Big Three networks from being major players in television production and syndication by placing strict limits on the amount of programming they could own and produce themselves. The rule, which became known in industry shorthand as "fin-syn," ensured that the Big Three networks had to go outside of their own walls to a Hollywood studio or independent producers for the bulk of their programming.

Daly knew the mentality of network executives. He had been at CBS in 1970 when the FCC voted in the original rule on financial interest and syndication, and when it was upheld seven years later in the form of consent decrees that ABC, CBS, and NBC signed with the Justice Department. Having witnessed the implementation of fin-syn, he knew the impact its reversal would have on the production of prime-time programming for the Big Three: once the networks' hands were no longer tied by the FCC, the market for programming would turn into the Wild West.

Hollywood's top studios and producers put up a good fight to save fin-syn. Daly, along with Hollywood's chief lobbyist, Jack Valenti, chaired the Coalition to Preserve the Financial Interest and Syndication Rule, a clutch of entertainment companies that had hundreds of millions of dollars in annual profits at stake if they lost the opportunity to produce shows for ABC, CBS, and NBC. As hard as they fought, Daly was savvy enough to see, based on the evidence coming out of the FCC and the federal courts, that repeal was inevitable. Daly tried to stall as long as possible by promoting the idea of an industry-backed "private solution," or a compromise agreement between the networks and studios to avert legislative action.

"I negotiated forever and a day. It was the first time I ever really negotiated where it was important to drag it on as long as I could," Daly says. "Because I came from CBS, from before there was a fin-syn, I knew what you could do as a network when there was no government to tell you what to do." Before fin-syn, networks routinely demanded that producers hand over a percentage of a show's long-term profits as a condition of getting on the air.

In the late 1960s, the campaign to enact fin-syn was initiated, quietly and effectively, by Hollywood rainmaker Lew Wasserman, who created one of the first integrated media conglomerates in the early 1960s with MCA/Universal. Wasserman leaned on his close ties with President Lyndon B. Johnson to push the regulatory initiative that would protect Universal's bustling television division at a time when it was the supplier of virtually every entertainment program on NBC's prime-time schedule.

Naturally, the networks hated having to suddenly play by government-imposed rules. ABC, CBS, and NBC were forced to divest themselves of their production and syndication operations. CBS's forced sale of its vast library, stocked with hits including *I Love Lucy*, begat a separate program distribution entity dubbed Viacom, which would grow into an industry powerhouse. One of the CBS executives to make the transition to Viacom was a young Jamie Kellner.

Lobbyists and lawyers for the Big Three sought to slay the fin-syn rule on and off for 15 years, but it was untouchable. Prominent independent producers like Aaron Spelling and Stephen J. Cannell were ready to bear witness before Congress, the FCC, and anyone else who would listen that the end of fin-syn would spell the end of their lives as small businessmen (which turned out to be true). Fin-syn even survived the deregulatory zeal of the Reagan administration in its first term. It was widely noted that Reagan's former Hollywood talent agent, MCA/Universal's Wasserman, made a personal appeal to the president in the White House to preserve the rules. Tongues wagged that leaving fin-syn intact was a gift from an old studio contract player to the town that gave him his start.

By the early 1990s, ABC, CBS, and NBC's battle to end fin-syn turned into a crusade when it became clear that Fox founder Rupert Murdoch was poised to reap untold riches from his gutsy gamble on a fourth network. Murdoch, his network competitors howled, had been given a host of special favors in Washington that allowed him to build his Fox empire in ways that ABC, CBS, and NBC could not. Murdoch made his big entrance onto the U.S. media scene in the mid-1980s with his purchase of a 50 percent share—soon to be 100 percent—of the then-ailing 20th Century Fox film studio. By the end of 1985, Murdoch had struck a deal to buy six top-market TV stations from billionaire John Kluge's Metromedia. The following year, Murdoch and 20th Century Fox Chairman Barry Diller embarked on their effort to launch a network with the aid of a sibling studio operation, which would supply much of the programming.

Murdoch's News Corporation ultimately received the FCC's blessing to produce and own much of the programming on Fox Broadcasting Co. through the 20th Century Fox studio operation. The commission decided that Fox had not yet reached the threshold of major network status where the fin-syn rule would apply. The FCC's rationale was that giving Murdoch a few breaks early on would be well worth it in the long run—if he succeeded in establishing a full-fledged competitor to the Big Three.

At the same time the multichannel cable revolution was taking root. MTV, CNN, ESPN, USA Network, Nickelodeon, TNT, Lifetime Television, and a host of other cable channels had become commonplace in America's living rooms after the rapid growth of cable's availability to television households. The Big Three turned up the heat on the fin-syn fight by arguing, in court and elsewhere, that they could no longer keep pace with their new broadcast and cable competitors under anachronistic FCC regulations. The FCC voted to loosen the fin-syn rules in 1991 with a convoluted proposal to give the networks some flexibility to produce a limited number of programs, but that decision was also challenged in court by ABC, CBS, and NBC.

In late 1992, a three-judge panel of the U.S. Court of Appeals for the Seventh Circuit remanded the revised fin-syn rules to the Federal Communications Commission. The judges gave the commission 120 days to come up with an acceptable legal rationale for maintaining the fin-syn status quo; otherwise, they'd have to revise the rules significantly. A year later, a federal court judge in Los Angeles issued a ruling that effectively overturned the consent decrees that had governed fin-syn since the 1970s.

"Certainly in 1993 with the entry of the Fox network, the substantial rise in the number of program producers, the dramatic increase in cable television stations, and the development in the sophistication of VCRs, the competitive climate today would unfairly penalize NBC, ABC, and CBS in the financing and syndication of off-network programming," U.S. District Court Judge Manuel Real wrote in his 10-page decision issued in November 1993.

By this time the commission was already chipping away at what had been the law of the land for networks and studios for nearly 25 years. The FCC's convoluted modifications to the rule only made the Big Three press harder to kill it off entirely. The legislative funeral for fin-syn was held on February 8, 1996, when President Bill Clinton signed the landmark Telecommunications Reform Act of 1996. After a decade of jousting and jockeying among media and entertainment firms, telephone giants, high-tech firms, consumer electronics manufacturers, and a host of other constituencies, the bill cemented the most sweeping changes to the nation's media and telecommunications law in more than 60 years by repealing fin-syn and other regulations, in a way that redefined the landscape of the media and communications industries.

Amid the regulatory upheaval, Bob Daly and Barry Meyer were increasingly convinced that Warner Bros. needed to take a cue from Rupert Murdoch and 20th Century Fox. Across town in Hollywood, executives at Paramount Pictures had been thinking the same way for some time. Launching a broadcast network was at the top of the 10-point strategic plan that Paramount Television Group chief Kerry McCluggage had drawn up after he arrived at Paramount in 1991 following a long run at Universal Television.

McCluggage had a reputation as a boy-wonder development executive during his 13 years at Universal. He famously became the youngest vice president in Universal Television's history at age 25. He was closely involved with a string of high-octane 1980s hits like *The A-Team*, *Miami Vice*, *Knight Rider*, *Quantum Leap,* and he helped shepherd the original *Law & Order* onto the air in his final year at the studio. During this time, McCluggage enjoyed a particularly close relationship with NBC's programming chief, Brandon Tartikoff. When Tartikoff left NBC to become chairman of Paramount Pictures in mid-1991, it came as no surprise to Hollywood insiders when McCluggage followed him to Paramount's Melrose Avenue lot. Tartikoff's tenure at Paramount did not last—he resigned after a little more than a year on the job—but McCluggage's did. He remained the studio's top television executive for 10 years.

Just as McCluggage was settling in at Paramount, he felt the same chill in the business climate that Meyer and Daly felt at Warner Bros. McCluggage wanted Paramount to create its own studio-branded broadcast network as a hedge against a grim future of closed doors at ABC, CBS, and NBC.

"We really felt that the studios that did not have their own distribution outlet would get leveraged in the marketplace by networks demanding ownership in the programming as kind of the price of admission for access to their schedule. And that pretty much played out," McCluggage says. "There was the battle about the financial interest and syndication rules, in which everybody said these bad things are going to happen. . . . But Congress, and for that matter the American public, really didn't care. They felt it was just a bunch of rich kids fighting over the last dime on the table."

Despite McCluggage's foresight, it took the galvanizing force of the threat of a competitor beating the studio to the fifth-network punch to prompt Paramount to act on its strategic plan and get serious about launching a network. When they got wind of Warner Bros.' plans, McCluggage and his top executives scrambled that summer to schedule meetings with key station owners. Though Warner Bros. had a lethal weapon in Jamie Kellner and its vast TV production operation, Paramount had its own armor: a billion-dollar asset called *Star Trek*. At the time, Paramount's *Star Trek: The Next Generation* and *Star Trek: Deep Space Nine* were among the most popular drama series in primetime. Fox and NBC had separately made big-money offers to Paramount to secure a *Star Trek* show, but Paramount had rightly figured it would make more money—from day one—by selling the show market-by-market to the highest TV station bidder in syndication, a form of television distribution more common to talk shows and game shows than high-end sci-fi dramas. But Paramount's gamble paid off handsomely.

McCluggage had another strategic reason for investing in a Paramount-branded network: Over the past few years, the studio had been acquiring affiliate stations in sizable urban markets like Boston, Philadelphia, Atlanta, and Miami. Those outlets would be important distribution building blocks for the network, and more important, they would help the company amortize the high cost of prime-time programming for the network. Since the days of David Sarnoff, William Paley, and Leonard Goldenson—the fathers of NBC, CBS, and ABC, respectively—the real money in network television has always stemmed from the network's owned-and-operated affiliate stations, rather than from the network operation itself. These key acquisitions would provide the studio with all of the reasons it needed to get a network off the ground.

The first thing Jamie Kellner had to do after he got serious about partnering with Warner Bros. was line up local television stations around the country to carry the new network. To attract top-dollar national advertising, the network had to be "cleared," in industry parlance, on stations covering at least 85 percent of the nation's 95 million homes with television. That meant recruiting station affiliates in more than 150 markets around the country. At that moment, nobody knew the TV station marketplace better than Kellner. He got his start in syndication sales, and for the previous seven years some of his most critical contributions at Fox had been keeping affiliates in the fold when times got tough. Kellner and his team at Fox had worked around the clock to help beef up the operations of the many sleepy independent stations that were suddenly doing big business after aligning with Fox.

Kellner had done his homework on the beaches of Long Island that summer; he knew there were enough unaligned independent stations out there that would welcome the chance to dump the sitcom repeats and chopped-up movies in favor of original prime-time programming with the imprint of a national network. His recruiting job would be toughest in the two most important markets, New York and Los Angeles. In those make-or-break markets, Kellner knew he had only two choices: Chris-Craft Industries, a tightly controlled company headed by the notoriously tough businessman Herbert J. Siegel; and Tribune Broadcasting, the TV station arm of the Chicago-based Tribune Company.

Chris-Craft and Tribune were the only station owners with powerful VHF outlets (Very High Frequency stations with the strongest signals and channel positions from 2–13) in New York and Los Angeles that were still independent, meaning they were not already affiliated with ABC, CBS, NBC, Fox, or PBS. The Chris-Craft and Tribune-owned stations mostly filled their prime-time hours with movies, syndicated programs, local news, sports, and event coverage. Because of this hodgepodge approach to programming, the stations could rarely compete in primetime on a sustained basis with Big Four network affiliates. Moreover, it was becoming harder and more expensive for local stations to buy top-tier movies from the major studios because of the flood of cable upstarts flush with money to spend and hours to fill. The same was true of local TV sports rights deals and the advent of regional sports cable channels.

Kellner could make a strong case to station owners for aligning with the WB by pointing to the Fox experience and the riches reaped by the owners of UHF stations (Ultra High Frequency outlets with weaker signals and channel positions from 14–83), who took a flier on that network. He spread the word among smaller station operators, and as predicted, there was enough interest to make a fifth network viable. At the outset, Kellner and Warner Bros. concentrated on Chris-Craft for stations in the top markets, in part because Warner Bros. was already in business with the company on a TV syndication experiment. Earlier in the year, Warner Bros. had joined with Chris-Craft and some of the strongest independent television stations in the country on a first-run syndication venture dubbed the Prime Time Entertainment Network (PTEN). It was a half-hearted attempt to put a network sheen on low-budget syndicated dramas produced by the studio, including *Kung Fu: The Legend Continues, Time Trax,* and the cult-favorite *Babylon 5.* PTEN was inspired in no small way by Paramount's success with its syndicated *Star Trek* dramas.

What PTEN had to offer was a national web of more than 140 stations signed up to carry the Warner Bros.-supplied programming in primetime a few nights a week. On paper, it seemed it would be easy enough to convert most if not all of those stations into the backbone of a full-fledged, Warner Bros.-based broadcast network. Chris-Craft executive Evan Thompson was head of the station manager committee that oversaw PTEN with Warner Bros.' executives.

Despite the corporate framework in place with Chris-Craft through PTEN, Kellner's preferred choice were the stations owned by Tribune Broadcasting. Tribune's stations were far stronger than Chris-Craft's, particularly in New York and Los Angeles. At the time, Tribune was the single-largest customer of Warner Bros., thanks to the studio's numerous long-term contracts with Tribune stations to license a slew of Warner Bros.-produced movies and television programs. But Kellner strongly doubted that Tribune would have much interest in becoming the backbone of a national prime-time entertainment network with a goal of expanding to six if not seven nights a week. Tribune had poured millions into making their stations the local titans in their market with the most coveted local sports rights and strong local news coverage. There was no way those stations, including WPIX-TV New York and KTLA-TV Los Angeles, would abandon their hard-won positions as local news and sports leaders for a network venture, or so Kellner thought.

With these obstacles at Tribune, the presumption was that Warner Bros. would have to make a deal with Chris-Craft. The company's chairman, Herbert Siegel, made his name as a top executive at the prominent Hollywood talent agency General Artists Corporation in the 1960s before he segued into business and investing. He took over boat manufacturer Chris-Craft in 1968 and built the company into a hodgepodge of units that at one time or another did everything from building yachts to manufacturing hospital laundry bags to owning major market television stations. (Siegel sold the boat business in

1981, but he held on to the Chris-Craft name.) He made a series of bold bets on amassing stock in Hollywood studios—Paramount, 20th Century Fox, and Warner Bros. through the 1960s, 70s and 80s—and then selling them at a premium.

Siegel was known to be cantankerous and tough in business. He earned his reputation as a hard negotiator who generally shunned the media and was not afraid to walk away from a deal at the eleventh hour. He tangled with billionaire oilman Martin Davis in the early 1980s for control of 20th Century Fox, and he clashed repeatedly with Warner Bros.' revered Chairman Steven J. Ross during the 1980s over Ross' management of the studio. By 1989, Chris-Craft owned 15 percent of Warner Bros.' shares, enough to hold up the studio's merger agreement with Time Inc. until Siegel secured a windfall of more than $2 billion for Chris-Craft's shares, and he agreed to resign as a member of the board of directors.

Chris-Craft had sought out its own network-like options in the past for its powerful station group, overseen by broadcast division head Evan Thompson. The company was publicly traded but tightly controlled by Siegel and his family members. His sons, John and William, held senior executive positions at the company. The company's profile in the television industry skyrocketed with its 1992 acquisition of the independent VHF station WWOR-TV in New York. WWOR was the perfect complement to Chris-Craft's KCOP-TV in Los Angeles. With a bicoastal presence in the nation's two largest markets, it was only a matter of time before Chris-Craft found a national network partner. The company did not have a station in Chicago, but it did have outlets in enough other good-size markets to make up for it: San Francisco; Phoenix; Baltimore; Minneapolis; Portland, Ore.; and Salt Lake City.

The Chris-Craft executives were not flashy Hollywood types. They were businessmen who happened to own TV stations. And they were sophisticated enough as investors to see that the television landscape was shifting fast under their feet.

"They knew they had to do something or they'd just have to sell the stations. And they didn't want to do that," says a lawyer who worked periodically for Chris-Craft in the 1980s and 90s. "They wanted to build something out of the station group they'd assembled."

Chris-Craft was ready to listen when Warner Bros.' executives began hinting at big plans far beyond the limited scope of the Prime Time Entertainment Network venture.

Late in the summer of 1993, Kellner, Meyer, and Bruce Rosenblum had dinner in New York at 21 with Herb Siegel, William Siegel, and station division head Evan Thompson. Neither side made any promises that night, and no overt deal points were discussed, but the participants certainly had the unmistakable vibe of a group of people who were on the verge of getting married, in a business sense.

"You could just tell by their attitude and demeanor that they assumed they were going to be our partner in the network, and we assumed we were going to do it with them. They were gung ho," Meyer recalls.

Everything seemed to be going as planned, until the following day, when Meyer and Kellner boarded a plane for Chicago. Meyer wanted to make a courtesy call at Tribune's headquarters because it was the smart and gentlemanly thing to do for the studio's biggest customer. The next morning, Meyer and Kellner walked through the imposing, neo-Gothic Tribune Tower headquarters building off Chicago's North Michigan Avenue. They were welcomed into a meeting with Tribune Broadcasting President and CEO Jim Dowdle and his No. 2 executive at the station group, Dennis FitzSimons. Kellner went through his finely tuned pitch for what was then called the Warner Brothers Television Network. They had no PowerPoint presentation or slick demo tape. Kellner had a flip-card presentation book that was well worn at the edges. It made Meyer think of Willy Loman.

Dowdle and FitzSimons listened intently to Kellner, who knew instinctively how to speak to his audience. The Tribune executives were the kind of rock-ribbed, red suspenders-wearing, consummate broadcasters that Kellner had befriended and worked with throughout his career. He knew what selling points would push their buttons.

He emphasized that with Warner Bros. as its network partner Tribune's stations would be ensured of having high-quality prime-time programming, and therefore higher ratings and advertising revenue would follow. Still, Kellner didn't think they were actually interested. He thought the Tribune executives were being respectful, even after Dowdle and FitzSimons asked Kellner and Meyer to leave the room for a few minutes so they could talk. After a short wait in an anteroom, Kellner and Meyer were ushered back in.

"We think we'd like to do this," Dowdle told them. "You can put us down as being very interested," FitzSimons reiterated.

Kellner could hardly contain himself, but the salesman in him kicked in and he kept his composure. They talked some more, and then Kellner and Meyer were offered the use of a conference room for their own privacy. Once the door was closed, Kellner's eyes were as wide as saucers.

"I'm not sure you understand what this means," he told Meyer excitedly. It had changed everything.

"We were absolutely shocked," Meyer says.

Not too long after the Warner Bros.' team met with Chris-Craft and Tribune, Paramount's Kerry McCluggage and syndication chief Steve Goldman paid their own visit to the Tribune Tower. The Paramount executives laid out their barely dry proposal for a network anchored by the male-centric *Star Trek* franchise. Dowdle and FitzSimons listened courteously. At the end, neither side beat around the bush on the big issue that all four executives had been thinking about since the meeting began.

Paramount owned TV stations in Boston, Philadelphia, and Atlanta; so did Tribune Broadcasting. The question of how they'd carve up the affiliation agreements seemed intractable. McCluggage and Goldman left Chicago certain they would never get over hurdles of partnering with Tribune and intent on making an agreement with Chris-Craft as soon as possible. After all, it wasn't as if Paramount and Chris-Craft were strangers. Most of the company's stations carried *Star Trek: The Next Generation* and *Star Trek: Deep Space Nine*, along with many other syndicated shows from Paramount.

• • •

When Kellner first approached Warner Bros. about the idea of partnering with him in a fifth network, he was confident that there were enough independent television stations left in major cities to support a fifth broadcast network. He didn't expect to have to compete for those stations against a well-armed, deep-pocketed Hollywood rival. The presence of Paramount in the market complicated Kellner's plans in more ways than one. To make the venture feasible for Warner Bros., Kellner and Bruce Rosenblum devised an elaborate formula for the network's affiliate stations to pay back to the studio a percentage of the incremental profits they earned through the higher ratings generated by WB-supplied shows.

Kellner dubbed the plan "reverse compensation," and he knew it wouldn't be an easy sell to station operators—especially to that particular breed of independent television station owners who were not accustomed to taking orders from anyone. At the time, the industry norm was for networks to pay their station affiliate for the use of their airwaves in primetime and other parts of the day. Early on, the typical reaction from station managers to Kellner's idea of "reverse comp" was either derision or disgust, depending on the executive.

But Kellner had to put reverse comp over because, unlike every other company that has launched a commercial broadcast television network in the past 60 years, WB parent Time Warner did not own a single television station to help it reap the rewards of owning a network. In the 1980s and 90s, Time Warner had picked cable television's subscription-based, hard-wired-into-the-home model over free over-the-air broadcast stations as the better long-term television distribution bet. The "fat pipe" of the cable wire would be able to deliver the greatest volume of data, video, telephone service, and high-speed connections into multiple outlets in the home, concluded the media giant's brain trust, led by chairman and CEO Gerald Levin.

In 1995, when the WB launched, Time Warner was the nation's second-largest owner of cable systems behind media mogul John Malone's Tele-Communications Inc (TCI). (In 2006, Time Warner was still No. 2 behind Comcast Corporation, the assets of which include most of the erstwhile TCI systems.) For more than 35 years, the Federal Communications Commission has maintained a cross-ownership ban that bars a single entity or individual from owning a broadcast television station and a cable system in the same television market. It was enacted a decade before America heard the cry "I want my MTV" in an effort to foster diversity and preserve competition in the television advertising and programming marketplace. Owning all of those valuable cable systems in major markets like New York and Los Angeles meant that Time Warner was effectively prevented from owning broadcast television stations in the most desirable markets. With no TV stations to bring in revenue, Warner Bros. needed some way of offsetting the cost of supplying the programming, let alone marketing and overhead costs, for the network. Enter Kellner's reverse comp.

"Networks are viewed as strategic assets that are meant to have an impact on other core assets of the company. In most cases, that other core asset is a TV station group," Barry Meyer says. "In our case, that other core asset was our programming. We saw this as a necessary strategic asset that would serve as a platform for us if the (major) networks started to do all of their own production in-house."

Had the WB been the only option on the table, Kellner was confident he would have had no trouble luring the strongest of the available independent stations out there. However, once a competitor hit the street with easier terms for station owners to swallow and the tangible program asset of a *Star Trek* series to boot, the odds were stacked against Kellner. Nevertheless, he wasn't about to quit, not with an 11 percent ownership stake in the venture.

"Jamie is an exceptional salesman," says Warner Bros.' Bruce Rosenblum, "and he can be very persuasive."

Kerry McCluggage had plenty of his own hurdles to clear in the weeks before and after the studio went public with its plan for a *Star Trek*-anchored network. McCluggage had sold his vision for the network to then-Paramount Communications Chairman Martin Davis and Paramount Pictures President Stanley Jaffe. Just weeks into Paramount's formal courtship of potential affiliates, however, the studio became ensnared in one of the fiercest, nastiest corporate takeover battles of the past 25 years.

In one corner was Viacom chairman Sumner Redstone, a self-made Boston Brahmin who had parlayed his family's chain of drive-in theaters into a powerhouse media conglomerate that encompassed MTV, VH1, Nickelodeon, the vintage CBS program library, and television and radio stations. Redstone had long coveted a movie studio, and in September 1993 announced his friendly $8.2 billion takeover of Paramount Communications.

In the other corner was none other than Barry Diller, who, after leaving 20th Century Fox about 18 months earlier, had cut an unpredictable path. Diller had surprised the industry a few months earlier when he invested $25 million in the cable home shopping giant QVC Inc. Using this new backing, Diller charged into the fray for Paramount, the studio where he had a long, successful run as chief in the 1970s and early 80s.

Initially, Paramount's Davis sought to keep the Viacom-Paramount merger on the fast track—the merger agreement called for Davis to become CEO of the combined company—but Diller went to court in Delaware to compel Paramount's board of directors to consider his group's higher offer valued at $9.4 billion. The court agreed. Redstone responded by arranging a quickie marriage for Viacom with Blockbuster Video in order to tap some of that company's cash reserves and increase his bid for Paramount.

As the corporate drama played out very publicly in the fall of 1993 and early 1994, McCluggage tried to keep his team moving and focused on the launch of the network. Paramount Television's leader poured himself into the design and launch of what would become UPN. Steve Goldman, a studio veteran who headed the syndication division, was McCluggage's right-hand executive in developing the business plan and recruiting the first affiliates to the new network. The hands-on approach taken by McCluggage and his top lieutenants would make it harder for them to hand over the reins to the newcomers who would be hired by the fall of 1994 to run the network.

McCluggage directed his group at the studio in program development, marketing, sales, and distribution to help him lay the foundation for what was then known as the Paramount Network. The network became a top priority for Paramount Television staffers because it was the top priority for their leader.

Jamie Kellner learned the television busi-ness from the bottom up, in the hardscrabble world of television syndication sales. A native of New York City, Kellner grew up on Long Island, the son of a Wall Street commodities broker. A contact made through a summer job while attending C.W. Post University there helped Kellner get a job in the management-training program at CBS in 1969.* Kellner bounced around as a trainee for a time before settling in to the network's program sales division, CBS Enterprises. He remained with CBS through the early 1970s, when the adoption of the financial interest and syndication rule forced CBS to spin off its vast program library into a distribution company dubbed Viacom Enterprises.

Kellner had reached the rank of vice president of first-run programming, development, and sales at Viacom by the time he left to join another independent distribution company, Filmways Inc., in 1978.

At Filmways, Kellner would distinguish himself by coming up with a solution to a problem that would make *Saturday Night Live* producer Lorne Michaels a small fortune and spark a lasting friendship between the two.

Filmways had the rights to handle the syndication of the reruns of Michaels' envelope-pushing NBC sketch-comedy series. Michaels had a sizable stake in any syndication profits from the show. But SNL's

----

* Alex Ben Block, *Out-Foxed: The Inside Story of America's Fourth Television Network* (1990, St. Martin's Press).

90-minute format made the show less attractive to TV stations. Kellner had the brainstorm to cut the 90-minute episodes down to a half-hour format and pack them with the funniest bits. Stations could program the half hours in tandem with other comedy repeats or air them back-to-back as an SNL-branded hour. The concept was a hit with station owners. Kellner's packaging epiphany made tens of millions of dollars for Filmways and for Michaels.

A short time after Kellner joined the company, Filmways was acquired by another independent, Orion Entertainment Group. Kellner was well-regarded by the new Orion regime and was appointed president of Orion Entertainment Group, giving him oversight of its network programming, home video, pay television, and domestic syndication divisions.

After several years with Orion, Kellner was recruited in early 1986 for the No. 2 job at Fox Broadcasting Co. by an executive headhunter who had a hunch his drive and competitiveness would be a good fit with Barry Diller's pugnacious management style. The headhunter proved to be right.

As a leader in the WB era, Kellner's style was to play it mostly cool and steely calm. He had a Mr. Spock-like detached quality at times. He wasn't easily excitable, yet he demonstrated such obvious passion and dedication that he inspired his team of young executives, none more than I. We appreciated the confidence he had in us. And what impressed us most was his innate ability to spot trends and opportunities, and then shift gears on a dime to capitalize on them. He's been an avid sailor since his youth—when he competed in yacht races off Long Island—and his ship's captain mentality shows in everything he does.

"Jamie's a sailor. He likes to find where the wind is," says Jordan Levin, a charter WB executive.

The fire in Kellner to prove he could do it all over again at the WB was stoked by a bitterness he carried with him after he left Fox.

Kellner, who was 45 at the time he left Fox, had never been happy about laboring in Barry Diller's shadow as the No. 2 executive at Fox Broadcasting Co. He resented being seen as Barry Diller's business and affiliate relations guy when his role as a leader and innovator had been much broader.

By the time Kellner formally announced his resignation on January 4, 1993, he was worn out after seven years of hard charging. His timing was also influenced by the changing of the guard at the White House that month. During his 1992 presidential campaign, Bill Clinton had vowed in virtually every stump speech to hike taxes on high-income brackets to give more relief and benefits to middle- and low-income Americans. The capital gains tax rate was a fat target for the new administration, and Kellner was expecting to see some significant capital gains once he left Murdoch's employ. Kellner wanted to cash out before the laws changed under Clinton.

Years before, Kellner had been given a 1 percent interest in the Fox network in recognition of his role in bringing it to fruition. That 1 percent did not include the hugely profitable Fox owned-and-operated television stations. Kellner's sliver was in Fox Broadcasting Co. itself, which meant it was hard to put a value on. What is a television network worth without the television stations to deliver profits? Nonetheless, by the end of 1992 Fox's network infrastructure—its national web of affiliate stations, the programming and marketing operations, legal, finance, and research departments, etc.—had some intrinsic value. Kellner was determined to receive his promised share of the wealth.

By multiple accounts, Kellner had a difficult time coming to terms with Murdoch on the years-old agreement.

"They fought over every million," says a knowledgeable source. In the end, Kellner is believed to have left Fox with a payout of $10 million–$15 million, but that payout, that 1 percent, was a sliver of what Kellner hoped to gain from his involvement with the WB. Despite the setback that Paramount's network represented, it was impossible to deter Kellner. Shrewd, calculating, and smart, Kellner was not about to let Kerry McCluggage or any studio get in the way of his vision for the fifth network. He had worked too long and too hard for other people to fall short of success now.

• • •

Warner Bros. beat Paramount to the punch
in taking its vision for a fifth network, complete with the reverse comp
strategy, to the independent station owners that both studios needed
to woo. But Paramount beat Warner Bros. to the formal announcement of a new network to the media by seven days in the fall of
1993.

Kellner and Warner Bros. had moved quickly to nail down an
affiliation agreement with Tribune following their surprisingly successful pitch meeting in Chicago in the summer of 1993. Kellner knew
Tribune's endorsement of his plan would speak volumes to the other
station owners he needed to court to bring his network to life.

Chris-Craft executives were none too thrilled about Warner
Bros. jilting them for their chief rivals at Tribune. When McCluggage
and other Paramount executives approached them only weeks later,
the Chris-Craft camp was primed for a big deal and very interested.
Besides, Chris-Craft was seeking a partnership that would allow them
to own at least half of the network that the company's stations carried. Herb and William Siegel and Evan Thompson knew during their
dinner at 21 that Warner Bros. would balk at forking over anything
but a minority stake. Paramount, on the other hand, was happy to
oblige Chris-Craft with a 50/50 deal.

On October 26, 1993, Paramount Communications and Chris-
Craft Industries issued a joint press release announcing the launch of
a broadcast network anchored by the latest *Star Trek* spin-off series.
There wasn't much fanfare to the announcement and scant detail offered about their plans, though the release did cite a January 1995
launch date.

At the time, *Star Trek: Deep Space Nine* had been pulling in
good ratings in first-run syndication for nearly two years. *Star Trek:
The Next Generation* was in its highly successful final season, with
cast members preparing to transition to feature films starting with
the late-1994 release, *Star Trek: Generations*. The confirmation

that another *Star Trek* television series was coming produced more ink than Paramount and Chris-Craft's plan to launch a new network did.

A week later, on November 2, Warner Bros. held a Tuesday-morning news conference in its executive dining room. Bob Daly, Barry Meyer, Jamie Kellner, Tribune's Dennis FitzSimons, and a number of other station-group owners were there in an effort to show that the "Warner Bros. Television Network" already had a groundswell of support where it needed it most. In truth, Kellner was personally disappointed by some of the no-shows among station operators whom he'd contacted about his plans for WB. Kellner had helped make a lot of station owners very rich with the success of Fox; he was hurt when some of those same owners opted to align with UPN rather than the WB.

The Warner Bros.' news conference drew a respectable media turnout, but the reaction from the press and the industry was charitably categorized as extreme skepticism. How could the marketplace support one new broadcast network, let alone two? And unlike Paramount, Kellner had no programming to speak of, save for the promise of Warner Bros. Television's track record. The insta-analysis in Hollywood on the two new networks was that one of the two would fold quickly, or they would merge, and even then it seemed more than likely that neither would make it to air.

By the late morning on that Tuesday, however, it was nothing but blue skies ahead for both camps. The aerial war was about to begin.

Kellner, Meyer, and Bruce Rosenblum, who had remained a key figure in planning for the WB, boarded a small jet borrowed from a friend of Kellner's for a barnstorming tour to recruit the independent station affiliates. The plane was small and rickety enough to make even the most frequent fliers squeamish—especially when they heard a loud thud and "Oh, shit" from the pilot as they were touching down in St. Louis.

"We get out of the plane and walk around to the front, where we see that the entire windshield is spattered with blood. *Spattered,*" recalls Barry Meyer. "And the pilot, who is still in the plane, looks at us and says, 'Hit a duck.' "

The dead duck was an apt metaphor for the challenges Warner Bros. faced in markets like St. Louis, a city that ranks among the top 20 television markets but had only one strong independent station up for grabs as the race between UPN and WB to line up affiliates began in earnest.

Kellner and Co. weren't the only ones burning up the skies in pursuit of station affiliates. Paramount's Kerry McCluggage and Steve Goldman were on the same quest in the Paramount corporate jet, oftentimes heading to the same cities as Team Kellner.

"We would just call (station owners) from the air, and say, 'We're here,' " McCluggage says. "We'd do as many as two or three stations a day in three or four different cities each day until we had the lineup we wanted."

The Paramount team's first stop was St. Louis. The city's lone independent station was owned by a local company called River City Broadcasting, whose leader, Barry Baker, was among a handful of entrepreneurial owners of midsize-market TV stations who were suddenly endowed, thanks to the Paramount–Warner Bros.' brawl, with increased clout in their dealings with the studios. This was because they owned multiple TV stations in markets where there weren't enough strong stations to go around for six networks.

Beyond the competition for networks and studios brought about by the sunset of fin-syn, there were additional upheavals in the station community that bred a gold rush mentality as Warner Bros. and Paramount were seeking to lock up independents. Outside of the two new networks, the market for buying and selling TV stations had been invigorated by recent FCC decisions that loosened restrictions on the number of TV stations a single entity could own.

The FCC's station ownership rules were designed to ensure a diversity of "voices" on the public airwaves and a tremendous variety of television station owners across the country, which was meant to guard against a Big Brother-ish monopoly of the medium. Hometown needs for news and information, and hometown values and standards would be of primary importance to locally based station management, if only because it was good for business. TV may have become the most influential mass medium, but no one would be allowed to amass too many TV stations in the United States under the federal government's regulatory rationale.

Acknowledging that broadcasters faced new competition from cable, satellite, Internet, and telephone company upstarts, however, the FCC in the early 1990s raised its limit on the number of stations a single entity could own by adopting a new formula that allowed for a maximum of 12 stations, so long as they didn't reach more than 25 percent of U.S. television households.*

But even more than the deregulation, the tradition-bound culture of Big Three network affiliate stations was shaken by the news that hit the wires early on the morning of Monday, May 22, 1994.

Rupert Murdoch had made headlines a few months before by spiriting a coveted National Football League TV-rights contract away from CBS. He brought the rights over to Fox, negotiating a $1.6 billion deal in the process. On that May morning, Murdoch unveiled another coup: signing long-term Fox affiliation pacts with 12 midsize-market TV stations that had recently been acquired by billionaire investor Ronald Perelman.

In one fell swoop, Fox lured away a dozen old-guard Big Three network affiliates, eight of them from CBS, in vital markets like Atlanta, Detroit, Phoenix, Dallas, Cleveland, Tampa, and Milwaukee.

The Fox-New World deal, as it came to be known in industry shorthand, demonstrated that nothing was sacred anymore, not even 40-plus-year affiliation relationships between station operators and their networks. All of a sudden, networks had to reach out to affiliate station partners they'd long taken for granted. Station owners had clout to demand more money, longer-term contracts, and concessions

---

*   Each TV market is ranked according to population size and the percentage of national television households that it represents. New York is the nation's largest market, encompassing 7% of all U.S. television households. Los Angeles is No. 2 at 5.3%, as of 2006.

from their networks. Frantic switching and swapping of network affiliations ensued among stations in markets large and small in the
two-year period that followed Murdoch's New World land grab.

And into this maelstrom of wheeling and dealing ventured emis-
saries from two Hollywood studios who were hell-bent on building
America's fifth broadcast network.

CHAPTER TWO

YOU'RE HIRED

Kerry McCluggage was leisurely making his way through 18 holes on a comfortable Saturday afternoon in September 1993 when his boxy mobile phone chirped. McCluggage had a funny feeling about the call. It had to be important if it was being put through to him on the golf course.

He was right. McCluggage's bosses, Paramount Communications head Martin Davis and studio chief Stanley Jaffe, came on the line to tell him about a takeover offer that had been tendered by Viacom and that it would be announced the following Monday. Davis and Jaffe tried to assure McCluggage that it was going to be an uncontested, friendly merger that would go smoothly for the studio and strengthen its operations in the long run. They told McCluggage before he had the chance to ask that Viacom chairman Sumner Redstone had pledged his full support for Paramount's new network. But McCluggage couldn't help wondering as he completed his round what it would mean for his baby.

Within weeks, McCluggage had a clear understanding of what it would mean, and it wasn't pretty. First, Barry Diller publicly badmouthed Paramount's plan for the network, saying that there was no demand for it in the marketplace and that he would shelve the idea if he got the studio. By the time Redstone's Viacom won the bidding war the price tag for Paramount had soared to $10 billion. The studio's new parent company couldn't afford to take on the kind of debt that it had projected (conservatively) to fund the new network, or Viacom could run the risk of running into trouble with its banks and Wall Street. McCluggage had no other option but to go to Chris-Craft's

Herbert Siegel and Evan Thompson and radically renegotiate their partnership agreement.

Paramount and Chris-Craft had already devoted many billable lawyers' hours to crafting a 50/50 partnership agreement. But in early 1994 it took a 180-degree turn. Chris-Craft's United Television and BHC Communications station units would have to bear the burden of bankrolling the entire network for at least its first two years of operations. Paramount would have an option to buy 50 percent of the network, and assume half of its debt, as of January 1997.

As strenuously as Paramount executives sought to reassure their partners that they would "option-in" as soon as possible, the damage was done. The sudden change in joint venture terms made Chris-Craft executives anxious about Redstone's level of commitment to the network. Under the reconfigured partnership that Chris-Craft and Paramount agreed to in the summer of 1994, the network's operations were governed by a lengthy operating agreement and an operating committee consisting of three members from the Paramount side and three from Chris-Craft. The operating agreement was carefully written so as to put checks and balances on both sides. The operating committee had to approve all major decisions on programming, marketing, personnel—basically any significant expenditure or initiative. This setup would prove crippling to UPN senior managers who had to maneuver a thicket of disagreements and bickering between the partners to get anything done.

"Operating committee meetings would go on and on while the partners argued over why the network was losing so much money. Chris-Craft would say it's because Paramount's shows were bad; Paramount would say that UPN's management wasn't picking the right shows or that the marketing sucked," says a former UPN executive. "They weren't throwing things at each other but there was anger. You'd have to be deaf, dumb, and blind not to notice it."

While the Viacom acquisition had unsettled the situation at UPN, by early 1994 plans were gelling between Jamie

Kellner, Warner Bros., and Tribune Broadcasting. It was time for Kellner to start scouting for executives to run his ambitious start-up. The countdown to launch day, January 11, 1995, had begun. Next to lining up affiliate stations to carry the network, Job One for Kellner was programming. Kellner knew from his Fox experience that the WB needed to have the right mix of people to develop distinctive original shows to give the network an identity in the minds of viewers. Because of the unique skill set he was looking for, Kellner was determined to hire a number of his former Fox colleagues. At the top of that list was Garth Ancier, who had been Fox's first head of programming. Kellner knew if he got Ancier he'd have enough of the charter Fox team to sell his new network as "brought to you by the same team that launched Fox" a decade before.

Ancier wasn't easy to get at the time. He was riding high as the producer behind the successful new syndicated daytime talk show hosted by Ricki Lake. The twentysomething actress best known for starring in the 1988 John Waters' movie *Hairspray* was an odd choice for daytime talk-show stardom. But somehow Ancier's bet on Lake paid off, and the show clicked with a coveted audience of young urban women. As its executive producer, Ancier stood to make a fortune from *The Ricki Lake Show*.

Early on, Ancier had been a protégé of NBC programming chief, Brandon Tartikoff, during Tartikoff's glory years in the 1980s. After leaving NBC for Fox in early 1986, Ancier developed a close working relationship with Kellner. Ancier's run at Fox had ended less than happily—he was slowly squeezed out of his role as head of programming by Barry Diller—but he remained friendly with Kellner. In the intervening years, Ancier logged a brief stint as head of Disney's television production unit, but mostly he worked as an independent producer.

In mid-January, Kellner traveled to Miami Beach to attend the conference and trade show exhibition of the National Association of Television Program Execuives. It's an annual television industry ritual that brings together various constituencies—network and studio executives, independent program distributors, television station owners, program buyers for foreign TV channels, TV advertising buyers, and a host of others—for a week of high-intensity networking and dealmaking, usually in a convention-friendly city like Las Vegas or New Orleans.

During the event's heyday, major studios and sizable independent distributors would lay out millions of dollars to hawk their wares each year at the NATPE convention. The trade show's floor was nothing less than a programming bazaar with major studios erecting $2 million booths outfitted with carpeted meeting rooms and catered by Wolfgang Puck. It was a natural place to meet with local station owners and prospective affiliates. Jamie Kellner had to be at the NATPE convention pressing the flesh in a big way if he wanted his network to be taken seriously by the operators of prospective affiliate stations.

In fact, Jamie Kellner had two pivotal meetings during his stay in Miami that week. The first was with Warner Bros.' Barry Meyer and Bruce Rosenblum, and key station-group owners who had committed to carrying the network in big markets, including Tribune's Dennis FitzSimons.

Kellner had recruited Warner Bros., Tribune, and a handful of other station operators to join his venture under very different business circumstances—before Paramount entered the fray. Warner Bros. had greenlighted the network-based financial models and projections, but these didn't account for the presence of a deep-pocketed direct competitor. Kellner felt an obligation to look his partners in the eye, and hash out this unexpected turn of events. When they gathered during the convention in Miami Beach, Kellner made it clear in his quietly intense way that the plans they'd discussed the previous summer had changed. Dramatically.

"I wanted to make sure they understood—it was a new game," Kellner says. "I told them it was going to take a lot more money and a lot more time to succeed." Kellner's forthrightness only endeared him to his partners.

Kellner's other big meeting that week was with Ancier, who was busy making the rounds at NATPE as the executive producer of the hottest new show in daytime. Kellner invited Ancier to lunch at South

Beach's trendy News Café, a few paces removed from the hubbub of the show floor at the Miami Beach Convention Center. If their industry colleagues saw them lunching together, the word that Kellner was courting Ancier might spread prematurely and complicate making a deal with the sought-after producer. Kellner already knew it was going to be difficult to cut a deal with Ancier because of his obligations to *Ricki Lake*. But the aura of success that Kellner saw around Ancier at the convention that year only solidified his resolve to make Ancier WB's founding entertainment president. Although Ancier had no shortage of lunch and dinner invitations that week, he went out of his way to make time for his friend.

A born eccentric with boyish charm, thick brown hair, and an ever-present sideways grin, Ancier was known among his industry colleagues as having an encyclopedic knowledge of television and a good ear for good ideas. The New Jersey native and Princeton University grad was viewed as a bright, lanky kid when he was appointed president of Fox at the age of 28.

Those of us who are fortunate to have worked closely with Garth know that one of his greatest strengths is his willingness to find ways to make unusual or convention-defying programming successful. Garth has a genuinely insatiable curiosity and drive to be innovative. He was working as a reporter for local NBC radio affiliates in Trenton, N.J. when he was a sophomore in high school. Before he was out of high school, he was producing a nationally syndicated radio long-form interview program called *American Focus,* which counted among its guests the philosopher Ayn Rand and actor Henry Fonda. He should never be underestimated, though his sweet nature sometimes makes him vulnerable to the attacks of others.

By the time they met in Miami, Garth was aware of Jamie's plan to launch a network with Warner Bros., but he had been so consumed with his own launch of *Ricki Lake* in the fall of 1993 that he hadn't given it much thought. When they were seated at the café, Jamie broached the subject in a low-key but direct manner.

"So you know I'm starting this thing with Warner Bros.," Jamie said. "Would you be interested?"

Jamie and Garth hadn't worked side by side in years, but there was still a professional shorthand between them. Yes, he was interested, Garth told Jamie, who appeared pleasantly surprised. The next step was for Garth to meet with Barry Meyer, Jamie told him. Once the business was out of the way, Jamie and Garth spent the rest of the meal talking about television, not in a WB-specific sense but as friends who never tired of talking shop.

Kellner and Ancier went to a dinner the following month in New York with Meyer. As far as Meyer was concerned, Garth had the necessary network bona fides, thanks to his Fox and NBC experience. And it was clear he already had a strong bond with Jamie. It was a dream scenario, except for the high-class problem of Garth's commitment to *Ricki Lake*, which was taped weekdays in New York and distributed by Sony Pictures' syndication arm. Sony expected Garth to devote all of his time to the show in his capacity as executive producer. But Garth brought his own leverage to the situation. His lawyers and his agents at Creative Artists Agency worked out a deal that allowed him to spend 50 percent of his time, or every other week, in New York producing *Ricki Lake*, and alternate weeks in Burbank. In his WB office, Garth had state-of-the-art videoconferencing equipment installed to help him keep tabs on the set from across the country.

Jamie agreed to the unorthodox arrangement because he knew Garth was right for the job. It would help immeasurably to have someone who had been through the birth of a network before and had dealt with the chaos and pressure. The WB didn't have the budget to pay huge salaries to its executives, but Jamie sealed the deal by offering Garth a two percent ownership interest in the network, a stake carved out of Jamie's 11 percent stake. There was a distinct possibility that 2 percent of the WB would never amount to more than red ink; on the other hand, it had the potential to be worth millions. Garth has always been a glass-half-full kind of guy.

"I don't ever enter something where I don't think we're going to make it. I don't go there in my mind," Ancier says. "You do the best you can, and you don't think about not succeeding."

Hiring Garth set the tone for what would become a crucial aspect of the WB culture, namely Jamie's decision to recruit a number of Fox alumni in marketing, advertising sales, publicity, and other areas. By doing so, Jamie assembled a hard-driving group of people who felt like they had something to prove. As much as the rivalry with UPN, the fire to show the industry that the Fox team could do it all over again was the decisive rallying factor for Jamie's cabinet at the WB.

Brad Turell, WB's longtime head of publicity, says the "hole-in-the-wall-gang" mentality among his fellow Fox alumni was highly motivating.

"Everyone had something to prove in that we could launch this network successfully and make it a hot network. That would validate our Fox days, and people would look back and say, 'Aha, this group did two networks successfully,' " Turell says.

Garth Ancier's contract to join WB as entertainment president came together at the same time that Jamie Kellner was finalizing contracts with two other Fox veterans, Bob Bibb and Lewis Goldstein, for the crucial job of selling America on the new network and its shows. Bibb and Goldstein were so well known as professional partners that they earned the nickname "BobaLew." The marketing pair met when they were young promotion department staffers working in a basement at NBC's Burbank compound in the early 1980s, and they have been joined at the hip as professional partners ever since. Ancier, a former colleague of Bibb and Goldstein's at NBC, brought them in to overhaul Fox's marketing efforts after it stumbled out of the gate in primetime.

Sandy blond, baby-faced, and amiable, Bob reflects the gentility of his Louisville, Kentucky, hometown. Lew's strong opinions and drive were shaped by his childhood experiences growing up in New Jersey and New York. Despite their differences, the two work shoulder to shoulder with remarkable unanimity.

The appointments of Garth, Bob, and Lew were announced in May 1994 with great fanfare, billed as the former Fox team reuniting with Jamie Kellner to do it all again for another studio across town.

Shortly before his news broke, Garth began putting out feelers for reinforcements under him in the programming department. Given his unusual work schedule, Garth knew he would need to lean on a key lieutenant to run things smoothly in his absence.

In typical Garth fashion, he started by making a realistic list in his head of the people he knew might be right for the job. It was a tough assignment because the person would have to be able to develop shows from scratch and help launch a business at the same time. Garth needed a seasoned executive, but there weren't many of those who would be willing to take a flier—and a pay cut—to work for a start-up venture. To further complicate the job description, Garth knew even then that the WB's programming needed to be distinctive by aiming for a more youthful audience than even Fox was courting at the moment. So his ideal executive couldn't be too seasoned or he or she wouldn't have the right sensibilities.

So in a roundabout way, I wound up at the top of Garth's list. I was not quite 30 and working in my second job as a development executive for a television network. Previously, I'd spent three years in the late 1980s working for *Saturday Night Live* producer Lorne Michaels in New York after graduating from Harvard University. It was at Harvard that I met my future husband, comedy writer-producer Greg Daniels. I moved to Los Angeles in 1990 after landing a job in the variety and specials department at ABC. That's where I first met Garth.

Garth and I worked together a few years before on an unconventional pilot for a sketch comedy series for ABC. Garth had been the producer, and we got along well, especially when it came to agreeing that the pilot we'd produced was hilarious but wrong for ABC in every way. Still, it had been a great experience and we kept in touch in the hopes of trying another project together sometime.

By the spring of 1994, when Garth called to recruit me to the WB, I was about to be promoted to head of the comedy programming department at Fox. (Oddly, my boss at the time would later become my direct rival at UPN.) I was coming off a great season, with two new shows I'd helped shepherd performing well enough in the ratings to be renewed for second seasons. I'd read in the trades about the new networks that were being put together by Warner Bros. and Paramount, but I hadn't considered them places I'd want to work. Why would I? I already had a good development job at a major network. But Garth was someone I'd always wanted to work with again, so I knew I couldn't go wrong by taking the meeting.

A week or so after he called, Garth and I wound up meeting when we both happened to be in New York. Over dim sum at a swanky Chinese restaurant on the Upper West side he sold me on the WB Television Network. His enthusiasm was utterly infectious, and the thought of working with him and Jamie Kellner was compelling indeed.

I didn't need much arm-twisting by the end of our lunch conversation, but I did insist on one thing. I wanted to oversee all of the network's program development, be it comedy, drama, or whatever else we might cook up.

"I'm going to take a chance on you; you have to take a chance on me," I told Garth. He barely blinked.

My meeting with Garth was quickly followed by a meeting with Jamie at his home in Beverly Hills. I hadn't spent much time at all with Jamie during our overlapping months at Fox. He resigned about six months after I arrived at the network in mid-1992 and, after all, I was a mid-level creative executive and he was the president of the network. I was nervous as I drove up to his local home that day in the Coldwater Canyon area of Beverly Hills. I knew from Garth that Jamie had some doubts about whether I was ready to be head of all program development. And in the days that had passed since my lunch with Garth, I became more and more excited about the opportunity, and the adventure that Jamie Kellner's new network venture seemed to offer. Even though I had a new contract that included a promotion sitting on my desk at Fox, I drove to Jamie's house in the early afternoon hoping like mad that I'd win him over.

Jamie was friendly as we shook hands in his wood-paneled den, but he also put me through a few paces, asking about my qualifications and my background. We found we had a mutual friend in

Lorne Michaels, which was a plus for me in his eyes. The one thing about that meeting I have often reflected on is how Jamie grilled me on whether I had the skills to develop drama series as well as comedies, given my background at Fox and ABC. The irony would become apparent years later when the WB's greatest successes came with drama series, while we struggled for years to find a truly distinctive comedy.

Back then, I assured Jamie that I was ready to grow creatively and was eager for the opportunity to make television history at the WB. By the time I left Jamie's house, we'd negotiated my responsibilities and my salary. I drove back to the Fox lot in West Los Angeles and gave notice that afternoon.

As soon as I started at the WB in early June 1994, I realized this was no regular No. 2 creative executive job. Garth had the loftier title of entertainment president, but he also had a clause in his deal that allowed him to spend only every other week working on the WB. The other half of his time was spent in New York producing *The Ricki Lake Show*. Garth's absences left me with far more responsibility and far less guidance than I knew what to do with. It was daunting. Jamie and Garth didn't help matters by waiting until my first day on the job to drop a bomb on me.

As I sat making a flurry of phone calls in our cramped quarters in the main executive office building on the Warner Bros. lot, Garth and Jamie approached me with a casualness that should have been a tip-off that they were about to surprise me.

"Uh, Susanne?" Jamie said.

"Yes," I replied putting the phone down.

"You know, we're having this affiliate meeting on August 11," Jamie said, his eyes darting around a bit.

"OK, great, I'll be there," I said with enthusiasm.

". . . and you have to have the new shows ready to announce by then."

It was a "you're kidding, right?" moment. I thought they were yanking my chain. Two hours of primetime in eight weeks? Most networks spend nine months or more on the creative development of each pilot. I had to come up with our first night of programming in less than a quarter of that time? It just couldn't be done, I thought, shaking my head.

Garth and Jamie were straining to look sympathetic. I asked them why they hadn't mentioned this August 11 date sooner.

"We were afraid you wouldn't take the job," Garth admitted.

"So are you excited about using Bugs Bunny as your mascot?" Sandy Reisenbach, Warner Bros.' top marketing executive, asked Bob Bibb and Lew Goldstein during their first meeting shortly after the duo signed on to the network.

A respected movie marketing executive, Reisenbach brought Bibb and Goldstein to his office on the lot on a typically June-gloomy morning in 1994 to discuss corporate-branding issues for the new network, particularly the use of Bugs Bunny, one of the studio's single most valuable assets. The character had been used in some of the earliest marketing materials for the Warner Bros. Television Network. Reisenbach assumed Bugs would continue to be part of the network's logo and image.

Bob and Lew weren't so sure. They loved the idea of using a character from the studio's animation treasure trove. They'd been responsible for resurrecting the use of 20th Century Fox's famed searchlight logo and orchestral fanfare on Fox Broadcasting's air; they knew how important it was to reinforce the network's tie to a household Hollywood brand name. Nonetheless, the contemporary Bugs Bunny was closely associated with children's entertainment and kid-oriented licensing and merchandising. Bob and Lew could foresee problems with the studio if the network ventured into programming that was deemed controversial or risqué. And from experience, the two knew that controversy and envelope-pushing was exactly what the network would need to stand out.

"What if we found another classic character that would be recognizable but not as kid-centric, and not as sensitive as Bugs?" they suggested after a respectful pause. Bob and Lew always spoke not in unison, but in the finish-each-other's-sentences manner common to happily married couples and successful business partners.

Reisenbach nodded. He invited them to poke around the studio's Termite Terrace archive and come back in two weeks with a proposal. Our marketing gurus immersed themselves in the task. They did their research and pulled together rough mockups of various options for review by Kellner and the core team. Bob and Lew were always very particular about the way they wanted to do things, large and small, but to their credit both always went out of their way to keep other department heads invested and up-to-date on their campaign plans.

At one of the first meetings they called to discuss marketing issues, however, Bob and Lew had no luck in getting a hearing from us, let alone any constructive feedback. They had the misfortune to schedule it for late afternoon on Friday, June 17. It wasn't just that it was a hot Friday afternoon in summer. It also happened to coincide with the bizarre spectacle of O. J. Simpson's white Ford Bronco leading the Los Angeles Police Department on a 60-mile slow-speed chase through several freeways and a nail-biting whirl through Sunset Boulevard and up to his Brentwood mansion.

While O.J. provided an unexpected distraction from our formidable workload that afternoon, I didn't have much chance to relax that summer. After getting over my initial panic at having to cobble together four shows in nine weeks, the first thing I did was to make the rounds of Hollywood's major production companies and talent agencies, searching for new and interesting projects. It's generally unheard of for network executives to drive to visit the sellers of programming, but we were a tiny start-up network based in Burbank. People would barely return my calls, let alone drive over the hill that separates Hollywood and Beverly Hills from the San Fernando Valley to pitch me in my office. So that summer, I spent a lot of time in my car—my sturdy, green, schoolmarm-ish Volvo 850 sedan that was old even then. I loved it—I felt like I was driving an impenetrable Swedish-made tank, fighting my way through the choked freeways and congested surface streets of Los Angeles' Westside.

Despite their news flash for me on the first day, Jamie and Garth treated me well. They couldn't have been more inclusive or welcoming. In that summer of 1994, the WB amounted to about 14 people—executives and assistants included—who all got along and worked hard together in cramped temporary office space in the aptly named Glass House building on the edge of the Warner Bros.' lot. There was a camaraderie developed in those days that the core group never lost, despite our ups and downs in later years.

The only bit of unvarnished criticism that I got was teasing from Jamie and Garth about my car. They didn't like my sturdy, leafy-green Volvo. It sent the wrong signal to the network's prospective producer and studio partners, they told me. To make matters worse, the WB's temporary offices were located across the way from the main administration building where studio Co-chairmen Bob Daly and Terry Semel worked. The boxy green thing was parked right outside the building in my reserved slot, where everyone who came to the lot for high-level business could see it.

Somehow, I kept putting off getting a new car. I wasn't trying to be defiant. I was just too busy driving around town trying to rustle up shows for the network. I felt like a traveling salesman. I had honed my pitch for the network—we were aiming for teens and young adults ages 12 to 24, the audience the other networks seemed to be ignoring, even Fox. Jamie and Garth hadn't given me much more direction than that. But that was all I needed.

I was working around the clock, but that really didn't matter to me. It was invigorating to be part of Jamie Kellner's kitchen cabinet that built and managed the network. During the summer and fall of 1994, the WB's staff fell into place, and in due time, we fell into a good groove.

My first hire was another young development executive from the Walt Disney Company's television production division. Jordan Levin was hired as senior vice president of comedy development, but he quickly took on a broader role that had him involved with all of our programming and development. Jordan and I had worked together on a Disney-produced pilot when I was at Fox, and it was clear in short order that Garth, Jordan, and I made a good team.

John Maatta, the former Warner Bros.' TV lawyer who officially became employee No. 1 of the WB in the summer of 1993, remained in his role as Kellner's consiglieri on a range of issues, including the network's dealings in the areas of public policy and lobbying. Tribune executive Mitch Nedick, another of Kellner's first hires at the WB, would last the entire run of the network as finance chief, then make the transition to CW. It was no accident that the charter WB team included senior executives from Warner Bros. and Tribune in important oversight roles.

"I thought it was a good way to have my partners feel comfortable by having key people in the company who had older relationships with them," Kellner says.

For the crucial job of overseeing advertising sales out of New York, Kellner brought in seasoned executive Jed Petrick, who had been third on the ad sales totem pole at Fox during Kellner's watch. In the early going, Petrick had the uphill battle of convincing Madison Avenue that the WB was going to survive, let alone thrive.

Hal Protter was an experienced local television station manager working at an independent station in St. Louis before he was brought in to the WB to help get the network's raggedy lineup of affiliates into shape. Protter had a pilot's license, which allowed him easy access to off-the-beaten-track markets. His specialty was the toughest cases—helping out the start-up stations that were new to their markets and looking to the WB to put them on the map. Under Kellner's leadership, the WB was aggressive in encouraging entrepreneurs of all stripes to invest in brand-new stations.

"Hal would deal with people who owned a chain of laundromats or made their money discovering oil and now wanted to own a TV station," says longtime WB executive Rusty Mintz. "He'd fly in to

Wichita Falls and find a way to stick a satellite [dish] on the top of a liquor store."

Mintz was working as a research executive in Warner Bros.' television syndication division at the time the opportunity to move to the fledgling network came up. At first Mintz hesitated; he wasn't sure about moving to an iffy start-up venture in a junior executive position. He knew the WB was talking to another research executive at another network. When those talks fell apart, Mintz became the "interim" head—for an interim of nearly a year. What that really meant was Mintz was acting as a one-man band in the high-pressure but little-recognized role of analyzing and interpreting the daily ratings tea leaves and other data for Jamie Kellner and his team. But Mintz didn't hesitate for long. It *had* to be more interesting than syndication research, he figured, plus it was a chance to work with Jamie Kellner, Garth Ancier, Bob Bibb, Lew Goldstein, Jed Petrick, et al, of Fox legend.

With so many pieces coming together, the team began to get to work. Bob and Lew spent their first few weeks on the job developing the network's on-air identity and logo. The Warner Brothers Television Network, as a name, was too big a mouthful for practical use. The network required something pithier for branding purposes. Bob and Lew latched on to the notion of calling it The WB. They thought it had a nice ring, à la The BBC. Bob would also explain to anyone who asked that he'd always liked how NBC, in its earliest days on radio, referred to itself as "the NBC."

Our marketing mavens went through a number of prominent advertising and design firms to find just the right look for The WB logo, one that would reflect Warner Bros.' mighty shield logo but would still allow the network to stand apart. They wound up with numerous slick presentation kits with lots of images and verbiage, but none of it really turned them on. One firm went so far as to suggest the network's logo become "W-Bee" and incorporate a bumblebee.

In desperation, the marketing duo wound up calling on a graphic designer friend who quickly came up with something that they did like. The design featured a small "The" adjacent to elongated "W" and

"B" letters in the familiar angular shape of the Warner Bros. shield. Their finishing touch: a 15-degree tilt to the "WB" coming out of "The." In their minds, setting off the "WB" with a slight tilt added a little kick to our image and further differentiated our logo from other Warner Bros.' brands.

Settling on the mascot wasn't hard once Bob and Lew had the chance to consider their options. They both responded to a long-forgotten character, a frog crooner who'd starred in the 1955 Charles M. Jones short *One Froggy Evening.* They didn't even know his name, but they liked his style as a high-kicking, high-strutting, top-hat-and-cane-sporting vaudevillian with a booming voice. He was all bright green torso, oversize mouth and bug eyes, skinny legs, and clever coloring to make him look as though he were wearing a tuxedo. He had the potential to be more cool than kiddie, which is what Bob and Lew had been concerned about in the first place.

Michigan J. Frog, as they learned after doing some research, had only starred in the one cartoon; he had no dialogue but belted out bluesy renditions of "Please Don't Talk About Me When I'm Gone," "I'm Just Wild About Harry," "Hello, Ma Baby," and his signature "Michigan Rag" ditty. Sadly, Michigan J. didn't work again for more than 30 years (except for a cameo appearance in 1975 on the cover of Leon Redbone's album *On the Track* for Warner Bros.' Records) until he appeared in a pair of 1990 episodes of the Warner Bros.' cartoon series *Tiny Toon Adventures* on Fox Children's Network.

Bob and Lew made an impassioned pitch for adopting the frog, and most impressively, they sketched out a strong vision of how he could be used for branding purposes. Their inspiration came from an unlikely source: the *New Yorker* and its monocle-sporting socialite-dandy mascot Eustace Tilley, who was a creation of the magazine's original art director, Rea Irvin.

"It was a way to give a personality to the logo and the network that went beyond just letters," Bob says.

Most of us were easily sold, but Garth was the exception. He never did become a fan of the frog—he felt it was hokey and signaled that the WB was a network for kids, not adults. Kellner characteristically backed the instincts of his marketing specialists. Besides, he loved Michigan J. and his boundless enthusiasm. Warner Bros.' leaders were also receptive to the idea of reviving a long-dormant character. Once animator Jones gave his blessing, Bob and Lew and their team scurried to produce dozens of funny, upbeat Michigan J. interstitials and promo spots—one that featured him strutting around to the "Dubba Dubba Dance" became a classic. In 1995, Jones even produced a follow-up to *One Froggy Evening*: *Another Froggy Evening*.

Because of the frog's natural showmanship, Bob and Lew seized on the chance to expand his "spokesphibian" role by having Michigan J. serve, in old-school fashion, as a commercial pitchman singing funny jingles for our sponsors, jingles that were penned at all hours of the day and night by our marketing department.

"We didn't have any well-known stars, we didn't have any completed shows at the start—we had to have something to promote," Lew says. "It came down to this darn frog."

Even before the Viacom takeover forced Chris-Craft and Paramount to overhaul the terms of their joint venture for the network, it hadn't all been smooth sailing between the two sides. The partners came from different worlds. Paramount executives were accustomed to the high life of Hollywood and the high stakes of the prime-time television business, where months of work and millions of dollars can be plowed into producing comedy and drama series that last no more than two or three episodes.

The Chris-Craft executives, on the other hand, were bottom-line businessmen accustomed to making money, not losing it. Paramount executives were frustrated by what they saw as tightfistedness and lack of quick decision making by the Chris-Craft representatives on the operating committee. From Chris-Craft's perspective, there was a feeling that the studio executives were dismissive and condescending to the station group's needs. There was a great deal of suspicion that Paramount was taking advantage of Chris-Craft in its accounting procedures for the shows that the studio produced for the network.

"It was a very difficult relationship," McCluggage says with understatement. "The first two years were extremely difficult, and it was made more difficult because we were working with a [network] management team that [Paramount] wasn't really comfortable with."

Indeed, nothing exemplified the gulf between the partners like the selection of Lucie Salhany to be the network's founding president and CEO. Salhany, a former Paramount executive and the person who succeeded Jamie Kellner as head of Fox Broadcasting Company, was Chris-Craft's choice. Her tenure began September 14, 1994, four months before the network was scheduled to make its entrance with four hours of programming on two nights, Monday and Tuesday.

The Paramount camp was more interested in other candidates, but Evan Thompson and William Siegel held firm, and because Chris-Craft held the purse strings, Salhany was in. McCluggage was incensed when word of Salhany's impending appointment leaked out to the media before the partners had ironed out all the details. At the time, Salhany was already in the spotlight; she had hastily resigned a few weeks earlier from the chairman's post at Fox after a rocky 18-month tenure. She'd been promoted to Fox Television chairman on January 5, 1993, the day after Jamie Kellner resigned. Salhany left her mark in history that day by becoming the first woman to head a national broadcast television network in the United States. I had seen Salhany in action during meetings at Fox. She always struck me as direct, intelligent, and passionate.

Salhany was also a well-known commodity to Paramount. She had a hugely successful run as the head of the studio's syndication division from 1985 to 1991. In that capacity, Salhany had been a prime force behind Paramount's celebrated revival of its *Star Trek* TV franchise with the premiere of *Star Trek: The Next Generation* in 1987, nearly 20 years after the original series had been cancelled by NBC. Most important to Siegel and Thompson, Salhany had deep roots in local broadcasting. She started her career programming *Star Trek* reruns and movies on a UHF station in her native Cleveland. Because of this background, she was already close to Chris-Craft's

Thompson and Siegel, having done business with them for many years.

Salhany's phone rang as soon as word spread of her resignation from Fox in July 1994. Chris-Craft's Evan Thompson was one of the first to call. She had a number of overtures, but she had always been particularly fond of Thompson. "It just made all the sense in the world," Salhany says.

For years—since Salhany left her home in Boston to work for Paramount in Los Angeles—she and her two sons had maintained a commuter relationship with her husband and their father, Boston restaurateur John Polcari. At her career crossroads between Fox and UPN, the family decided that Lucie and the boys would stay in Los Angeles for another three years, until their oldest son reached the seventh grade. So Salhany sent her lawyers off to negotiate a three-year contract with Chris-Craft while she took the rest of the summer off with her family.

Salhany was born to be a trailblazer, and she was nothing if not tough. Not two weeks after she started her first job at Fox (running the 20th Century Fox TV production operation), Salhany was diagnosed in the summer of 1991 with breast cancer. After making a big career change after a long and prosperous run at Paramount, Salhany was too competitive to let an illness, even one as grave as breast cancer, slow her down. Few in the industry, few even in her own family, knew that Salhany underwent chemotherapy during her first year at Fox.

A compact brunette with engaging, saucer-shaped brown eyes, Salhany grew up in Cleveland in a tight-knit family of Lebanese descent. Her father owned a grocery store where her mother also worked. Watching their struggles as small business owners made a big impression on Salhany.

"We came from very little . . . but I had a great family life," Salhany says. "With my mom and dad, life was always about being happy and about being the kind of person you needed to be without lying or cheating, and about having no regrets."

As a female executive in broadcasting in the 1970s and 80s, Salhany didn't have many role models. Moreover, Salhany made her mark in areas of the broadcasting business that were considered off-limits to women, namely programming and syndication sales. Her career began in the era of *The Beverly Hillbillies, Batman, The Smothers Brothers Comedy Hour,* and the original *Star Trek.* After high school and a brief stint at Kent State University in the mid-1960s, she returned home and got a job as a secretary for the program manager at independent UHF station WKBF-TV in Cleveland.

"A month after I got there, I said 'This is what I want to do,'" Salhany says.

From Cleveland, she moved on in 1975 to a job as program manager in the top 10 market of Boston, at independent station (and future WB affiliate) WLVI-TV. After four years there, she segued to a higher-profile position as head of programming for Taft Broadcasting, a large TV station and program distributor based in Cincinnati, though Salhany worked out of its Philadelphia offices. In its heyday, Taft owned a clutch of TV and radio stations, Hanna-Barbera Productions, Quinn Martin Productions, program distributor Worldvision Enterprises, and theme parks, among other assets. Paramount Pictures came after Salhany in 1985 to run its syndication division, an unprecedented move for a female executive at the time.

Salhany credits much of her success to the confidence she gained from her parents.

"My mother was very strong," Salhany says. "She used to say to me, 'Just throw your shoulders back, walk tall, and look 'em in the eye.' And a lot of times, when I would walk into meetings and I was petrified, I'd remember that."

When she signed on with Chris-Craft to run UPN, Lucie Salhany knew exactly what she was stepping into. She knew she wasn't popular with the regime at Paramount, so she made it a condition of her employment at UPN that she was to report directly to Evan Thompson and William Siegel rather than to Kerry McCluggage or the operating committee. The "dysfunction junction," as one UPN veteran put it, between Paramount and Chris-Craft made things much harder for those who were laboring round the clock to get the network up and running by January 16.

Because Chris-Craft controlled the finances, they had the final, final say on everything, though the Paramount side had some sway, if only through the programming the studio produced for the network.

"At that point, because Chris-Craft was funding everything, there was no need to be polite. And they weren't," says the former UPN executive.

Salhany's management style could also be exacting on her staff. She was excitable; many UPN alumni have stories of her going "ballistic" when things didn't go swimmingly. But she was also the type to cool down quickly. Her moods could be erratic, which in and of itself was nerve-wracking, longtime associates say.

"Her management style was good on some days—not good on other days," says another former UPN executive. "She loved to stir it up with Paramount. We'd say, 'Lucie, we have to work with these people,' but she just had that streak in her."

The mischievous streak in Salhany led her to go out of her way to needle Paramount executives with whom she was not on great terms. Once when Paramount was throwing a UPN-related party, Salhany sent out a network-wide e-mail with an unmistakably nasty message that went something like: "Drink their drink, eat their food, call their women ugly. Have a good time. I'm not going."

It created a firestorm among the partners that never really died down. "It began a war," Salhany says. "It was just a nightmare. They were sooo mad at me."

Salhany expected her staff to roll with the punches—after all, she was running a start-up television network, not a preschool. She inspired great loyalty and respect among the rank-and-file, but she also left some emotional scars.

"If there was a problem, Lucie could reach down your throat, rip your heart out, pull it back out, and show it to you," says a UPN alum. "She could be horrific."

At other times, she was the consummate office den mother. In the hectic months before the launch, executives remember plenty of late nights when Salhany would pop out of her office and order people to reconvene at her home so she could whip up some food for them.

"There were a lot of us who just loved working for Lucie because no matter what you knew, she cared about us and she cared about what we were doing," says charter UPN executive Marna Grantham. "You wanted to work hard for her."

UPN spent its formative months crammed into a portion of the ground floor of the large Marathon office building on the Paramount studio lot. It was a warren of windowless offices, cubicles, and desks shoved into every available corner. There was the constant din, which would rise to a roar by late afternoon. Dozens of frantic executives and assistants were there working the phones and pounding on computer keyboards in a scramble to get everything ready for launch night.

Most of the charter UPN team consisted of people who were hired after Lucie Salhany, which meant they came aboard with the clock ticking down to the launch.

"We just grabbed people we knew to come work with us," Salhany says. "I called people and said, 'You've just got to start. You don't have a choice.' It was a miracle we made the launch date. . . . But those were the best days for me because they were the most fun."

There was a tiny coffee nook in the UPN office space that was nearly filled up by a gigantic all-purpose coffeemaker. It became a prime hub of activity and conversation for a group of people in need of frequent caffeine fixes.

"The machine was huge, and it would spew out anything: cappuccino, tea, hot chocolate, latte—whatever," says Kevin Tannehill. "A lot of people would swear that if it wasn't for that machine, the network would have never have gotten on the air."

Tannehill had been the first executive hired specifically for the network venture; Kerry McCluggage brought him in to help line up affiliates. Tannehill's original business cards billed him as head of distribution for the "Paramount Network." An experienced syndication sales executive with the perfect background and relationships for the job, he spent most of his first year on the road for the network, but toward the end of 1994, as D-Day drew near, he spent most of his time in the pressure cooker of UPN's temporary office space. It was intense and exhausting, but it was also an exhilarating start-up experience that none of them will ever forget.

"Our interoffice communication consisted of jumping up on our desk and yelling over the cubicles. We had this start-up mentality. And we all looked upon it, even though it was stressful and long hours and everything, as a fun time," Tannehill says.

In contrast to the situation at the WB, where Barry Meyer and Bob Daly mostly left Jamie Kellner alone to run the network as he saw fit, UPN executives from the two parent companies had far more direct involvement in the management and development of the network, specifically from Paramount Television Group chairman Kerry McCluggage and Chris-Craft's Evan Thompson. The level of control McCluggage intended to exert over UPN, even after Salhany was hired, led to sparks between the two of them. Salhany was even known by her staff to refer to McCluggage as "Carry my luggage."

Among the first issues that Salhany butted heads with McCluggage over was the selection of the network's name. Paramount had commissioned a new slate of proposals from advertising and marketing firms. McCluggage and Salhany sat through a number of what Salhany considered "stupid" presentations of potential monikers, such as "Blade." Finally, she blew up.

"I said, forget this. *For-get it*. We'll call it United Paramount Network—UPN. If someone comes up with something better, we can change it," Salhany says. "Paramount went crazy. They hated it."

The network had been developed under the assumption that it would be branded as "Paramount." But Salhany and others convinced Chris-Craft that they needed to protect themselves in case Paramount did not exercise its option to buy into the network. "United" came from the United Television division within Chris-Craft that owned the top UPN affiliates. Salhany won the name fight, and she had her freshly hired marketing executives whip up the network's original circle-triangle-square logo, which was also used over Paramount's protest. "They thought it was old-fashioned," Salhany recalls. (In

UPN hieroglyphics, the circle stood for United, the triangle represented Paramount's snowy mountaintop logo, and the square signified a television set.)

Still, Salhany's frustrations mounted. She felt the network was getting second- and third-best from Paramount in the programming department. The two comedies Paramount had reserved for UPN were both "busted" pilots that had recently been rejected by other networks, one by NBC, the other by Fox at Salhany's direction.

Salhany also had fierce battles with Paramount over the network's handling of its marquee property, *Star Trek: Voyager*. Before Salhany signed on, Chris-Craft and Paramount came up with an arrangement in which UPN would pay nothing upfront to Paramount for supplying the show, but Paramount would keep all of the advertising revenue it generated. Tannehill and his distribution team were also focused on clearing the show on an ad-hoc, syndication-like basis in markets where the network did not yet have an affiliate station.

Voyager was an easy sell, given the strength of *Star Trek: Next Generation,* which had ended its seven-year run a few months earlier with huge finale ratings. Meanwhile, its successor *Star Trek: Deep Space Nine* was still going strong. In Salhany's view, that left little incentive for UPN to lure new affiliates if stations could acquire the network's strongest show on an à la carte basis. Salhany felt the studio was treating *Voyager* like a syndicated show that happened to run on UPN stations, to the detriment of the network's potential growth.

Paramount, on the other hand, needed to be sure it would recover its $2 million to $2.5 million per episode production costs on the show. And the markets where *Voyager* was cleared as a syndication sale—rather than a commitment from the station to carry UPN's entire lineup—were generally in smaller markets where the network had little hope of finding an affiliate because there weren't even enough stations to go around for the Big Four networks.

Without *Voyager,* UPN's cash flow was held to a dribble from what it could generate from a forgettable inaugural lineup of shows. The Hawaiian detective-adventure drama *Marker* starring Richard

Grieco was a pale attempt to reproduce the *Magnum, P.I.* milieu. Rapper Sir Mix-A-Lot took a Rod Serling turn as host of the Las Vegas-based mystery anthology *The Watcher*. The two sitcoms paired with *Voyager* on Monday nights were both Paramount-produced pilots that had been rejected by other networks: *Pig Sty*, revolving around five guys sharing a Manhattan high-rise apartment, and *Platypus Man*, featuring comedian Richard Jeni as the host of a TV cooking show who was desperately seeking Mrs. Right. (I'd been involved with the development of *Platypus Man* the previous season at Fox.)

Salhany had come aboard the network so late in the premiere planning that she didn't even appoint a head of programming for UPN until mid-October, barely two months before the launch. Michael Sullivan was a former ABC executive and producer of the family comedy *Growing Pains*. Given the timing, Sullivan knew he had no shot at developing anything original for UPN's launch slate. His focus from the start was beyond the January 16 launch date. He needed to get material ready to be called up when the inevitable first wave of cancellations came. From the look of things, Sullivan concluded after his first week on the job, he would have to move quickly.

"*All in the Family?*"

"No."

"*Peyton Place?*"

"Yes."

"*Emergency?*"

"Definitely *not* a WB show."

Garth Ancier, Jordan Levin, and I had one big thing in common: we truly loved television. During the countdown to launch phase in 1994, Jordan would frequently put me and Garth through impromptu drills in which he'd pick a random show out of a TV encyclopedia, and we'd discuss whether it would be right for the network we were trying to build. He'd distribute copies of the Big Three networks' prime-time schedules from a random year, and we'd debate whether any of the shows belonged on the WB.

Like Garth, Jordan was the TV-freak kid who had grown up making his own prime-time scheduling notes in the margins of *TV Guide* every week. Jordan's father, Bob Levin, worked in advertising and then as a movie marketing executive for Disney and other studios. Jordan had insider exposure to the entertainment business at a young age, but it was balanced by the experience of growing up in Chicago and spending time in real-world locales like Houston. And like me, Jordan was in the sweet spot of the WB demographic as a 27-year-old, upwardly mobile, professional urbanite.

Jordan knew he'd made the right move in following Garth (Jordan's boss at Disney) to the WB network after he showed up for the first day of work wearing a tie. Jordan made a point of extending a polite greeting to Kellner, who was in his usual Oxford-and-chinos uniform. When Jamie saw Jordan, our leader grabbed a pair of scissors and cut off his tie. Jamie wagged his finger in a friendly way and informed Jordan that he was only to wear a tie for special occasions, "when we're asking people for money."

Jordan smiled, happy to comply.

"There was real awareness among us at the time that even though there was a tremendous amount of work . . . there was a sense that this was probably going to be the best work experience of our careers," Levin says.

The camaraderie among us only grew when we moved out of our temporary digs to our permanent space on a smaller lot known as the Warner Bros. Ranch at the end of August. The ranch, as it was known, was down the street and around the corner from the big lot, but it was also a world apart. The 32-acre lot, once used for producing Westerns, was tucked into the edge of a residential Burbank neighborhood on one side and the start of a commercial strip on the other. Symbolically, the move gave us the breathing room to do our own thing under Kellner's direction.

As exciting as it was, there was a sobering quality to our new space. The headquarters of America's fifth television network consisted of three industrial-size trailers laid out in a U-shape in the corner of a black asphalt parking lot next to three clusters of soundstages.

The prop department whipped up a wooden deck and short staircase leading to the main entrance in an effort to mask the fact that the offices were in, well, trailers. The gallows humor spewed from all of us, even Jamie. We were working in a trailer park. We joked that there was a steering wheel hidden somewhere, and if Warner Bros. decided to give up on the network, they'd just pull it out and drive us all onto a storage lot somewhere.

In fact, our trailers were quite large and spacious. This was quite noticeable when we first moved in because there were so few of us. The interior was set up to function as a workspace for a minimum of 100 people, with cubicles and assistant desks waiting for the staff to claim them as their own.

As the January 11 launch date approached, Jamie and Garth began to get more and more media inquiries about what we were up to, and requests by reporters and photographers to visit the new network's offices. Jamie has never been a press hound, but he understood the importance of free media for a start-up enterprise. One day, after we'd been in the trailers about a month, Jamie advised us at the close of a meeting to "look busy tomorrow" as if we weren't, because a writer from the *Wall Street Journal* was scheduled to visit. We scrambled to put on our best face. Our gray-colored reception area and main conference room were still barely decorated, plus the place had the feeling of a ghost town with so many empty desks and unassigned telephones and computers. Worse, the nearly empty space had a disconcerting echo.

Bob and Lew quickly worked their magic on the situation. They grabbed anything they could get their hands on—designs for Michigan J. Frog promos, affiliation contracts, ratings reports from the top 50 television markets—anything that was lying around, and began distributing them on desks. They had assistants make photocopies to generate more material. Then they scurried around distributing paperwork, coffee cups, pens and pencils, candy wrappers, family photos—anything that would make the offices and cubicles look lived in. We tacked up paperwork and WB promo materials on bulletin boards and turned on all the computers.

By the next morning, Bob and Lew had half-eaten bagels and half-full Snapple bottles strewn around on desks. We threw sweaters, baseball caps, and all kinds of clothes and office-type toys around the space in an effort to give the impression that we were a bustling operation.

We were proud of our handiwork. More than one person observed that we were decorating the set of our own show. Our plan worked—so much so that we didn't have to read any references to the network being "under-populated" or having "eerily empty offices." In a few years time, when we *were* a bustling operation, bursting out of our available space in the trailers, those of us who remembered the prelaunch days would smile among ourselves as we remembered those half-eaten bagels.

When we first opened the doors to our trailers, we expected that we would need to fight to win viewers. We expected an uphill battle in getting the entertainment industry to take us seriously. We didn't expect to have the roughest time of all with our sibling studio, Warner Bros. Television.

At the time, Warner Bros. Television was the undisputed king of prime-time production. For years, under the leadership of President Leslie Moonves, the studio sold more shows to ABC, CBS, NBC, and Fox than any other Hollywood shop. That fall, Warner Bros. Television had hit two home runs out of the park with two new hit shows on NBC, the comedy *Friends* and the medical ensemble drama *ER*.

Moonves didn't want to have much to do with the little ol' WB. He was too busy wooing A-list talent and cutting deals with the Big Four to trifle with a network that didn't even have an affiliate in many big markets—at least that's how it seemed to us. Furthermore, it was no secret, even at the time, that Moonves was angry at not being brought into the loop earlier on plans for the launch of the WB. Moonves didn't want to run the network per se, but he wanted to have oversight of the network with Kellner reporting to him. Given where Jamie Kellner was in his career, that never would have happened.

In retrospect, Warner Bros.' Barry Meyer concedes it was a tactical mistake to keep Moonves out of the loop for as long as they did in 1993.

"It was the strength of Jamie Kellner's personality that was pushing this thing through then, that was for sure," Meyer says. "And Les, well, he's no shrinking violet."

Because Moonves had no incentive, financial or otherwise, to send any of his hot properties to the WB, we had to sift through rejects from Warner Bros. Television and from other networks in the mad scramble to find the shows that we could parade before the August 11 affiliate meeting. We needed to have something tangible in the programming department to show them or we would start losing affiliates. From Warner Bros. Television, we were offered a pilot for a comedy series starring Shawn and Marlon Wayans that NBC had turned down. The pilot wasn't terribly funny, but Shawn and Marlon were. They clearly had raw potential. We found a companion piece to the Wayans show in another passed-on Warner Bros. TV pilot starring comedian Robert Townsend in a fairly conventional urban domestic sitcom dubbed *The Parent'hood*. Townsend was the closest thing we had to an established star.

Garth convinced his old friend, writer-producer Ron Leavitt, to create a raunchy domestic comedy in the vein of Leavitt's *Married . . . with Children* for our inaugural slate. *Married* had been Fox's first breakout comedy hit during Garth's tenure as head of programming, and Garth's support of the show early on had made Leavitt a rich man. Around the office, we referred to Leavitt's show, *Unhappily Ever After*, as "Divorced . . . with Children," and in fact it was a pale imitation of the Fox hit, which was still running at the time the WB went on the air.

The show we were most excited about was *Muscle*, from Paul Junger Witt and Tony Thomas, partners behind such successful TV comedies as *The Golden Girls*, *Soap*, *Benson*, and *Empty Nest*. Warner Bros. had recently signed lucrative film and TV production deals with the duo's Witt-Thomas Productions. The talented head writer for *Empty Nest*, Rob LaZebnik, was game to be experimental with a new show for a new network.

Muscle was an ambitious half-hour show that was part farce and part soap. It was set in an upscale New York City gym. It alternated between comedic bits involving the gym staff and its colorful patrons and a murder mystery involving the death of the late gym-chain mogul, his young widow, and her fast-living stepson. The show was so tongue-in-cheek that the first episode opened with actor Adam West, of *Batman* fame, playing the gym-chain magnate who drops dead after walking in on his philandering younger wife. *Muscle* was hard to follow, because of its large cast and intricate plots. There was too much story packed into 22 minutes of program time. But Witt and Thomas believed in the format. If they were going to take the risk of producing for a brand-new network, they were at least going to have fun and dare to be experimental.

The chilly relations between the WB and Warner Bros. Television didn't warm up, given all the problems that plagued the production of *Parent'hood* and *Wayans Bros*. In the weeks leading to launch, *Wayans* in particular was in big trouble. Jordan and I had been pressing for information on how things were proceeding on the set. We wanted to read the scripts for upcoming episodes so that we could get out in front of any problems or weaknesses as soon as possible.

After weeks of stonewalling, David Janollari, the Warner Bros.' TV executive in charge of comedy programming, came to our conference room on a rainy day in late October to tell us exactly what a mess *Wayans* had become. "We have nothing," Janollari admitted, making no attempt to sugarcoat the situation. The executive producers had quit. There were no scripts in preproduction because there were no scripts written at all. Stars Shawn and Marlon Wayans weren't being entirely cooperative either. The list of problems went on and on.

David was not cavalier about the situation. He seemed genuinely at a loss. There weren't many talented comedy writer-producers available for hire at that time of year—by the fall all of the best talent is committed to shows for the season. Garth, Jordan, and I knew David from our previous jobs, and we knew him to be a sharp executive and good person. None of us could have known on that dark day that Janollari was also destined to play a key role at the WB in its final years.

When it rained on the trailers that housed the WB, you could hear every drop inside. The soft drumbeat and the gravity of our problems led the four of us to pace around the conference room for too long, whining, grumbling, and cursing anyone we could blame for our fate. At one point, I noticed that there was a large hunk of leftover birthday cake and a stack of small paper plates and plastic forks on a small table in the corner. The conference room must have been used earlier in the day to celebrate a staffer's birthday. It struck me that the network must really be growing now if there were cake and punch get-togethers that I didn't even know about.

Jordan paused his migration long enough to grab a hunk of cake and prop himself up in a corner. He stabbed at it angrily with his fork as he ate.

"So what are we going to do?" I said, slumping down in a chair. Things looked bleak. We felt especially bad because we felt abandoned by the one studio that was supposed to take care of us. We knew that Janollari was rooting for our cause, but we had our doubts about his superior.

"I just sat there with a fork and kept eating this cake—the entire cake—trying to soothe myself with food," Levin recalls.

As the holiday season approached, the grow- ing staffs of the WB and UPN labored round the clock in a whirlwind of last-minute preparations and tasks that had to be done before their respective launch dates. Whether it was the *Wayans* problems at WB or *Star Trek* issues at UPN, both sides had their work cut out for them as they tried to conjure up the shows that would introduce their networks to the viewing public. I lost a lot of sleep in the months preceding our debut because I knew that *Wayans* and the other shows were far from the best we could do. It was the best we could do with the material and the time allotted. But that harsh reality didn't make for much of a slogan, and it wasn't conducive to good ad copy in our teaser spots: "Here's the best we could do in nine weeks!" Garth and Jamie kept telling us not to worry, and to just keep pushing on.

As the activity within each network picked up, so did the activity at the corporate level among the parent companies of both networks. More than once during the 12-year war, the sides submitted to cease-fires to quietly explore the feasibility of joining forces as a single, stronger network. Time and again, the main obstacles to the union came from how station affiliation assignments would be divvied up between Tribune and Chris-Craft and who would run the combined networks. In late 1994, Sumner Redstone got a call in New York from Warner Bros.' Bob Daly. Daly and his top Warner Bros.' executives wanted to talk to Redstone and Jonathan Dolgen about their respective network ventures. They set up a dinner date at the original Spago eatery on Sunset Boulevard in West Los Angeles.

When they gathered a week or so later, Daly, his Warner Bros.' co-chairman and CEO, Terry Semel, and Barry Meyer were pleased to hear that Redstone and Jonathan Dolgen were on the same page with them about the two-network race. It made no sense. Anybody could see that there was really only enough room out there in the station marketplace to support one new network, not two.

In between much convivial conversation and Wolfgang Puck's delicacies, the Warner Bros.' executives laid out a proposal for Redstone. Chris-Craft and Tribune would split the two biggest prizes— New York and Los Angeles, and from there on out it wasn't too hard; the two station groups were actually pretty complementary in their station holdings.

"We can wait until we both lose $300 million, or we can merge these networks today," Daly told Redstone that night.

"Sounds smart to me," replied the seventysomething billionaire who'd parlayed his family's small chain of drive-in theaters into a global media powerhouse.

But even with all his clout, Redstone wasn't in a position to OK any deal. Chris-Craft was calling the shots and paying the bills at UPN for at least the first two years.

So Daly and Meyer took their pitch to Chris-Craft executives.*

"I told them, 'This is nuts. We're all going to lose a lot of money. We could be strong by putting the best affiliates together,' " Daly says. "We tried a few times to get Chris-Craft to the table, and they never would do it."

Without Chris-Craft's cooperation, there could never be any deal on UPN's side. So despite the fact that the high-level executives from both parent companies recognized the market could not and would not sustain two start-up broadcast networks, there would be no turning back. As the 1994 holidays wound down and the final pieces of each network's lineup fell into place, there was an overwhelming sense of inevitability in both camps. There would be only one victor in this battle; second place was as good as last. With January 11 and January 16 right around the corner, all we could do was focus on our shows and plot our long-term strategies. And wait for the other side to falter.

---

* Multiple sources with knowledge of the talks recalled Chris-Craft executives balking at the proposal, but others disputed the assertion that such a specific swap offer was ever proposed to Chris-Craft.

CHAPTER THREE

THE NIGHT IS YOUNG

Like most news of real consequence in network television, the verdict on the WB's opening-night ratings performance arrived early the following morning. Most weekdays, the television industry gets its first glimpse of the previous day's ratings by 9 a.m. Eastern time. Those on the West Coast get to wake up to the news of how their networks and shows fared with America the night before. By sunrise in Hollywood, the raw data detailing each major broadcast network's performance in 56 large U.S. cities, encompassing more than 70 percent of the nation's 110 million television households, are available in 15-minute increments. More detailed reports on prime-time ratings for a host of narrowly defined demographic groups—women between the ages of 18 and 49, men in the 25–54 range, female teenagers, boys age 2–11, and on and on—flow in within a few hours.

The final verdict on each network's prime-time performance is set in stone most days by 10 a.m. Eastern with the release of the "finals," or the numbers that ratings provider Nielsen Media Research guarantees have been checked and double-checked for glitches in its national web of electronic monitors implanted in 6,000-plus representative homes across the United States.

With rare exceptions, those final numbers are the most important yardstick for measuring commercial success in television. Ratings are the currency of the realm, the basis for all advertising sales. As such, every morning a small army of research executives working for all manner of entertainment, media, and marketing firms scrutinize the daily ratings reports for insights and ammunition. No one expected the opening-night ratings for the WB and UPN to determine each network's long-term fate. But they would be a strong indicator of which network would win the first round in the court of public perception that a "fifth network" had arrived.

As the WB's launch party at Chasen's restaurant wound down around midnight on the soggy Wednesday night, there was already nervous anticipation among all of us about the arrival in fewer than six hours of the first-ever WB ratings. Rusty Mintz, the WB's executive in charge of ratings and research, knew that his job performance for the rest of his tenure at the network would likely be judged by how quickly he analyzed and distributed those first-night ratings to Jamie Kellner and the rest of us. Rusty shared in the toasts and celebration at Chasen's but was strict about limiting his revelry. Single and in his early 30s, Mintz made sure he got back to his apartment in the Los Feliz area of Los Angeles in plenty of time that night to be rested and ready for his early-morning duty. He lay down in his bed and squeezed his eyes shut, but he had too much adrenaline in him to fall asleep. His ears were still buzzing from the din at Chasen's. It's not every night you raise the curtain on a new network, Rusty thought as he peeked at the clock next to his bed.

Mintz rolled around for what seemed like an eternity until he finally dropped off. He woke up after only an hour or so. His room was pitch black, but he convinced himself that he'd overslept. He bolted out of bed, threw on a pair of jeans and a shirt and tore out to his car. He was well on his way to the freeway on-ramp that would take him to Burbank before he realized it was 3:45 a.m. Screw it, he thought. He decided to drive to the main Warner Bros.' studio lot and wait.

The big lot was eerily quiet at 4 a.m., Mintz thought, looking over his shoulder periodically as he hustled over to the white, single-story box of an office building on the far edge of the lot that housed the studio's television division. He was lucky the security guards knew him from his previous syndication research job or they never would have let him on at that hour of the morning. Once he got to the building, Rusty made a beeline for one particular computer in the research department that he knew was the first point of entry for the studio's daily Nielsen data dump. He pulled up a chair and sat staring, half-asleep, at the blue-ish glow of the PC monitor.

At about 6 a.m., Jamie Kellner was the first to call for the verdict. Mintz wasn't surprised. Nor did Jamie seem surprised when Rusty read him the numbers. The WB's opening-night ratings weren't just unimpressive. They were anemic. The network generated a mere 2.0 household rating, which translated to an average of about 2 million households and just under 3 million viewers for our two-hour program slate. The meager numbers made it plain there wasn't much interest in or awareness of the network, even in the top Tribune markets where the WB had strong affiliates. By any measure, the WB had limped out of the gate.

Kellner convened a company-wide meeting that Thursday morning in which he knew he'd have to be a combination of General George S. Patton, Anthony Robbins, and Winston Churchill to keep the troops motivated. While he did his best "we haven't begun to fight" to keep morale at healthy levels, in truth he wasn't surprised or disappointed by the numbers from the first night. They hadn't spent much on advertising and promotion. He knew better than anyone the limitations of the WB's distribution base. For weeks leading up to the launch, Jamie and Garth went out of their way to manage our expectations for the initial ratings. From the standpoint of the general public, we were still an unknown commodity, which meant we had plenty of chances to get it right with the right shows.

Most important, Jamie and the other Fox alums advised us, we couldn't get bogged down in the industry or media gossip mill about the WB-versus-UPN or predictions of our demise. Given the prominence of Warner Bros. and the players involved, it was inevitable there would be scrutiny of our performance in industry circles. All we could do was keep working hard, continue to staff up, and focus on finding the WB's signature shows.

On that Thursday morning after the launch, the two of them assured us that Warner Bros. and Time Warner were firmly behind the WB, that one night did not make or break a network and that we were on the right track. There was some eye rolling among the staff at that suggestion, but even if we didn't exactly believe him, we appreciated the effort Jamie made to buck us up. After a while, his confidence spread.

"There wasn't an overwhelming sense of panic, no matter what the public perception was," says Jordan Levin. "There was a sense of history there with Garth and Jamie and Bob and Lew and Jed. They kept saying, 'We've done this tour before. This isn't nearly as bad as it was at Fox at the beginning.' "

At UPN, the reaction to those first overnight numbers was decidedly different. Early on the morning of Tuesday, January 17, after UPN's simultaneous premiere parties in Hollywood and New York, Lucie Salhany got a call at home from Kevin Tannehill, the executive who had played host at the New York party. At first Salhany thought Tannehill was just being overzealous in checking in with her about the event. She was worn out from the pressure-cooker feeling of the night before and the nonstop pace of her job since she'd joined UPN four months earlier. But after a minute on the phone with Tannehill, she was howling with laughter. He regaled her with the drama of the missing *Star Trek: Voyager* dubs and how they wriggled their way out of what would have been a disastrous stumble in the biggest media market in the world. Salhany hadn't known the full extent of what had gone wrong in New York until then.

"We almost didn't have a show to show these people, Lucie," Tannehill told her. "You know how embarrassing that would have been?" But Salhany couldn't answer. She was gasping for breath between laughs.

Salhany might not have been so easygoing about the New York snafu had she not woken up to mind-bendingly good news. UPN had rocketed out of the gate with more than 21 million viewers tuning in to the two-hour *Star Trek: Voyager*. That was at least 18 million more than checked out the WB's maiden voyage five days earlier. With its first broadcast, UPN beat ABC, CBS, NBC, and Fox affiliates in many big cities where UPN had its strongest stations. The performance was a testament to the drawing power of a *Star Trek* franchise and to the fact that Paramount spent a small fortune in advertising to promote *Voyager*'s premiere date.

UPN staffers celebrated that morning in their cramped quarters on the Paramount lot with bagels and champagne. The congratulations rolled in all morning for what had been an impressive debut—a 13 household rating—a performance the network would never equal, let alone surpass, again. But on that morning after the four-month mad dash to get UPN up and running, Salhany and her staff took the time for a few bows. Even the feuding partners behind the network were celebrating that day. Many of them framed the front page of the following day's edition of *The Hollywood Reporter* with its banner headline: "UPN sets sail in 1st place."

The mood at UPN didn't drop much even after the sobering news of the ratings for the network's launch of its second night of programming on Tuesday. The debuts of dramas *Marker* and *The Watcher* hadn't come anywhere near beating the major networks, even on UPN's strongest stations. They did better than the WB's ratings, but not by all that much.

No matter. UPN had won the first round in the court of public opinion. It was the one to watch.

"We were the fifth network," says former UPN publicity chief Kevin Brockman. "We were winning the spin war. We had the magazine covers and the *TV Guide* covers. If you'd asked anyone in the industry which of the two networks was more likely to survive, it'd be us. We just had it."

Or so they thought. The one thing they didn't have, and wouldn't have for a long time, was a really big hit show. *Voyager* by the end of its first season settled into credible, but not impressive, ratings territory. It was by far the most-watched program on the network, but for Paramount, it was a ratings disappointment compared to *Star Trek: The Next Generation* and *Star Trek: Deep Space Nine*. It never was the kind of talked-about show that UPN desperately needed to lure viewers. Nor was *Voyager* particularly popular with ardent Trekkies. The series' premise was built around the *Voyager* being a lost starship that had been hurtled, as if by sling-shot, by a freak storm into a distant part of the galaxy—a place so remote that the return trip home would take 75 years. With that plot device, *Voyager's* captain and crew members didn't get out of the ship much at all, which gave the writers a limited canvas for storytelling in the first season.

Nobody at UPN much liked to admit it, but it became clear after just a few weeks that *Voyager* was both the network's biggest asset and its Achilles' heel. *Voyager* was an island unto UPN, pulling in an older, whiter, more affluent, and more male viewership than anything else—by far—on the network. As such, UPN's programming executives always had an impossible time finding suitable companion shows for its marquee property. Salhany had warned her bosses at Chris-Craft about the uniqueness of the *Star Trek* demographic, which she knew well from experience in launching *Star Trek: The Next Generation* when she was at Paramount in the 1980s.

By the end of its first mini-season, January to May 1995, every show on UPN's inaugural slate except *Voyager* would be canceled. Lucie Salhany counseled her troops just as Kellner had counseled his. Keep moving, keep focused. The first year is about learning to crawl.

Despite the WB's wobbly start, Jamie Kell-ner was in his entrepreneurial element. No matter how many potshots the industry took at the "frog" network, the WB was on the air. He had faith that his new team would pull together to find and market the hit shows we needed to put us on the map. WB was Kellner's fief and he ran it as such, but he did not have total autonomy. Warner Bros. was not a silent partner. In addition, Bob Daly loved being back in the weeds of prime time, strategizing once again, some 16 years after he left CBS for Warner Bros., and the studio chairman made a point of attending the WB's pilot screenings and fall scheduling meetings. Bruce Rosenblum also remained intimately involved with the WB in the two years that had passed since he helped Kellner draft the blueprint for the network. Rosenblum was a regular presence at the WB's company-wide staff meeting that Jamie presided over every Tuesday morning.

At those staff meetings, everyone, from assistants to top managers, was encouraged to speak their mind: about the state of the network, the industry, pop culture, and the shows the WB was putting on. Jamie encouraged staffers to speak freely if they didn't like a show or something else about the WB. It was clear he genuinely enjoyed debating about the industry, trends, gossip, and new creative ideas. The 10 a.m. Tuesday ritual became a good way to keep track of the company's growth, as it became a tighter and tighter squeeze to get the entire company into our main conference room each week.

Shortly after the launch, ratings guru Rusty Mintz became the unofficial emcee of the meetings. Lanky and clean-cut, with a natural deadpan in his voice, Rusty would open the meetings with some ratings information from the past week followed by a few jokes. We were a tough crowd, so most weeks Rusty worked on his material in advance.

Mintz had another sacred responsibility as the keeper of The Gong. After the WB moved into its trailers at the ranch, Kellner had a large, saucer-shaped gong hanging in a circular wrought-iron frame placed in the WB's lobby. Whenever the network hit a ratings milestone or sold a commercial spot for a record price or signed a new affiliate, the staff would squeeze into our narrow, low-ceilinged lobby and cheer as Mintz let loose and hit the gong, releasing a resonant minor-key note that would reverberate off the aluminum trailer walls.

Most of the time, the only discord of note that flared in the Tuesday staff meeting was between Kellner and Rosenblum. The two knew each other well from long before the WB came along, but they often had contradictory perspectives on how the WB should be run and where the television business was headed. The debates between Kellner and Rosenblum could be fascinating as they batted around big-picture concepts and issues. At times, though, there were fundamental clashes. What was good for Warner Bros. Television was not always so good for the WB, and vice versa. Rosenblum was tasked with representing the studio side and its investment in the network. Jamie Kellner's only interest was in building the strongest network possible, no matter what.

The room would invariably grow quiet when Jamie and Bruce would go at it—respectfully, for the most part. It was easy to tell when Jamie was really annoyed. He'd show it in his own steely-caustic way. Bruce would always try to keep a smile on his face, but there were times when we knew he too was fuming. Those of us on the sidelines around the conference-room table would squirm, as if we were watching our parents fight.

Aside from the occasional intra-family squabble, the meetings were a productive and reliable way to gauge where we were as a company on a week-by-week basis. Often, I would use the meeting as a chance to bring up new ideas or directions that I thought we should gain. These ideas were constantly in flux. We were trying to ramp up our script development for the WB's first full-length season, which was a sizable undertaking. Whereas before we had been working toward the launch date, the new deadline we were racing toward was May 22—the day we were scheduled to join the annual network ritual of the "upfront" unveiling of our programming plans for the 1995–96 season to advertisers and media in New York City.

We were happy to shift gears from the launch-panic mode of the previous few months to a slightly more conventional program-development process, but I still felt like I was flying blind. I had no idea what my budget was or how much money I had to spend on scripts. At ABC and Fox, I'd worked within strict budgets, and knew exactly how much I could spend each year on contracts with creative talent. This was not the case when the WB began. Our inaugural slate of shows had been such a scramble to pull together that there hadn't been time to think about long-term budgets. Now the focus was to prepare for a full September–May prime-time season with two nights of programming—three hours on Sunday and two hours on Wednesday. In order to do this, I needed to get at least two dozen projects percolating. Or so I thought.

Garth, Jordan, and I spent a lot of time talking about our approach and our basic development philosophy on how to approach our shows. We'd all seen the good, the bad, and the ugly of how the modern network television sausage factory works. We agreed that in our collective experience, the best approach was to hire interesting creative people with strong visions for their characters and settings, and then let them do their thing. We vowed never to "note" our writers to death. I had strong feelings about how writers should be treated. After all, I married one!

Following this plan, Jordan and I found plenty of interesting things to choose from, and we recited our pledges to everyone in the industry who would listen. Despite our best intentions, we were still facing a lot of skepticism and snubs, making it a struggle to get the time of day from the representatives for A-list creative talent. By necessity, as well as by our own dare-to-be-different design, we trained our focus on finding fresh talent.

One of the only heavy hitters in the industry to respond to our desperate cry for help in programming that first year was the mighty Creative Artists Agency. The agency's leadership was very savvy about working within our constraints (read: lower pay for their clients) in the short term to help seed a new customer for their clients over the long term. Of course, I never forgot the helping hand they gave us when we needed it most. Most of the WB's first shows were stocked with CAA clients, including Robert Townsend and Shawn and Marlon Wayans. The smart, young agent assigned to oversee our network, Steve Smooke, consistently delivered for us, bringing to the WB budding superstars like Jamie Foxx.

"The WB in the beginning was one of the best experiences I ever had in terms of honesty, depth of character, and of caring about what they did," says former CAA Co-chairman Lee Gabler. "They would sit around a table and talk about things like they were running CBS, NBC, ABC, all at once. It was just infectious. You just wanted to be involved with people that were that committed."

We recognized at the outset that our area of weakness as executives was the hour-long series form. Jordan and I both came from a background of comedy and specials. Garth's big successes at NBC and Fox had come in the comedy realm, not drama. We loved to spend time analyzing what we liked and didn't like, and asking why so many shows were formulaic—the cop show, the lawyer show, the medical show, etc.—and stale.

We wanted our hour-long series to play more like mini-movies and be built around enigmatic youthful characters—not the case of the week or the disease of the week. "A cinematic feel" was our catchphrase. Garth was a fantastic mentor, helping us hone our vision for what would become the WB's signature program genre—the coming-of-age teen dramedy.

We were also still struggling with our late start, again, to pilot season. From late summer through late fall, network programming executives are consumed with taking pitches from writers and their agents on ideas and concepts for series pilots. Once an idea is commissioned, writers tend to hibernate for a month or so with their laptops or legal pads. First drafts are usually turned in to the commissioning network from late November to early December. Around mid-January, the much-maligned "network notes" are delivered to the writer(s), and rewriting ensues. By the time the second and third drafts are in the works, programming executives have a pretty good sense of whether the project has any hope of getting to the pilot stage.

Because we had experienced such a massive scramble for shows in preparation for the launch, we had essentially missed the chance to develop scripts for fall 1995 on the regular pilot schedule. In the spring of 1995, as we were pounding the pavement for fresh material, the major networks were already shooting their pilots for the year.

In addition to being behind schedule, I knew we were also up against financial constraints, only I wasn't exactly sure what my limitations were. I prodded Jamie every time I saw him to tell me how much money we had to spend on development. When we ran across a few things that I wanted to try that were on the high end of the script sale, I hesitated. I didn't want to blow my entire budget on a few expensive scripts. I finally called Jamie and demanded to know the figures. He couldn't brush me off this time.

"Is this a trust issue for you?" I asked in exasperation. "I don't understand why you feel like you can't share the budget with me?"

"I just don't want you to feel limited," Kellner said in a quiet but clear voice. "If something great comes along, I want you to come back to me for more money. I don't want you to limit yourself."

I was relieved. His answer demonstrated why he was such a good programmer even if he wasn't schooled in creative development and production per se. I had to promise him, as if reciting a Girl Scout pledge, that I would come back to him in an instant if I found something great. In that regard, Jamie was a development executive's dream boss.

And then he gave me the round number: $1 million.

That was enough to buy only about 12 scripts. A dozen swings at bat to launch a new night—it meant that at least four new shows would have to be ready to go for September. Plus we needed a few midseason replacements. I hadn't been expecting an ABC- or Fox-size budget, but I expected more than 12 scripts.

After I got off the phone with Jamie, I found Jordan and told him the number. From his time at Disney, he'd also been accustomed to having vast resources at his fingertips. Jordan was sitting in a chair in front of my desk with his legs propped up on another chair. He looked like he was deep in thought.

After a long pause, Jordan abruptly swung his legs down to the ground, reached across my desk, which was covered in scripts and videos, and grabbed a packet of yellow Post-it notes sitting atop a pile of scripts that seemed to be headed for an avalanche. He pressed a dozen Post-its onto the wall beside my desk and numbered them 1 through 12.

For the rest of pilot season, every time we heard a pitch, we'd look over at the row of Post-its and think, "Is this good enough to be one of the 12?"

• • •

Because of their revenue limitations, both UPN and the WB were forced to get creative in the kinds of deals they were able to put together. Just as Fox had a decade earlier, the WB and UPN worked out agreements with Hollywood's creative guilds—the Screen Actors Guild, Writers Guild of America, and Directors Guild of America—that called for a reduced rate on the minimum standard fees and residual payments that networks are obligated to pay creative talent on shows. Such breaks from the unions representing actors, writers, and directors were vital to giving us the chance to grow and compete with our larger network rivals.

Even with the reduced rates, there were many revenue shortcomings, and it was because of this that the goal of getting shows rerun in syndication was even more important for UPN and the WB than it was for the Big Four networks. Syndication profits from Warner Bros.- and Paramount-produced shows from the WB and UPN would help the studios offset the high costs of running their networks.

In the era when UPN and the WB were born, producers of prime-time series made most of their money from syndication sales, or when local TV stations and cable channels purchased the rerun rights to specific shows. In most cases, the producers and studios who put together the shows would lose money on the initial prime-time run of a show because the license fee the network paid for the show would rarely cover all of the production costs. For producers and studios, the gap between what the network paid and what each episode cost to produce is known as the "deficit." In recent years, the deficit typically ranges from $300,000 to $1 million or more per episode for a high-end series, sometimes much more if the show has highly paid stars. Studios absorb those production deficits in the hope of making their money back, and then some, through syndication sales. If the show lasted long enough to rack up about 100 episodes, or at least four seasons at 22–24 episodes per season, the studio would be able to sell the rerun rights in syndication. The 100-episode milestone was (and still is) significant for syndication sales because it allows flexibility in scheduling those reruns. Having 100 or more episodes means that a local TV station or cable outlet can run the show on a Monday–Friday basis without having to show the same episodes more than once over a few months' time.

The more successful a program was in its initial run, the more money it typically commanded in syndication fees. Paramount and Warner Bros. knew that shows debuting on UPN and the WB were not likely to garner the kind of money in syndication as a hit coming from ABC, CBS, Fox, or NBC, but both studios felt that in time they would achieve parity. Not only were the new networks investments, their programming was an investment as well.

On paper, the business models dictated that Paramount would be the primary supplier of shows to UPN, just as Warner Bros. would be the dominant producer for the WB. In practice, however, getting the two sides of the same factory to work together became inordinately complicated for both networks due to executive ego clashes and conflicting agendas.

It was also understood that both networks could not rely exclusively on their studio siblings to provide every one of their shows. UPN and the WB would never be taken seriously as networks within Hollywood's creative community if they didn't do business with other important producers. But first, UPN and the WB both had to scale mountains of skepticism. Despite the ties to two of Hollywood's major studios, many in the industry doubted whether UPN or the WB would last another four months, let alone the four seasons needed to get a show to syndication. And even if one or both survived, few believed that shows coming off the WB and UPN would be worth anything to syndication buyers, given their lower profile on fledgling networks.

With all of these unknowns, it was something of a miracle that the Walt Disney Company's television division agreed to produce Ron Leavitt's comedy *Unhappily Ever After* for the WB's launch slate. We weren't surprised when they sought to do it on the cheap—super cheap. The show was bawdy and sophomoric. Its gimmicky nature was accentuated by the presence of a large, wise-cracking, scraggly bunny puppet named Mr. Floppy, who regularly conversed (in Bobcat

Goldthwait's voice) with the show's used car-salesman father, whose family had thrown him out of the house.

During our first few years, the WB paid production companies and studios a standard program license fee of $350,000 to $400,000 per episode for a half-hour show. UPN's fees were in the same ballpark as ours. At the time $450,000 to $500,000 was the norm for the Big Four. Both the WB and UPN were a bit more competitive in the hour-long arena, with license fees of $750,000 to $850,000 per episode at a time when the going rate for ABC, CBS, and NBC was about $900,000 to $1 million.

The bigger problem for the start-up networks was that, beyond the license fee, the producers and studios were very wary of spending much money on production of a WB or UPN show. Because they depended on syndication sales to reimburse them for their deficits, many producers and studios felt there was unsettlingly little reassurance that they would ever get their money back. Disney had such doubts about the syndication viability of *Unhappily Ever After* that it refused to absorb any deficits on the show. That meant production costs had to be slashed even further than the shoestring budgets we were prepared to work with.

"Ron Leavitt and the staff literally had no offices of their own," Jordan Levin recalls. "They would work out of a conference room, all of them. The craft-services table was one of those variety packs of Frito-Lay chips. That and some card tables in the green room—that was it."

Paramount Television produced every show on UPN's inaugural slate, which consisted of two nights of programming to the WB's one, with the exception of the Tuesday drama *Marker,* the Hawaii-based private-eye drama starring Richard Grieco. *Marker* hailed from the independent company run by veteran producer Stephen J. Cannell, who also owned a few TV stations, including the UPN affiliate station in Cleveland, Ohio. UPN and Cannell were a natural fit—Cannell was known for high-octane action dramas; UPN was targeting a young male audience. And as an independent producer, Cannell had every incentive to help build a new network and another potential customer.

(Cannell produced one of Fox's first successful series, *21 Jump Street,* which also featured Grieco.) But by 1995, due to corporate media consolidation and the sunset of fin-syn, indies like Cannell were a dying breed. Two months after UPN's debut, Cannell sold the bulk of his Cannell Entertainment to Ronald Perelman's New World Communications for $30 million.

While these financial limitations for programming were challenging, the fact that they were the same on both sides seemed to level the playing field at the outset. The programming issue for UPN and the WB was about who could work within limitations the best. Because industry analysts, independent producers, and studios all doubted the long-term viability of both networks, we were forced to get creative in order to overcome that start-up stigma.

Lucie Salhany rarely saw eye to eye with Kerry McCluggage on programming matters, a fundamental disconnect that was a source of conflict between them throughout her tenure.

Salhany was singularly unimpressed by what Paramount had to offer the network. For Salhany, Exhibit A in the why-bother category was the fantasy Western *Legend* starring Richard Dean Anderson, who was long removed from his *MacGyver* heyday. The show appeared in April 1995 and was gone by August. It replaced another show Salhany loathed, the mystery anthology *The Watcher*. A ratings bomb, *Watcher* only ran as long as it did (through early April) because UPN had nothing else in the larder.

A few months after UPN went on the air, Paramount Television learned that ABC was planning to cancel the studio's family sitcom *Sister, Sister,* starring twins Tamera and Tia Mowry, after one season. The cancellation of a show after one or two seasons is the cruelest blow for a studio; the show has been in production long enough to rack up millions of dollars in deficit spending, yet it hasn't produced enough episodes to bring in meaningful syndication dollars.

Paramount urged UPN to pick up the show, but Salhany balked. *Sister, Sister* would be a bad fit with the rest of UPN's programming, she thought. How could a network aimed at young men throw on a *Parent Trap*-esque show about twin sisters who find each other at age 14 after being separated at birth? At the time, Salhany and her troops were pulling together the network's first full-season slate, and it was stocked entirely with hour-long drama series. Even the shows in the works for the network's planned expansion to Wednesday night in March 1996 were hard-edged dramas. UPN had no rational place to put *Sister, Sister*, Salhany argued—at times loudly.

Paramount found a ready taker for *Sister, Sister*, not at Fox, NBC, or CBS, but at the WB. Setting aside the corporate battle of the "netlets," as *Variety* branded the pubescent networks, the WB was a natural place for Paramount to go with the wholesome family comedy, given its tonal similarity to the WB's *The Parent 'Hood*. But the deal between UPN's sibling studio and its start-up rival raised eyebrows in industry circles and fueled scuttlebutt about the ill will between McCluggage and Salhany, and between Paramount and Chris-Craft.

"They went up one side of me and down the other," Salhany says. "From Paramount it was, 'You should have taken it; you people don't know what you're doing.' There was always pressure to take Paramount shows, even if they weren't right for us. I would say, 'You can't do that and be true to your affiliates.'"

Paramount's deal with the WB came together as both start-ups were preparing for their initiation into the annual ritual of the network upfront presentation, a splashy two- to four-hour event in New York City where networks tout their plans for the upcoming season's prime-time programming to advertisers and the media. These events are typically scheduled during mid-May at grandiose venues such as Radio City Music Hall, Carnegie Hall, Lincoln Center, and Madison Square Garden. Unless they joined the parade of presentations, the WB and UPN would never be seen as full-fledged networks.

The mandate of the upfronts is to get advertising buyers enthused about the network and its shows for the upcoming season.

Within weeks of those presentations, a frenzy of buying and selling advance advertising commitments erupts, in a marathon of deal-making that often runs around the clock for days until the networks have sold most of their available ad spots for the coming season.

Network executives often fiddle with their program scheduling plans until the final hours before the presentation starts, particularly when it comes to giving a thumbs-up or thumbs-down to new shows. It's not unheard-of for a pilot to be picked up and dumped, then picked up again on the day of a network's presentation—sometimes entirely as a result of financial or deal-point concerns, sometimes because an executive's spouse really hates a certain pilot. The run-up to upfront presentation day is a chaotic time at any network, let alone for a fledgling network going through it for the first time.

The negotiations between McCluggage, other Paramount executives, and the WB executives on picking up *Sister, Sister* were businesslike and entirely unremarkable. All of the principals involved knew one another from past jobs, but Paramount did make us sweat a little more than necessary by dragging its feet on confirming that it would accept our offer for the show. That made things more difficult because we had to have a Plan B if we didn't get the show. We wanted it to be the 8 p.m. cornerstone of our Wednesday night lineup that consisted of the same shows as our previous Wednesday schedule sans *Muscle* (which became our first cancellation at the end of the season). We wondered if Paramount would pull a fast one and move *Sister, Sister* to UPN at the last minute.

Jamie Kellner and the rest of us had already gathered at our hotel in New York when the call from Paramount finally came—on the afternoon of the day before our upfront. Plan A, it was, to our great relief.

From Madison Avenue's perspective, the timing of UPN and the WB's entry into the marketplace couldn't have been better. The television advertising market was on fire in the mid-1990s following a downturn in the early-1990s recessionary period. The entrance of Fox and the rapidly growing cable arena had been good for the industry in a rising-tide-lifts-all-boats kind of way. But despite the vast expanse in the supply of national television advertising time, the Big Four networks were still able to command enormous annual price hikes of 10 percent to 20 percent during this period, even as the size of their audience continued to erode slowly but surely, in the face of new competition. The bull market conditions for television advertising mirrored Wall Street's wild ride in the 1990s. Because of the ad rates that ABC, CBS, NBC, and Fox were commanding, the WB and UPN were welcomed by the powerful media buying agencies that decide where Fortune 500 companies spend their TV advertising dollars. Although the WB and UPN had their limitations as start-ups, the entry of two new national broadcast networks into the marketplace gave media buyers some leverage against the aggressive price increases sought each year by ABC, CBS, Fox, and NBC.

Throughout his career, Jamie Kellner had gone out of his way to maintain strong relationships in the advertising and media-buying worlds. He knew how to speak their language, and he knew how important it was for a start-up to have Madison Avenue rooting for you as an underdog. He'd done a masterful job in selling Fox to advertising's stodgy elite back in 1986, and as such, Kellner was very particular when he was casting about for an executive to oversee the WB's advertising sales department in New York. When he approached his former Fox colleague Jed Petrick about the job, Petrick was more than interested, though he had to serve out the last few months of a contract with another company before he could move to the WB in October 1994.

Shortly before he started, Petrick made a round of calls to key advertising contacts and learned something alarming. Many of the most important media buyers in the industry were skeptical that the WB would actually get on the air. There were rumors that Time Warner had been getting squeamish about the cost of launching a network. The chatter in New York media circles was that Time Warner was far more interested in buying NBC or CBS. Petrick called Kellner and bluntly told him they had a big problem. Kellner didn't have to be told twice. To greet Petrick on his first day, Kellner rounded up Bob Daly and Barry Meyer, Time Warner's Gerald Levin, and Tribune's

Dennis FitzSimons for a show-of-force presentation at Time Warner's New York headquarters to about 100 media buyers. It was a well-timed and effective move. The WB's initial fleet of advertisers included numerous blue-chip companies, including Anheuser-Busch, Nestlé, General Motors, Bristol-Myers, Kraft Foods, and National Dairy. None of those advertisers saw any of the WB's shows or even a list of its station affiliates until two days before the network launched. They went on blind faith in Kellner and his team, Petrick says.

"The buying community almost universally rooted for the WB. Only a few of them felt we would succeed, but as a group, they truly hoped we would," Petrick says.

UPN was also well received by the advertising community because it had a successful, known commodity in *Star Trek* to offer. Internally, however, advertising sales were the source of much angst for Salhany and her team. For the first two years of its existence, UPN didn't have a dedicated advertising sales department. Paramount already had control of all ad revenue for the network's most attractive property, *Star Trek: Voyager*. In an effort to save on UPN's overhead costs at the outset, the partners agreed to let Paramount's existing Premier Advertiser Sales division handle all of UPN's ad time.

The Paramount executive who headed Premier did not report to Salhany, not even on UPN matters. This frustrated UPN's chief executive to no end, and Salhany fumed as the lack of a dedicated advertising sales force left her network with zero presence on Madison Avenue.

"We couldn't possibly ever catch up under those terms," Salhany says. "Jamie Kellner and Warner Bros. did it properly. They had their own sales arm, they hired the best people, and they treated it like a network. Whereas we couldn't because we had this weak and ill-conceived operating agreement."

The WB's advertising sales advantage would prove a vital component in our success a few years later when we became the darling of advertising buyers. But the WB's first upfront presentation was an inauspicious debut.

We couldn't have hoped to fill a large hall, so we went for the hipper (or so we convinced ourselves) Roseland Ballroom for our Monday, May 22 event. The floors were dance-hall sticky. There were rats in the bathroom, and there were reports of a giant puddle of murky water in the men's room from a backed-up drain. The smell was enough to keep people from staying through the entire presentation.

All WB hands arrived at Roseland early that morning to pitch in with the set-up and to rehearse our presentations—at least parts of them. Garth Ancier cringed when he saw staffers hanging up fliers and banners featuring the call letters and logos of the WB's various affiliate stations. The liberal use of silvery duct tape screamed "start-up network," he observed. It reminded him of some of the rocky early presentations Fox had mounted.

Jordan Levin couldn't contain himself when he saw the banner for the network's affiliate on the island of Guam. Considering all the holes in the WB's affiliate lineup in the continental United States, it struck Levin and others as funny that the WB was covered on a U.S. protectorate near the Philippines with a population of 150,000.

"We've got Guam," Levin said over and over, pointing to the flag of the U.S. protectorate that was taped up next to the station's call letters.

More laughs had to be suppressed when the representative from the WB's Baltimore affiliate station showed up a little early. He stood out, even among the WB's eclectic group of affiliate station managers because he was an undergraduate at Towson University, in the Baltimore suburb of Towson, Maryland. The TV station was run by the university and thus could only be received by TV sets on the campus and immediate surrounding neighborhood. However, it was the only outlet available to the WB that would cover even a sliver of what was then the nation's 24th-largest TV market. The station embraced us wholeheartedly, taking on the call letters WMJF-TV in honor of Michigan J. Frog. (Our affiliate relations chief Hal Protter learned the hard way that he had to pay a student to stay at school during holiday break periods to ensure that the station stayed on the air.)

The clinking of glasses from the open bar in the rear of the ballroom nearly drowned out Jamie and Garth as they made the opening remarks to the advertising buyers. Garth told them they were taking "dead aim" at the kids, teens, and young adults ABC had left behind with the dismantling of its "TGIF" Friday comedy lineup.

"For those of you who thought we were going to try to out-Fox Fox in program content, you can relax," Jamie added.

The clinking grew louder as Garth and I embarked on what remains one of the most uncomfortable experiences of my professional life. The only thing I can say in our defense is that it seemed like a good idea at the time. Thinking like a talk show producer, Garth had the idea that we should bring out a few director's chairs and present our shows á la *Regis and Kathie Lee,* including interviews with the stars of our shows. These segments would be more entertaining for buyers than the average network rah-rah-rah with meaningless statistics and charts. It all sounded good, in theory.

In practice, it was something else entirely. Something bad. Our stars were as unprepared as we were. It's harder than it looks to have a casual conversation with unknown actors. We brought out Jackie Guerra, the Latina star of our comedy *First Time Out*; Ellen Cleghorne, of *Saturday Night Live*, who played a single mother in the sitcom *Cleghorne!*; and our big star that year, Kirk Cameron, the former heartthrob of ABC's *Growing Pains* who tried unsuccessfully to navigate the transition from kid to adult actor with our sitcom *Kirk.*

I kept straining to think of things to ask that wouldn't sound inane. I never had so much appreciation for those people who are comfortable ad-libbing in front of a crowd or a camera. Afterwards, Garth was easygoing about the whole thing. He agreed it hadn't gone too well, but he was always adventurous about that kind of thing, always willing to chalk things up to an "interesting shot." Me? I was embarrassed beyond belief. On top of everything else, pictures from the incident confirm that even my hair was a frizzy mess during the whole event. From that day forward, I've been obsessive about planning and rehearsing every detail whenever I'm called on to perform as an executive. Especially in New York in the springtime.

UPN held its first May upfront presentation five days before the

WB at the Theater at Madison Square Garden. Thanks to the halo effect of *Voyager*'s strong premiere, UPN drew a good crowd of media buyers. Its presentation was slicker and more polished than the WB's. Salhany touted the network's ratings and distribution advantage over its rival, the extraordinary *Voyager* premiere numbers, and the network's plan to expand to Wednesday night the following March. Plus, her hair looked great.

"Dramatically different" was part of UPN's sloganeering that year. After flopping with *Pig Sty* and *Platypus Man,* the decision was made to go entirely with drama series for UPN's first full season. Entertainment president Michael Sullivan touted the network's new dramas as shows that "could not be found on any other network."

The shows were a mixed bag of action, fantasy, and sci-fi vehicles with stars that were a mismatch for a network that professed to be courting a young male audience. *Deadly Games* starred Christopher Lloyd, known to viewers as the space-cadet stoner Jim Ignatowski of *Taxi*; he was cast as the evil supervillain of a video game come to life and bent on destroying Los Angeles. *Live Shot,* starring TV staple David Birney, was a soap opera set in a TV newsroom where bed-hopping among the staff was the primary agenda. *Swift Justice* was a run-of-the-mill gumshoe drama about a cop who "breaks all the rules." *Nowhere Man* was an ambitious thriller in the vein of *The Fugitive* about a photojournalist pursued by a secretive underground government that destroyed his identity. *The Sentinel* revolved around a cop who came back from a trip to the Peruvian jungle with heightened sensory perception and visions that made him a "human crime lab." Of the lot, only *Sentinel* would survive its first season, in part because it was produced at some expense by Paramount.

After getting through their first upfront, UPN executives returned to L.A. to prepare for another big move. Since its inception the network had been housed on the Paramount lot, but that May it moved to newly renovated offices on Wilshire Boulevard in West Los Angeles. The move sent a message to Paramount executives that could not have been clearer. Even in the best of traffic conditions, UPN's new offices were a good 30-minute drive on surface streets from the studio's lot in Hollywood. The site was, however, convenient to Chris-Craft's offices in Beverly Hills.

Salhany took an active role in redesigning the interior of the three-story Italian villa-style building to her liking. She wanted plenty of open spaces for people to congregate and a big wide staircase connecting the first two floors so people would interact more freely than they might in an elevator. The network's staffers were going to have to work long and hard in those offices the next few years. She wanted them to be comfortable.

"What I really wanted was a big warehouse with offices, so everybody could be in a big room together communicating with no walls. But you couldn't do that," Salhany says. "So when I met with the architect I told him I didn't want anything hidden. I wanted everything with glass walls facing the common areas so that when you walked in, it would feel very open."

When they finally moved in, Salhany gave everyone, from assistants to executive vice presidents, a modest budget for decorating their office or cubicle. She'd always felt it was unfair that only top brass got such luxuries. It was her housewarming present to the staff.

"Everybody went out to flea markets together and picked out tables and chairs to refinish," Salhany says. "There were certain things that were uniform about the offices, but everybody got to go out and pick out a few of their own things. People worked long, long hours. This was going to be home for them."

In the summer of 1995, the media world was abuzz with talk of wheeling and dealing, mergers and acquisitions, stock prices and initial public offerings. You couldn't escape it. The Walt Disney Company shocked the media and business worlds with its stealth $19 billion acquisition of ABC. CBS was the subject of many rumors until it was purchased by Westinghouse Electric Corp. for $5.4 billion. A start-up software company called Netscape upended the rules of the stock market in the dog days of August by going public at $71 a share, after being priced at $28. Jamie Kellner kept telling us we were fortunate to live in interesting times. I agreed with him, most days.

There was rampant speculation in the business press about further studio-network hookups in the wake of the Disney-ABC pairing. At the WB, we were nervous that Bob Daly would feel renewed pressure to buy a "real" network. There were persistent rumors that Time Warner wanted NBC, which we figured meant curtains for little 'ol us.

Time Warner was involved in a mega-bucks merger in the summer of 1995, but it wasn't with NBC. Time Warner boss Gerald Levin was negotiating with Ted Turner to buy out his Turner Broadcasting System Inc. cable empire, home to powerhouse cable channels CNN, TNT, TBS, and the Cartoon Network, among other assets. The $7.5 billion deal promised to fortify Time Warner's position in the cable business and had the bonus of reuniting Warner Bros. with its pre-1948 film library, which had been sold off long ago. We never saw it coming until the first rumors of the deal leaked in the press in late August, but it was a no-brainer for Time Warner. Despite the upside for the studio, all of us worried that the merger might make them less enthusiastic about backing a fledgling broadcast network.

Bob Daly and Barry Meyer seemed to go out of their way to reassure us that the strategic rationale for launching the WB was still sound. In this era, the Hollywood mindset remained broadcast-centric. The thinking was that Turner's powerful cable channels would never be able to draw as large a crowd or as much money for a 30-second commercial as even a struggling broadcast network because cable was still not as readily accessible to viewers as free over-the-air broadcast TV.

As the TBS acquisition proceeded, we continued to enjoy incredible freedom in pursuing new shows for the network. Nobody came and curtailed our budgets, so in time we stopped worrying about the merger. We wouldn't find out until months later what having Ted Turner in the Time Warner fold as a major shareholder, division head, and board member would mean for the WB.

The legendary chairman of TBS was no fan of the WB. He

thought it was an expensive toy for the already over-pampered War-ner Bros.' executives. He didn't seem to care much for Jamie Kellner, and he was incensed that Jamie had a piece of the WB, by many ac-counts. He wanted to see Time Warner go after an established broad-cast network, or plow the money devoted to the WB into better programming for his cable channels, TNT and TBS in particular. Turner let his feelings about the WB being a losing prospect be known during meetings of the Time Warner board. Turner kept up his cam-paign, and some of it spilled out into the media, which reported his "kill the WB" crusade. But Daly and Time Warner CEO Gerald Levin were highly effective allies who kept the "mouth of the South" at bay and maintained the board's support for us.

Serendipitously, just as Turner was raising questions about our relevance in the new Time Warner, the WB got some good news in the programming department: the move to pick up *Sister, Sister* had been a smart one. The comedy quickly became our highest-rated show, which wasn't saying a lot, but it was still growth. More important, *Sister, Sister* and the audience it attracted helped point our compass in the right direction. Our marketing gurus, Bob Bibb and Lew Gold-stein, were among the first to zero in on the research data showing that in many large markets, *Sister, Sister* was routinely drawing more than half of the teenagers watching television at the time it aired. The fact that we drew bigger crowds with PG-rated fare than we did with the bawdy humor of *Unhappily Ever After* or *Wayans Bros.* was in-triguing.

"We all thought, 'I think we have a niche,'" says Bibb. "We'll let Fox be the bad-boy network, and we can be the place for the good teens, the kids who are home watching TV rather than out getting into trouble. We can be their comfort food."

Salhany never ceded an inch to Paramount in her opposition to *Sister, Sister*, even after it was clear that the show was a boon to our cause at the WB. But the mere fact that a Paramount-produced show was on our air seemed to heighten the hostilities with UPN. As far as the industry was concerned, our success with the show had been

UPN's failure. We knew that had to be grating on the ultracompetitive Salhany.

One of the more entertaining aspects of the UPN-versus-WB feud to outsiders was how strenuously executives at both networks denied that they were in competition with the other. Kellner and Salhany were particularly indignant on this point.

"We're really not competitive," Kellner told reporters during one of the television industry's twice-yearly press junkets held in Pasadena, California, days after the WB and UPN launched in January 1995. "But it makes a nice story."

The WB's wobbly debut hadn't tempered any of Kellner's bravado, and Salhany wasn't the type to hold back either. There was no love lost between the two from the moment Salhany arrived on the Fox lot in 1991, and it became apparent that she was a contender for higher office.

"You just could see them clawing away at each other," says a former head of a Big Four network. "People knew about their history and thought it was kind of funny, like a soap opera."

Despite Kellner and Salhany's public protestations, staffers at the two networks felt as if they were working in a foxhole every day. The mantra at UPN was, "Kill WB." Salhany sparred with Kellner almost as much as she did with the Paramount executives, which endlessly irked Kerry McCluggage and his boss, Viacom Entertainment Group's chairman Jonathan Dolgen, who was Sumner Redstone's top lieutenant in Hollywood.

"It was a game. It used to just go round and round," says a founding UPN executive. "Anytime we could get anything on (the WB), we'd put it out there. It was just all about who could outmaneuver and tackle. We'd go toe to toe with them, even when we were clearly winning."

On our side, WB staffers ate up every piece of news and gossip about our rival. In the WB conference room, the standard-issue magnetic scheduling board was divided into six columns, one for WB, ABC, CBS, NBC, Fox, and finally, "other." In hindsight, it's comical.

We couldn't even put their name up on our board. We saw them as the enemy in the worst way.

At the end of our first year on the air, we brought in a seasoned executive who would prove himself to be an invaluable field marshal for Jamie in the war of words and deeds between the start-up networks. Publicity executive Brad Turell was another former Fox colleague of Kellner's. Turell arrived at the WB in December as the replacement for our first head of publicity, Jim Yeager. Yeager had exited the network in October after repeated clashes with Garth over our publicity strategy. Their fights were not pretty. It seemed out of character for Garth to be as tough as he was on Jim. Garth was one of the most easygoing executives I've ever worked with, but he can be ruthless if he doesn't think a person is doing their job well.

Yeager was one of the few early high-level WB hires who didn't have a long history with Jamie. Yeager was close to Warner Bros.' Bruce Rosenblum, who had recommended him for the job. In the beginning, Garth was particularly peeved that the WB was generating more advance publicity for the Michigan J. Frog mascot (which he loathed) than we were for the four new shows we were working on. Yeager after a while got so frustrated he told Garth in no uncertain terms what he thought of our shows. Things went downhill from there. It was no surprise to any of us that when Yeager got an offer to work for Universal Studios's theme park division, he jumped.

In contrast to Yeager, Turell was schooled in the Fox tradition of making noise and grabbing headlines by (virtually) any means necessary. Turell was pugnacious, known for unleashing tirades on reporters who wrote things that he, or Jamie, didn't like. He was a tireless spin doctor and an invaluable strategist to his boss. He never missed an opportunity to emphasize the "we've-done-it-before, we'll-do-it-again" spirit among the Fox alums running the WB.

In his Fox days, Brad epitomized a new breed of cocky, whip smart, hypercompetitive network executives. Tall and animated, he developed a reputation for playing hard and partying hard, though he was always highly regarded as a good guy to have with you in a fox-hole. By the time the top PR job at WB opened up, Turell by his own admission was in need of a job. He'd left Fox not too long after Kellner in 1993 and had since bounced around from producing concert specials to doing PR for a film company. By the end of 1995, he had a growing family and was in need of a steady paycheck.

We were just as anxious to fill our void on the public relations front. Jamie and Garth knew that the network was in for some renewed scrutiny from the media and from their industry colleagues as the WB's and UPN's one-year anniversaries approached. Our big fear was that the WB would be written off as a dud in the inevitable round of UPN-versus-WB stories that were in the works.

Turell had the good fortune of arriving at the WB just as the circumstances were stacked to allow him a number of big wins right off the bat. He also had an instinctive understanding of how to turn the incessant competition with and comparison to UPN into a galvanizing, rallying force that could be used to our advantage. And we needed any advantage that we could muster at the time because there was no other way to spin it. UPN was winning.

WELCOME TO SUNNYDALE

By the start of WB's second year on the air, we had a few things going for us. *Sister, Sister* had done better than we expected in the ratings. *The Parent 'Hood* was qualitatively better than it had been at the start and would soon gain national media attention for some of its issue-oriented episodes, particularly one dealing with how the middle-class African American family at the center of the show dealt with an unpleasant incidence of racial stereotyping. And our Kids' WB! children's programming block had gotten off the ground on weekday afternoons and Saturday mornings with beautifully produced Warner Bros.' cartoons. Most important, those kiddie cartoons made money for us and Warner Bros. right off the bat. It wasn't enough to put us in the black, by any means, but it helped offset the bills for our prime-time programming. One of the shows developed for Kids' WB!, *Pinky and the Brain*, was so funny and hip that Rusty Mintz had the brainstorm to give it additional exposure as the 7 p.m. anchor of our inaugural Sunday night lineup. The animated series about two genetically altered rats on the loose from Acme Labs in New York generated more buzz for us than anything else on our slate when the WB's second night of programming bowed on September 10.

UPN wasn't doing much better than we were, programming-wise. They had *Star Trek: Voyager* and that was it. But they had a stronger and larger lineup of affiliate stations nationwide, and that ensured that they would continue to beat us until we came up with a hit that would make viewers take notice. We needed a slam-dunk success to anchor the network. By the beginning of 1996, we knew that our tent-pole show was not going to be *Cleghorne!* or *First Time Out,* two comedy series that we'd had high hopes for back in the fall. But hope springs eternal when you're a creative development executive—it has to or you'll never last in the job. As we made plans to adjust our Sunday night lineup, we were very excited about one particular mid-season replacement series that was in the works. It was our first stab at a drama series.

Months before, Jamie Kellner reached out to a high-powered friend to give us a much-needed boost in programming and publicity; Aaron Spelling was happy to take the call from his pal Jamie, even though Viacom owned about two-thirds of his company at the time. We were thrilled to learn that the legendary producer had agreed to develop a few projects with us.

Spelling and Jamie became tight when Spelling's soaps *Beverly Hills, 90210,* and *Melrose Place* were hits for Fox in the early 1990s. In his trademark Texas drawl, Spelling would tell us later that getting the call from Jamie reminded him of the call he'd received years before from Barry Diller drafting him to do *90210*. Kellner knew the mere fact that Spelling agreed to produce a show for the WB would generate a fair amount of buzz and free media attention. And he believed that the famously prolific producer, then in his early 70s, still had a Midas touch for appealing to mainstream America, especially young America.

Garth Ancier and I worked closely with Spelling and his producing partner, E. Duke Vincent, in developing two projects in 1995. One of them was *7th Heaven*, the gentle family drama destined to become synonymous with the WB as our longest-running and most-watched show. But before *7th Heaven*, we put another Spelling series on the air that was almost as important as *Heaven* in the life of the network, in its own way.

Savannah was a classic Spelling soap confection about three contemporary Southern belles. It carries the distinction of being our first hour-long series, and it was the first WB show with any real flair. Most important, *Savannah* was the first show to become a rallying cry for the WB's senior management team, from programming to marketing to affiliate promotions and advertising sales. There wasn't anything quite like it on TV at the time, not even Spelling's ongoing Fox serials. The show's deep-South setting had a sexy cachet, thanks partly to the prominence that Savannah, Georgia, plays in John Berendt's best-selling 1994 novel *Midnight in the Garden of Good and Evil*. After a rough first year of being deep in sixth place, we saw *Savannah* as our best hope of garnering some attention from viewers.

As a series, *Savannah* was vintage Spelling: fantastic plots, bitchy dialogue, low-slung blouses, spiky heels, and big hair. The leading ladies were then-unknowns (Shannon Sturges, Jamie Luner, and Robyn Lively) who were cast as much for their figures as their acting skills. The entire network coalesced around the show's January 21 premiere, from the Southern-mansion motif featured at our company events that winter to the flood of on-air promotion and off-air advertising that we gave it in advance of its premiere. The initiative came together naturally under Jamie's direction as it became clear that *Savannah* had promise. It was the first example of what would become a hallmark for the WB: picking a single show to funnel most of our marketing dollars and energy into each year.

The marketing campaign that Bob Bibb and Lew Goldstein orchestrated for *Savannah* set the tone for what would become known as the WB's well-oiled "marketing machine." Bob and Lew always impressed us with their impossibly high standards, their creativity, and how they never reined in their ambition because we were a start-up. On the contrary, they seemed energized by the challenge of having to convince viewers to check out a new show on a network they'd never heard of. Their dedication was inspiring.

The sense of Southern mystique in *Savannah* and different way of life gave the marketing chiefs a lot to work with. The *Savannah* marketing visuals keyed in on the white-columned mansions and other anachronisms redolent of *Gone with the Wind*. At one point, as we were hunkering down to set the final details of the launch, Bob and Lew abruptly, and quietly, disappeared. We found out that they had become so wrapped up in giving the show a sense of place that they'd hopped a plane to Atlanta. They planned to hire a film crew to get additional footage of the city of Savannah and of the exteriors used in the show for the promos and print ads.

It was an impulsive act, one that was not entirely thought out by the time Bob and Lew were in the air. When they arrived in Atlanta, they faced up to the fact that they barely had any money to pay a crew, and they had no contacts for hiring film crews and photographers in that part of the country. Finally, after calling friends back home in Hollywood, Bob and Lew were put in touch with a wild-eyed local helicopter pilot who was game to do it for a few hundred bucks. A Directors Guild of America-sanctioned shoot, it wasn't.

"The guy broke every known aviation rule," Goldstein says, by flying his helicopter dangerously close to the ground while another man leaned out a window with a camera.

Weeks later, after the marketing team had distributed the first batch of *Savannah* promos to WB and Spelling executives, Aaron Spelling called Bob and Lew directly. He wanted to know how he could get that aerial footage for use in the show's opening title sequence. "Where'd you get that shot?" Spelling's raspy, pipe-smoker's voice cut through the hum of the speakerphone in Bob's office. Without exchanging so much as a glance, Bob and Lew demurred on cue about the source of the footage.

Our new publicity chief Brad Turell also scored a few quick wins in the press department. He hosted a *Savannah* press event at Santa Anita racetrack that was well attended by journalists (it was part of the semi-annual press junket in nearby Pasadena), who gave the WB more column inches and respect than we'd ever received before. A number of seasoned writers who remembered Jamie and Garth from the Fox days sidled up to them to strike up a conversation about way back when. It made Turell confident that his image-shaping plan was working.

On the night of the two-hour *Savannah* premiere, the show opened with a three-minute introductory spot featuring a grandfatherly Aaron Spelling, who cheerfully highlighted the major theme of the marketing campaign as he sat on the edge of a desk and spoke directly to viewers.

"No matter where you're from, it seems the Old South holds a special fascination for us, even today. . . ."

By WB standards of the day, *Savannah* had a strong opening. More significant, it performed well with the same demographic groups that were responding to *Sister, Sister*—teenage girls and young women in the 12–24 age bracket. All the arrows were pointing in the direction of the niche that we would come to identify as "the WB demo" in the years ahead.

"After *Savannah*, there was a period when we never looked back," Turell says.

Two nights after the WB got a lift from the debut of *Savannah*, UPN notched its success story for 1996 with the January 23 premiere of *Moesha*. In a quirk of prime-time fate, the half-hour comedy series came from Big Ticket Television, a start-up subsidiary company of none other than Spelling Television. The domestic comedy about an African American teenage girl growing up in Los Angeles came to UPN from an unlikely source: CBS.

The show starring budding R&B singer Brandy Norwood had been developed as a pilot for CBS by veteran writer-producer Ralph Farquhar, whose resume stretches back to *Happy Days*. *Moesha* was in no way a fit for CBS in the era when its hits included *Touched by an Angel* and *Walker, Texas Ranger*. Farquhar and others involved with the show were aggressive in shopping it to other networks. UPN was not a natural choice, given its manly Trekkie bent in 1995, but producers who have genuine affection for a pilot will take a meeting with anyone who will listen. Lucie Salhany jumped at the chance to pick up *Moesha* when Farquhar brought it in, not too long after the network settled in to its space in West Los Angeles.

Moesha was a big departure from the drama-heavy young male strategy UPN had been pursuing. The UPN team had to have noticed the ratings the WB managed to deliver in key markets with our urban comedies. *Moesha*'s successful opening gave Salhany and her team a confidence boost when they sorely needed one. Other than *Star Trek: Voyager,* the network had no successes to speak of in its first year. Its first two comedy series, *Pig Sty* and *Platypus Man*, flamed out quickly, so the network loaded up on fantasy and sci-fi dramas for the fall of 1995 and for the network's expansion to Wednesdays in March 1996.

By the fall, on *Moesha*'s lead, UPN had shifted its programming strategy entirely and loaded up two nights of its three-night schedule with six sitcoms featuring predominantly African American casts. As a bid to generate higher ratings, it was a sound strategy. Ethnic and urban-centric comedies played to the strengths of the audience attracted by UPN's largest affiliate stations. Not surprisingly, though, the shift raised red flags within the Paramount camp who wanted to stick with the original plan. The concern was that, over the long term, the emphasis on courting African American and Hispanic viewers would hurt and inherently limit the network's appeal to more mainstream audiences. It is a cold fact of the television advertising business that programs that attract a largely minority audience command lower advertising rates, from a smaller pool of advertisers, than shows with broader appeal.

"The feeling was that one night of black programming is good business; more than that is not," says a UPN veteran.

Young, urban minorities are considered the low-hanging fruit in television. They tend to watch more TV than other adult demographic groups, and younger viewers are far more likely than their parents to surf the TV dial and seek out provocative new shows. They were among the first to embrace Fox. It made sense for any start-up broadcast network to court young urban viewers.

Salhany took her programming cues from the types of shows that did well outside of prime time on UPN's owned-and-operated stations. The Chris-Craft and Paramount-owned stations carried a heavy load of repeats of comedies purchased in syndication, such as Fox's *Martin* starring Martin Lawrence; *Living Single* starring Queen Latifah; and *The Fresh Prince of Bel-Air* starring Will Smith.

Moesha's success, relative to the dramas UPN had tried, validated Salhany's shift in prime-time strategy, in her view. Kerry Mc-Cluggage and others were frustrated that Salhany was pulling away from targeting young men with action-adventure shows. Salhany and programming chief Michael Sullivan were quick to point out that those kinds of shows were hard to do on UPN's beer budgets.

"On a weekly series budget you can't do a lot of action. The studios weren't willing to put up a lot of money on top of our license fees," Sullivan says. "We had to make the best of the best material we could get."

For UPN in its second year, the solution was more comedies aimed at the *Moesha* demographic and fewer sci-fi and action dramas. It was a decision that would hasten the end of Salhany's run as CEO.

After getting *Savannah* off to a good start, our focus turned to nurturing the other Spelling series in the works. I knew when we made the deal with Spelling that he was virtually guaranteed that both pilots, short of being train wrecks, would get on the air; who were we at a little start-up network to say no to a legend of primetime? When the time came, however, I was pleasantly surprised that we wholeheartedly wanted to put both shows on our air. *7th Heaven* was so strong Jamie wisely banked on it to lead our expansion to Monday night. We got the jump on the 1996–97 season by launching *7th Heaven* and our new Monday night on August 26 during the dog days of summer. That Monday night *Savannah* also relocated from its Sunday time slot to be *7th Heaven*'s companion in the 9 p.m. hour.

It was clear as the key elements of writers, producers, and actors fell into place on *7th Heaven* that it was a contender, and much sturdier (better writing, better actors) than its sibling, *Savannah*. About halfway through *7th Heaven*'s first season, the cast and crew had gelled so completely that it had the aura of a show that could go the distance.

7th Heaven was born out of one of our many brainstorming sessions about old shows that we liked and program genres that were not on the air at that moment. Garth Ancier pushed us to have Spelling tackle a contemporary take on a family drama á la *Eight is Enough*. Spelling was game, but he kept talking about doing a heavy emotional drama along the lines of *Family*, the acclaimed ensemble show he'd produced for ABC in the late 70s. We wanted a lighter touch. I suggested that to do that, we should shop around for a comedy writer who was ready to try something different. No network at that time was focused on developing the next great light family drama. I wanted a comedy writer to guard against something too sappy.

Jamie Kellner loved the idea and our approach to it, because it was not like anything else on the air. He knew it would play well in markets where WB was not on the radar, and he knew instinctively it would get us some attention with advertisers. I beat the bushes among my agent contacts for the right writer. It wasn't an easy sell at the time but eventually a friend suggested a woman who'd just come off a stint as supervising producer on the NBC comedy *Mad About You*. I loved her writing samples from *Mad About You* and another NBC comedy, *Blossom,* before I met her. After we met, I was convinced Brenda Hampton was the right person for the job.

Hampton got into television writing through a circuitous route. A native of Georgia, Hampton worked for the Navy writing how-to manuals before she decided to head to Hollywood to make it as a TV writer. Brenda likes to say she was surprised to receive the overture from Spelling and figured it was a long shot for anything to come of it, given her background as a comedy writer, but she eagerly took the meeting because she wanted to be able to go home and write "Dear Diary: Today I met Aaron Spelling." Fortunately for us, Brenda and Spelling also hit it off from the start.

For me, meetings with Aaron Spelling never failed to be a slightly surreal experience. It made me feel so much like I'd made it—not in an arrogant way, but in the pinch-me realization that Susanne Lieberstein from Westport, Connecticut, had progressed enough in her career to be in this storied producer's palatial shag-rug-lined office. And he couldn't have been nicer about it. He was never condescending when it came to age or the experience differential between us. He spoke to me as a professional when we were in a business context, and outside of work he was a courtly and generous friend.

Brenda's first pass at the script that would become *7th Heaven* was solid but not exactly what we were looking for. It was very straightforward family stuff. Garth and I were talking about the script in my office one day, and how to make it more distinctive when Jamie sauntered in.

"Why don't we make the father a minister?" he suggested. Garth and I were surprised but also intrigued. I wondered if it was a spontaneous notion or something Jamie had been thinking about for a while. Either way, the more we kicked it around, the more we liked it. Spelling was wary at first. Wouldn't that turn off a large chunk of the show's potential audience? It could dampen the show's foreign sales, he also observed. But he too trusted Jamie's instincts, and Brenda also responded enthusiastically to the idea, which took her back to her church-going youth in Atlanta. She became the intelligent designer behind the Rev. Eric Camden and his wife, Annie, and the ensemble of characters that surrounded them. It quickly became clear that Brenda had a deft touch in writing wholesome material that wasn't nauseatingly syrupy or speechy. She got away with a lot—like naming the Camden's family dog Happy—by mixing the basic four-act television episodic drama structure up with a lot of humorous moments, and a lot of plot.

Brenda endeared herself to us and to Spelling by consistently giving us quality work, on time and on budget. She always kept things fresh and regularly brought in new faces. She was never cowed by an actor demanding more money. Brenda had a standard speech she gave anyone who fussed too much: "Good-bye and good luck. I'll write you out of the show so fast and have someone new and fabulous in here tomorrow."

The other coup at the outset with *7th Heaven* was the casting of Stephen Collins in the lead role. Collins was a name-brand actor with a "quote," or a minimum fee that has to be met before he would even think about taking a role. We had been talking to Beau Bridges for the role of Rev. Eric Camden, but Bridges' quote was too high and he wasn't about to budge. After we gave up on Bridges, Collins' name was on a short list of strong candidates drawn up by our head of casting, Kathleen Letterie. A group of us gathered in a small conference room to hash out the list. Most of us were still pouting about losing Bridges.

"Stephen Collins?" she read.

More than a few eyebrows went up. After a beat, the first comment came from Mitch Nedick, our head of finance and administration. At the WB, it wasn't unusual for Mitch, an operations guy, to sit in on creative meetings. At other networks, it would have been.

"I've always liked him," Mitch said. The rest of us began nodding. The more we batted his name around, the more we were convinced he was the perfect Rev. Eric Camden. And he was available. We got even more excited after we saw how much natural chemistry Collins had with Catherine Hicks, the veteran TV actress who was cast as Camden's soul-mate wife, Annie. You just *bought* them as a couple. In television, when you're asking viewers to warm up to characters for what you hope will be 100-plus episodes, you've got to get the casting alchemy just right or you're doomed.

Kellner felt as a programmer that family-friendly was the way to go for the WB when all of the broadcast competition was headed in the other direction. He knew that if properly done, the show would stand out among the quality-TV advocacy groups and the advertising agencies who for years had been bashing the major networks for abandoning overtly family-friendly shows in favor of edgier, grittier fare like cop shows, medical dramas, and legal potboilers. He came up with a mouthful of a slogan for us, declaring the WB to be "a friendly place where American families can watch television together." It was designed to impress Madison Avenue more than anything else. It certainly didn't roll off the tongue as an on-air slogan or ad tagline. Around the office we had a thousand variations on it, none of them G-rated.

Another influence on our thinking at this time was a book that was making some waves as a non-fiction best seller, *Reviving Ophelia: Saving the Selves of Adolescent Girls*. It was published in 1994 by Nebraska-based clinical psychologist Dr. Mary Pipher, whose views were based on 25 years of private practice. Pipher's thesis in *Reviving Ophelia* sounded the alarm that popular culture in the United States was destroying the souls of adolescent girls—even many of those from stable, loving families.

Pipher argues that the barrage of media and advertising messages urging girls to be beautiful, thin, and sexually voracious beyond their years was hitting overload for America's female preteens. Women in late-20th century America were growing up with raging insecurities, low self-esteem, and other neuroses. Girls were bred in the culture of victimhood, leading to all sorts of unhealthy behaviors that complicate their ability to maintain close relationships, Pipher warned.

Jordan and I both had baby daughters at home. As young parents, we were horrified by Pipher's thesis. It got us thinking about the absence of strong young female characters in prime time at the time the WB went on the air. ABC had flamed out that same season that the WB went on the air with a show that endures as a critical and cult fave, *My So-Called Life*, featuring the ingenue Claire Danes as a typically tormented 1990s teen. We looked into the possibility of picking up the show, but it was an expensive production from A-list producers Ed Zwick and Marshall Herskovitz, the Emmy winners behind *thirtysomething*. We simply couldn't afford it.

As we focused on finding strong female characters, Jamie Kellner reminded us of another subgenre, the light fantasy/horror dramas in the mold of his favorite from the mid-1970s, Darren McGavin's *Kolchak: The Night Stalker*. Jamie pushed us to keep an eye out for off-the-wall shows like *Kolchak* that could make you laugh and gasp in the same scene. Our solution walked through the door a few weeks later in the guise of a charismatic artiste named Joss Whedon, who brought us a pitch for a show based on his 1992 movie *Buffy the Vampire Slayer*.

• • •

Once *Moesha* hit in early 1996, UPN went headlong into the urban-ethnic comedy business. The network that billed itself as "dramatically different" in its first full season, in 1995–96, with no half-hours on its three-night schedule, wound up stacking its 1996–97 season lineup with six urban-skewing comedy series, four on Monday and two on Tuesday. They were in the *Moesha* vein, meaning that they were built around personalities who rated highly with African American viewers. But none of them were as well crafted as *Moesha* under the direction of producer Ralph Farquhar. He built a deep bench of talented African American writers from a range of backgrounds—from Ivy League grads to single moms—and Farquhar and others took great care in schooling them in the art of being a television writer and show runner.

UPN's new shows that season included *In the House*, starring rapper L.L. Cool J and Debbie Allen, which UPN rescued from cancellation after one season on NBC. (NBC dropped the show even though it was produced by its fledgling in-house NBC Productions unit. Fin-syn was history by this time, after all.) *Malcolm and Eddie* was a buddy comedy starring former *Cosby Show* kid Malcolm Jamal-Warner and Eddie Griffin; *Goode Behavior* featured Sherman Hemsley, former star of *The Jeffersons*, as a reformed con man living with his nephew while on parole; and *Homeboys in Outer Space* was exactly what it sounded like: a *Star Trek* farce about two 23rd century guys traveling the cosmos in a "Space Hoopty."

Also noteworthy about UPN's strategy shift was the fact that each of the new comedies hailed from a production entity other than Paramount. *Moesha* was the only one to come from an affiliate of Viacom, Spelling Television's Big Ticket Television imprint. *Malcolm and Eddie* came from Sony Pictures' TV production unit. *Goode Behavior* was a last-ditch effort from the once-proud MTM Productions to turn a profit, about a year before the company was acquired by Rupert Murdoch's News Corp. *Homeboys in Outer Space* was a Walt

Disney Company production. The lack of Paramount investment in the network's new direction spoke loud and clear to the television industry about the state of the UPN partnership.

During the Television Critics Association press junket in Pasadena, California, in July 1996, Salhany hosted a state-of-the-network Q&A session with reporters, who were eager to share their thoughts about UPN's new lineup. Salhany had been prepared to field a few pointed questions about the racial tilt of the network's new lineup, but she hadn't anticipated the depth of the outrage about what some writers viewed as modern-day Stepin Fetchit material. For a few minutes during Salhany's executive Q&A session, a handful of top critics debated which of the new UPN comedies was the worst of all. (Opinion was divided between *Goode Behavior* and *Homeboys in Outer Space*.) Salhany instinctively did her best to deflect the heat by turning the question of racial insensitivity back on the group of largely white male television critics and journalists.

When grilled about the propriety of stacking a night and a half with African American comedies, Salhany shot back that she was "concerned about terms like *'ghettoizing'*" being used to describe UPN's scheduling tactic.

The ferocity of the criticism unleashed that day took Salhany and UPN entertainment president Michael Sullivan by surprise. Sullivan knew that none of the network's new shows were going to win Emmys, but he was surprised at how harshly UPN was viewed for targeting the young African American niche. In his view, it wasn't about racial exploitation; it was simple supply and demand. Like the WB, UPN was looking for underserved audiences, the viewers who were not being as heavily courted by the larger networks.

"Look at where both networks were most successful: with shows featuring African Americans and teens," Sullivan says. "We always found in casting that if we were looking for a young African American male lead, we always had multiple good choices. If we were casting for a thirtysomething male lead in a drama, it was always hard because we were last on the list for that talent pool."

The instant response to *Moesha* proved that there was an audience out there for programs with an African American sensibility; the same was true for the WB with the strong ratings for *The Wayans Bros., The Parent 'Hood,* and other shows generated in African American households. The Monday night block of urban comedies that UPN established in the fall of 1996 would serve the network well, in good times and bad, through its last nights on the air. In time, UPN's comedy bench would grow to include some well-regarded series, including *The Parkers,* a spinoff of *Moesha*; and the sexy-ensemble *Girlfriends.*

More significantly for Hollywood's creative community, the volume of African American comedies on UPN and the WB opened doors in the industry for many black writers, directors, producers, actors, and others, particularly women. UPN and WB provided a springboard for such prominent writers and producers as Mara Brock Akil, creator of *Girlfriends* and alumnus of *Moesha* and *Parent'Hood*; Sara Finney and Vida Spears, former writers on ABC's *Family Matters*, who moved through *Moesha* on their way to creating *The Parkers.* Eunetta Boone, a former newspaper sportswriter, worked on the WB's *Parent'hood* before creating UPN's father-daughter sitcom *One on One.* Felicia Henderson served a stint on *Moesha* before spearheading Showtime's critically praised television series adaptation of the feature film *Soul Food.* The WB gave a prime-time showcase to the multi-talented Jamie Foxx at a key moment in his career with *The Jamie Foxx Show,* which ran for five seasons beginning in 1996. Cedric the Entertainer became a superstar comic among African Americans in large part by costarring on the WB's *The Steve Harvey Show.*

The WB faced many of the same criticisms over our casting and scheduling decisions, though not to the same degree as UPN. One thing that set us apart was that by the fall of 1996, when UPN came under scrutiny, we'd made an effort to blend the comedies on our schedule. Sunday night that season opened with two comedies with white leads—Kirk Cameron in *Kirk*, and Joey Lawrence in *Brotherly Love*—leading into *The Parent 'Hood* and *The Steve Harvey Show.* On Wednesday that season we had white actor Mitch Mullany starring with an ethnically diverse supporting cast in *Nick Freno: Licensed Teacher*, bookended at 8 p.m. by *Sister, Sister* and at 9 p.m. by *The Wayans Bros.*

In terms of programming strategy, we found it telling that for years the only comedies that worked well for the WB were those with a largely African American focus. We took our shots at every kind of half-hour comedy imaginable, but until singer-actress Reba McEntire worked her magic for us with *Reba* in the fall of 2001, the only half-hour shows that performed for us at all were the strongest of our African American comedies.

It was incredibly frustrating to have some critics and pundits paint every one of the WB and UPN's African American comedies with a broad brush based on the assumption that they were all low-brow, bawdy, and produced on the cheap. I'd experienced some of that bias during my time at Fox working on *Living Single* and *Martin*. To me, such stereotyping of an entire genre of programming was racially insensitive, not to mention disparaging to the audience who watched those shows.

The mastermind of *Buffy the Vampire Slayer* came from a show business family. Joss Whedon's grandfather, John Whedon, and father, Tom Whedon, were prominent television writer-producers in their day. Joss's prime influences were comic books, with their emphasis on melodrama and big ideas, and Shakespeare, from whom he learned the art of weaving character, humor, and mythos into writing. Joss's deep voice, natural intelligence, and intensity lent him a gravitas beyond his years; his tendency to mumble and ramble completed the auteur package in a way that was charmingly genuine when he arrived in our offices in the fall of 1995.

Joss was a rising star screenwriter at the time, and he'd worked on TV shows, including a top 10 hit, ABC's *Roseanne*. But he still looked like the one-time video store geek that he really was. He had worked the counter for a time at a video shop in the Pacific Palisades near his family's home. When he first shopped his work in Hollywood, Joss had wavy strawberry-blond hair flowing down to the middle of his back.

For all his eccentricities, Whedon was serious about getting into the family business. He penned sample "spec" scripts for influential comedy series of the moment: Fox's *Married . . . with Children* and Showtime's *It's Garry Shandling's Show.* Shortly thereafter, he hooked up with an ambitious young agent, Chris Harbert, at the talent agency that represented his father. In no time, Joss was a member of the writing staff at the only show he wanted to work on, *Roseanne,* during the 1989–90 season.

When he knocked on our door with *Buffy* five years later, Joss was better known as a high-priced movie script doctor on such blockbusters as 1994's *Speed.* He was on the verge of scoring the biggest hit of his career as one of four credited screenwriters on the Pixar/ Walt Disney Co. hit *Toy Story.* While Joss was working on *Roseanne,* he'd penned a spec feature script for a movie about a high school girl who fends off vampires in her spare time, as a chosen one, or "slayer." He handed it to Harbert while they were backstage at the taping of *Roseanne*'s last episode of the season.

After many twists, turns, and compromises in getting the financing for the film, the movie starring Kristy Swanson was produced and it landed a major studio distributor, 20th Century Fox. *Buffy* had been Whedon's passion project, but getting it released was a mixed blessing. The final product was not the movie he would have made, and he was disappointed, to say the least, with the results.

Three years after *Buffy* fizzled at the multiplexes, Whedon was busy making big bucks on movies—his own scripts and rewrites of others. He was not the one actively looking to resurrect *Buffy* on television. That job fell to an executive at the production outfit that took on the *Buffy* movie, Sandollar Productions, headed by prominent talent manager turned producer Sandy Gallin.

Gail Berman joined Sandollar as its head of television development shortly before the release of the *Buffy* movie. A former Broadway producer, Berman read the film script and thought the character would be perfect for a TV series. But nobody paid much attention after the movie came and went quickly. Berman put the script on the good-ideas-but-can't-make-them-happen-right-now shelf.

When UPN and the WB came along, Berman started eyeing the *Buffy* screenplay again. She set her sights on pitching it as a pilot for the 1996–97 television season, which meant she made the rounds with it in the early fall of 1995. Before she could offer it for sale, Berman had to clear through a thicket of rights issues with the original producers and director, Fran and Kaz Kazui. In doing so, she found something interesting in Sandollar's original distribution contract with 20th Century Fox: a mistake. The studio had failed to secure the TV spin-off rights to the movie, which has been a standard part of movie deal-making in Hollywood for years. It was an oversight, but there it was, or more to the point, wasn't. Berman proceeded as if she could shop around as a free agent for the best network and studio home for the show.

She made contact with Whedon's agent for what she figured would be a pro forma call to get Whedon to waive his right to be involved with the show. Whedon was becoming a player in the film business. There's no chance he'd want to revisit *Buffy the Vampire Slayer* as a TV series, Berman thought. She couldn't have been more wrong. In her first phone conversation, they spoke excitedly at length about *Buffy*'s potential.

"We talked all about the notion of female empowerment and teenage fears, and the fact that there were no young female lead series other than *Blossom* on the air at the time," Berman says. "I don't think there were any people on Earth other than us who were really passionate about it. Everybody else was like, 'Oh, god, that's a tired old idea.'"

Whedon and Berman put together a short pitch reel consisting of scenes from the 1992 movie and a range of "beautiful images" to set the tone of what they hoped to accomplish with the show. Berman focused on selling *Buffy* to Fox as an 8 p.m. coming-of-age drama. It was teen angst writ large, with cool special effects, great dialogue, and a couple of good gasps every hour. It was like nothing else in prime time at the moment, and at that moment Fox was definitely in need of a fresh hit. Whedon shone in the pitch meeting with Berman and a handful of Fox development executives. At the pitch, Whedon, then 31, displayed his all-consuming passion for the project and a mastery of the characters and stories he intended to tell. Berman thought she had the deal nailed, but to her shock, Fox passed. Berman had expected that Whedon's heat as a feature writer would make it a cinch for Fox to at least pick up the script for development. Berman was later told that Fox was moving away from teen-centric shows, and that *Buffy* felt too similar in tone to the network's existing show *Party of Five*.

Berman quickly set up two more pitch meetings, one at NBC, the other at the WB. She knew *Buffy* didn't have a prayer of landing at NBC. She simply wanted Whedon to get another chance to refine the pitch he would have to kill with at the WB a few days later. The more she thought about it, Berman realized the WB might be an even better home than Fox for the show. Because it was such a struggling enterprise, Berman figured the WB would focus more of its money and attention on an unusual show such as *Buffy*. She was right.

The moment Joss entered my office, it was apparent that he was unlike anyone we'd met with before. Joss Whedon is sui generis. He had all the gravitas and tortured-genius attributes we grew to love even then: furrowed brow, penetrating hazel eyes, deadpan delivery, and deep baritone voice. I had approached the meeting with some skepticism. I'd seen the *Buffy* movie and thought it was cute and original, but nothing more, not the "cinematic feel" we'd been looking for. I was wrong.

Joss told me everything he *didn't* know about *Buffy* the TV series upfront, and that impressed me. He didn't know if the show was an hour or half-hour. He didn't know if it should be more drama than comedy or the other way around, if it should have a laugh track or not. What he did have down cold was the world that *Buffy the Vampire Slayer* inhabited. He sketched it out in Dickensian detail, explaining what powers the various types of vampires, slayers, and watchers wielded, and why. When we asked if the show really required the older "watcher" character of Rupert Giles, Whedon launched into an eloquent lecture on the history of watchers, their origins in England, and why it was absolutely vital that the character remain in the show.

The overall vision that Joss pitched me was more intriguing than anything I'd seen in the movie, and more compelling than other pitches I'd heard in our search for a strong young female character. We bought *Buffy* the TV series in the room.

After we commissioned the *Buffy* pilot script from Whedon and Sandollar Productions, Berman had to do some more maneuvering to settle the question of which studio would produce the pilot, 20th Century Fox Television or Warner Bros.? Jamie insisted that it go to Warner Bros. Television, on the assumption that 20th Century Fox wouldn't be as willing to absorb the deficits required for the show's visual effects and post-production needs. He figured it was better off in-house where there was a corporate reason to invest in it. Meanwhile, 20th Century Fox lawyers threatened to sue Sandollar if 20th didn't get the TV series. The last thing Berman wanted was for *Buffy* to get tied up in a legal dispute with Fox, even if there was a glaring error in the film contract. She agreed to go with 20th Century Fox Television, which proved prescient because Warner Bros. TV's business executives were balking at spending the extra money *Buffy* required.

At 20th, *Buffy* had an important champion in Peter Roth, president of the television production unit. He liked the script and recognized that there was nothing else like it on television at the time. Twentieth had barely done any business with us before. But at that moment, Roth was in the midst of carrying out a corporate crusade to rapidly grow the Fox studio's television production operation. The goal was to make it a player in selling comedy and drama series to ABC, CBS, and NBC, as well as to its sibling network. They were striving to overtake Warner Bros. as the No. 1 supplier of shows to Fox and all other broadcast networks.

Roth kept on the WB and Berman about *Buffy* and went to bat with his bosses to secure the extra money that Joss' vision demanded.

In the effort to stretch our development dollars further, we usually commissioned 25- to 30-minute "pilot presentation" episodes for our hour-long series prospects, as opposed to full 40-to 45-minute pilots. The shortened presentation format can make it tough on writers and producers to establish character, setting, and tone for a series; on the other hand presentations are slightly less arduous to produce than full-length pilots.

In short order, we had a deal with Joss and 20th Century Fox TV. Soon we were ensconced in *Buffy* casting sessions.

At the time she came in to audition for the series, Sarah Michelle Gellar was not a well-known actress, but she was a pro. She'd been on the ABC daytime serial *All My Children* for two years (she earned a Daytime Emmy award for best young actress the year before she auditioned for *Buffy*), and she'd logged numerous TV movies, guest shots, and commercial spots. It's a well-known part of *Buffy* lore that the naturally brunette Gellar first auditioned not for the lead role of Buffy but for the supporting role of the sexy campus vampire Cordelia. Whedon had been attached to the idea of another actress playing Buffy Summers, but in our view that actress didn't capture all of the character's youthful contradictions.

Gellar nailed the part of Cordelia during her reading. We'd seen every actress between the ages of 18 and 24 in town during the *Buffy* casting process (or at least those willing to audition for a WB series with a funny name), and still we were stymied on the lead role. After Gellar's reading, the large group of us—which included Joss, Gail Berman, Peter Roth, Garth, Kathleen Letterie, and Marcia Shulman, a well-known independent casting director—couldn't stop talking about how fantastic she was. After a few minutes, Peter leaned over to me and whispered that he thought Sarah should read for the lead role. In another corner of the room, it turns out Garth was saying the same thing to Kathleen at just about the same time.

Sarah came back to read for *Buffy* the next day, but realistically, I think she got the job as soon as Peter and Garth made the suggestion. Letterie had taken a general meeting with Sarah a few months before *Buffy* came along, and she struck our chief talent scout as a name to remember.

"She was so poised and so much in charge of herself and her career," Letterie says. "I remember thinking this is the most together 18-year-old I've ever met, *and* she could act."

For *Buffy* in particular, it helped that Sarah was not a waif but rather a natural athlete. Joss intended to give parts of his show a Hong Kong action-flick feeling. His leading lady would have to be able to keep up with him.

The coda to our *Buffy* casting saga came a short time later when we finally found our Cordelia. We'd been kept waiting all afternoon for a meeting with an aspiring actress who only had a handful of credits to her name. Most of the same large group wound up waiting in a conference room so long we ordered pizza. Another hour later, we had finished eating and were wrapped up in a lively conversation about what makes good television. Finally, a leggy, shapely brunette with a hairdo right out of *Charlie's Angels* burst into the room, all in a fluster because she'd had trouble finding the ranch, and then when she got to the trailers she'd been sent to the wrong room.

Kathleen and I and the others exchanged glances as Charisma Carpenter huffed and puffed and told the story of her troubles in getting to the audition. She was worth the wait.

"Because that's exactly what Cordelia would do. Keep everyone waiting and then come in and selfishly be unaware of things," Jordan Levin says. "She was perfect."

Joss Whedon could have made a lot more money working on movie scripts during the time he was devoting to resurrecting *Buffy* as a TV series. One thing about his auteur quality made us nervous, however. He insisted on directing the pilot. I wanted to support Joss' vision in crafting the show, but the WB didn't have money to burn. I had to think hard before recommending that we gamble nearly $1 million on a presentation with a first-time director.

Finally, Joss' agent, Chris Harbert, laid it on the line with me in a conversation that was friendly but pointed. Joss directs or he walks, Harbert said, over and over without wavering. There would be no bringing in a co-director or even a shadow director. The way Joss felt about *Buffy*, I knew it wasn't an empty threat.

So we caved. Amazingly, Jamie Kellner backed us. He could see how strongly we felt about the show. The fact that Jamie backed us only made us work harder to turn *Buffy* into a hit. Jordan demonstrated how much of a cause the project had become for us one afternoon in the spring of 1996 while he was in his office watching a tape of the dailies from the presentation shoot. Two talent agents who were visiting the network on unrelated business wandered into Jordan's office unexpectedly. The man and the woman happened to work for the same agency that represented Whedon. The woman took one glance at the footage and declared: "That show will never work."

"Oh, really? Why not?" Levin asked, bristling.

"Because that girl has no presence. She's not a star."

"Oh, yeah," Levin spat, "well, maybe I ought to call your agency and tell them that the show they're packaging will never work because you saw 10 seconds of the pilot and you don't think Sarah Michelle Gellar is a star."

Before he could stop himself, Jordan threw the videotape at the woman's head. It left a dent in the wall that he made a point of not repairing for a long, long time.

The pilot story revolved around Buffy Summers and her divorced mother moving from Los Angeles to bucolic Sunnydale, California, as Buffy is about to start her sophomore year in high school. She already knows she's a vampire slayer—Buffy was kicked out of her previous school after burning down the gym to deal with some nasty vampires. But her hopes for a fresh start are torpedoed not long after their arrival when Buffy discovers Sunnydale sits at the edge of an invisible Hellmouth that is home to hordes of bloodthirsty creatures.

The production of the original *Buffy* pilot was rough in parts— no doubt about it. Joss was schooled in the basics of television directing each day of the shoot from veteran 20th Century Fox physical production executives assigned to his pilot. We were fortunate in that the studio had seasoned line producers on staff, and as a result, Joss didn't have too much trouble with the mechanics. The genius part of him soaked up their tutorials like a sponge. When the final 30-minute product was assembled, it was clear Joss had a knack for capturing the action sequences with a Hong Kong-esque style that was exciting to see on the small screen. He had a good feel for the scary scenes and the special effects-driven sequence, limited as they were in the presentation reel. But dialogue-rich, character-building sequences that are vital for a good pilot were something of a problem. Joss had captured most of them with a handheld Steadicam that lent a frenetic feel, making it harder to absorb his very witty dialogue and the character insights those sequences offered. We were in a quandary. It was too good to pass on but not quite ready for prime time.

At the WB, before any pilot was given a greenlight to go on the air as a series, it had to pass muster through a sometimes tough screening process with Jamie Kellner; Warner Bros.' Bob Daly, Barry Meyer, and Bruce Rosenblum; Tribune executives; and perhaps the toughest critics of all, the WB's other department heads, including Bob Bibb, Lew Goldstein, Jed Petrick, and Brad Turell. Most of the time, the screenings were held in plush projection rooms on the Warner Bros.' lot. The fanciness of the surroundings (compared to the WB's trailer chic) always seemed to turn up the pressure even more.

I was well aware that *Buffy* was going to be a hell of a sales job on our part. We knew we had to sell the promise, the raw talent that was clearly on screen. For all its shortcomings, the show was very stylish and cutting-edge, in an indie film kind of way. It was the most creatively original thing we'd produced in our 18 months on the air.

Jordan often wrote out our selling points for me on one or two index cards in preparation for pilot screening nights. I usually did the talking by introducing the pilot and explaining why we thought it was right for our network. Jordan wouldn't hesitate to jump in if he didn't think I was doing a good enough job selling the show, especially if it was something he cared about.

Jordan wrote out at least six cards for me when the brain trust gathered to see *Buffy* during our pilot screenings in the spring of 1996. We knew the show was at a disadvantage from most of those who would judge it just because of its campy name. We hoped they wouldn't remember the flop movie from a few years back, but realistically, we knew they were industry pros, not rubes. Of course, they'd remember.

"This show and this character are going to speak to the young audience we're going after," I said in my best Sally Field-impassioned voice. "There is nothing like *Buffy* on the air right now. There are no female role models like this, and there's no cool and creepy-scary TV show like this out there, with the exception of *X-Files* and look what a hit that is for Fox. . . . We will get attention with this show, because it looks different, feels different. . . ."

Watching it in that important company on the large screen seemed to magnify every flaw, every rough-cut aspect of the visual effects. The stiffness of the dialogue seemed more pronounced in part and only in the presence of so many middle-aged men did I become more sensitive to the level of sexually tinged violence in the show—an area we would struggle with for the show's entire run.

It was quiet when the screen went blank again. Nobody declared it a travesty. Nobody said much of anything, until the pause was broken when several in the room spontaneously began offering specific suggestions for fixing it. Jamie suggested we move the setting to a college, a New York University–type campus, where the characters study by day and fight crime and vampires by night. Others raised concerns about the suburban setting of the show; might life at the local school and mall prove too limiting for a horde of vampires?

For about a half-hour after the screening, we made our plea. Bob Daly and Barry Meyer seemed to be going out of their way to be respectful of our feelings. There were none of the loud "who'd spend money on this dog meat?" recriminations that I feared.

I finally interjected and begged them to reconsider the show as is, for the most part, with some key fixes. We needed more money and more time to rework the presentation into something we could put on the air.

"Joss is worth it. There is something here," I said, putting my palms together as if I were praying. We trained our puppy-dog gazes on Jamie Kellner and Bob Daly.

I almost felt uncomfortable to be fighting so hard for it, but I had such a strong gut feeling. "I'm telling you, I know it's worth it."

Finally, Jamie stood up and spoke from the center of the box-shaped room.

"If you feel that strongly about it, do it," Jamie said, without condescension, but rather with that shrug of the shoulders that made it sound as though I hadn't really needed his permission to pursue it (which was absolutely not true, no matter how nonchalant he was). Barry Meyer quickly concurred with Jamie.

Jamie was ready to move on with the rest of our pilot screenings. He had his own golden-gut instinct that year about *7th Heaven*. He couldn't wait to get it on the air and see how the public and advertisers would react to such wholesome entertainment. Jamie was personally invested in selling this G-rated concept to the advertising community. But once he had given Jordan and me the go ahead on *Buffy*, we immediately began to worry about how this push on family-friendly shows would allow us to put on the air a show called *Buffy the Vampire Slayer*.

After we made it through our May 1996 upfront presentation pushing the family theme, without any reference that a project called *Buffy the Vampire Slayer* was in the works, we kept in close contact with Joss and Gail Berman. We kept telling them "all is not lost on the *Buffy* front." They assumed, naturally, that we were stringing them along.

"When you're a producer and you hear, 'All is not lost,' you pretty much assume there's no hope," Berman says.

Still, Gail hounded me about the project and whether it would be picked up or released back to 20th Century Fox and Sandollar. Finally, there was a meeting among the key players: A handful of us from the network, Joss and Gail, and Peter Roth. We asked Joss to make a handful of not-major changes that included recasting the crucial supporting role of Willow, which went to starlet Alyson Hannigan, and an adjustment to the script to make it crystal-clear to viewers that Sunnydale lay at the opening of Hellmouth and was steadily being invaded by vampires. And we all agreed the pilot needed to be re-shot.

After we got the commitment to re-do *Buffy*, I felt relieved and grateful, but also incredibly anxious. I had promised the CEO of the network and our parent company that *Buffy* would be a hit. Now all I had to do was deliver.

In the fall of 1996, Kevin Williamson, who was a budding screenwriter in Los Angeles, got a call from Paul Stupin, a television producer that he'd worked with the previous year on an autobiographical pilot script for Fox called *Dawson's Creek*.

"They read *Dawson's Creek* at the WB," Stupin informed Williamson. "They love it."

Stupin was breathless. Williamson was surprised. He'd been heartbroken the previous year when he found out just before Christmas that Fox had passed on shooting a pilot of his autobiographical ensemble piece. Williamson was warned by writer friends that he could expect four or five more strikeouts before he'd see his first pilot script produced. He was so despondent he went out and bought a young golden retriever and named it Dawson. He figured it would be his only lasting memory of the experience.

When Stupin called, Williamson was preoccupied with the impending release of the first film that he'd written, a hot horror movie called *Scream*, not to mention the handful of other projects he had percolating. Stupin had told Williamson a few weeks earlier that the studio that initially backed *Dawson's*, Columbia TriStar Television, was trying to revive the script's fortunes by sending it out at the start of the 1996–97 pilot season to ABC and the WB. But in his mind, it was over. Even his agent told him to "go write something else" for television, Williamson recalls.

Upon hearing from Stupin that WB executives wanted to meet with him as soon as possible, all Williamson could think of as he paced around his West Hollywood apartment was: "What is the WB?"

Williamson may not have heard of us, but we were already very impressed with him. I first heard the title *Dawson's Creek* over a lunch meeting at a Studio City restaurant. Jordan Levin and I were having a casual "what should we develop this year?" lunch in the late summer of 1996 with two executives from Columbia TriStar Television, Sarah Timberman and Carolyn Bernstein. It's the kind of lunch all network development executives have with their studio counterparts at that time of year, part of the ritual preamble to the January–April marathon of pilot season.

We gave Sarah and Carolyn our well-rehearsed speech about looking for new voices and a cinematic sensibility to all of our projects. They glanced at each other and told us, practically in unison, that we had to read a fabulous script that Fox had inexplicably turned down from a young hotshot screenwriter. Sarah and Carolyn emphasized that it was the best pilot they'd read in years from a wonderfully talented fresh voice. Jordan and I had a lot of respect for Sarah and Carolyn, but that's the kind of thing you hear all of the time from producers and studio executives.

This time, of course, they were right. Kevin Williamson's work made me sit up straight in my chair after a night spent in my den hacking through a two-foot pile of scripts. It was past 11 p.m. by the time I finished it for the first time. I had to fight the urge to call Jordan late at night to make sure he read it as soon as possible too. I sat there in the middle of the night in my den, too excited to crawl upstairs to bed, rereading the script to make sure I loved it as much on the second and third time.

At that moment, Kevin was a few months away from igniting his movie career with the success of the teen horror romp *Scream,* released in December through Dimension Films, a label run by indie film darlings Bob Weinstein and Harvey Weinstein of Miramax Films fame. Williamson was prolific; for the next three years, he wrote himself into a reputation as the Weinstein brothers' go-to rewrite guy.

But you wouldn't have known this from the unassuming young man who walked into our offices a few days later with Sarah and Carolyn smiling behind him. Kevin painted quite a tableau of his vision for his coming-of-age story rooted in the lives of four high school sophomores in a small coastal New England town. His inspiration for the show was largely his own youth spent growing up in Oriental, North Carolina. There really was a Dawson Creek "where the kids all used to hang out," Williamson assured us with a Southerner's flair for storytelling. We fell for Kevin almost as much as we were intrigued by his show.

Kevin was all youthful exuberance that day, sporting a sweet grin, tousled sandy blond hair, and deep-blue eyes. He was dressed in screenwriter-formal attire: light cotton pants and a polo shirt. His manners were impeccable; he was humble and charming with a lilting North Carolina accent that came out more as he grew more animated. He kept assuring us that he wouldn't be afraid to "fictionalize" his story with new characters to keep things entertaining. Kevin described *Dawson's Creek* as a blend of two shows he remembered fondly as a kid, *James at 15*, the 1977–78 NBC drama about the trials of a precocious 15-year-old; and *Apple's Way*, the 1974–75 CBS drama starring Ronny Cox as an eccentric, strong-willed architect who moves his family from the big city to rural Iowa for a different way of life.

On the surface, *Dawson's Creek* revolved around the heavy-petting love lives of its four principal teenage characters, but what really drove the show was how the teenagers were reacting to real-world issues enveloping them and their families. In many cases, the kids were more together than their parents. The 15-year-old pillars of *Dawson's Creek* were Dawson, scion of a prominent family whose happy facade is cracking; Joey, the tomboy from the wrong side of the tracks who realizes she has more than platonic feelings for her childhood friend Dawson; Pacey, Dawson's slacker-dude friend with a knack for getting into scrapes; and Jen, the sexy outsider who stirs things up by moving to fictional Capeside, Massachusetts, to help her family take care of her ailing grandmother. The pilot begins as the four are starting their sophomore year in high school.

Garth Ancier and I were taken with every word of Kevin's pilot script. There was nothing we felt we *needed* to change. But something he'd said during the pitch about Pacey having an affair with his English teacher caught my attention. Kevin suggested that their romance would blossom with a kiss in episode six. I thought it'd be a good idea to speed that up and put it in the pilot. It was provocative. Kevin took my suggestions to heart after we talked about how a show like this needed to be stoked with a lot of plot twists every week. Kevin very clearly articulated a story arc for Dawson and Joey that would see them finally kiss at the end of the thirteenth episode, or halfway through the first season (we hoped). Kevin understood that if we hoped to build tension in the show by stretching out the Dawson-Joey relationship, there had better be plenty of other stuff going on to keep the audience engaged.

As we prepared to move forward with shooting the *Dawson's Creek* pilot, we had no inkling that it would be the WB's first blockbuster hit. All I knew was that we had the same gut feeling about the talents of Kevin Williamson and the show he pitched us as I'd had when I first met Joss Whedon. Our job was to support them, keep problems at bay, and do everything possible to make these shows successful. My job depended on it.

There was a good deal of skepticism around the UPN offices as the buzz grew in the industry about the new WB show based on the movie *Buffy the Vampire Slayer*. Some had heard that hotshot screenwriter Joss Whedon had put his film career on hold to helm the vampires-in-high-school show. UPN's programming and marketing executives decided that they had to see the show. It didn't take too many calls to friends in the industry for them to turn up a copy of *Buffy*'s two-hour pilot.

A sizable group of UPN staffers, not including Lucie Salhany, made a lunch date in early March out of the screening in the network's main conference room. It was a blurry dub of a dub with a muddy soundtrack, but they could see past those technical limitations.

"What the . . . ?"

"This looks so cheesy. . . ."

"So there's supposed to be a big stash of vampires under the surface of this suburban California city. Yeh, right. . . ."

Catty comments and snarky observations sailed around the room. There was snickering and tsk-tsking. But even the show's most vocal detractors stayed to watch all of the two-hour episode.

When it was over, a number of senior executives dismissed it as weak and a bad fit with what little audience the WB had, namely moms and young kids. Meanwhile, the younger UPN executives left the room shaking their heads, suspecting that the WB had a hit on its hands. UPN's leaders didn't see it, but *Buffy* had something. The younger executives understood it didn't look like anything else on TV, and it was absolutely of the moment in its use of fashion, music, slang, and settings. It was also well written and engaging in ways that you wouldn't expect from something called *Buffy the Vampire Slayer*. It was, in short, a show they'd watch.

But as 1996 came to a close, UPN's owners had bigger issues to worry about than WB gaining traction with *Buffy*. Throughout the year, speculation had been snowballing about whether Viacom would exercise its option to buy a 50 percent stake in UPN. That option, which came up in January 1997, amounted to owning half of a growing pile of debt from programming and marketing expenditures.

The strife between the partners had become stifling, UPN alumni say. Chris-Craft executives still suspected Paramount was using UPN to offload its dead pilots and sop up a higher-than-normal percentage of the studio's overhead costs. The view from the Viacom side was that Chris-Craft executives, chiefly Evan Thompson and Bill Siegel, were slow to react and make decisions and were overly cautious about spending money. To Viacom, Chris-Craft wasn't thinking about UPN as a national network service but more parochially as a program service for its big-city TV stations.

Under the UPN operating agreement, the partners agreed on a budget every season for the network. When UPN went over the agreed-upon budget for the quarter, individual expenditures had to be approved by the partners at the operating committee meetings. And that meant just about everything had to be approved that way because, by numerous insider accounts, the partners always approved unrealistically modest budgets.

"Every year, the partners would bullshit each other about how great it was going to be," says a senior UPN executive. "And every year, from the beginning, it was terrible."

Paramount brass were also frustrated with Chris-Craft's slow pace of deal-making in buying television stations. The Paramount Stations Group swooped around the country looking for stations to buy, or better yet swap with other station owners to avoid heavy tax bills. Chris-Craft purchased stations in Baltimore and Tampa Bay, Florida, during the UPN years, but on the whole it was not as active as Paramount had hoped. At the time, Chris-Craft was sitting on a war chest of more than $1 billion in cash. Paying for acquisitions wasn't the issue.

The cycle of distrust and financial struggle continued. By many accounts, McCluggage and his boss, Viacom Entertainment Chairman Dolgen, thought Salhany was petty, childish, and almost always looking to stir up trouble between Chris-Craft and Viacom. And when she wasn't fighting with them, she was sparring with the WB's Jamie Kellner, which also drove the Viacom executives crazy.

In time, the speculation about Viacom picking up its option spread beyond the UPN building. Salhany was convinced that Jamie Kellner helped fuel a rumor that Viacom refused to buy half of UPN unless Chris-Craft agreed to replace Salhany as CEO. Regardless of whether or not Kellner had started the rumor, it happened to be true, and soon Viacom's distaste for Salhany was conventional wisdom in the television business.

"The Paramount people hated me at that point. I think they would have rather shot me than have me stay," Salhany says.

Beyond the hostility in the air and the punishing hours of being a CEO, Salhany had another urgent reason to prepare her exit from UPN: her husband, John Polcari, was facing severe health problems. He nearly died during UPN's first year due to complications from an eye infection. He spent weeks at Cedars-Sinai Medical Center in Los Angeles, and at one point even had last rites administered before he pulled through. Later, he suffered a heart attack.

After her husand's brush with death, it was clear to many who knew Salhany that it was only a matter of time before she moved on. As 1996 progressed, the commuter relationship that she and her sons maintained between Hollywood and their home in Boston had finally begun to take its toll. After his brush with death, this arrangement was out entirely. By then, the older of Salhany's two sons had reached middle-school age. Salhany remembered the promise she made to herself, and to Chris-Craft's Bill Siegel and Evan Thompson, when she took the UPN job. The time had come to move back to Boston.

"I don't think there would have been any condition where I would have stayed (in Southern California)," Salhany says.

By the end of 1996, Chris-Craft executives were eager to see Viacom acquire half of UPN. The terms of the purchase had been largely spelled out at the time the revised operating agreement was set in 1994. All Viacom needed to do was cut Chris-Craft a check for $160 million for a 50 percent stake. But before Viacom would do so, executives there wanted Chris-Craft to assure them that Salhany would be replaced as CEO. The rumors floating around the industry for months had been true. Viacom would not buy in to UPN so long as Salhany remained in charge.

Chris-Craft Chairman Herbert Siegel didn't often weigh in directly on UPN affairs. His son William served as his lieutenant in overseeing the family's sizable investment in the network. But out of an abundance of loyalty and gratitude, the Chris-Craft mogul quietly intervened on Lucie Salhany's behalf to keep the paramount troops from sacking her before she could arrange a graceful exit. The Chris-Craft camp felt strongly that for all she'd done for UPN, Salhany deserved the dignity of managing her own resignation.

Herb Siegel called Viacom Chairman Sumner Redstone in late

1996 to request a high-level partners meeting. A small group from each company convened in a private room at the Beverly Hilton Hotel. The Chris-Craft chairman agreed to begin looking for a successor, so long as Redstone agreed to give Salhany six months to work through the transition. Redstone and Co. harrumphed about Salhany's short-comings during the past two and a half years, but ultimately they had a handshake agreement. Viacom delivered the $160 million check to Chris-Craft not long afterward.

For all its struggles, UPN maintained its ratings lead over the WB for the remainder of the 1996–97 season. The advantage was largely due to the superiority of UPN's station lineup. In hindsight, UPN veterans say the cushion of the better stations lulled them into complacency. As long as the WB was out there, there was always someone UPN could say it was beating.

In spite of their leadership woes, this confidence led to a sense of ease among the UPN staff by the end of 1996. The WB had generated a little sizzle with *Savannah* at the start of the year but the ratings didn't hold up, let alone grow. Making things worse for the WB was that the network's move in the fall into family-friendly territory seemed to be an uphill climb. Initial viewer reaction to *7th Heaven* was lukewarm at best, and the ratings and advertising boost that Kellner had been hoping to cash in on failed to emerge. While younger staffers at UPN had been concerned by what they saw on the *Buffy* tape, whether or not the show would succeed was still anyone's guess. The higher-ups at UPN were confident that Buffy would tank, but they were also preoccupied with the search for Salhany's successor.

By year's end, the unofficial search for Salhany's replacement had officially begun with whispers and phone calls placed to Hollywood's top television executives. No one, least of all the UPN partners, knew who it would be, but everyone knew that person had better be good, and ready for a fight in every aspect of the business.

CHAPTER FIVE

I DON'T WANT TO WAIT

As 1997 dawned, a big point of focus for both networks was the need to extend their contracts with affiliate stations. The chase to lure the strongest station affiliates had never really let up, but the heat was turned up again toward the end of 1996 because the clock was ticking on many of the WB and UPN's original three-year affiliation contracts. UPN and the WB had signed mostly short-term contracts when they were beating the bushes for station partners in late 1993 and 1994. At the time, the rivalry between the start-ups, coupled with the affiliate musical chairs in the broader market, ensured that neither netlet had the clout to sign many stations for more than two or three years.

The WB's affiliate relations executives and their counterparts at UPN knew that the second go-round with some of their stations was going to be tough. Station owners were no fools. They would be even more aggressive about asking for money and extra compensation for carrying the network. The operators knew full well that the WB and UPN had settled into a kind of stasis. Neither could really claim victory—not since UPN's premiere night—but neither seemed in danger of going away thanks to the wherewithal of their parent companies. The parent companies needed stations to cooperate or all their investment in building a broadcast network during the previous three years would go down the drain.

"It was affiliate wars, part deux," says UPN distribution chief Kevin Tannehill.

While UPN was focused on cherry-picking the best of WB's lineup, Jamie Kellner was spending a lot of time thinking about the smallest markets. There were plenty of places in the country where neither the WB nor UPN had much hope of landing a full-time affiliate. Jamie had faced the same distribution quandary at Fox during the late 1980s. He thought long and hard about the solution he had devised back then, and then improved on it. Jamie's solution for Fox had been to court the mostly mom-and-pop cable operators in small-to-tiny markets. He convinced many of those operators to set aside a channel on their systems, which had plenty of available channel space, to carry Fox's prime-time programs. The cable operators would get high-quality original fare that local viewers would undoubtedly seek out after hearing so much about edgy shows like *Married . . . with Children* and *The Simpsons*.

When it came time to roll out the same concept for the WB a half-dozen years later, Kellner formulated a plan. He would lean on Warner Bros. to use its vast library to provide a range of daytime and early evening programming for the cable channels he was hoping to secure. And in a twist on what he did at Fox, Kellner set out to recruit the strongest broadcast TV stations that were in the same local markets as the cable operators to adopt the WB-branded cable channel. Under this new arrangement, the broadcast TV stations would handle the cable channel's local advertising, sales, and marketing needs—in exchange for a cut of the station's advertising revenue. In this manner, the local broadcaster would have the perfect platform to promote the WB-branded cable channel, and those station executives would have the right local-yokel advertising contacts needed to make the most of the ultracheap ad time available on the cable channel.

Warner Bros.' technical operations department took on the challenge of meeting the WB's needs in smaller markets with great vision and determination. The main hurdle was to find a way to streamline the technical aspects of running a TV station—the need for round-the-clock staff to schedule and monitor the airing of programs, commercials, station identification breaks, and so on. The local cable operator would not have the spare manpower or the financial incentive to monitor such things on the WB's behalf. The operations of the WB-branded cable channel had to be 95 percent automated (other than ad sales and marketing) to make them financially and technically viable for the WB and the local cable operator.

Warner Bros.' executives took their needs to IBM headquarters in New York. Engineers at IBM worked with the Warner Bros.' Technical Operations department to devise a "station-in-a-box" technology that allowed WB to send out daily feeds of programming plus the commercials for the pre-programmed breaks. The feeds were sent to dozens of small cable operators using sophisticated digital encoding from an automated hub located in an industrial stretch of West Los Angeles near Los Angeles International Airport.*

In the tight-knit station community, Jamie's bold plan didn't stay quiet for long. UPN executives savaged Kellner's concept as detrimental to God, country, and the American way of life because it embraced cable as a method of distribution for WB programming. Nevermind that Fox had been doing so for years. UPN executives raced to their phones and fax machines after managing to get copies of the WB's station-in-a-box pitch materials. They sent it off chapter and verse to station owners and business writers in the hopes of generating some critical media coverage, and they reached out to UPN affiliates in the affected markets to make sure none had the notion of jumping ship. UPN executives expertly played the broadcast-versus-cable card that resonated with many station owners.

At the WB, we had no idea Jamie's small-market initiative would be branded controversial until we got word of UPN's smear campaign. From there, we countered with unadulterated outrage. Brad Turell had to be scraped off the ceiling after a few conversations with journalists who had clearly had the UPN briefing. There was heated talk of suing UPN and Paramount for slander and interference with trade but, of course, it was just talk.

Jamie kept cool through it all. His industry peers had a field day

---

* In 2005, IBM and Warner Bros. were honored with a joint technical Emmy Award for developing the "station-in-a-box" technology, which the National Academy of Television Arts and Sciences called "a breakthrough solution in television engineering."

dissecting his business proposal idea to connect all of these small cable channels into one sizable regional force. The new mini-network, first dubbed "the WeB" and later the WB 100-Plus Station Group, could serve as one-stop shopping for advertisers and program suppliers looking for a more efficient way to do business in smaller markets. As usual, the television industry would embrace Jamie's innovative thinking—after the dust settled.

UPN, meanwhile, made fast work of most of its affiliation renewal negotiations.

"Going into 1997, we were the ones with the momentum. We had a slight statistical ratings advantage. We were the ones poaching them," UPN distribution chief Kevin Tannehill says. But Tannehill was expressly told by his bosses in early 1997 not to engage in affiliation renegotiations with one particular station-group owner. Baltimore-based Sinclair Broadcast Group was the second most important affiliate owner outside of the stations that Chris-Craft and Paramount owned and operated.

Sinclair is run by the enigmatic David Smith, whose father was among the pioneers in broadcasting who used UHF technology to bring new TV stations to markets that previously only had two or three. Smith became a player on the national TV scene in the mid-1990s as his company amassed an arsenal of the kind of independent and Fox-affiliated television stations that spend a lot of money buying sitcom rerun rights, talk shows, and other syndicated programs from Hollywood's major studios. Sinclair owned UPN affiliates in such vital arteries as Baltimore, Cincinnati, and Pittsburgh. Paramount and Chris-Craft knew the WB camp had to be reaching out to Smith all the time. The partners wanted to handle the Sinclair renegotiation with kid gloves at the highest levels.

So they did. The upshot of those talks would be a ground-shaking event for UPN.

Nearly a year after that first presentation pilot screening where I begged for *Buffy the Vampire Slayer*, it was time to celebrate. Joss Whedon's agent, Chris Harbert, threw a small party at his Santa Monica home on a balmy Monday night, March 10, 1997, the night of the premiere. It was a low-key gathering of friends and coworkers who'd been through the *Buffy* battle together.

For the show's premiere, Joss and his team re-shot and extended the material in the original pilot presentation, and stitched it together with the second episode to make the debut a two-hour "event." Bob and Lew came up with a provocative 90-second trailer that introduced the concept of Buffy as the mysterious, once-in-a-generation chosen one, a slayer tasked with keeping evil at bay. The trailer opened with pan shots of vintage black-and-white photographs of stern-looking women, Gothic churches, scenes of mayhem, and a cemetery—all from pictures our marketing mavens found randomly in antique stores.

"In every generation, there is a chosen one . . . ," the voice-over intoned.

Joss didn't particularly care for the spot, but there was no arguing its effectiveness. It explained the *Buffy* mythos brilliantly and succinctly, and it set a certain tone for the series. Buffy Summers was a hero, not a victim. Viewers with any appetite for fantasy, action, and horror would have to stay tuned.

The atmosphere that Monday night in Harbert's home was casual and comfortable. Joss and Gail Berman were cheered as conquering heroes, deservedly so. I was proud to see such a positive reception to something we had all worked so hard on. I'd limped my way into the party, having broken my leg a few weeks earlier in Aspen, Colorado. It wasn't just the effect of the painkillers; the sweet feeling of accomplishment and vindication was swirling all around us that night, even before we saw the first Nielsen numbers.

During a toast by Garth Ancier, he memorably confessed that he'd be happy if the show pulled in a modest household rating. The verdict was in 12 hours later: *Buffy* finished with a 3.4 household rating, which translated into almost 1 million more households than we were pulling in on average in the same time slot with *Savannah.* For the WB, it was a big, big number. There was jubilation at the ranch that day. Whoops and hollers and high-fives were exchanged in the hallways. Kellner convened a margarita party that afternoon for the entire staff in the main executive conference room.

As with the gong ceremonies, Kellner appreciated our need to let off steam and toast our wins. Early on, after we moved into the trailers, we had assistants buy a bunch of blenders for the office, and we always kept a stash of bar salt, Triple Sec, and lime juice on hand. The celebration that spilled out all through our trailers the day after the *Buffy* premiere was a particularly momentous occasion. A large group of us were chatting and guzzling drinks in the conference room when Warner Bros.' Bob Daly and Barry Meyer walked in on our soirée. With suits and ties and an aura of authority about them, the two men stood in stark contrast to the mostly under-35 crowd in the room. But Bob and Barry were always gregarious and warm. They said their hellos and how-are-yas, and shook many hands as they made their way across the room.

Jordan and I later confessed to each other that our first thought when we saw Bob and Barry was that we had done something wrong. Bob in particular made me nervous as he approached. He made a point of letting us know that he hadn't forgotten how hard we'd fought to keep *Buffy* alive when no one else thought it had a prayer.

"Let this be a lesson to you," Daly said, gently wagging his finger. "If you disagree with us, then don't listen to us. You stick with what you think is right for the WB." For years afterward, Barry Meyer encouraged me to trust my instincts and fight for shows I believed in. Two years later, we developed a successful *Buffy* spinoff series, *Angel*, around the popular good vampire character played by David Boreanaz.

The heat generated by *Buffy the Vampire Slayer* came at the perfect moment for us. The same month *Buffy* bowed, Tribune demonstrated its eagerness to increase its investment in the WB. In March 1997, Tribune paid $21 million to boost its holdings by nearly 10 percent, to 21.9 percent, from the 12.5 percent interest it purchased for $12 million in August 1995.

Around this time Jamie also set into motion his own long-sought entry into station ownership—WB affiliates, of course. He set up a private venture in which he was the majority shareholder; it was designed to benefit the WB much in the way the Paramount Stations Group had helped shore up UPN's distribution by acquiring or building stations in areas where the network was weak.

Jamie had hoped to bring in Warner Bros. as a minority partner in his station group. He pitched the idea to Bob Daly, but it ultimately was a nonstarter with Time Warner at the corporate level. The media giant was heavily invested in cable systems through Time Warner Cable. Even with the WB in the fold, Time Warner brass decided it made no sense for the company to pursue a minority stake in a small group of broadcast TV stations.

Jamie was disappointed but not surprised. While Warner Bros. was not involved, they allowed him to hold on to the name he'd selected for his new venture, Acme Television, derived from the ubiquitous brand name seen in Warner Bros.' Road Runner cartoons. Acme was formed in February 1997 with the acquisition of an existing WB affiliate, KWBP-TV, in Portland, Oregon. Jamie tapped Thomas Allen, who had been chief financial officer at Fox during Jamie's tenure at the network, and the experienced station executive Douglas Gealy to run the company. Jamie was to serve as chairman and CEO. The company sold itself to Wall Street effectively with a simple strategy of buying underperforming stations or building new stations to fill in the black holes in the WB's affiliate lineup. For Jamie, Acme was all business, which meant that the WB was not the only network that Acme would support, and in the years ahead Acme would acquire both the WB *and* UPN affiliate stations in Albuquerque, New Mexico.

Within three years, Acme would expand to 10 stations in such strategically important markets as St. Louis and Salt Lake City, and it would have a successful initial public offering. It would also stir a hornet's nest of resentment among some Warner Bros.' and WB insiders, who frowned on the idea of Jamie holding a CEO position outside of the WB with a company whose business model relied on being a WB affiliate partner. In the view of many, even those who respected and admired Jamie, the advent of Acme was fraught with potential conflicts of interest with his day job. The Warner Bros.' legal department had its hands full crafting waiver and disclosure agreements for Jamie to sign that would effectively tie his hands whenever Acme had direct dealings with the WB.

Jamie didn't seem to care much about the eyebrows he raised with the launch of Acme. He genuinely loved the TV station business and the old-school broadcaster circles he'd grown up with in his career. Wall Street was incredibly receptive at the time to new station-ownership ventures, even those like Acme, which planned to build some of its stations from scratch. And while his new start-up had ruffled some feathers at Warner Bros.' corporate level, in the end Acme was seeking to add affiliate stations to the WB and boost viewership. It was a double-edged sword for the network, but Jamie argued vehemently that the station group would help us compete with UPN.

Even with Tribune stepping up and Acme coming together in early 1997, Jamie wasn't satisfied. He had his eye on an offensive strike at the competition. He wanted to make headlines for the WB with an affiliate grab that would be hard for UPN to recover from and give the WB an upgrade in markets where it sorely needed them. And he knew exactly who he needed to go after: the 800-pound media gorilla of Baltimore, Sinclair Broadcast Group.

Sinclair had five UPN affiliate stations in important markets where the WB was barely on the radar: Baltimore; Pittsburgh; Cincinnati; San Antonio, Texas; and Oklahoma City, Oklahoma. Jamie began courting Barry Baker, Sinclair's CEO-designate, a seasoned station executive who Jamie already knew well. Baker's own TV station group, River City Broadcasting, had been acquired by Sinclair the year before for $1.2 billion. Baker's River City headquarters in St. Louis had been one of the first stops for the Warner Bros.' and Paramount planes in the fall of 1993. Outspoken in the press and in industry circles when it suited him, he was known as a savvy station operator and wily negotiator. And his bargaining position had only grown stronger after joining forces with the family-controlled Sinclair.

The WB was already in business with Sinclair in some smaller markets. Jamie knew that Sinclair's hard-nosed president and CEO, David Smith, was all about the bottom line. It would take real money, not reverse compensation deals, to convince him to switch his larger-market stations from UPN to the WB. But paying Sinclair stations for carrying the WB would repudiate everything Jamie and Warner Bros. had said in the station community for the past four years about the network's unique need for reverse compensation.

Yet after two years on the air, Jamie and Warner Bros. had learned a very important lesson: the merest increase in the network's national ratings always brought in far more in advertising revenue than it did in increased reverse comp payments from affiliates. That meant that it was in the WB's best interest to line up the strongest affiliate stations it could find in mid- and large-size markets to beef up its national ratings average.

Sinclair was asking for a boatload of money in exchange for a long-term affiliation deal. While initially some at the WB balked at the figures, when Warner Bros. crunched the numbers, they found it would be money well spent in terms of increased advertising revenue. Regardless of the bridges the WB might burn with other affiliates by paying Sinclair upfront, the move was a shrewd one because it would strengthen the WB's distribution in key markets where the network had barely been visible before.

Kevin Williamson had never tackled a television pilot script at the time Stupin and Columbia TriStar Television first commissioned *Dawson's Creek* from him in 1995. The studio sent over a number of episodes of *My So-Called Life*, which had just been cancelled by ABC. The show hadn't found a large audience, but it had a hard-core cult of fans after just a few episodes. Kevin sat in his apartment and timed out the acts between the commercial breaks with a stopwatch to determine how many pages he should write for each act.

Because the pilot script was for an hour-long show, we had to turn it into a 30-minute pilot presentation as we had with *Buffy*. The hardest thing about turning that script into a 30-minute pilot-presentation reel was finding the right actors with the right chemistry, usually the case with any pilot. We knew we had to have fresh faces. Our head of casting, Kathleen Letterie, worked day and night to find leads and audition tapes.

All of the characters were crucial to getting it just right, but none more so than Joey, the tomboy struggling to shed her cocoon and become a young woman. After all, it's Joey's internal revelation about her romantic feelings for Dawson that is the engine of the pilot story. At one point we were strongly considering 24-year-old actress Selma Blair for the role. She had a mere handful of credits to her name at the time, and she had the spunky brunette quality of the character (Selma Blair would later land a lead role on the 1999–2000 season WB comedy *Zoe, Duncan, Jack & Jane*). But Kevin hesitated long enough for Letterie to come in to Jordan and me one day with a reel from a drop-dead gorgeous 17-year-old in Toledo, Ohio.

Katie Holmes was a discovery Kathleen had made about a year before at a modeling event in New York. Kathleen had met with her a few times in Los Angeles and had even sent her in to read for the lead in *Buffy the Vampire Slayer*. Although she was not right for the role of Buffy, Katie's striking beauty and natural charisma made a big impression on Kathleen, who was determined to get her on a WB show. When *Dawson's Creek* came along, Katie was at the top of Kathleen's list.

The only hiccup in bringing her in for an audition was that Katie at the time was playing the lead in her high school production of *Damn Yankees*. She wasn't about to let down her classmates, or give up the spotlight, at Notre Dame Academy, a prestigious all-girl Catholic school in Toledo. So she sent along an audition tape shot in her basement that featured a dramatic scene between Joey and Dawson, with her mother handling Dawson's lines. Her decision to stick it out with *Damn Yankees* even as Hollywood beckoned was so in character for her, and for Joey Potter, that we were sold on her for the role long before she made it to our offices for a meeting.

"As soon as we saw Katie Holmes on that tape, I was like, 'How fast can she get here?,' " Williamson recalls.

Katie, the youngest in a tight-knit family of four sisters and a brother, wasn't a total novice. She'd done some modeling, and she'd spent time on the audition circuit in Los Angeles, landing her first small film role in 1997's *The Ice Storm*. She was still charmingly green when we first met her, but she wouldn't be for long.

Another cast member who came to us early on in the casting process was Joshua Jackson, who we at first considered for the role of Dawson. After batting around the issue for a while, nobody felt he was quite right for the title role, but it became clear that Pacey was a perfect fit. Josh was 18 and a pro, with a long list of film and TV credits to his name by then. More important, he was fine with the best-friend role.

Michelle Williams was a commanding presence at all of 16 years of age when she came in and nailed the part of Jen. Unlike Katie, whose older sister chaperoned her during production of the pilot because she was not yet 18, Michelle had taken the legal step of becoming emancipated from her parents at age 15. She was an incredibly motivated, take-charge kind of person who'd grown up in rural Montana and took a methodical approach to her goal of becoming a movie star. Ironically, Williams was the one member of the *Dawson's Creek* Fab Four that we had some doubts about in terms of acting range. Of course, she's the one who has gone on to earn great reviews for her work on the big screen, including an Academy Award nomination for her supporting role in 2005's *Brokeback Mountain*.

The toughest role of all to cast was our leading man—a dilemma that is also par for the course during pilot season. We were days away from flying the cast and crew to the location site in Wilmington, North Carolina—about two hours away from Williamson's hometown—to begin production. Kathleen came through at the eleventh hour, running into my office with a videotape in one hand and a resume in the other.

"I think this guy might be the right one," Kathleen said excitedly.

"MIGHT be right? He HAS to be right. He HAAAS to," I screeched, letting my anxiety out without even thinking about it.

Before I had the chance to apologize, Kathleen had popped the tape into my VCR. The lanky young man on the screen was handsome but not matinee-idol handsome or stallion-handsome. He mumbled so much we couldn't hear his lines. His hair was disheveled, and so was his Oxford shirt. His dark brown blazer looked worn, and his face wasn't exactly clean shaven. He looked very much like the college student he was, at Drew University in New Jersey, who had two little-seen indie movie parts to his credit.

We weren't totally sold on the tape, but we were desperate enough to bring James Van Der Beek out to Los Angeles for a closer look. When James arrived, Kevin tried to coach him a bit before the audition for the network and studio brass.

"Be *bigger*," Kevin told James in the hallway outside our conference room, waving his arms around as if he were trying to take flight. "Try to be bigger in your delivery. You're mumbling."

To Kevin's surprise, James had pointed questions for him. He wanted to make sure that Williamson wanted to do a serious, high-end ensemble drama along the lines of *My So-Called Life* and not a pure soap à la *Beverly Hills, 90210*. Kevin assured him that *Dawson's Creek* was his passion project as a writer. James must have believed him, because he was great in the audition. He came into the room wearing a beret, which threw me off at first, but as soon as he removed it, I could see he was our Dawson, even if he was still mumbling.

As excited as we at the WB and Columbia TriStar Television were about shooting *Dawson's Creek,* the project was not high on the industry's radar screen as it was coming together in the spring of 1997. It was a 30-minute pilot (it actually came closer to 40 minutes) made for very little money for a network that many in Hollywood still sniffed at. It was about as anonymous as it could get, shooting in North Carolina with a cast of unknowns.

Jordan made the trip on the WB's behalf, and it was a bonding experience that left him, and by association, the network, with a rock-solid relationship with the show's key players. During production of the pilot, the *Dawson's* cast and crew bunked at the local Howard Johnson motel, right across the street from one of Wilmington's hot spots, the local Hooters restaurant. The conference room where the actors and Kevin held their table-read rehearsal sessions was right next door to the hotel's swimming pool. The room was damp, moldy, and noisy with pool sounds seeping through the walls. The budget for the 30-minute presentation was just over $1 million, which was modest even by WB standards at the time.

The situation called for guerrilla filmmaking at its most inventive. Everybody who was on hand was expected to pitch in, including Jordan and Columbia TriStar Television executives Sarah Timberman and Carolyn Bernstein. Jordan, Sarah, and Carolyn spent an afternoon at a nearby mall looking for authentic teen clothes and accessories to augment the show's wardrobe racks. The three executives also served as chauffeurs and companions to the actors and crew members during the 10-day shoot.

Despite the rustic conditions, the cast gelled quickly in a way that was amazing to see; it was evident even in the daily footage I was scrutinizing back in Burbank. Jordan kept reporting back to me that the stuff they were getting was fabulous and that our young actors were supremely talented and motivated. I was excited but still cautious. You can't count your chickens on a pilot until you've seen the whole package put together in a final cut.

Before the pilot was even finished, Jordan wrote a passionate speech about why we absolutely positively had to greenlight *Dawson's Creek* as a series. Fortunately, we never had to deliver it. The pilot was universally well received by all of the people who mattered. Warner Bros.' cochairman Bob Daly was particularly effusive. In May, we triumphantly screened a few clips of *Dawson's Creek* at our 1997 upfront event and brought the cast out to dazzle the advertising buyers. We announced the show as being in reserve to lead our big expansion to Tuesday nights in January 1998.

Everyone at the WB had wild faith in the show because the pilot had turned out so well and because the process of pulling it together had been so charmed, relative to most pilot productions. The credit goes to Kevin Williamson's talent, and his wonderful collaboration with producer Paul Stupin and pilot director Steve Miner.

There were a few final hurdles to overcome, however, once it was a certainty that the show was going to air. One of them was the need to get filmmaker-mogul Steven Spielberg's OK for the show's liberal use of Spielberg's name, likeness, and works to help define the personality of our lead character, Dawson. The character worshipped the director, and aspired to be like him, just as a young Kevin Williamson had been in his youth. Spielberg pictures, Spielberg movie posters, and Spielberg's name were featured throughout the pilot script. The legal departments of the WB and Columbia TriStar both instructed producers to get Spielberg's sign-off on the heavy usage to ensure he wouldn't sue. Otherwise, they'd have to change the character's obsession to a fictional director. To avoid this, we tried every avenue to get in touch with Spielberg.

We knew how to reach Spielberg's handlers, of course, but we also knew that first he'd have to make time to screen the pilot before approving a legal waiver for *Dawson's Creek*. Therein lay the problem—obtaining 30 spare minutes in the life of one of the world's most famous movie directors. By late summer, we were getting antsy about the lack of contact with Spielberg's office.

Finally, word came to the studio through Spielberg's representatives that he'd screened the pilot and thought it was very good. He could see the potential. He would give us his go-ahead under the condition that the show make no reference whatsoever to his wife, actress Kate Capshaw, or to his children. That was fine by Kevin and all of us, though it did require excising Capshaw from a few photos visible in Dawson's room in the pilot.

Of course, the news was also exciting because it was confirmation that Steven Spielberg agreed with us. *Dawson's Creek* had the makings of a hit.

• • •

By the time the WB was starting to take off, Lucie Salhany was preparing to wind down. In January 1997, Salhany and other UPN executives traveled to New Orleans for the annual National Association of Television Program Executives business conference and trade show. NATPE was always old-home-week for Salhany, who would invariably run into dozens of old friends and colleagues from her days in local television and syndication.

At the convention, Salhany made a point of asking Evan Thompson and Bill Siegel to save some time for a private lunch for the three of them. When the trio met in the Big Easy, Salhany reminded them of the timetable she'd laid out for herself two and a half years earlier when she took the job. She told them she did not want to sign another long-term contract as CEO of UPN, even if Chris-Craft was prepared to fight its partner on her behalf. She would step down later in 1997 when her successor was in place.

After she laid it all out for her bosses in a matter-of-fact way, Salhany the warrior let a few tears roll into her gumbo.

"It has been quite a ride," Salhany said as the trio lingered over their meal, swapping stories about good times and big deals they'd pulled off together, most of them long before the advent of UPN.

Thompson and Siegel couldn't help but feel sympathy for Salhany's situation. Both had spent many hours with her at the hospital when her husband's illness was at its worst. They knew she was preparing for a major lifestyle change. And though it was largely unstated during the lunch, Salhany, Siegel, and Thompson all knew that Viacom was never going to stand for Salhany continuing as the network's leader. Instinctively, Salhany knew she had to bow out gracefully sooner rather than later, or she would lose the ability to control the timing and spin of her resignation announcement. She was unaware of the agreement Herbert Siegel had initiated with Sumner Redstone a few months earlier.

Salhany decided that she would make her news official shortly after the network's May 20 upfront schedule presentation. During the months leading up to that May date, one of the few people at UPN that Salhany confided in about her plans was publicity head Kevin Brockman. Salhany and Brockman had developed a strong working relationship during the previous two and a half years. They trusted and respected each other. What's more, Brockman had come to her early in the year because he wanted to be let out of his contract so he could take a high-profile job as head of publicity at ABC Entertainment under its newly appointed president, Jamie Tarses.

"I think the fact that ABC would come after me speaks volumes about what we've accomplished . . . ," Brockman said. Salhany had been staring at him sternly from behind her large desk, arms folded and lips pursed. After a few minutes, she exhaled and began waving her hands for him to stop.

Before Brockman had the chance to really pour on the emotion about what they had accomplished as a group, Salhany informed him that she planned to resign. Salhany swore Brockman to silence and gave him one more task before he moved on. She instructed him to write a press release announcing her resignation from the network and stash it in a password-protected file in his computer. Brockman was on the job at ABC for two months before he got the call from his old boss asking him where that release could be found.

In fact, Salhany's original plan to hold her announcement until after UPN's upfront presentation was scuttled by the press. The rumors of her departure swirled to a peak in the first few days of May, when executives at UPN, Viacom, Paramount Television, and Chris-Craft began getting phone calls from reporters from major newspapers inquiring about Salhany's status. In the late afternoon on May 8, Salhany learned that a number of news outlets had confirmed the story enough through other sources that they were going to run with it for the following day, whether she commented or not. That was the day Salhany placed the call to Brockman.

After her resignation became official, Salhany and Chris-Craft had one last surprise in store for Paramount's Kerry McCluggage and Viacom Entertainment's Jonathan Dolgen. Salhany was leaving the network, but she was to be appointed one of Chris-Craft's representatives on the operating committee, meaning that she would remain a regular, undoubtedly vocal, presence in the big-picture management of UPN.

McCluggage and Dolgen were aghast. But other than grousing, there was nothing they could do. It was Chris-Craft's prerogative to appoint its own operating committee members. To the Viacom camp, it was yet another example of petty, defensive, destructive behavior on the part of Chris-Craft. Indeed, relations between the partners were so touchy in this period that Chris-Craft quietly talked to executives at Universal Television, among other entities, about their interest in possibly buying out Paramount's stake in UPN.

About a month after Lucie Salhany announced her plan to step down, the charter UPN executive team staged its last hurrah. It would endure as the high-water mark of UPN–WB bashing in the 12-year battle of the networks. June 10, 1997 became known as "Salhany's last stand."

UPN opened its annual post-season meeting with affiliates on that postcard-perfect morning. The event took place at the plush Paramount Theater on the studio lot, right outside the rectangular office building where UPN had been cobbled together a few years before. Salhany telegraphed her pugnacious mood with a brooch she sported on the lapel of her bright-white power-executive pantsuit. It was a ceramic figurine depicting a plump green frog with a dagger stuck into its chest. The eye-catching accessory drew a fair number of comments from affiliate managers and the handful of reporters who covered the meeting. Some of them asked for tight closeups of Salhany with the frog-pin visible to run in their newspapers and magazines. It was the perfect illustration of the blood feud between the networks. Salhany cheerfully obliged.

It wasn't something she'd talked about much since the WB emerged with its Michigan J. Frog mascot, but, in fact, UPN's leader had for years been an avid collector of amphibian knickknacks: pins, figurines, toys, jewelry, ceramics—if it had a frog motif, she wanted it. The infamous frog with a dagger in its heart came to her in the mail at UPN anonymously a few days before the affiliate meeting. There was no name on the package, just a note saying "Saw this, thought you'd like it," Salhany recalls. Nobody ever claimed credit for sending it to her, even after pictures of her wearing it ran in numerous publications.

After participants that day milled around for half an hour or so in the theater's circular lobby, they went into the meeting, which began shortly after 9 a.m. Salhany walked out on the small stage to a podium. After a little chit-chat, she opened her speech to the station executives with a call to arms.

"Let me share with you the three biggest lies that Warner Bros. tries to pass off as the truth . . . ," Salhany said with fury in her voice. She listed the WB's shortcomings and challenged its claims of growth and momentum. She repeatedly accused them of lying. Most everyone in the room understood the subtext. Rightly or wrongly, in her mind Salhany blamed Jamie Kellner and his lieutenants for talking trash about her and UPN in important circles.

At the 1996 affiliate gathering, Salhany made a big point of warning the affiliate managers that it didn't matter whether they liked the network's shows or not because they were not the target audience. The following year, she made much the same argument, but with far less conviction as they trotted out the stars of new shows, which included a comeback bid for stone-cold comic Andrew Dice Clay. He played the street-tough head of a Los Angeles record label in the comedy *Hitz*. UPN also rescued another Paramount-produced sitcom that ABC jettisoned after one season. *Clueless* was based on the studio's hit 1995 movie about the exploits of a Beverly Hills princess. Salhany didn't even try to explain how the show that didn't click for ABC was a fit with UPN's urban comedies and action-fantasy dramas such as *The Sentinel* and *Star Trek: Voyager*.

As the meeting went on, the WB flogging continued. Distribution chief Kevin Tannehill had the crowd chanting "Dump the dubba, dump the dubba," in a play on the WB's on-air jingle "Dubba-Dubba-W-B!" During another tirade, Salhany punctuated a point about the WB's misleading propaganda, particularly its short-lived effort to

brand itself as a family-friendly network in the *7th Heaven* mold—
until *Buffy the Vampire Slayer* came along.

"They're not the family network. I can say I'm six feet tall, blonde,
and with black eyes," but that wouldn't make it true, she said.*

Later, Viacom Chairman Sumner Redstone came out on stage
for brief remarks in a thinly veiled effort to telegraph the parent
company's continued support for the ailing network, despite all the
industry gossip about the enmity between the partners. The ever-
charismatic Redstone even paid his own tribute to Salhany when she
joined him on stage.

"You might not be a blonde . . . but you are six feet tall," Redstone said with his trademark grin. The lanky, redheaded mogul gave
the compact Salhany a sideways hug around the shoulders as the station executives rose for a standing ovation.

But the vehemence of the attacks on the competition didn't sit
well with some in the room, especially those who also owned WB affiliate stations. UPN's rank-and-file staffers heard it in the comments
from affiliate managers as the morning sessions broke up and the
group filed out of the theater for a luncheon set up in another building. Some of them were clearly appalled.

Nevertheless, to Salhany, the WB was already hitting below the
belt by attempting to sow seeds of doubt about UPN and about her in
the marketplace.

"Compete with us on programming needs, or distribution, OK,"
Salhany says. "But there was no need for them to start really slinging
mud. . . . So you want to sling first mud? I'll sling second mud. It was
totally unnecessary."

Of course, it didn't take long at all for
word of the UPN fusillade to filter over the Cahuenga Pass to the
ranch. With such a clear opening to pounce on, publicity chief Brad

---

* *Daily Variety*, June 11, 1997, *The Hollywood Reporter*, June 11, 1997.

Turell had free-rein to mount an aggressive counterattack. His response was deliberately muted on the first day, but Turell and WB executives dined out for weeks on the material handed to them that day by UPN executives. And within a month, the WB would strike back in a very public way at the heart of UPN's strength over the WB, namely its distribution advantage.

"Ms. Salhany's comments seem desperate. Her statements are not factual and, beyond that, we choose not to engage in a mudslinging contest that could discredit us or our industry," Turell told reporters that day.*

Jamie Kellner ate it up. He looked like the Cheshire cat from *Alice in Wonderland* most of the time. Only a few of us in his inner circle knew that something was in the works that would strike back at UPN in a much more damaging way than a few barbs tossed at an affiliate meeting.

Kellner, Barry Meyer, and Bruce Rosenblum had been on the phone and in meetings with Barry Baker and other Sinclair executives for weeks, hammering out the details of the affiliation pacts. It all came to a head during the Fourth of July weekend in 1997, when the principals were scattered all over the country for the holiday but spent most of their time on conference calls with one another. Kellner was on a boat off the California coast; Barry Meyer was at his home in Los Angeles in the midst of throwing a 76th birthday party for his mother; Bruce Rosenblum was vacationing with his family at the posh Hotel del Coronado outside San Diego. Baker was on a barge in the Chesapeake Bay with a massive fireworks display going off in the background.

Sinclair's David Smith and Barry Baker had been in talks on and off for months with the WB and UPN, and they had been candid about that fact with both networks. With many of its UPN and WB affiliation deals coming up at the same time, the company wanted to consolidate its portfolio and steer all of its affiliation pacts toward one

----

*　*The Hollywood Reporter*, June 11, 1997.

of the two networks. That would give Sinclair maximum clout as an affiliate owner, Baker says.

"We thought we could be a kingmaker in terms of giving one of the [networks] a distinct advantage. And we listened to both sides," Baker says. "At the end of the day Warner Bros. paid us an awful lot of money. It was pure cash, plain and simple."

Paramount and Chris-Craft made a full-court press to renew the Sinclair stations, and they also tried to sweeten the offer by discussing the possibility of station swaps or other business between Sinclair and Viacom, and Sinclair and Chris-Craft. But the simple truth was that neither Paramount nor Chris-Craft had been as forthright as Kellner in terms of what they were prepared to offer.

By early summer, with barely six months to go on the existing UPN affiliation contracts, Sinclair's talks with UPN were dragging on. The WB's offer was straightforward: $84 million for a 10-year deal beginning in January 1998. Sinclair and the WB camp had agreed on giving themselves an informal deadline of early July to reach a deal or move on. When the time came, it wasn't a hard choice. At Sinclair, money doesn't talk; it swears.

Sinclair got lucky in betting on the right netlet, aligning with the WB just as it was taking off with cutting-edge shows that skewed younger. But Baker makes no pretense of having a strong instinct one way or another that summer.

"There was no belief that anyone had a magic formula by then for programming," Baker says. "It was, 'Who's going to pay us for the distribution system?' And it was an awful lot of money to charge for UHF distribution systems, considering that Fox had paid their stations nothing. It was a huge deal for the business in that way."

On July 14, 10 days after the WB deal was finalized over the four-way phone call, Baker met Kerry McCluggage and Steve Goldman for breakfast at a hotel in the Universal Studios complex that lies between Hollywood and the San Fernando Valley. The trio made some small talk, but Baker didn't waste time in telling McCluggage and Goldman, in a matter-of-fact tone, that his company had just signed a 10-year pact with the WB that would be announced later in the day.

McCluggage and Goldman were stunned. Baker picked up the check.

The news hit the UPN office hard later that morning. The WB orchestrated the timing of the release for its day at the summer Television Critics Association press tour presentation in front of 200 or so reporters from the U.S. and Canada. Kellner fairly gloated about his stealth maneuver. He called it a "cataclysmic blow" to UPN.

"Sinclair was a tough issue that was really ugly. But you can't say surprising," McCluggage says. "Dave Smith always had just a different point of view about the affiliations that wasn't about loyalty or building a network for his stations. It was 'Who's going to pay me the most money?' And when that's how someone approaches a transaction, you're always going to be vulnerable."

Kellner maintained his clear-eyed logic about the rationale of the deal being worth it in the long run when grilled by the trade press or ribbed by colleagues for changing his tune on the WB's need for reverse comp. And he steeled himself for the stampede of other station executives who would demand their compensation.

In August, UPN would sue Sinclair on the basis of fine print in the original affiliation contracts. Those deals included a provision that gave the network a three-year option to renew the agreement unless station owners provided written notification to the network of their intent to drop the affiliation within 180 days of the contract's expiration. UPN contended in its lawsuit filed in Los Angeles Superior Court that Sinclair had missed the deadline for proper written notification, and therefore it was obliged to continue with UPN through January 15, 2001.

Sinclair countersued in Baltimore Circuit Court, asking the judge for a speedy ruling on whether the affiliation station switches could proceed as planned in January. Sinclair's Baker and Smith were so irate at the litigious reaction that they yanked the network from their other UPN affiliates not affected by the deal with the WB. That meant crippling sudden blackouts for UPN in the top 40 markets of Indianapolis and Kansas City, among others. It was a nightmare scenario for UPN and its advertisers.

• • •

The jolt of the Sinclair affiliation grab slowed the headhunting effort to find Salhany's successor. By mid-summer, the contenders included two prominent cable programming executives: Rod Perth, entertainment president at USA Network, and E! Entertainment Television President Lee Masters. Len Grossi, Salhany's trusted No. 2 executive on the business side, and Paramount Stations Group President Tony Cassara were also considered. By mid-August, the partners had agreed on a dark-horse candidate.

Dean Valentine was the Walt Disney Company's top television production executive. He'd worked at the studio for nearly 10 years, and before that he'd worked in comedy development at NBC. He was the consensus choice, but not in a begrudging way for either side. Valentine was endorsed for the Chris-Craft camp by a former Chris-Craft executive, Rich Frank, who had gone on to work with Valentine in Disney's television division. The Paramount side was familiar with Valentine from industry circles. He was known for being offbeat in his taste in material. Both factions hoped his sensibilities would be right to bring in a young male demographic.

UPN's rank and file had high hopes too. At UPN and elsewhere, Lucie Salhany was generally well liked and respected by her staff for her accomplishments. But on her worst days, UPN's leader could be moody and unpredictable, irrational and angry for no good reason.

"We all liked Lucie, but Lucie could make you crazy," says a former senior UPN executive. "When Dean came in, we were hoping for someone who wouldn't make you so crazy all of the time."

Although her departure was drawn out over the tumultuous summer following the Sinclair–WB pact, Salhany couldn't help but feel nostalgic in her waning weeks at UPN. She wasn't just leaving a job, she was saying good-bye to an industry she loved. She was wistful, but ready. Those conflicting feelings were reinforced around the time of the fall season launch, when Chris-Craft threw a going-away party for Salhany at Drago, a posh eatery in Santa Monica not far from UPN's offices.

The highlight of the gathering was a Salhany retrospective video that staffers had assembled. The reel chronicled major moments in her UPN tenure; they also had some fun with clips of an "Ask the Manager" segment she had done in the 1970s during her days as a station executive in Boston. But the thing that made the crowd roar was a plain title-card slate featuring the famous Salhany bon mot that epitomized her feisty spirit.

"Drink their drink, eat their food, and call their women ugly. I'm not going."

Once her departure was official, Valentine quickly made it clear to the staff that he had earned his reputation as an iconoclast. As is usually the case in network regime changes, as Valentine settled in, other top executives tendered their resignations not long afterward, including executive vice president Len Grossi and entertainment president Michael Sullivan. Weary of the dysfunctional UPN partnership, Sullivan had already been planning to move on when his contract expired later that year.

Dean Valentine was not a total stranger to UPN. The Walt Disney Company was one of the few major studios willing to produce shows for UPN and the WB in their first years. Lucie Salhany considered him an important outside supporter of the network. During Valentine's tenure as president of Walt Disney Television and Walt Disney Television Animation, Touchstone Television produced the network's ambitious conspiracy thriller *Nowhere Man* in the 1995–96 season. The following season, Touchstone gave UPN the sci-fi spoof *Homeboys in Outer Space*.

Highly intelligent and cultured, Valentine is a natural contrarian, a cynic with a good sense of humor who loves to thumb his nose at authority, say friends and colleagues. He has an irascible charm, but even his admirers characterize him as "brash," "arrogant," and even "antisocial" at times. Balding, with a closely cropped thin beard, Valentine favored a California-casual wardrobe that ran toward over-size work shirts and jeans. He came across then as a "Los Angeles Lenin," according to a favorable 1998 profile in the *New Yorker*.

In another life, Valentine might have been a rabble-rousing college professor. Working in the entertainment business served him well, however, if only because it allowed him to earn enough to support his modern art habit. Valentine has a world-class collection of contemporary works, and he remains prominent in New York and Los Angeles art circles. During his nearly four and a half years at UPN, Valentine lined the walls of the network's offices with items from his vault. Some of the pieces were so avant-garde and off-putting that they added to the stressful working environment of a struggling network, UPN alumni say. Valentine's office was adorned with, among other oddities, a large, rusty, corrugated metal sign that spelled out Dean Martin, and a 9-foot papier-mâché rendition of a can of Raid bug spray.

Later, Valentine commissioned artist Barry McGee to do an oversize piece on the exterior wall of the network's executive conference room. The final product was a bright blood-red wall with disembodied heads sprinkled around. Until the last days of the network, the floating heads bore down on the UPN brain trust, long after the rest of Valentine's collection had moved on with its owner.

Born in Romania, Valentine and his family fled the oppressive conditions for Jews in the Soviet-dominated state by moving first to France, then to St. Paul, Minnesota, and finally to Queens in New York City by the time he was a preteen in the 1960s. Once in New York, Valentine absorbed everything the city had to offer like a sponge. He attended the Bronx High School of Science and then learned the classics at the University of Chicago, where he received an Artium Baccalaureates degree in 1976.

After college, he returned to New York, and like his father, worked as a freelance writer and editor. He spent years with Time Inc., moving from publication to publication as a Mr. Fix-it editor, including a stint as an articles editor for *Life*. He was on assignment for *Life* in Los Angeles in the spring 1985—doing a story about a man's effort to erect a mechanical pterodactyl in Death Valley—when he accompanied the journalist friend he was staying with to a weekend softball league game. That day, Valentine met a person who would change the course of his career, NBC's Brandon Tartikoff.

Within a few months, Valentine was heading west after Tartikoff offered him the chance to join NBC's comedy development team in a midlevel executive position.

"I found television to be exciting. There was an energy to it," he says. "I always liked TV a lot more than I liked journalism."

Valentine was schooled in the realpolitik of the network television business during his nearly three-year stint at NBC. In 1988, as NBC was undergoing an executive shakeup, Valentine saw an opening in television development down the street at Disney, where executives Michael Eisner and Jeffrey Katzenberg were in the midst of what would prove a historic turnaround. The bonus for Valentine in working at Disney was that he had always been crazy about animation, going back to *Steamboat Willie* and *Silly Symphonies*. Valentine eventually roamed all over the Disney lot, working on a number of projects and supervising everything from children's animation to television movies. He was also closely involved in the development of the Touchstone-produced sitcom smash for ABC, *Home Improvement*.

In 1996, shortly after Disney completed its acquisition of ABC's parent company, Capital Cities/ABC Inc, Valentine made a play for a top programming job at the network. But Disney's newly appointed president, former superagent Michael Ovitz, had other ideas, namely a hotshot NBC executive named Jamie Tarses. Valentine was unhappy about being passed over.

Once the UPN opportunity came along, it took a month of wrangling with Eisner and Katzenberg for Valentine to extricate himself from his Disney contract. As a result, portions of his employment contract had been hastily put together in an effort to make a formal announcement on September 16, 1997, at a morning news conference at the Beverly Hilton hotel. By then, it was common knowledge in the industry and had been reported by industry trade papers that Valentine was UPN's new CEO.

Valentine made light of the situation during the news conference, where Lucie Salhany sat by his side. "I was actually at Disney only for one year. I've been negotiating with UPN for the past nine," he quipped.

· · ·

Dean Valentine left mixed first impressions on the staff he inherited. Some liked his brash confidence and directness. Some didn't.

"He acted as if he'd become the president of NBC," says Kevin Tannehill.

But Valentine was not a typical Type-A workaholic chief executive. UPN executives recall impromptu lunch invitations with the boss that would run more than three hours, including long drives to restaurants far from UPN's offices, complete with detours to artists' studios and funky galleries. Valentine was good company on a one-on-one basis, if you could spar with him intellectually, former UPN associates say. If not, you wouldn't be hanging out with him for long. He does not suffer fools. At times, he could be dismissive to the point of rudeness of executives who worked outside of his programming and marketing comfort zone in areas like affiliate relations and the Paramount Stations Group.

When he was evaluating the opportunity to take the reins at UPN, Valentine could see that the WB was starting to get its act together in both programming and distribution; UPN wouldn't be able to remain complacent for much longer. Television was the ultimate pop art to Valentine. With a network, he had a large canvas to work with: 10 hours a week in prime time, 8 p.m. to 10 p.m. Monday through Friday. He was brought in with a mandate from the partners to expand the network from three to five nights of programming per week, which he would undertake the following year.

Valentine came to UPN with a fully formed vision, almost a calling, for where he wanted to take the network. He firmly believed that there was a blue-collar, silent-majority demographic out there just waiting for some meat-and-potatoes entertainment fare. Not every show had to be about young, good-looking people in New York or Los Angeles. NBC was at the peak of its "Must-See TV" prime with *Friends*, *ER*, *Frasier*, *Seinfeld*, *Mad About You*, and *Law & Order*. Valentine was convinced the plethora of witty urbane shows was turning Joe Six-Pack and his girlfriend away from broadcast television. He wanted UPN to be the anti-*Friends* network, just as Fox's *Married . . . with Children* had been a reaction to the wholesomeness of *The Cosby Show.*

Valentine's vision for targeting the teaming masses instead of the $75,000-plus income households wasn't a hard sell to the UPN partners. From her new perch in the monthly operating committee meetings, Salhany was quick to voice her doubts about the viability of Valentine's strategy, given the network's history and the audience profile of most of its station affiliates. Both the Chris-Craft and Viacom camps were concerned about the network becoming too narrowly defined as catering to the young African American audience. By the time Salhany left, the network was carrying two-hour blocks of sitcoms featuring predominantly African American casts on Monday and Tuesday nights, followed incongruously on Wednesday by the sci-fi/fantasy dramas *The Sentinel* and *Star Trek: Voyager.*

"We looked at the numbers and said, 'Gee, what's it going to look like in a certain number of years if you continue to go this way?' It looked really, really bad," Valentine says. "So it was my decision, rightly or wrongly, to make as radical a break as possible from that strategy and go another way."

In his first months on the job, Valentine spent a good deal of time sitting just outside his office on the terraces that Salhany had been so adamant about including in the building. Cigar in hand, he pondered the practicality of his middle-America vision and how he should execute it. Marketing was crucial, but the bottom line was that it was all about the shows. If he could come up with one hit show, one good comedy, UPN and his own reputation would be made.

Valentine's sharp focus on programming often made for a difficult fit with Tom Nunan, the executive he brought in to replace Michael Sullivan as head of programming. Nunan came to UPN after two years at NBC, where he'd been responsible for beefing up the network's small in-house production operation, NBC Productions (later NBC Studios), in the post-fin-syn environment. Nunan spent about $70 million in two years on development deals with writers and producers, which led to such shows as *The Pretender*, *Profiler*, and *Will & Grace*. But in time, Nunan missed working on the programming side rather than in production. Before NBC, Nunan was a top comedy programming executive at Fox, where his staff included one of his new rivals—namely, me. I knew Tom to be a talented executive and a funny, warm person, if prone to micromanagement at times.

Nunan and Valentine had worked together when Valentine was selling prime-time shows at Disney and Nunan was a development executive at Fox. Nunan appreciated Valentine's warped sense of humor and considered him a friend. When Valentine moved to UPN, Nunan's name was mentioned by mutual friends as someone to consider as his lieutenant in programming. Nunan, then in his early 30s, formally joined the network in the first week of October. He'd had some interaction with the Salhany-era UPN team through the NBC Studios-produced comedy *In the House*, starring L.L. Cool J.

But after working at NBC and Fox, Nunan was not prepared for the budgets and resources he faced as executive vice president of programming at UPN. He was "shocked" by the open warfare between the partners in the monthly operating committee meetings. He was surprised at how little they committed to program development or marketing campaigns. After Nunan settled into the job, he realized the most troubling thing of all was the lack of a clearly articulated programming vision for the network at the highest level.

Valentine had his ideas, but Nunan wasn't sure if Dean was on the same page as the operating committee. For several reasons, Nunan also didn't know whether the potential that Dean saw in middle America actually existed. None of the UPN principals, in Nunan's view, really understood what it would take to make UPN succeed.

"What we learned at Fox was that we weren't thought of as a 'network' by the viewer," Nunan says. "Our programming was seen as alternative to the mainstream, so it had to be. UPN didn't *get* that."

The long lead time that we enjoyed for the launch of *Dawson's Creek* gave our marketing geniuses, Bob Bibb and

Lew Goldstein, the opportunity to shine in a way that many of us felt was their finest hour at the WB. And for the network, the stakes this time around were incredibly high. We were using *Dawson's Creek* to launch our fourth night of programming, on Tuesdays, and the show's premiere was strategically scheduled to come a few nights after our new Sinclair-owned affiliate stations made the switch in those five important markets.

The poster and print advertising campaign materials for the show emphasized James Van Der Beek looking wistful and handsome as he stood in a small rowboat floating all alone on the still waters of the show's namesake creek. About halfway through the photo shoot with James, Bob and Lew had one of their joint brainstorms to throw a tweedy, elbow-patches kind of blazer over Van Der Beek's jeans and T-shirt. It complemented the Dawson look perfectly. For that touch and so many others, Williamson was impressed and grateful for Bob and Lew's instinctive understanding of the style and tone he was striving for in his labor of autobiographical love.

"It just *worked*. They made it seem so special with that campaign," Williamson says. "I remember watching the promos at home and going, 'Wow, I wrote that?' There hasn't been a campaign that good for a show since. You couldn't turn around without seeing that boat."

Bob and Lew focused on the key art shot of James in that boat for weeks in advance of the show's January 20, 1998 premiere. The promo spots gradually evolved to include tight closeup shots of classically beautiful Katie, and Michelle and her angelic face. Then we added Joshua and ensemble shots that screamed coming-of-age drama.

Bob and Lew even get the credit for suggesting the Paula Cole ballad "I Don't Want to Wait" to be the show's evocative theme song. Kevin had the Alanis Morissette tune "Hand in My Pocket" in mind when he first wrote the pilot for Fox. When we tried to clear the rights to use Morissette's tune, we got an unambiguous answer: No. Meanwhile, Bob and Lew were looking for a contemporary love ballad to use in the promo spots for the show. They came across Cole's lilting falsetto in "I Don't Want to Wait" shortly after the song was released as a single in fall 1997. It was building momentum at the time but by no means a hit.

Kevin fell even harder for the idea of Cole's song as his theme than he did for "Hand in My Pocket." The song's wistful sentiment about a wife and mother impatient to know "right now" what life has in store for her and her family set the perfect atmosphere for the show. Never mind that it also mentioned "the war of '44" and "granddaughters"; it was ideal as far as Kevin was concerned. Only trouble was, Cole also turned us down. She didn't want to license her song for use every week as the theme. To make the impasse even more frustrating, Cole happened to be a Warner Bros.' recording artist.

Kevin despaired. We kept trying to reach Cole and her manager, or anyone who could get to her to make sure she'd actually seen the pilot. We idealistically clung to the notion that if we could just get her to watch the first episode, she'd change her mind. Finally, as time was running out for us to make a deal or move on, Kevin took some advice from a writer friend and sent Cole a handwritten appeal along with a copy of the pilot. He told her the genesis of *Dawson's Creek* and where it came from inside of him, as one writer to another. A few days later, we had her signature. (Within a few weeks of the show's premiere, "I Don't Want to Wait" was climbing the Billboard Hot 100 singles chart, and it peaked at No. 11.)

It felt like slow torture having to wait until January to take the wraps off *Dawson's Creek*. But it was the smart move.

In the months leading up to the *Dawson's Creek* premiere, Jamie and the scheduling team brainstormed to have *Buffy* producers whip up a two-part cliffhanger episode to draw attention to our expansion to Tuesday. The first installment, "Surprise," ran January 19 in *Buffy*'s original Monday 9 p.m. slot. We followed it the next night with the conclusion, "Innocence," in the show's new 8 p.m. Tuesday berth to feed a healthy audience into the 9 p.m. premiere of *Dawson's Creek*.

Despite all of the attention we'd lavished on *Dawson's Creek*, we did not throw a big premiere bash. When the big night came, Kevin Williamson and a small group of writers and producers gathered in L.A. for a low-key sendoff party at the home of one of the staff writers.

The cast members, however, were with Jamie, Garth, and the rest of us in New Orleans. The premiere came while the TV industry was gathered in the Big Easy for the annual NATPE convention, which for me meant presentations and meetings and handshakes with affiliate station managers. Often, there was a fair amount of jousting over some kind of nonsense with UPN. (In 1998, however, the television industry's conclave was interrupted by events in the real world—the sex scandal that exploded that same week involving President Bill Clinton and a former White House intern named Monica Lewinsky.)

By this time, after four years of hard driving at the WB, I was tired of traveling for the network. I'd had my fill of the industry conference circuit. So to make the latest trip bearable, I asked my mother to meet me in New Orleans so we could have some fun and see the sights after I finished my work for the WB.

We brought the four *Dawson's Creek* stars to New Orleans with us to get our affiliates enthused about the show. (Kevin couldn't make it because of an existing commitment to a film project.) James, Katie, Joshua, and Michelle together were something to experience. Their charisma was kinetic, and they very clearly enjoyed each other's company. The show exuded authenticity because the four actors were close in age and temperament to their characters.

Jamie initially thought of hosting a big blowout dinner with the cast and top affiliate station managers at a four-star New Orleans restaurant. But then he decided against it. We had an intimate affair—the core WB executives, plus my mom and the actors. We watched the show premiere at 9 p.m. like the rest of America (we hoped).

We reserved the backroom of a quaint seafood restaurant in the French Quarter for about a dozen of us. We should have asked in advance if they had cable. The rickety old TV set mounted on the wall of the private room was older than the actors and could barely pick up the over-the-air signal of our local New Orleans affiliate station.

We finally got something resembling a picture after twisting and turning the rabbit ears on top of the set.

Like the TV set, the accommodations were anything but fancy. The room was dark and musty with little ventilation, and on top of everything else, some of the seafood dishes we ordered didn't smell so good when they arrived at the table. Yet it was impossible to bring down our mood. We had a famously good time that night, drinking the vintage wines ordered by our sommeliers, Jamie and Garth, and toasting what we hoped would be a prosperous future. The actors were not only humble, they were downright naïve. I'll never forget being with James, Katie, Joshua, and Michelle on the night their lives changed forever.

"We just knew that because of this show, these kids were going to see their lives change radically. And they were just clueless. They had no idea," Garth Ancier recalls. "But we just knew. It was a pretty exciting moment to be there with them as it happened."

CHAPTER SIX

CHARMING MIDDLE AMERICA

As he began his first full year on the job at UPN, Dean Valentine was ready to test-drive his theory that Middle America was prime-time television's Great Untapped Audience. The first show Valentine picked up at UPN shortly after the start of 1998 was a quick six-episode revival of the 1970s confection *The Love Boat*, from Aaron Spelling. TV ironman Robert Urich led the ensemble crew.

It was no accident that Valentine responded to the notion of re-uniting Spelling and Urich, who had a hit together in the late 1970s with the slick ABC detective drama *Vega$*. ABC's youthful prime-time profile in the late 1970s was exactly what Valentine was striving for, albeit in contemporary fashion. ABC's success in that era drove the television industry's move toward a demographic-specific focus on ratings and advertising sales from the mass-appeal yardstick of household ratings.

In many respects, Valentine was ahead of the curve in seeing the red state/blue state divide that has cleaved American politics and culture in the post-Clinton era. He picked up on the thriving us-against-them sentiment that cuts both ways, from the prevailing media and cultural elitist view of rubes in "flyover country" to the distrust of Hollywood found in many quarters, not just the Bible belt, for what some view as its over-eagerness to embrace a liberal anything-goes attitude in everything from sex to spirituality. He paid attention to how many politicians and preachers were playing the immoral-Hollywood card in an effort to win votes and headlines and applause from the pews. But what alarmed him most was how the anti-

Hollywood feeling was spreading among soccer moms and NASCAR dads, mainstream folks who could hardly be called evangelicals or passionate activists.

The viewing public was losing interest in network television because network television had lost much of its interest in them, or so Valentine believed.

"Television is a mirror. People are looking for a mirror of their own lives in the television. And that mirror was completely broken in the American broadcast landscape when I took over UPN," Valentine says. "What America looked like if you were watching television, was a bunch of loathsome upper-middle-class New Yorkers and a bunch of equally repellent teens with infinite amounts of money, doing incredibly well in the economy. They all had great jobs, they all had no problems, except their zits or their boyfriends or their girlfriends or whatever . . . As a kid who grew up in Queens, I found it personally repellent. And I found it a business opportunity."

Valentine saved the news of his six-episode pickup of *Love Boat* for his first appearance as UPN's leader before the firing squad at the winter edition of the twice-yearly Television Critics Association press junket in Pasadena. Valentine mentioned *Love Boat* as being part of a shift to a more middle-America–centric programming strategy. But he didn't really sell his vision, not in the fiery way he would a few months later during the run-up 1998–99 season launch. First, Valentine wanted to see if his new-model *Love Boat* would float.

WB publicity chief Brad Turell was speech-less when the first overnight numbers rolled in the morning after the premiere of *Dawson's Creek*. He was sitting in a hotel conference room in New Orleans looking at a fax from Warner Bros.' research department in Burbank. A few other executives wandered into the conference room suite while Brad was on the phone with Burbank. Every one of them was smiling big.

The fax he was holding had eight small grids of ratings tables laid out in two vertical columns, with every other box shaded to make it easier to read. The tables detailed the show's performance in demo-graphics ranging from kids 2 to 11 to men 50-plus. The sea of digits and percentages all boiled down to one impressive number: 41.

"*Dawson's Creek* did a 41 share in female teens," Turell read out loud to himself as his convention-weary mind processed the informa-tion. It meant that the Tuesday 9 p.m. premiere of *Dawson's Creek* drew nearly half of the teenagers in the country who were tuned into network or cable television in that hour. A 41 share of any demo was an eye-catching number by any network's standard.

Later that morning we moved from our hotel to the carpeted Warner Bros.' booth on the exhibition floor in the Ernest N. Morial Convention Center in the heart of New Orleans. In years past, we couldn't help but feel like a guest in their house, awkward and never knowing quite where to stand. We all tended to wander off to look for friends and colleagues at the other major studios' booths. But that year, when *Dawson's Creek* premiered, none of us minded being there at all. Word of our fantastic premiere spread quickly on the trade show floor. The setting made the experience all the more intense be-cause we were all there together, the WB troops and plenty of our friends and industry peers, in hotels and a convention center in New Orleans for 72 hours. We were surrounded by a sea of well-wishers and high-fivers.

We weren't surprised at all that the pop culture press had taken to *Dawson's Creek*. They loved having good-looking newcomers to put on their covers and in photo spreads. But we were pleasantly sur-prised at how much attention we got from the business press with the show's strong premiere numbers. The business press and industry trades were still eager to declare a winner in the then four-year-old saga of UPN versus WB. By the time influential media outlets like the *New York Times* gave us a second hard look on the heels of the big *Dawson's Creek* opening, we also had *7th Heaven* and *Buffy the Vam-pire Slayer* to point to as defining the WB demographic. We had a good hook and a good growth story, with *Buffy* staying strong with young adults and *7th Heaven* growing steadily in its sophomore year. Our champions weren't shy about pointing out how glaringly obvious it was that our first big out-of-the-park, insta-hit came from a studio other than Warner Bros. Television.

Although we couldn't quite see it that morning, it would become clear in a matter of weeks that the WB's growing teen appeal would allow us to ride a pop culture explosion whipped up by the release in December 1997 of director James Cameron's long-awaited epic *Titanic*. Our *Dawson's Creek* premiered a month after *Titanic* began its long, historic run in theaters. Cameron's three-hour visual effects epic was fueled by repeat business from teenage girls and twentysomething women on a par with Rudolph Valentino and Tab Hunter among teenage girls. The boom in affluent, educated teens and twentysomethings was "discovered" by the pop culture and lifestyle press as *Titanic* steamrolled to an astounding $600 million at the domestic box office.

Titanic's popularity kept it in the multiplexes for months after its release. But it was still just one movie. The WB had the same crowd flocking to the network every week. It was nothing short of a business miracle laid on the WB at a crucial moment in our history. Overnight, WB ad sales chief Jed Petrick was fielding calls from advertisers trying to get into the following week's episode. Advertising buyers who were attending the convention in New Orleans went out of their way to corner Jed at the Warner Bros.' booth. That had never happened before. At the Tuesday staff meeting the week after the *Dawson's* premiere, hours before the second episode aired, Petrick was patched in as usual by phone from New York. He drew a long and loud round of applause when he announced: "This sales department is *done* begging for its dollars."

Still, in television, big opening nights for new series are a double-edged sword. Most of the time, e.g., *Star Trek: Voyager*, it means there's nowhere to go but down—often precipitously—in the weeks to follow. As huge as *Dawson's Creek* was in its premiere, Brad Turell knew he'd be on the phone putting a careful spin on the second-week ratings with reporters to make sure the show didn't get pummeled as a flash in the pan. There was no way *Dawson's* could come close to those premiere numbers again, Turell told himself. The intensity of his spin on the week-two numbers would depend on how much of a plunge the show took in the female teen and young adult demos we'd bragged about so much the previous week.

Once again, the morning after the second episode aired, the numbers shocked everyone. The ratings had actually increased from the premiere. This was not just great news; it was the Holy Grail. *Dawson's Creek* was going to be a big, signature hit for the WB.

"There was delirium around the building," Turell says.

Earlier in the day, before the ratings had arrived, Turell had taken up Lew Goldstein on an offer to go to a UCLA basketball game that night. Turell had been preoccupied all day with a full-court press telephone campaign to get major media outlets to note *Dawson's* gravity-defying performance. He hadn't had much time to bask in the moment. But as he settled into Goldstein's Toyota Land Cruiser in the dark WB parking lot for the trek in rush hour traffic from Burbank to UCLA's West Los Angeles campus, Turell felt a rush come over him stronger than any narcotic could produce. His teeth were numb for the first part of the traffic-snarled drive as he and Goldstein bantered excitedly about how *Dawson's* had changed everything. It came as sweet vindication for members of the kitchen cabinet who felt they were denied their share of the credit for the launch of Fox.

"It was such an amazing redemption for this team," Turell says. "And nobody could take it away from us this time. We built the WB, and we were going to run it."

The *Dawson's Creek* explosion even managed to overshadow another milestone in the competition between the WB and UPN that actually came a few days *before* the show's premiere. For the first time since the ratings race between the two networks began in January 1995, the WB tied UPN in the season-long standings. By the end of the third week of January 1998, the WB was matching UPN's overall average rating (the average since the start of the season in September for all programs) for the 1997–98 season with an average 3.0 household rating and a 5 share. That translated to an average audience of about 4.5 million viewers each week, which was better than most of basic cable by a margin of a few million but still significantly lower than Big Four network standards, then and now.

A year before, in a morale-boosting session held as part of a WB company retreat, Jordan Levin had drawn with a marking pen on a large piece of easel-paper two intersecting arrows, one pointing down labeled UPN, the other pointing up labeled the WB. He saved that paper and scotch-taped it to the wall in the hallway outside his office. As the WB's ratings momentum steadily grew throughout 1997, Levin and others had periodically logged milestones with the date on the sheet next to the WB arrow. By the time *Dawson's Creek* wrapped its first mini-season in May 1998, the paper looked like the inside of a high school yearbook—a blur of exclamation points, witticisms, and the enthusiasm of people who know their best years are still ahead of them.

One of the indelible moments for all of us during the charmed year of 1998 came in mid-May while we were flying to New York on a Time Warner jet to our upfront presentation. Rusty Mintz, our hard-working research and scheduling maven, had jokingly made a promise to Jamie Kellner years earlier that if any of our shows ever managed to hit a double-digit share of the audience (i.e., a 10 share or greater in its time slot), he would shave his head.

That long-ago conversation was the last thing on my mind as the core group of WB executives milled around the plane, enjoying the corporate luxury of our surroundings and trying to prepare for the presentation of a slate of new shows in which we had the utmost confidence. Rusty, Jordan, Garth, and I were huddling over some paperwork when Jamie Kellner rushed up to us with an ear-to-ear smile on his face instead of his usual sly grin.

"You're *bald*, buddy!" he said, pointing a finger at Rusty. For a moment, Rusty was taken aback, but there was no mistaking Jamie's jovial mood. Jamie reminded us of the old wager that had been witnessed by an entire staff meeting. He showed us a printout of a ratings report and, sure enough, our little show that could, *7th Heaven*, had hit a 10 household share in its most recent airing. I thought Jamie was going to burst. It was clear he was equally as excited about the show hitting a new all-time high number as he was about calling Rusty on the kind of thing you might say in a meeting but never expect to make good on.

Two days later, about an hour before the start of our affiliate meeting, which followed our upfront presentation at the Sheraton Hotel and Towers, Rusty had his thick wavy head of hair shaved down to a Marine-style buzz cut. Jamie brought him up on stage during his address to the affiliates as if he were a trophy. I doubled over with laughter.

But that was nothing compared to the howling Rusty provoked about two weeks later. Jamie, Garth, and I were leading a meeting in our main conference room to brainstorm fall launch strategies with Bob and Lew and a large group of staffers. Suddenly, Rusty walked in the door at the opposite end of the room with an old-fashioned-looking barber in tow, complete with a short white smock and terry-cloth towel over his arm. Rusty sat in a chair without saying a word, not even darting a glance at us. In a matter of minutes, the barber pulled out a set of buzz clippers and shaved Rusty completely bald—shiny bald. For about 15 seconds all we could hear was the low hum of the electronic razor. And then it was near-pandemonium as everyone in the trailers came in to rub Rusty's chrome dome for good luck. As near as I can recall, we hauled out the margarita supplies later on to toast a man who truly kept his word.

As we were toasting our progress, *Dawson's Creek* was in the midst of shooting a new season. From the time that filming had begun the previous spring, we were aware of how special the show was because of how the production process went uncommonly smoothly. Finishing out a show's first 13-episode order is the high hurdle that makes or breaks a show. Writers and producers usually have months to live with and perfect a pilot. And then they have to deliver another episode, just as good if not better, on a 10-day turnaround.

When the *Dawson's Creek* contingent returned to Wilmington in fall 1997, a few months after the pilot shoot, to begin production of the remaining 12 episodes, creator Kevin Williamson went with them. He rented a house in Wilmington overlooking the coastal waters of the North Atlantic and relived his youth, pounding the episodes into shape and, as promised, taking plenty of fictional liberties to keep the story lines moving. Visits from family members would jog the North Carolina native's memory on bits of dialogue or moments in time. Many of the episodes had been mapped out and written in Williamson's head by the time we handed him the 13-episode order.

"Because the first six were in my head, I could write them like the wind," Williamson says. "After that, the development process began."

There were other developments between the time the pilot was shot in spring 1997 and the time the cast reconvened in the early fall for series production. During the pilot shoot, our oh-so-vulnerable Joey, actress Katie Holmes, had very clearly nursed a crush on costar Joshua Jackson. Kevin Williamson even searched out a DVD box set of the *Mighty Ducks* hockey movies in which Jackson had appeared and left it as a gift for Holmes in her trailer.

When cast and crew reunited after the series was picked up and set for a January premiere, Josh and James Van Der Beek decided to room together in a loft in downtown Wilmington. Their friendship deepened during the first few months of production. But after a month or two, it became apparent that Katie was dating James. They made a handsome couple, on screen and off, but it was not meant to be. In due time, Katie began a romance with Josh that would last on and off for two years. Shortly after that, James and Josh stopped being roommates. These behind-the-scenes tensions among Katie, James, and Josh never spilled over onto the set in a way that significantly interrupted production, thank goodness. But the triangle was a constant subject of chatter among the crew, a soap-within-a-soap that was discussed openly, if affectionately, by the people whose names scroll by in fine print on the show's end credits.

Williamson's nostalgic reverie was interrupted toward the end of the first season production cycle by the bare-knuckle reality of the independent film business. In spring 1998, Harvey and Bob Weinstein dispatched a pair of "goons" to Wilmington to lock Kevin in his waterfront house until he completed the outline for *Scream 2* and finished punching up the dialogue on another movie Miramax had in the works. Kevin's attention had been diverted for most of the past 14 months or so by the production of his autobiographical TV series. The Weinstein brothers were not pleased.

For more than a week, Kevin was confined to his bedroom and his laptop computer while he finished his outline and worked over the other script. He had to ask permission to use the bathroom, something he joked about with us long after the fact. We were dumbfounded. True to his genial genius, even when being held as a highly paid hostage, he somehow got it all done.

After production on the last of the 13 episodes was finished and Williamson had returned to Los Angeles, Columbia TriStar Television showed its appreciation with the customary largess that studios shower on writer-producers who deliver shows that look to be long-term players. The studio, owned by Japanese consumer electronics giant Sony Corp., sent to Williamson's home a truckload of "more electronic equipment than I had seen in my life," he says. "Widescreen TVs, subwoofers, speakers—stuff I didn't even know existed at the time."

The timing of the *Dawson's Creek* onslaught was heaven-sent for the WB in more ways than one. Shortly before the show premiered, Ted Turner, the WB's biggest detractor on the Time Warner board of directors, once again cranked up his efforts to shut down the WB. By many accounts Turner had a personal dislike for Jamie, and the feeling seemed to be mutual. Turner was still outraged that Jamie and a handful of insiders had been granted an ownership interest in the WB, knowledgable sources say. As Turner pressed the issue, Time Warner Chairman Gerald Levin asked Warner Bros.' Bob Daly to make a presentation to the board on the long-term strategic plan for the WB.

The WB's good karma held sway. Daly's presentation in mid-1997 convinced the board to continue to support the WB. Turner was quieted, at least temporarily. Levin did ask Daly to come back in six months with a new forecast for the network. When the time came,

Daly had *Dawson's Creek*, the Sinclair switchover, and other recent victories to spotlight. With a hand that strong, the board had no intention of disrupting the momentum of what appeared to be a thriving little business for Warner Bros.

"Turner knew we needed a network," Bob Daly says. "He just felt that if we got rid of the WB, I'd be on his side to push for [the purchase of] NBC. And I did push for NBC. But I always felt that it was a long shot and I thought it was necessary for us to keep the WB."

If Turner felt vanquished by Jamie Kellner then, it was nothing compared to what was in store for Jamie and the house that Turner built in just a few years. While Daly had kept the sharks at bay, in a short time the threats to our future would seemingly disappear altogether, amid much breathless talk in Hollywood, Silicon Valley, and Wall Street about the "new economy" and new paradigms for media and entertainment companies in the Internet age.

The arrival of a new boss and a new head of programming at UPN inevitably raised the network's competitive metabolism. As experienced executives, Dean Valentine and Tom Nunan could see the threat posed by the WB's steady progress, and they recognized distinctive, well-made shows when they saw them. In desperation, UPN made a lame attempt to distract from the *Dawson's Creek* premiere by airing on that Tuesday night a pair of cheesy tabloid specials, *Real Vampires . . . Exposed!* and *Alien Encounter: The Incident at Lake County*. UPN's bloodsuckers and aliens were no match for the WB's good-looking stars.

It was hard for UPN's new regime to watch the WB's rocket take off just as they settled into their roles. But Valentine's first small victory at UPN was not far off. His bet on a refurbished *Love Boat* had been a pretty good one. The show had a respectable opening on a Monday night, April 13, drawing about five and a half million television homes, or enough that UPN could brag about generating its best ratings in the time slot in two years. It wasn't *Dawson's Creek*, but it was a start. More important, the response to *Love Boat* and its overtly corny and cheesecake elements only reinforced Valentine's conviction that there were plenty of people out there yearning for a few mindless comedies and softer, slicker dramas to relax with after a long day at work. *Love Boat* premiered four weeks before Valentine would put his professional reputation on the line in campaigning for his middle-America strategy at UPN's upfront presentation for the 1998–99 season.

Valentine's confidence in his plan came across as smug arrongance to many inside and outside the network. He had been thinking about this for years—ever since the success of NBC's *Friends* had spawned a slew of imitators that inundated the airwaves in the mid-1990s. Valentine had another reason for disdaining the *Friends*-ification of network TV. After the Walt Disney Company completed its purchase of ABC in 1996, Valentine made a big play for a top programming job at the network. But he was passed over in favor of NBC executive Jamie Tarses, who was closely associated with the development of *Friends* and that network's brand of Must-See TV—comedies revolving around witty, urbane singles. She brought that focus to ABC, which made it harder for Valentine, as the head of the network's new sibling TV studio, to interest the new regime in the low-brow and middle-of-the-road program concepts that interested him. His resentment toward Tarses was barely concealed by the time he arrived at UPN. He was eager to prove the new ABC regime wrong by developing some blue-collar hits for his new network.

Valentine wasn't shy about voicing his views concerning what was wrong with network television. And he could be very persuasive, in an if-you-build-it-they-will-come sort of way. In the four months between the May upfront and the fall 1998–99 season launch, Valentine would undertake a whistle-stop tour to sell his vision far and wide to anyone who would listen. In an industry full of double-talking executives, Valentine was admired by many for having the courage of his convictions.

By the time *Love Boat* premiered, series pickups and marketing plans for the Middle America push were well underway (even if Valentine didn't know quite how he was going to pay for it all). It didn't matter that *Love Boat*'s audience sank by half in its second airing and went down every week from there. Valentine's vision was about to be realized. He would renew *Love Boat* for another season.

It wasn't quite the back-to-young-men route Kerry McCluggage had envisioned after Salhany's departure, but even the ever-feuding UPN partners agreed it was important to support their newly appointed CEO. The network was looking to make a quick expansion to a Monday to Friday programming slate with the addition of Thursday and Friday nights. That was a hard thing to do without an overriding "big idea" to drive the development of shows, marketing plans, and media spin.

Valentine made the decision to launch both nights at the same time in the fall. He envisioned incorporating the network's expansion as part of the overall marketing plan for UPN's new direction. Touting the fact that the network was becoming a real five-night-a-week service would be part of the splash UPN desperately needed to make with viewers. The inaugural Thursday night lineup was the long-delayed movie night, which featured B- and C-grade sci-fi and thriller TV movies, most of them from Paramount. Valentine figured Friday night would be the perfect new time slot in the fall for the reconstituted *Love Boat*.

Surprisingly, as the network embarked on such a significant strategy shift, little effort was made to analyze or quantify Valentine's Middle-America concept, according to former UPN insiders. There was little research done on the viability of such middle-brow programming thrust vis-à-vis the audience profile of UPN's most important affiliate stations. Nor was there much of a research effort undertaken to understand what made Valentine's broadly defined blue-collar demographic tick.

"It was very much on the fly," recalls Tom Nunan. Valentine had a surprising degree of autonomy, if not unlimited resources, to call the shots at UPN in his first months on the job. He had more say in the final decision-making process at his network than his counterparts at the larger networks. As such, the programming and marketing departments took their cues from Valentine. UPN's chief executive paid particular attention to the development of comedy series because of his background at NBC and Disney. He knew that one big comedy hit can turn around a network. Valentine was looking for shows that were broad, irreverent, even sophomoric by design—the antithesis of *Friends.*

Valentine was keen to find a show with *Home Improvement* attributes that would appeal to guys' guys. The result was titled *Guys Like Us,* just to drive home the point. The "us" in question were Jared and Sean, two odd-couple roommates—one black, one white—in Chicago whose bachelor-pad world is turned upside down when Jared's excitable 6-year-old kid brother, Maestro, moves in. *Guys* was also envisioned as a way of building a bridge between the black audience that came to UPN for *Moesha* and *Malcolm and Eddie* and the dwindling base of young white men who tuned in for *Star Trek: Voyager* and to a lesser extent for the other sci-fi and action fare.

Another sitcom that made the cut was *DiResta,* a domestic comedy cut from *Honeymooners'* cloth. It starred the New York City transit cop-turned-comic John DiResta as—what else?—a New York transit cop ("a guy with a big heart and an even bigger mouth," according to UPN's promotional materials) who lives on Long Island with his nutty family. Jackie Gleason, he wasn't, but *DiResta* was virtually assured a spot on UPN's schedule because Valentine loved John DiResta's standup act.

Valentine's pet project was a comedy inspired in his mind by the British comedy series *The Black Adder,* which starred Rowan Atkinson, aka Mr. Bean, in odd historical sketches and settings. Valentine was more invested in the half-hour pilot that became *The Secret Diary of Desmond Pfeiffer* than any other UPN show that year.

Valentine had the idea to do a series of costume-drama farces that could satirize contemporary culture. The outrageous concepts and period garb would allow for broad silliness, to keep the show from being too high-brow for Valentine's long-neck-drinking target audience. He settled on the Lincoln White House in the midst of the Civil War as the opening backdrop for the series. And he began casting about for a writer who would be a good fit stylistically with his outré vision.

Valentine had a wish list of scribes he thought had the right stuff to handle the balance of lowbrow and smart. However, even if he could have recruited them, he couldn't afford them. He finally cut a deal with the veteran comedy duo Mort Nathan and Barry Fanaro who were under contract to Paramount at the time. The duo had worked on hit shows like *The Golden Girls* and *Benson*. They had been the creators of one of UPN's first short-lived series, *Platypus Man*, starring comedian Richard Jeni.

Nathan and Fanaro suggested having the show revolve around a black English butler who happens to be the only sane one of the bunch. Valentine liked the idea of being provocative and politically incorrect. One thing all Americans with a fourth-grade education know about Lincoln is that he "freed the slaves" by signing the Emancipation Proclamation, which helped set in motion the Civil War and his own demise. Why not tackle head-on one of the most explosive issues in American history with humor, so that it didn't feel like homework but couldn't help but make the audience think?

"The whole point of the show was to be funny, but it was also to be able to explore some of these issues more seriously over time in a comedic way," Valentine says.

The "brilliant satire," as Valentine billed it, amounted to character actor Dann Florek portraying Honest Abe as a sex-crazed moron who engages in "telegraph" sex, one of the many un-funny jokes regarding the Monica Lewinsky sex scandal that had enveloped President Bill Clinton. And the show's idea of a running joke was obtrusive mentions that the lead character's name was pronounced "Puh-Feiffer"—the "P" was *not* silent.

In addition to the unique brand of comedy Valentine was championing, there were dramas he greenlighted that went against the grain of the cop, doctor, and lawyer themes that were then dominant in prime time. Of all the shows that made the cut, *Legacy* might have been the most unusual choice for the network at that moment in its history. The hour-long drama was UPN's stab at *Dr. Quinn, Medicine*

Woman, with a serial about Irish horse farmers toughing it out in 1880s-era Kentucky. It was a potboiler in a dusty, period setting revolving around the lives and loves of the sprawling Logan clan. It was complete with the family's prodigal son Sean falling head over heels in a frowned-upon love affair with the family's black housekeeper.

The network's two other new dramas that fall had sci-fi and fantasy themes. *Mercy Point* was essentially a futuristic *ER*, revolving around earnest young doctors working the graveyard shift at a space station hospital. *Seven Days* was about a former CIA operative who's recruited into a secretive government program that allows agents to travel back in time seven days before a major disruptive event to prevent it from happening. (In the show, the Feds had discovered the key to time travel by dissecting the spacecraft that famously crashed in Roswell, New Mexico, in 1947.) The show hailed from writer-producer Christopher Crowe, who was a close friend and a favorite producer of Kerry McCluggage's. (He was the creator of the inaugural UPN show that Lucie Salhany hated so much, *The Watcher*.)

In the months leading up to the launch, Valentine's pronouncements about the state of the network television business were enhanced by a flattering profile in the *New Yorker* magazine that ran the week the TV industry gathered in New York for the network upfront presentations. The story portrayed him as a colorful raconteur who had advanced in the entertainment industry by going against the grain. As a former journalist, the attention his campaign was receiving from august institutions like the *New Yorker* and the *New York Times* thrilled him to no end and reinforced his conviction that he was on the right path, friends and colleagues say.

"We're going against the current—but we're headed for the mainstream," Valentine told a gathering of UPN affiliates in June at the ritzy Ritz-Carlton resort hotel in Laguna Niguel, California.

"Because in the obsessive quest for the 18–34 demographic, what's being ignored is the largest 'niche' audience in the country. A niche so large it's not a niche at all because it constitutes the majority of people in this country. I'm talking, for lack of a better term, about the American middle class."

During the affiliates' conference, Valentine made a point of showcasing *Pfeiffer* as the one to watch next season by screening the pilot for the station managers on the first day of the meeting. Some of them mustered a few kind words for the show when asked for their reaction, but UPN staffers couldn't deny the uneasy vibe in the room when the lights came up. As the station executives filtered out of the ballroom, several network executives heard the manager of a prominent UPN affiliate station say, to no one in particular, "Well . . . we're puh-fucked."

After *Dawson's Creek,* writers started to get what we were looking for, and more of them came to us. The 1998–99 pitch season was unlike any we'd had before, as we began to hear more pitches than ever. We delighted in the process of meeting amazingly talented writers and helping to shape their series concepts.

Separating a good pitch from a fantastic pitch was and still is one of the most fascinating things about being in the television business. J. J. Abrams and his then-producing partner Matt Reeves walked into our office in early fall 1998 with a fantastic one for a show called *Felicity.* J. J. Abrams, the cocreator of ABC's *Lost* and *Alias* and writer-director of *Mission: Impossible 3,* is by far one of the best I've ever worked with in terms of pitching stories and shows. He's charming and funny. He brings heart to a pitch and can tell you clearly why anyone would or should care about the world he's describing. But the single most impressive thing about J.J. is the depth of the analysis he lays out in a compelling, almost professorial way. He can tell you everything about every character and their story arcs. And he can also tell you how and why his show fits into your network, into the television business and the world at large, *and* how the audience will relate to it.

The *Felicity* script was shopped around to various television networks, though J.J. and his handlers had targeted the WB from the start. Even after ABC expressed interest, his reps rightly surmised that the project would get more TLC and more pop culture buzz by going with the WB than one of the Big Four. That decision spoke volumes about how far the WB had come in barely a year's time. It wasn't a hard decision for us to commission a pilot for *Felicity*.

We bought the pitch and commissioned a pilot for *Felicity*. J.J. and I would have our differences on *Felicity* during the show's four-season run, but I never forgot how impressive it was to hear him sketch out the five-season arc for his heroine, Felicity Porter. He had thought through the beginning, middle, and end of the love triangle that drove the show about an idealistic girl from California who follows her high school crush to school in New York, based on an item scrawled in her senior yearbook. We all felt that this passionate young guy with the geek-chic horn-rim glasses was a massive talent just waiting to explode.

Around the same time that we got into business with J.J. and Matt, we dove into another project with Aaron Spelling. We were already thinking along the lines of doing a drama about sisters, a kind of younger, sexier version of the series *Sisters* that had aired on NBC a few seasons before. But we needed to give it a WB twist. One of the shows we'd often talked about during rounds of our "is this a WB show?" game back in the early days was Sally Field's 1960s farce *The Flying Nun.*

All of these ideas were in my mind as I sat down one afternoon for a meeting with Constance Burge, an inexperienced but promising young writer from Spelling Television's stable. After hearing the kinds of themes that we were interested in Connie worked with the development team at Spelling and came back to us with an intriguing pitch for a show about the supernatural adventures of three very different sisters. The series that became *Charmed* revolved around a trio who discover that they are witches when they are reunited as young adults in San Francisco and find themselves back in the Victorian house where they grew up with their grandmother. We loved it.

Spelling and his team had been great to work with on *7th Heaven* and *Savannah*, and we were confident that the same would hold true a third time. We were jazzed when Aaron told us he'd recruited Shannen Doherty for the anchor role as Prudence Halliwell, the alpha sister of the three main characters: Pru, Piper, and Phoebe Halliwell.

The media was taken by the fact that Spelling and Doherty had now patched things up, nearly five years after Spelling booted her from his Fox soap *Beverly Hills, 90210* for what he viewed as unruly behavior. Who better than the bad girl of *90210* to play a sexy young witch? Holly Marie Combs, who played Piper, was never anything but a total pro and a delight to work with. Combs was trained in the David E. Kelley school of TV from her prior stint as a teenage daughter on CBS's small-town drama *Picket Fences*. The casting of Alyssa Milano, all grown up from her *Who's the Boss* years, as Phoebe was a smart move that also got a lot of attention. Aaron Spelling picked up the phone and wooed Milano at the last minute after the actress who played her role in the original pilot, Lori Rom, bowed out because, as she explained to us, she could not reconcile her spiritual beliefs with the witches-and-warlocks theme of the show.

There were sparks between Shannen and Alyssa off screen, but they were good together on camera until Shannen departed after the third season under much the same circumstances as she left *90210*. Rose McGowan, then best known as the girlfriend of shock rocker Marilyn Manson, neatly filled the Doherty void by signing on as Piper and Phoebe's long-lost half sister Paige Matthews in the fourth season. (From then on, *Charmed* carefully avoided the *Charlie's Angels* revolving-cast syndrome and remained a bastion of stability through its eighth and final season.)

"There was a tradition at the WB where every year, one pilot was just really special," Garth Ancier says. "It was a great feeling of sitting in that little [network] conference room and putting up that [standout] pilot, and you'd just say 'Ahhh.' Because you just knew."

A few weeks before America had the chance to judge UPN's *The Secret Diary of Desmond Pfeiffer* for itself, Danny Bakewell entered the picture. Bakewell, a Los Angeles-based civil rights activist known for his bare-knuckle tactics, got wind of *Pfeiffer* through a *Los Angeles Times* article on the brewing controversy about the show. African American activists were calling on UPN to yank the pilot episode because of reports that it included a scene that depicted a lynching, complete with men in hoods; producers insisted it was only a hanging, and of a white character at that. (The scene was ultimately cut.) Bakewell and others effectively hammered the point that the show "trivialized the history of slavery" in America before any of them had seen it. Some of the sins attributed to *Pfeiffer* in the media coverage of the controversy were patently untrue. But it didn't matter. *Pfeiffer* had become a cause celeb, one that "probably belongs more to the history of race relations in the United States than it does to UPN per se," Dean Valentine says in retrospect.

In a *Los Angeles Times* story about the growing storm, Valentine had been defiant about the show and its propriety. A few months before, Valentine had recruited an NBC alumnus, Paul McGuire, to run the network's publicity department and raise the network's profile, as Brad Turell had done for the WB. Before Valentine got on the phone for the interview with a *Times* reporter about *Pfeiffer*, McGuire stressed the need for Valentine to choose his words carefully and not say anything that could be taken as inflammatory.

McGuire could only shake his head and groan as he heard his boss declare at the start of the interview: "We have nothing to feel bad about, and we're not going to feel bad about it. They can march up and down the street all they want." On the morning of Thursday, September 24, Bakewell's Brotherhood Crusade, the Hollywood chapter of the NAACP; local Nation of Islam members; and other advocacy groups followed through on the protest threat. McGuire was forced to brave the chanting crowd of about 200 people, some carrying camera-ready signs declaring "Slavery is not funny" and "Stop the big white liars."

McGuire had driven from his home in Pasadena to the Paramount lot in Hollywood that morning in preparation for doing as much damage control on the protest as he possibly could. As McGuire and Paramount publicity executives watched the gathering crowd from different vantage points on the lot, it was finally decided that the network's head mouthpiece should go down to the street and speak to them. That day, McGuire, a Bostonian with a wry sense of humor, earned the respect of his industry colleagues. He walked coolly out of the Paramount Television executive office building, snaked his way through the studio's courtyard plaza, passed the crammed visitor parking lot, continued down the narrow pathway that runs alongside the security gate and guard hut, and walked down to the sidewalk in front of the studio's ornate wrought-iron gate that sits majestically off Melrose Avenue. As he first caught sight of the faces in the crowd, McGuire knew that if nothing else, he would have one hell of an angry-mob story to dine out on for years.

In conversing with Bakewell and other protest leaders, McGuire noted that he'd tried to set a meeting between Valentine and Bakewell the previous week and that calls to the Brotherhood Crusade office hadn't been returned. He read portions of a statement that he'd just sent out to the press detailing UPN's position that the show was by no means racially insensitive or demeaning to the history of blacks in America. The statement cited examples in the pilot where the Pfeiffer character and black characters in general are portrayed as more rational than the buffoonish white characters.

Despite McGuire's entreaties, the protestors weren't buying it. They wanted a sacrifice from the network and the studio. UPN would not pull the show's scheduled October 5 premiere. After McGuire made the network's case and respectfully bowed out of the sidewalk summit, he hustled back to his office and sought to do whatever damage control he could with major news outlets for the rest of the day. The protestors milled around outside the gate for another hour or so, until the last TV cameras and photographers left.

A week later, the Los Angeles City Council, of all governmental bodies, weighed in with a resolution to have its human relations committee "review" the pilot episode to see if it might incite racial strife in the city. Valentine was apoplectic in the face of the council members' shameless grandstanding.

"Anybody who has seen the pilot and whose brain hasn't been fried by the surfeit of political correctness would find nothing racially offensive about it," Valentine said, calling the council's motion a "pathetic affront to abridge freedom of speech under the most specious argument."*

Within a few days, however, UPN decided to swap the *Pfeiffer* pilot with the second episode for its premiere. The network said the switch was made because executives felt the second episode was funnier. Nobody bought that either. In a further attempt to smooth over the situation, McGuire thought it would be a good idea for them to do some public relations outreach. He accepted talk show host Tavis Smiley's offer to do an interview on the Black Entertainment Television cable channel with *Pfeiffer* star Chi McBride and entertainment president Tom Nunan.

Smiley didn't hold back once the camera was on. Nunan was pretty well pummeled, and McBride looked miserably uncomfortable. When it came time for the call-in segment, the haranguing from viewers was even worse. Until a call came in from a young man identifying himself as "Sterling."

"Well, you know, I hear the show's pretty good . . . ," the caller said, to Smiley's surprise.

McGuire was sitting in his UPN office fuming as he watched the live program. It wasn't exactly the reasoned discourse about the controversy that Smiley had promised, in McGuire's view. But he had to grin a bit through his grimace when he recognized "Sterling" as the voice of Lonnie Moore, one of Nunan's two office assistants.

The *Pfeiffer* debacle made UPN a punchline in industry circles, especially after people saw the show. But, in fact, the period during the protest had its genuinely scary moments. Death threats were lobbed by phone, fax, and e-mail to Valentine, programming head Nunan, and McGuire. The trio had round-the-clock security following them to and from work each day for a few weeks that fall.

And what was it all for? A 2 share—a mortifyingly low turnout, even for a four-year-old network—and savage reviews. Despite the hubbub and all the free advance publicity, *Pfeiffer* didn't even draw

- - - - - - - - - - - - - - - -
*　*The Hollywood Reporter*, October 1, 1998.

television rubberneckers, or anything remotely resembling affection from critics. Longtime TV pundit Ray Richmond opened his review in *Daily Variety* with the observation: "It is rare that prime-time auds are treated with quite as much disdain." * *Pfeiffer* bombed mercilessly in its premiere, along with the rest of UPN's Monday comedy lineup, which was the centerpiece of its "UPN for UPS" campaign.

"When the ratings from the premiere came in, it was just like a flat line. Every show had the same rating, which was horrible," Mc-Guire says. "All that heat and no ratings spike. I shut my office door, put my head down on the desk, and realized it was the wrong week to quit smoking."

Desmond Pfeiffer was puh-finished by the end of the month.

Less than six weeks into the new season, it was painfully, embarrassingly obvious that UPN's new lineup had gone over like a lead balloon. All of the Monday comedies save for *Malcolm and Eddie* would be canceled by January (though *DiResta* remained on the air until March). Valentine yanked *Mercy Point* off the schedule after three airings, mostly because he hated the show. It was replaced by the incongruous pairing of the clip show *America's Greatest Pets*, and another short-lived sitcom, *Reunited*, starring Julie Hagerty of *Airplane!* fame.

Love Boat: The Next Wave didn't survive the rerouting to Friday and would be sunk by the end of the season. None of the other dramas caught fire, though *Seven Days* lasted three seasons and the horse farmers of *Legacy* got a season-long reprieve. The only shows that had any kind of traction that fall continued to be *Moesha* and *Star Trek: Voyager*, and they didn't get any help by having the schedule crumble around them.

The UPN ratings debacle that fall was so severe the network was forced to give up millions of dollars worth of additional commercial time during the months ahead to make it up to advertisers. Most television advertising time is sold on the basis of a minimum guaranteed rating for any given show, which translates into a guarantee from the

---

*   *Daily Variety*, October 2, 1998.

network that a show will attract a bare minimum number of viewers in various demographic groups. If the actual rating delivered falls below that guaranteed bare minimum rating, the network has to compensate the advertiser in the form of additional commercial time, aptly known in the industry as "make-goods." Those "make-goods" would only add to UPN's projected $300 million loss for 1998. While the partners had braced themselves for a rising tide of red ink that year because of the cost of adding two new nights of programming, they weren't prepared for the street protests and an alarming ratings downturn across the board. By the end of 1998, it was virtually impossible for UPN to get a cent approved by the operating committee for additional programming or marketing funds.

At the outset of his tenure at UPN, Valentine felt supported by the operating committee. They were "with me up until October" when bad news arrived, Valentine says.

"All of a sudden, the existing UPN audience saw the change in direction and they said, 'It's not for me anymore.' And the new folks hadn't come in yet. And that terrified the owners of the network so much that they pulled back on the finances to a radical degree," Valentine says. "And from my point of view, that ended the United Paramount Network. Not because it wasn't [pursuing] my vision anymore, but because the financial support for the network dried up."

With a belly flop that big, UPN went into crisis mode. Valentine and his department heads began having brainstorming sessions every night at 7 p.m., but with Valentine's tendency to run on his own clock, the meetings usually started around 7:30 or later.

"It was like a war room, every single night for a couple of months," Nunan says. "We had to figure out what to do."

During this crisis period, Valentine's lack of traditional leadership instincts became all the more apparent, according to insiders, and increasingly it was clear that his actions did little to solve the multitude of problems the network was facing. Staffers were either bemused or demoralized, but nearly all were looking around for other jobs. While the outward perception of the network head in this time of crisis was that he did little to alter his management strategies, Valentine's inner circle, which included Nunan, McGuire, and business affairs chief Layne Britton, saw a more nuanced picture. In crisis, Valentine became more rational, a little less inflexible, less mercurial. He impressed his core team by not passing the buck or laying the blame for the DOA fall launch on anyone but himself.

"Dean always took responsibility for everything," Nunan says. "And he had a sense of humor about it."

Valentine openly criticized his decision to spend the bulk of his fall marketing budget on so-called image advertising, or spots designed to telegraph the overall shift in tone at the network, as opposed to so-called tune-in advertising designed to drive viewers to a specific show ("Watch *Moesha!*") at a specific time ("tonight at 8 on UPN 34!").

By the accounts of multiple insiders, Paramount pushed UPN to spend more of its off-air marketing budget on basic cable channels, including some of those owned or co-owned by Viacom, rather than focus on inexpensive local radio spots in key markets as UPN had in the past. The network under Lucie Salhany always plowed the vast majority of its marketing dollars into local radio; it was impossible to tailor national cable spots to local market needs. At the suggestion of Paramount, Valentine agreed to shift the network's limited funds into cable during that first year, and he came to regret it.

As UPN's fall 1998 launch was struggling to get off the ground, the WB's fortunes were summed up by the names of two new shows that did good business for the network: *Charmed* and *Felicity*. From its opening night on October 7, 1998, *Charmed* was a workhorse for the WB. The fantasy drama conjured up numbers that were well beyond expectations, with a turnout of 7.7 million viewers. The show's ratings consistently held up for the network despite cast changes and numerous time slot shifts over the years—the ultimate battle scars for a television series.

Felicity was a surprise of an entirely different sort. What shocked us about *Felicity* was how virtually every major TV critic and pundit in the country placed it on their "best new shows of the season" list that fall, and lauded Keri Russell for her performance. Her doe-eyes and angelic halo of curls were peeking out everywhere that fall, thanks to another masterful marketing campaign orchestrated by Bob and Lew. All of the critics raved about the authenticity of the pilot script. They would remember the name J. J. Abrams.

Of the two shows, we had anticipated a bigger turnout for *Felicity* than *Charmed*, if only because it had intense heat going into its September 29, 1998 debut in the 9 p.m. time slot following *Buffy the Vampire Slayer*. It turned out to be the opposite, but no matter. *Felicity* had respectable ratings, and it earned its keep in free gushy ink. Together, *Felicity* and *Charmed* cemented our position as a network with a roster of successes. The strength of the programming, marketing, and casting departments at the WB not only created a niche for the network, but a new program genre for the business, at least for the moment. Young, advertiser-coveted viewers seemed to be flocking to our teen fantasies.

As our lineup coalesced in the fall of 1998, we embraced our alternative status and did a better job of any network in creating a cohesive network identity with our shows and our branding and marketing campaigns. Even the soundtracks to our shows and promos were infused with great music by cutting-edge artists who enhanced our overall image with teens and young adults. "A WB show" became a distinct program genre unto itself in industry shorthand; it meant a teen angsty feel-good milieu that challenged the industry axiom that "viewers don't watch networks, they watch shows." In our heyday, viewers came to us to watch "WB shows." We had a potent combination of people who really were dealing with adolescence and those who wanted to revisit that experience.

"We had fantastic-looking people in their twenties, playing characters in teenage scenarios. It gave some of our audience the momentary escape to youth, that phantom zone of your life before there are mortgages, jobs, taxes, babies, when you have the freedom to define your personality," says marketing chief Bob Bibb. "It was a fantasy zone we created. We always said that if we get the teens to the set, the 45-year-old moms are going to find us too."

At our peak, the WB also had a stable of rising stars that viewers came to connect to the network all the time—even off screen. They became walking, talking marketing machines for the network with every magazine cover and gossip item. Brad Turell ran the network's finishing school for starlets, and he worked tirelessly to get our stars on magazine covers and *Entertainment Tonight,* and to position them to take advantage of promotional opportunities and old-fashioned press-the-flesh events and headline-seeking stunts. Turell made sure he was tight with key magazine editors in the WB demo: *Seventeen, Jane, YM,* and later *Teen People.* He knew their publishing schedules better than they did, and he made a point of having an insouciant in-genue at the ready—hair and makeup costs covered—when bigger names would invariably fall out of planned cover shoots on deadline. The summit of Turell's idol-making career was a two-page "The Women of the WB" photo spread that ran in the 1998 year-end issue of *Entertainment Weekly* magazine. Staffers at the network ogled the pages when the issue came out. They were drooling not so much at the curves on the eight women—*7th Heaven's* Jessica Biel, *Buffy the Vampire Slayer's* Sarah Michelle Gellar, *Dawson Creek's* Katie Holmes and Michelle Williams, *Felicity's* Keri Russell, and *Charmed's* Holly Marie Combs, Shannen Doherty, and Alyssa Milano—but at how the spread signified the WB's ascent.

In spite of all of this good news, there was trouble on the horizon: Tension erupted one day when I heard Jamie yelling in his office.

"I can't believe he would do this to me. I can't believe he'd leave *me!*" Jamie sputtered. Soon he was pacing furiously back and forth in my office, absolutely incredulous at the news he'd just been given by Garth Ancier. He felt hurt, angry, and insulted.

"I will *never* hire that man again. I can't believe he wants to go there. Why would he do this to me?" Jamie continued.

Garth had just told Jamie he was going to accept a job offer to become the head of programming at NBC. It was early December, at the end of our charmed year. The holidays were approaching, the days were getting shorter, and Garth's contract was coming up in just a few months. Jamie had known that Garth was being pursued by NBC and by a former Fox colleague of theirs, Scott Sassa. Sassa had been NBC's head of programming but was being promoted and needed to replace himself.

Working at the WB hadn't been just another job for any of us. We were a professional family of people on an all-consuming mission to build a network. And right then, we were two and a half months into the start of what was clearly going to be our best season yet. We'd worked like dogs to get there. As Jordan and I walked to our cars every night, we used to compare the weight of our bags filled with all the scripts we were bringing home to read.

Because of the vision that we shared and the closeness among all of us, Jamie genuinely never thought Garth would leave his WB kinfolk to go to NBC. To Jamie, the upside at the WB was so much greater than at NBC, which anyone could see was heading for an inevitable downturn after a long run as the dominant network of the 1990s. Given our wild momentum, the last thing Jamie wanted to see at this point was a shake-up among his core executives with a departure, even if Garth had always been a little more detached from the day-to-day commitments than the rest of us because of his *Ricki Lake* commitments.

It wasn't that Jamie was caught unprepared in terms of naming a successor for Garth. I had it in writing in my employment contract with the WB that I would be promoted to entertainment president once Garth cut his next deal and got a new title. The previous year, I had been seriously tempted by an offer to return to Fox, this time in a powerful job as Peter Roth's No. 2 executive in programming. I had great respect for Roth from my experiences working with him on *Buffy the Vampire Slayer* and other projects. I was so torn about whether to go to Fox or stay at the WB that I actually went to a psychic. I'm not a big "believer" in psychics, but I was desperate.

Jamie wound up giving me the entertainment president commitment in my contract and a fractional (and by that I mean a sliver) stake in the network to keep me from going to Fox. The psychic had told me that I was going to stay where I was. I'm not sure if I listened to her or to my own instincts, but I sent my regrets to Peter Roth. (As the executive turnstile would have it, we'd be working closely together soon enough.)

After Garth made his decision, he made a point of coming to me to explain his rationale. He didn't need to. I understood. He was distraught by how hard Jamie had taken the news. He hadn't seen that coming, at least not with such vehemence.

"As much as I love the WB and as much as I'm proud of all that we've accomplished here, there's no way I can turn this down," Garth told me.

Going to NBC was like going home for him. He started there as an intern after graduating from Princeton in 1979. He had worked as an assistant to Brandon Tartikoff when Tartikoff was skillfully leading NBC through a tough rebuilding phase. He'd learned programming at the knee of the contemporary master, who, tragically, died young of cancer in 1997. There was no way Garth could turn down the chance to go back to NBC as entertainment president.

Jamie stayed angry at Garth for months, and even tried to buy back Garth's two percentage points in the network, but Garth wouldn't sell. I never saw Jamie in a more emotionally volatile state than I did in this period.

In all of this high drama, the exhaustion factor cannot be ignored. We had all been pushing so hard for so long that we were wiped out. Tempers felt permanently frazzled. The intensity of the blowup between Jamie and Garth put a temporary cloud over what was a momentous occasion for me: my promotion to entertainment president.

After the DOA fall launch, UPN senior executives suddenly became experts in ratings and the audience profile of their stations. Tom Nunan and others spent time on the road talking to affiliate station managers and scrutinizing what worked on UPN's strongest affiliates. They finally settled on a raunchier, edgier version of the network's original focus on young men, only this time with body-slamming wrestlers and sophomoric comedies rather than the 1980s vintage action-adventure dramas that Kerry McCluggage made his name on at Universal.

At first, Dean Valentine found the retrenching process painful and infuriating when the partners made it clear they had lost faith in his Middle-America idea. It was also made apparent that his job depended on getting the network's $250 million to $300 million annual losses under control, or UPN would have to drop one of its newly launched nights.

Valentine thought about resigning—it was his bullishness and conviction that got them into the mess—but it didn't feel right.

"I'm not a quitter," Valentine says. Instead, he guided the network through its next big phase of courting young men with rowdy and randy programming, but his heart was never in it again. His job as CEO of UPN became an exercise in giving himself on-the-job instruction on how to run a business, skills he had always felt he was lacking.

"It became a process of managing losses rather than the process of growing a network," Valentine says. "As difficult as it was, I didn't like the idea of just walking. I had come up to bat only one time. But I never believed that we could ever grow the network from that point onward."

The WB's fast rise hadn't taken any of the steam away from the network's competitive ferocity. The bulletins of bad news for UPN that seemed to come every day were devoured around the WB offices with glee. The ability to gloat from such a high perch about the flailing enemy was more than just a morale boost for the Burbank mob. It was a safety-valve release of pent-up stress for a team that had been going pedal-to-the-metal for more than four years by that time.

Brad Turell in particular kept our competitive spirit running high virtually all of the time. Sometimes his intensity backfired on him, like the time he had to write a letter of apology to Aaron Spelling for issuing a press release that savaged the ratings for Spelling's UPN series *The Love Boat: The Next Wave*.

Brad's press release was mean-spirited, starting with the headline " 'The Love Boat' Continues to Sink." It contained even more barbs directed at a show from a producer that we happened to be heavily in business with. UPN's public relations department was smart enough to make sure that a copy of Brad's release was faxed over to Spelling's office. They were not amused.

As if having to write a mea culpa letter to Aaron Spelling wasn't bad enough, Brad had to read about his PR debacle on the front page of *Daily Variety* a few days later (thanks to UPN's enterprising press department, no doubt). The article didn't mention Brad by name, but everyone in town knew who was behind the move described in the story as "stupid and obnoxious" by an unnamed Spelling Television executive.*

Despite the occasional misstep, however, the streak that started at the WB with *Savannah* only made us work harder, and strive to be more creative, more inventive, and more ahead of the curve, because more was expected of us. What none of us expected was the high-class headaches that our stunning successes would create, coming as they did against the backdrop of the dot-com mania and the easy money that seemed to be floating all around us.

A parade of venture capitalists and Silicon Valley types came pounding on our doors, telling us that TheWB.com domain name alone was worth $500 million. Big-money offers flowed in almost daily from dot-com outfits that wanted to partner with the WB in order to harness the youthful cachet of *Buffy the Vampire Slayer, Dawson's Creek,* et al. We listened to all of the partnership and licensing proposals that came to us, but Jamie wound up turning every one of them away. He presciently told us that they were flimsy companies with no cash flow—hardly worthy business partners for the network we'd worked so hard to create.

By the beginning of 1999, Jamie's refusal to jump into an IPO left some of the WB's top echelon grappling with feelings of bitterness toward our leader. Many of us had pangs of guilt for our feelings, but we also couldn't fathom Jamie's objections to the idea of setting up

---

*   *Daily Variety,* May 4, 1998, "WB, Spelling: 'Love' Lost."

TheWB.com as a distinct business from the WB, so more of the rank and file could share in the network's success through a public stock offering.

Our passions were stoked by the bubble-madness of the moment. Every time you picked up a newspaper or magazine, every time you turned on the TV, there was another report of another startup dot-com venture making millions for its twentysomething founders. And these were businesses with a lot less going for them than the WB.

Jamie's steadfast opposition to TheWB.com was bad enough in the eyes of his loyal lieutenants. But the situation became far worse when he began preparations for a public stock offering of his Acme television station group. All of a sudden, the embers created by TheWB.com standoff turned into a fast-moving brushfire. The heat stirred by Acme Communications' initial public offering would be the first blow to the all-for-one, one-for-all corporate culture that Jamie had tried so hard to establish at the WB. The Acme IPO left a deep divide in our trailers that would have a lasting effect on the psyche of the network.

CHAPTER SEVEN

SMACKDOWN

In the wake of the fall's train wreck, UPN's focus turned to ensuring a successful send-off in January 1999 for *Dilbert*, a half-hour animated rendition of the popular newspaper comic that skewers corporate-cubicle culture. Dean Valentine had gone out of his way to land the TV series rights to *Dilbert* when the project was shopped by Sony Pictures' television arm shortly after he arrived at UPN. Valentine had to put some extra money on the table to convince Sony's television executives to go with UPN rather than an established network. Valentine assured them that he would make *Dilbert* the centerpiece of the network's schedule, and its marketing budget. There was no chance that *Dilbert* would get lost in the shuffle on UPN as a cartoon series might on one of the Big Four networks.

Because of the longer lead time required for animation production, the earliest *Dilbert* episodes could be ready was midway through the 1998–99 season. By that time, after the woeful performance at the start of the season with *Secret Diary of Desmond Pfeiffer*, the pressure was on Valentine and programming head Tom Nunan to deliver a success.

"We knew we had to get *Dilbert* right," Nunan recalls.

Nunan was never big on the idea of doing a TV show based on the daily three-panel comic penned by Scott Adams, which was limited in its storytelling and character development. Nunan made no secret of his skepticism about the project. He doubted whether viewers would be able to connect with a cartoon character of such bare-bones design. It bugged him that the title character's eyes didn't even have pupils.

Because *Dilbert* was a well-known commodity, UPN and Sony were able to recruit an A-list comedy producer, Larry Charles, to spearhead the television adaptation as executive producer and show runner. With Charles on board, *Dilbert* seemed to have all the elements—a seasoned producer, a well-known voice cast including Daniel Stern, Chris Elliott, and Jason Alexander, and built-in name recognition with viewers. The conditions were ripe for a big opening night on January 25.

As is customary with a high-profile new show, UPN executives set up a meeting with Charles to discuss the marketing and advertising plans for *Dilbert*. The executive in charge of marketing for the network, Rob Rene, was a Valentine recruit who was never well liked or well regarded by his colleagues. Rene had come to UPN in February 1998 to fill a newly created position that gave him broad responsibilities for the network's marketing and advertising activities, and by the time he arrived at UPN, his career path had been a circuitous one. He'd served a stint as an investment banker at Oppenheimer & Co., worked as an advertising account manager at Madison Avenue giant Young & Rubicam, and prior to UPN served as head of marketing at the ill-fated Americast television service that the Walt Disney Company tried to launch with regional telephone partners. Earlier in his career, Rene worked in development at Universal Television on shows like *Miami Vice* and *Magnum, P.I.* With this background, he'd amassed a range of experience but none in the functions he was hired to carry out for UPN.

By many accounts, Rene came in with a head of steam and little else. Numerous senior executives who had reported directly to Valentine now had to report to Rene, which couldn't help but roil the ranks. His first major effort for the network had been the bungled fall launch campaign.

Rene had called the meeting with Charles on developing a marketing strategy for *Dilbert*. But the timing ultimately conflicted with Rene's vacation plans in Hawaii. So Rene instructed his staff to set up a conference call so he could lead the meeting by speakerphone from

Hawaii. Rene had been vocal with other staffers who were set to participate that he would be the one to steer the discussion with Charles, even if it had to be by speakerphone.

"He told everybody: 'Remember, this is *my* meeting,'" one participant recalls.

Even by the standard of television comedy writers, Larry Charles is known as an eccentric. He can afford to be. Charles earned his bona fides as one of television's most sought-after comedy writers and show runners with his work on NBC's *Mad About You* and *Seinfeld* in the mid-1990s. Charles usually looks like a cross between a rabbi and a member of ZZ Top's entourage, with an ever-present pair of dark sunglasses offset by long hair and a scraggly salt-and-pepper beard. Despite his unconventional style, Charles is known as a consummate pro, the kind of show runner who can parachute into any project and make it respectable, on time, and on budget, or at least close enough.

On the day of the *Dilbert* meeting, Charles showed up at UPN's offices wearing a colorful set of pajamas—which for him was normal attire for such a meeting. He was ushered into the conference room, where a half-dozen network executives were waiting to greet him enthusiastically. Charles was considered an incredible "get" for UPN. (*Dilbert* was the first show that UPN got ahold of that actually made me and others at the WB a little nervous.)

As promised, Rene handled the pleasantries and introductions by phone. He thanked Charles profusely for coming in and assured him that the network had no more important priority in the coming year than *Dilbert*. Charles responded with what seemed to everyone in the room to be the only logical thing for a producer to say at the start of a marketing brainstorming meeting.

"Tell me what you're going to do for this show," Charles demanded in a voice louder than most people tend to use when talking into speakerphones.

His words hung for a while in the silence that followed. The muted crackle and hum of a long-distance connection on a speakerphone was the only sound heard in the conference room. It was obvious that Rene was still connected but just didn't know what to say. Any of the other executives present could have jumped in and bailed Rene out with a verbal soft-shoe. But as the pause grew uncomfortably long, all anyone could think of was Rene's "it's *my* meeting" directive. Nobody said a word.

Finally, Rene spoke, promising that the network planned to generate many thousands of "impressions" for the show. Rene's slightly out-of-context use of marketing jargon made his colleagues think it was something he'd picked up from reading an issue of *Advertising Age.*

Charles, sensing blood on the tracks, refused to give Rene any slack.

"Wow. Impressions . . . ," he said with more than a hint of incredulousness. "OK. But I'm a TV guy, Rob. Tell me, what's an impression?"

Rene was left dangling by a thread on the phone for another 10 minutes, babbling about "impressions." The others remained mute, struggling to contain their smirks. Charles eventually leaned back in his chair and said, to no one in particular: "I think we have our first episode."

Charles wasn't laughing. "He was serious and pissed off," recalls one participant.

"*My* meeting," the staffers snickered as they left the conference room and left Rene stewing in Hawaii. A few months after the embarrassing meeting with Charles, Rene headed for the exit at UPN with two years left to go on his employment contract.

Even with the poor impression that the marketing team made, *Dilbert* got off to a good start, by UPN standards, and in fact, UPN did spend a fair amount to promote the show's premiere. It worked, but only for a moment. Viewership declined steadily in subsequent weeks and never recovered. A month after its premiere, however, UPN gave the show a full-season, 22-episode pickup for a second season. It was a costly, showy gesture, the same as the WB had done with *Savannah* three years before.

By then, however, Dean Valentine barely gave a damn. He had become miserable within weeks of the start of the 1998–99 season. He had long ago lost the support of the operating committee and was under orders to find another programming strategy—quick. Both the Paramount and Chris-Craft camps were spooked by how swiftly the network went into ratings free-fall. The ever-feuding partners managed to find common ground in mandating that Valentine get the losses down from more than $200 million in 1998, or the network would suffer the humiliation of cutting one of its nights. Valentine didn't take it personally, but for him, UPN was over as a creative endeavor.

"We had no money for additional production, which is really what should have happened if it had been a serious company running UPN," Valentine says. "You've either got to close it down or make it work. [The partners] always kind of kept splitting the difference."

For Valentine, the worst thing about the budget crisis and the partners' loss of confidence in him was that he was forced to rely on Paramount to supply UPN's programming. It seemed to Valentine that UPN was forced to swallow a whole lot of Paramount's chaff in the form of unsold pilots, busted theatricals, and other cost-absorbing items. He'd never been impressed with the output of Paramount Television under Kerry McCluggage, but now it was becoming a bigger problem. In addition, the longstanding cold war between the UPN partners had become even worse after 1998's losses. The tension between Chris-Craft and Paramount took its toll on Valentine, just as it had on Salhany. Unlike his predecessor, who was aligned with Chris-Craft, Valentine seemed to UPN insiders to tend more to his relations on the Paramount side, though Chris-Craft's Evan Thompson also remained a constant presence in management of the network.

"Kerry and Evan were the guys. Dean would always say, 'Well, I gotta check with Kerry,' or 'I gotta call Evan,' " a former senior UPN executive says. "He always had to work both sides and he would, by dribbling out information."

Star Trek: Voyager continued to be a constant source of tension.

For the show's fourth season, the deal between Paramount and the network was renegotiated to be a standard program licensing agreement rather than the original arrangement of UPN paying no license fee for the show but rather turning over all of its national network advertising time in the show to Paramount. According to UPN insiders, Chris-Craft executives never let go of their suspicion that Paramount was chiseling them on *Voyager* and making more money on that one show than they were putting back into the network and on and on. Paramount scoffed at the idea that the studio was rolling in profits from short-lived shows it produced for UPN. In frustration, Kerry McCluggage and Viacom's Jonathan Dolgen more than once offered to let Chris-Craft invest in any Paramount-produced UPN show—their choice—if they were convinced the studio was making so much money off of them.

Valentine often found both sides pulling him aside at network events or calling him on the QT; they would implore him not to "take any shit" or some such colorful description from the other partner.

"It would take six months for Jonathan Dolgen to schedule a meeting with Bill Siegel to talk about something important to the network," says a former senior UPN executive. "It was preposterous. The network really deserved more professional management."

Despite the hole they were in, the senior executives circled the wagons and continued to strive for a solution to their programming woes. The UPN braintrust batted around all kinds of way-out options in their search for a new game plan from late 1998 to early 1999. Public relations chief Paul McGuire only half jokingly once suggested they start their own roller ball league. The comment drew chuckles, but the idea wasn't far removed from the conceit of the program that would restore some of UPN's dignity by the end of 1999.

After weeks of nightly war-room brainstorming sessions fueled by a vending machine diet of Cokes and candy bars, in early 1999 UPN had settled its focus on a program form that has been a part of the prime-time landscape on and off since the late 1940s: wrestling. The gaudy theatrics of professional grapplers was perfect for UPN at that moment, in more ways than one, Valentine would realize. Valentine set his sights on cutting a deal with the hottest property in wrestling, the World Wrestling Federation.*

Valentine knew the WWF was in the market for a broadcast network outlet because he had been pitched the idea months earlier by WWF proprietor Vince McMahon and his adult son Shane. They'd been escorted to UPN by their handlers at the William Morris Agency. At the time, Valentine hadn't given the WWF a definitive answer. He was mildly interested in the idea of doing female wrestling. It wasn't something the WWF had offered per se, but Valentine figured nobody else on television was doing it, so why not UPN? But he was also in the midst of plotting his blue-collar revolution for the fall of 1998 and didn't give much thought to what wrestling might do for UPN.

The WWF at the time was becoming a huge draw on cable's USA Network and a growing pop culture phenomenon among young men. The Connecticut-based company profits from a never-ending cycle of arena tours and pricey monthly pay-per-view events that rake in hundreds of millions of dollars annually. Vince McMahon has thrived by paying special attention to the theater of wrestling, particularly his characters and story lines. He's a spandex Svengali, creating stars out of Dwayne "The Rock" Johnson, "Stone Cold" Steve Austin, rough-tough lady wrestlers Sable and Chyna and others with careful marketing and soap opera plots, complete with cliffhangers and blood feuds. For all the tawdriness of their product, Vince McMahon and Linda McMahon, his wife and the company's shrewd CEO, have infused their wrestling extravaganzas with a kind of sleazy-homey atmosphere, with them as patriarchs and their adult children, Shane and Stephanie, as key players and competitors in the ring.

By the late 1990s, the WWF was ready for the big leagues on a broadcast network to capitalize on its rising popularity. The WWF's top-rated USA Network program, *Raw,* and the tours were great starting points, but being on the prime-time schedule of a broadcast

---

*   The company changed its name to World Wrestling Entertainment after losing a protracted legal battle with the non-profit World Wildlife Fund for the trademark use of "WWF" in 2002.

network, even one in UPN's state, would pump the WWF up to the next level of visibility and profitability.

Tom Nunan couldn't stomach the idea of UPN devoting two precious hours of its prime-time schedule to wrestling. He thought it was "crap" that would send the wrong low-brow message about the network to the creative community that UPN needed to court. But after UPN had met its Waterloo the previous fall, the network was too desperate to worry about prestige. Valentine knew the McMahons were prepared to write UPN a check to essentially rent two hours a week on the network, 52 weeks a year. He believed he could capitalize on the WWF's young male "dude" demographic and turn it into a new "strategic direction" spin. He knew he could sell that to his masters on the operating committee, to the media, and to the entertainment industry. UPN would transform itself once again, this time into a testosterone-driven young male alternative to the female-centered WB.

The deal to bring the WWF into the UPN tent was the smartest move Valentine could have made in an impossible situation. The association with the raunchy wrestlers would give UPN a new focus for its programming and marketing efforts. Better still, the WWF would pay UPN for the privilege of using its airtime. This decision to court the WWF would prove to be Valentine's lasting legacy at the network, so much so that wrestling would eventually make the transition to the UPN–WB successor network, CW.

"It was a marketing tool, and it was a marketing tool that, for better or worse, set UPN on a certain course," Valentine says. "Wrestling was getting hot in the culture—you could just see it. And I knew I could spin that into a young male [target audience] story that would fit in with the WB's young female story."

Late in 1998, a few months into the third season of *Buffy the Vampire Slayer,* Sandy Grushow, the president of 20th Century Fox Television, set up a lunch date with Jamie Kellner.

Jamie Kellner (*left*) and Warner Bros. executive vice president Barry Meyer symbolically break ground on the WB Network in early 1994. As the WB's first photo-op, this was one of the few times Kellner appeared at a network event in formal attire.

Jamie Kellner celebrating with the WB's Michigan J. Frog at the network's low-key launch party, January 11, 1995.

Crucial members of the WB's launch team (*from left*): Marketing chiefs Bob Bibb and Lew Goldstein, programming president Garth Ancier, Warner Bros.' Barry Meyer, and Tribune's Dennis FitzSimons.

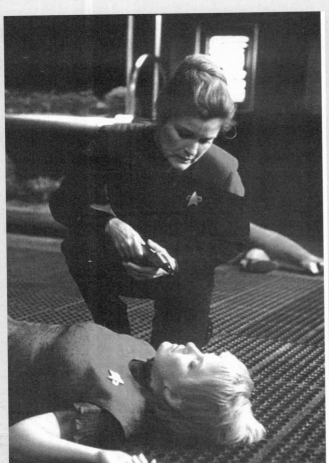

Star Trek: Voyager, the show that launched UPN, would see its greatest success on the network's launch on January 16, 1995. UPN would never again match its opening night audience of 21 million. (*CBS Photo Archive*)

Lucie Salhany, UPN's first president and CEO, brought a fierce competitive spirit to the network's competition with the WB and her dealings with Paramount executives. (*Berliner Studio/BEImages*)

Producer Aaron Spelling surrounded by the belles of *Savannah. From left:* Jamie Luner, Shannon Sturges, and Robin Lively. Spelling's stature in the industry lent credibility to the WB in its early years.

The Aaron Spelling–produced family drama *7th Heaven* overcame a slow start to become the WB's most-watched and longest-running series. (*The WB/James Sorenson*)

Joss Whedon's *Buffy the Vampire Slayer* was the WB's first breakout success: it provided a strong, young female heroine who resonated with the target audience and developed a rabid following. (*"Buffy the Vampire Slayer"* ©1997 *Twentieth Century Fox Television. All Rights Reserved.*)

Most WB executives were not much older than the stars of the network. Here I am in the middle with *Buffy the Vampire Slayer*'s Sarah Michelle Gellar and *Dawson's Creek* star James Van Der Beek.

Warner Bros.' Bruce Rosenblum (*left*) and WB Network's Jordan Levin were pivotal players in the WB saga, but the two would eventually clash over the management of the network.

Dean Valentine's offbeat taste in shows and his contrarian personality made him an unusual choice to follow Lucie Salhany as network CEO of UPN. He would quickly lose the support of UPN's owners after his first programming slate took the network to new ratings lows. (*Berliner Studio/BEImages*)

Despite some off-screen drama between the cast members, the teen coming-of-age show *Dawson's Creek*, inspired by creator Kevin Williamson's youth in North Carolina, became the signature hit that put the WB on the map with viewers. (*Courtesy Sony Pictures Television*)

This was taken shortly after I became WB entertainment president, just as the network began to break through with a strong roster of distinctive shows.

Paramount Television's *Star Trek: Voyager* was UPN's first program—and its first to last long enough to make it to syndication. Here network and studio executives celebrate the show's one-hundredth-episode milestone. *From left:* Paramount executive Tom Mazza, *Voyager* star Kate Mulgrew, UPN's Dean Valentine, *Voyager* executive producer Rick Berman, and Paramount Television chief Kerry McCluggage. (*Berliner Studio/BEImages*)

In 2002, to salvage the network, CBS's Leslie Moonves selected Dawn Ostroff to take over for Dean Valentine as UPN president. (*John Paul Filo/ The CW © 2007 The CW Network, LLC. All Rights Reserved.*)

Jordan Levin and a cavalcade of WB stars at the network's 2003 upfront presentation in New York. Levin was four months away from being formally named Jamie Kellner's successor as CEO. (*Kevin Mazur/ Wireimage.com*)

A big part
of UPN's
comeback
hinged on its
ability to catch
the reality-
programming
wave with
the runway
competition
series *America's
Next Top
Model*, hosted
and produced
by Tyra Banks.
*(Bill Inoshito/
UPN ©2006
CBS Corp.)*

Leslie Moonves, Barry Meyer, and Dennis FitzSimons stunned the
media world on January 24, 2006, with the stealth announcement at a
Manhattan news conference that UPN and WB would merge into the
CW. *(Jeffrey R. Staab/CBS ©2006 CBS Broadcasting Inc. All Rights
Reserved.)*

Grushow brought along his top dealmaker at the studio, Gary Newman. Grushow and Newman wanted to talk to Jamie about 20th Century Fox Television's contract with the network for *Buffy*, which at the time ran for another two years, through the 2000–01 season. They met at Adriano's Ristorante, a popular industry pasta eatery near Mulholland Drive in the hills of Bel Air.

Grushow and Jamie were old friends from their days at Fox, where Grushow was a hotshot in the marketing department before rising up the programming ranks. He was named Fox entertainment president in late 1992 during Jamie's waning months at the network. Jamie had called Grushow when he was assembling the WB to see if he had any interest in joining him at his new venture.

After some friendly small talk, the conversation got down to business with the kind of frankness that only former colleagues who've been in the trenches together can share. Grushow and Newman tried to impress upon Jamie that 20th had given *Buffy* the TLC as if it were being produced for the Fox network. Newman reminded him of how he'd personally gone to bat for *Buffy* with Fox's senior management while he was serving as interim head of Fox Television, before Grushow was tapped to run the studio in early 1997. Grushow noted how he'd also recognized the show's promise and had continued to support it and *Buffy* creator Joss Whedon.

By the third season, 20th Century Fox Television was running a budget deficit of $450,000 to $800,000 on each episode, for which the WB paid a license fee of $1.1 million. Those were high deficits for a WB show for sure, and they were also high proportionate to the level of red ink that 20th would be willing to absorb on projects produced for a Big Four network.

Nonetheless, Grushow and Newman explained, 20th had not scrimped on *Buffy*'s visual effects or other production needs. When the actors, including star Sarah Michelle Gellar, asked for more money in light of the show's success, the studio dug deep and gave her and other actors big raises. When Whedon asked to upgrade the show's film stock from 16 mm to 35 mm, at a cost of about $20,000 per episode, 20th said yes in recognition of his hard work and dedication.

Fox had consistently gone the extra mile for the show that veritably defined the WB demo, Grushow and Newman stressed, as if they were lawyers methodically laying out an opening argument.

But now 20th was looking at $85 million in debt before *Buffy* made it to syndication. The 20th executives offered to strike a new deal that would extend the WB's hold on *Buffy* from two to four more seasons in exchange for a higher license fee to help offset the deficits.

The answer from Jamie over lunch that day was a quick, emphatic "No." Jamie assured Grushow and Newman an early contract renegotiation was not in the cards. The WB was striving first and foremost for profitability, and they weren't about to take on any more debt if they didn't have to. Kellner was firm. The table conversation remained friendly as they wrapped up the meal. But from that day on an ominous feeling surrounded 20th's dealings with the WB.

"There was a tension that was, for the most part, unspoken in the relationship because we all knew this big battle was coming," says Newman, who would become president of 20th Century Fox Television alongside Dana Walden when Grushow was promoted in late 1999 to a higher post overseeing the Fox network and the TV studio.

Not long after that awkward lunch date, the first warning shots were fired in January 1999 during the winter edition of the Television Critics Association press junket in Pasadena, California.

Grushow was asked during an open Q&A session with a panel of top studio executives whether he anticipated a battle with the WB over the *Buffy* renewal. He was pointedly asked whether he would be willing to move the show to 20th's sibling network, Fox, if the WB would not meet his asking price. A media-savvy executive who barely hides his ambition, Grushow possesses the shoot-from-the-lip cockiness common to the first wave of Fox network executives. As such, he responded without much hesitation that he would indeed take *Buffy* to the highest bidder if the WB continued to "lowball" the studio.

"Fair market value is fair market value," he said, especially for a show that had proven so valuable to the WB.*

Jamie was irritated when he heard about Grushow's remarks. The WB's leader had long been an advocate of fiscal discipline, frugality among executives, and the importance of a business operating within its means. Jamie wanted the WB to get over the hump to profitability as soon as possible for his own benefit as an owner as well as for the long-term health of the network. That meant adhering to budgets and financial planning.

In his view, 20th stood to make a fortune off a hit show that had shown every sign of being the kind of hard-core cult favorite that would be ensured a long life in reruns, not to mention sequels, spinoffs, and ancillary products. Jamie resented Grushow's public posturing for a new deal at a time when the WB's contract still had another two seasons to go. He felt it was a below-the-belt tactic from a media giant that could afford to shoulder some debt on the show until it hit the syndication jackpot. In his public statements on *Buffy*, Jamie insisted that WB had developed the show internally at the network and served it up on a silver platter to 20th—a view that is not consistently shared by others who were involved in the launch of *Buffy* as a TV series. The studio should have been grateful, not grabby, Jamie thought, just as fervently as Grushow and his bosses believed that 20th should be compensated for its exemplary handling of *Buffy*. It was a fundamental clash of business interests and the egos of executives with long histories; for Jamie, that didn't just apply to Grushow but also to Rupert Murdoch and to News Corp. President Peter Chernin, who worked closely with Jamie at Fox.

Those of us on the sidelines at the WB watched this prolonged and unusually public war of words over *Buffy* unfold with a mix of amusement and alarm; I wanted to believe it wasn't anything more than executive saber-rattling. I was feeling very reassured about our

- - - - - - - - - - - - - - - - - -

*   *Daily Variety*, January 14, 1999, "Bloody 'Buffy' Spectre Eyed by Studios, Webs."

future by some news about Warner Bros. Television that broke around the same time the *Buffy* spat began. Warner Bros.' Bob Daly and Barry Meyer implemented a regime change at the TV division in February 1999. Tony Jonas, who had been Leslie Moonves' successor as president in 1995, was out. The new recruit was none other than Peter Roth, the executive who had championed *Buffy* during his time as president of 20th Century Fox Television.

Roth is well known in the industry as a warm, bear-hugging executive with a keen ability to connect with creative talent. He tackled the challenge of improving relations between Warner Bros. Television and its sibling network with high-minded determination. It was a considerable task. The gulf between the studio and the network was made clear by the studio patronage of the WB's biggest successes: both *Buffy* and the later spin-off *Angel* hailed from 20th Century Fox TV. *7th Heaven* and *Charmed* came from Viacom-owned Spelling Television. *Dawson's Creek* flowed through Sony Pictures Entertainment, and *Felicity* hailed from Walt Disney Co.'s Touchstone Television unit. Even with our children's programming, our best shows came from outside of Warner Bros.

When Roth arrived on the Burbank lot in early 1999, he didn't need to be told by Meyer that his top priority was thawing the iceberg between the network and studio and getting a few Warner Bros.-produced hits on the WB. Roth went so far as to institute not only regular meetings between studio executives and their network counterparts but semiregular cocktail mixers at Hollywood night spots—neutral territory—in an effort to bridge the communication gap.

"I would tell my staff, 'I don't want to see any two Warner Bros. Television executives standing together. I only want to see groups of network and studio people together,' " Roth says. "After a while, the communication began to flow easier."

As 1999 progressed, so did the WB. On February 8, 1999, the network hit a high-water mark that would stand for the rest of its days. On that Monday night, 12.5 million viewers tuned in to see the birth of twins in the Camden family on *7th Heaven*.

All of our fantastic momentum made Jamie a star performer for Time Warner on the endless circuit of investment conferences hosted by big Wall Street firms. At one such event in 1998, Jamie dazzled analysts and money-managers with a bullish presentation about the WB's near-term prospects. Afterward he headed over to the WB's New York offices at 1325 Avenue of the Americas.

Before heading to his own office, Jamie dropped by the 32nd floor to speak to advertising sales head Jed Petrick. The WB's ad sales department worked in a large open area with Jed's office tucked into a far corner. As Jamie strolled in that day, he was feeling good. He spoke in an uncharacteristically loud tone in order to project his voice into Jed's office.

"Hey Jed, can we bill $450 million this upfront?" Jamie bellowed. "Because I just told the whole investment community that we could."

The reply was swift from the soft-spoken Petrick.

"Are you kidding me? Oh man. . . ."

The WB had generated about $310 million in upfront sales the previous year. Meeting Jamie's lofty projection seemed like a terrible long shot, even in a bull market for TV advertising time fueled by the influx of dot-com dollars. And yet when the numbers were tallied that summer, the WB had pulled in some $455 million at an average year-over-year rate increase of 29 percent.

"Some advertisers paid [rate increases] as high as 45 percent more than they had the prior year. I had been selling commercial time for 20 years at that point and had never seen an advertiser pay that much more on a year-to-year basis," Petrick says. "It was *the* killer upfront."

To Jamie, the gains registered by the WB didn't seem so crazy. We got lucky, for sure, on the back of hard, hard work. Most important to Jamie, we had huge upside potential. The WB was unquestionably hot, but its advertising time still sold at rates that were usually 20 percent to 30 percent or more below the price of a 30-second spot on ABC, CBS, NBC, or Fox. In our fight to bridge the gap, Jamie and Jed hammered home a simple message to Madison Avenue: the WB was a more efficient buy for advertisers seeking a young demographic because it offered concentrated youth. Precious few people over the age of 50 were watching our shows, which meant that advertisers got more bang for their buck than on shows airing on the Big Four nets with a broader range of viewers.*

"We are not in the same business as ABC, CBS, NBC, and Fox anymore," Kellner told *The Hollywood Reporter* in June 1999 after achieving the $455 million upfront milestone. "We're in our own discreet little world." †

I knew how well the WB was doing as a business—you couldn't miss it. It seemed that every other week there was a new story in *Forbes* or *Fortune* or *BusinessWeek* or *Time* or *Newsweek* about our growth, about how we were the only broadcast network that had any room to grow and about how we were able to reach young people better than any other network.

I knew all that to be true, and still, I worried constantly about UPN as competition. We were gleeful and smug about their disastrous launch in the 1998–99 season when we were so hot. But I always worried about the day when they'd finally get their act together. I fretted about this, that, and the other in the spirit of gallows humor that was pervasive at the WB. But I sincerely began to worry when we found out that UPN was getting wrestling. Or more accurately, that the World Wrestling Federation was buying Thursday night on UPN. I worried still more when I heard that Dean Valentine and Tom Nunan were telling writers and agents and studio executives and others in the

---

* Most programs that rate highly in the adults 18-49 demographic still draw a large, if not larger, group of viewers aged 50 and up, who generally watch more TV and are easier for broadcast networks to lure than viewers aged 18-49 or younger. Advertisers tend to pay a premium for shows that draw high concentrations of younger viewers.

† *The Hollywood Reporter*, June 1, 1999.

creative community that they were doing another 90-degree turn from Middle America to go after young men with broad, silly, guy's guy shows to capitalize on the WWF demo.

I wasn't surprised at their choice at all. I'd thought for a while that they should be going after that audience. There had to be room out there for a network to put a male spin on what we had done with teenage girls and young women. I could see UPN capitalizing on the wrestling base to relentlessly promote new shows. I thought they might get creative in picking up shock-value fare that would draw the WWF audience to check out the network on other nights. I was horrified by the idea that they could out-strip our growth if they came up with a few shows that worked. By and large, UPN still had the better station lineup, even with all of our success.

Jamie told me repeatedly not to worry. He didn't think wrestling would have an impact on UPN, based on the track record he'd seen there during the previous five years.

"Ratings are ratings," I told Jamie more than once. "The WWF will help UPN."

"No, Susanne, advertisers will discount it because it's wrestling," Jamie would reply. "It's just something UPN acquired. It's not like they've created their own hit show."

"No, they're bringing eyeballs to the network. Wrestling is going to help build them, one way or another." I was convinced.

But Jamie and I didn't have much spare time on our hands for debating UPN as the summer wore on. I became completely distracted by the great Hair Crisis of 1999 involving *Felicity* star Keri Russell.

Keri is a born actress, and despite her natural beauty and early success, she's a very down-to-earth and lovely person. She garnered a boatload of press during the show's first year, which can be a hard thing on the psyche of a young and talented actress. She won a Golden Globe Award for *Felicity* after the show had only been on the air for four months. Yet Keri was already a veteran when she signed on for *Felicity*. She'd been working as a dancer and actress since she was a preteen, having logged two years in the early 1990s as a Mouseketeer in one of Disney's *Mickey Mouse Club* revivals alongside Christina

Aguilera, Justin Timberlake, and Britney Spears. She'd guest starred on *7th Heaven* and costarred in a short-lived Aaron Spelling soap for NBC, *Malibu Shores*, among other projects.

When production began on *Felicity*'s second season in the summer of 1999, I remember getting a phone call from producer J. J. Abrams with some bad news. Keri had decided to chop off most of her hair—the beautiful curly crown that had been such a distinctive feature of the show. We were all dismayed at the surprise she sprang on us when she reported for work on season two, especially when we saw just how much of a bob she'd gone for.

At least that's how I remember it. Others, including Abrams, recall a different scenario. They remember the haircut being a point of discussion before the scissors came out, and that it was part of her character development for season two. Abrams and his partner Matt Reeves figured that an impetuous change of look would be just what a young woman would do at the start of her second year of college as a rebounding move after a tough break up, as Felicity had endured at the end of season one.

Whether it was scripted or not, all I remember is seeing red about the whole thing. We tried to get Keri to consider using hair extensions to ease the audience into her look but she and J.J. would have none of it. I didn't even try to hide my anger at the situation. In hindsight, with more experience under his belt as a producer, J.J. says he's a little more sympathetic to my point of view, and to the negative reaction the shift provoked in many fans.

"It was like we pulled off Groucho's mustache, or turned Santa's red suit green," Abrams says. "It was a massive shift for the character. But I think if the ratings had picked up that season it wouldn't have been nearly such a problem for everyone."

Felicity was never the same after Keri lost her curly mane. The show's ratings went down in season two after we moved it to Sunday night and away from the cushy time slot following *Buffy the Vampire Slayer* on Tuesday. But the critics stopped raving as hard too. The blunt cut made Keri, then 23, look much more grown up. She didn't exude the virginal vulnerability that made the big city such a sexy backdrop for the Felicity Porter character. With the bob, she looked like any other too-hip female undergrad from someplace else living it up in New York City.

While I was grappling with the fallout from an ill-timed haircut, Jamie had another focus entirely. His Acme station group had grown to 15 stations by that fall. Acme was preparing for an initial public stock offering in September. As with most IPOs, it was designed to give Acme ready access to currency for cutting deals as it pursued station acquisitions and licenses to build new stations from scratch. Of course, the IPO also stood to enrich Kellner and his Acme partners. The prospectus Acme filed with the Securities and Exchange Commission raised hackles as the document circulated around the WB in the summer of 1999.

The 140-page prospectus clearly laid out how Acme's business strategy was intertwined with the WB. It touted the network's rapid growth during the past two years as key to Acme's strategy of seeking out midsize markets where the WB had no outlet or needed an upgrade to a stronger station. The prospectus cited the familiar refrain that Jamie was working with a core team of Fox veterans who knew how to build a network, citing by name me, Garth Ancier, Bob Bibb, Lew Goldstein, Jed Petrick, and Brad Turell.

No one begrudged Jamie his success, or his ability to profit from his sweat-equity in the WB, but his continued opposition to the offers for TheWB.com left the rest of us feeling as if we were missing out on the gold rush. His heavy reliance on the WB brand for his private Acme venture smacked of hypocrisy. As he moved closer to Acme's IPO, his actions were increasingly frowned upon by executives within the network, Warner Bros., and Time Warner. None of the other Warner Bros.' division heads had an equity interest in any of the units they supervised, let alone a publicly traded side business intertwined with Warner Bros.' assets.

Eventually the tension built to a head. A small group of us who were closest to Jamie eventually asked for a meeting with him in the conference room that separated my office from his. It was right before the start of the fall 1999 season, which is a hectic time under the best of circumstances, and right before Acme's September 30 IPO date. We told him we thought the situation was unjust, and that in our view we should be granted at least a small ownership position in Acme and TheWB.com. Jamie didn't like what he was hearing one bit. The tone of his voice was angry and bitter. He felt we were being ungrateful after he'd given us all the chance to grow and shine and have the invaluable experience of working with him on a start-up network.

Confronting him was one of the hardest things we ever had to do, because we all respected and admired Jamie enormously. He was a father figure, no question, and we treasured our chance to help him build the network from scratch. But we had a hard time reconciling his stance on TheWB.com and Acme with the sentiment he'd shared with us about his desire to avoid the Fox syndrome at his network. Hadn't Jamie felt undervalued by Rupert Murdoch and Barry Diller during his years at Fox? Wasn't he going to right some of those wrongs by fostering a true team atmosphere at the WB? Or was the WB simply his vehicle for making the fortune he missed out on at Fox? Those were questions we felt entitled to ask after five years of killing ourselves for the WB. Frankly, it was maddening to think that Jamie's partners in Acme stood to make more off of the WB than we did.

Most of us had families to support, mortgages to pay, school tuition fees to cover, and all kinds of other obligations. And we knew from comparisons with friends and colleagues at other networks and studios that the WB's pay scale was low. Yet other than Garth decamping to NBC, the core team that created the network out of whole cloth in the summer and fall of 1994 was still intact. We loved the WB. We felt just as much pressure to guard its future as its founder did. A handful of us had fractional ownership stakes in the network that had been granted by Jamie. But those stakes were illiquid until somebody, i.e., Warner Bros., was prepared to buy them out. That day wasn't all that far off, but we didn't know that at the time of the furor surrounding the Acme IPO.

I feared Jamie would take the conference-room confrontation

personally, and from the second we all started talking I could tell he did. He did a slow burn that was actually not so slow, and the meeting was over. Later that day, Jamie called me into his office and erupted. It was so out of character for him. He never lost his cool in front of us. I was reduced to tears pretty quickly, which only made me more upset. I like to think of myself as a professional. I'll cry at a good movie, or a good script. I'll cry at a sappy McDonald's commercial at home if I'm in the right mood. But not on the job. Real executives don't cry at work. That day, however, I couldn't stop myself.

"Susanne, how could you do this to me?" he yelled. "You've all turned on me. Why would you try to undermine me like this? You've all had a good experience here. . . ."

As upset as I was, I could see that he was genuinely hurt too. Jamie thought I was instigating a revolt against him in the office. I was totally exasperated because it was simply not true. He accused me of being the "ringleader" in a plot to turn the staff against him.

It was true that co-workers would come into my office for impromptu meetings on work-related matters, and during that time we would often wind up talking about Acme or TheWB.com. In those days, it seemed that every time we turned around, there was another headline about the roaring stock market (though you wouldn't know it from Time Warner's share price) and big media mergers and acquisitions. We couldn't help but notice what was going on in the world around us, and there was resentment that we weren't reaping anything from the gold rush when TheWB.com option seemed so ideal. Still, at no time did I ever plan a meeting of the division heads to strategize on ways to undermine Jamie. I knew what a vital leadership role he played at the WB.

It was also true that I and the other division heads at the network felt it was patently unfair that Jamie had been able to start Acme, yet we couldn't do anything with TheWB.com. We'd made plenty of contributions to what everyone at Warner Bros. and Time Warner was talking about as "a $1 billion asset." I left Jamie's office that afternoon thinking that it might be time for me to move on. Nothing was worth this stress and anxiety, I thought. Right around this time, we'd also gotten the news that Bob Daly and Terry Semel were stepping down as the heads of Warner Bros. after nearly a 20-year run together. I was thinking of passages and new chapters and what I wanted to do in my life and in my career. It was the low point of my seven years with the network.

Jamie was chilly toward me for a while but not in an overtly punishing way. I was so rattled by the whole thing that I cut off all discussion that came up about Acme or TheWB.com. People at the network knew not to even use the words in my presence. And although Jamie eventually came to realize that there was no conspiracy against him, there remained a ton of frustration.

In the end, Jamie took steps to allow a number of WB insiders to participate in the Acme IPO at preferential pricing. But as Acme prepared for its debut on the NASDAQ index, Warner Bros.' corporate officers got wind of the plan to allow WB executives into the IPO. John Schulman, the studio's long-serving, highly regarded, no-nonsense executive vice president and general counsel, was by many accounts aghast at the notion of Kellner picking favorites among his staff to allow into the IPO on preferential terms. Schulman's office pushed back so hard on employee participation in the IPO that it created a new wave of us-against-them angst among the WB's senior managers toward the studio. The situation was sorted out with a compromise that allowed Warner Bros.' counsel to review and prune a list of employees suggested by Jamie.

Acme wound up with a respectable debut at $33 a share, but with it the misery index at the WB went considerably higher.* Things were never quite the same after this period. We had to wonder, at times, whether Jamie was focused on the WB's success or on securing a big payout for his stake after he got the network over the hump to the break-even point.

----

*   Acme's stock price climbed as high as $36–$37 per share early on but it didn't stay there. Acme fell below $10 per share by the first anniversary of its IPO and has rarely climbed back into double-digit price territory since then. In 2005 and 2006 the stock hovered around $3–$4.

• • •

After being in the shadow of the WB for nearly three years, UPN finally claimed some of the spotlight on August 26, 1999, when World Wrestling Federation bouts began their Thursday-night residency on the network. The WWF essentially rented UPN's Thursday night 8–10 p.m. network lineup for 52 weeks a year, filling the time with fresh WWF bouts—no repeats, no pre-emptions. The WWF controlled all the advertising sales and kept the proceeds. WWF chief executive Linda McMahon extracted such favorable deal terms because she realized that UPN needed the WWF as much as the WWF needed a network.

Landing the WWF was likely the move that saved Dean Valentine's job in 1999, UPN veterans concur. It spared the network the indignity of having to cut back a night; in fact the network finished ahead a few million dollars on Thursday, compared to the red ink generated on its other four nights. Giving over two hours of prime time a week to the WWF saved UPN the $30 million to $40 million it would have spent on license fees alone for comedy or drama series to fill those slots. UPN's initial deal with the WWF called for the network to earn a fixed percentage of *SmackDown!*'s net advertising revenues (minus the $300,000 production cost of the show), or a minimum, eight-figure guarantee of around $20 million per year, whichever was higher.

The move to the broadcast TV big leagues was like putting the WWF on steroids. The company saw its advertising revenue from TV programs alone spike from $30 million in 1999 to nearly $78 million in 2000, the first full year of the UPN contract. The figure rose to $90 million the following year. (Not surprisingly, the WWF had its highly successful IPO in October 1999.) While UPN didn't control the ad revenue, it did get to claim the ratings delivered by *WWF Smack-Down!* on the toughest night of the week to program. *SmackDown!* quickly became the highest-rated program on the network, week in and week out. The boost to UPN's overall average ratings helped the network do a little better in its advertising rates for other shows.

SmackDown! also gave UPN a base from which to promote the rest of its lineup, which had veered into WWF-friendly sophomoric territory with inane comedies like *Shasta McNasty* and the self-conscious parody of spy dramas, *Secret Agent Man*. Most important, for many at UPN, the success of wrestling gave them something they could use to jab back at the WB at a time when the frog net seemed to have the teen-Midas touch.

Unfortunately for UPN, the network's moment of chest beating lasted all of two weeks. On September 7, 1999, the Tuesday after Labor Day, the network's future was thrown into serious doubt once again when Sumner Redstone's Viacom confirmed to Wall Street and the world that it had struck a nearly $40 billion deal to buy Mel Karmazin's CBS Inc. The acquisition would add one of the Big Three networks to Viacom's arsenal of MTV, Nickelodeon, VH1, Comedy Central, the Showtime pay-cable-channel, Paramount Pictures, Blockbuster Entertainment, and other entertainment assets.

The catalyst for the Viacom-CBS deal lay in a vote held a month earlier by the Federal Communications Commission to loosen decades-old television and radio station ownership restrictions. Since the dawn of commercial broadcasting in the 1940s, the FCC had barred a single individual or business entity from owning more than one television station in a TV market and more than one of the Big Three networks in the interest of maintaining diversity on the public airwaves. The major networks and other Big Media concerns lobbied hard for years to do away with the so-called "duopoly rule" as it applied to stations. They finally succeeded in the laissez-faire atmosphere for telecommunications policy in Clinton-era Washington. (It didn't hurt that Big Media and Telecom companies were spreading tens of millions of dollars in campaign cash around Washington in those years.)

What had been an outright ban on owning more than one station in a market was revised to allow for multiple station ownership in certain larger markets so long as two conditions were met. There had to be a minimum of eight other TV stations left in the market after the combination, and the combination could not involve more than one of the top four stations in the market, as judged by ratings and revenue.

Before the dual-ownership ban was lifted, Viacom would have had a much tougher time melding the station holdings of CBS with the Paramount Stations Group. The combined company would have had to sell off stations in multiple markets where CBS and Paramount both owned a station. With the duopoly rule change, however, the combined Viacom-CBS would likely have to sell only a handful of smaller-market TV and radio stations to win the FCC's blessing of the merger.

Most of the staffers at UPN and the town at large considered the deal in more simplistic terms that Tuesday morning as they absorbed the news. If Viacom was about to get its hands on a real network, why would Sumner Redstone need UPN?

"It was completely demoralizing," said a senior UPN executive. "We could tell Dean [Valentine] didn't know what was going on. We thought it was over."

By then, UPN executives were accustomed to having any glimmer of good news quickly trampled by unforeseen bad developments.

"It was uncanny. There was never any sustained sunshine in the operation," said another former senior executive from the Valentine era. "Any time we'd have some moment of success, a bigger black cloud would open up somewhere."

Sumner Redstone and then-CBS Inc. chief executive Mel Karmazin said they wanted to keep the network operating, but they had to acknowledge in the same breath that the FCC would have the final say in light of its existing dual-network ownership ban. The conventional wisdom was that a rule that predated by decades the emergence of the WB and UPN, and Fox for that matter, would not apply to a prospective combination of ABC, CBS, and NBC and an "emerging" network, a term the commission had coined in the 1980s to characterize Fox in its infancy.

In discussing the merger plans with reporters and Wall Street analysts in the days and weeks after the deal came together quickly during the Labor Day holiday weekend, Redstone and Karmazin said that they planned a full-court press in Washington with lawmakers and regulatory agencies, and that they would lobby the UPN point hard. Karmazin was characteristically blunt about the situation: either Viacom gets to keep its half-interest in UPN, or it shuts down. There were no likely suitors on the horizon for the money-losing venture. However, Robert Johnson, the billionaire founder of Black Entertainment Television, made a point of telling reporters that he'd invest in UPN if, in exchange, he could secure the right to run repeats of some of its shows on his BET cable channel.

UPN staffers were skeptical about getting lip-service from Sumner Redstone and Mel Karmazin regarding UPN while the merger approvals were pending. They knew Viacom would jettison its half of UPN in an instant if it became a sticking point in winning regulatory blessing for the CBS merger agreement.

In addition to worrying about Viacom's true post-merger intentions toward UPN, there was the added drama of how Chris-Craft was going to react to the Viacom-CBS union. For those who had even a little understanding of the dynamic between the UPN partners, there was no reason to wonder. There were no congratulatory notes from Herb Siegel to Sumner Redstone that day. The only notes Chris-Craft executives were writing were to their lawyers.

"Chris-Craft went berserk," said Valentine.

Relations between Paramount and Chris-Craft had already deteriorated to a state of virtual noncommunication. Once the Viacom-CBS merger was announced, there was officially no communication between the UPN partners because both sides were well aware that Chris-Craft was considering mounting a legal challenge to the merger.

"It was just a continuation of the paralysis of the network. They used the network like dysfunctional parents use children as a hostage in their dealings with each other," Valentine says. "It was a mess. And the messier it got, the more determined I was that I wanted to walk out standing."

In the view of Chris-Craft executives, Viacom's stealth deal with

CBS confirmed their worst suspicions about what they saw as Viacom's duplicitous motive for maintaining UPN. From Chris-Craft's perspective, Viacom wanted to keep UPN afloat to help Paramount Television clean up its financial messes from bad bets on bad shows that could be burned off by programming them on UPN, accusations that Viacom's Jonathan Dolgen and Paramount's Kerry McCluggage consistently and strenuously denied. But all Chris-Craft executives could see was red—the red tide of $800 million-plus in losses the network had piled up since its January 1995 launch.

Instead of the expected headlines about Chris-Craft filing a lawsuit against Viacom, word surfaced in October in the business press that Viacom, Rupert Murdoch's News Corp., and possibly other media giants were eyeing a buyout of Chris-Craft's stations. Chris-Craft had let it be known through their bankers and Wall Street advisors that they would entertain offers for their stations, and in fact CBS had been in discussions with Chris-Craft about a buyout of the stations even before CBS's merger talks with Viacom came together. Even with the ill will between Chris-Craft and Viacom, Sumner Redstone's media conglomerate was the most logical buyer for those stations. Chris-Craft's managers had an obligation to negotiate in reasonably good faith or face legal action from outside shareholders.

CBS's then-chief executive Mel Karmazin handled the talks with Chris-Craft on behalf of Viacom-CBS, as those two companies awaited regulatory approvals of their megamerger. Karmazin didn't have a tortured history with Chris-Craft as Viacom and Paramount executives did. But Karmazin has never been accused of being a diplomat, and he is not known to be willing to overpay to seal a deal.

Thickening the plot, Tribune Company was also quietly in discussions with Chris-Craft on a station buyout deal that would have altered the course of history for both the WB and UPN had it come to fruition. But for all of the suitors, price was the impediment to getting to the finish line with Herbert Siegel.

Siegel wanted at least $3.5 billion for the stations, or $95 to $100 a share, while Viacom-CBS's offer for Chris-Craft was in the range of $80 to $85 per share. News Corp. didn't make much headway with Chris-Craft that fall and winter either. Rupert Murdoch, who had a long history of tangling with Siegel, went on record in November 1999 as saying News Corp. wouldn't bid for Chris-Craft "unless something changes dramatically." At the time, News Corp. was disadvantaged by the weak stock price for its Fox Entertainment Group subsidiary, which had been spun off the year before in an effort to achieve higher valuation on Wall Street for Fox's entertainment businesses. The slumping Fox shares made it more costly for Murdoch to use them as currency in a deal for Chris-Craft. As Fox Entertainment Group's share price improved during the ensuing nine months, News Corp.'s evaluation of the deal that Siegel sought would change—dramatically.

In September 1999, the WB announced a new five-year affiliation agreement with its station partner, Tribune Broadcasting, that included a provision for Tribune to absorb a greater share of the network's losses than it had in the past.

At that point, the WB had grown strong enough to command such favorable terms. The network was on its way to recording its first-ever profitable quarter at the close of 1999, a $3 million operating profit in the fourth quarter that meant for the first time we took in more than we laid out in overhead, expenses, programming rights, marketing and advertising, satellite time, and such. It was a sweet feeling for WB staffers when the fourth-quarter numbers were tallied a few months later, and Time Warner management bragged about the WB's first precious black ink, though our full-year losses for 1999 still ran a sobering $92 million.

The WB's heat in prime time fueled the network's rise, but it would never have made it over the hump to that first profit without a $100 million assist from the Japanese animation import Pokemon. The cartoon series about a troupe of catlike characters had sparked a national craze with kids in Japan, and it did wonders for our Kids' WB! weekday and Saturday morning programming block. The show had been a savvy pickup spearheaded by Jed Petrick, who was introduced to the Pokemon phenomenon by an independent children's program distributor.

With the wind at our back, even on Saturday mornings, Jamie made a bold prediction in the press release announcing the Tribune affiliation deal: the WB would hit the break-even ceiling by the end of the following season.

CHAPTER EIGHT

SUPERMAN AND SUPER DEALS

There was no contest in the WB-versus-UPN fight as the two networks approached their fifth on-air anniversaries and the calendar made its momentous turn in January 2000. While UPN twisted and turned as it awaited decisions on its post-merger fate, the WB was caught up in what was ballyhooed as the biggest and boldest media merger yet. It came just ten days into the New Year.

Time Warner would never be the same after January 10, 2000, when the company unveiled its all-stock buyout agreement with America Online. The world's largest old-media concern was about to be acquired by the highest-flying new media player in the New Economy marketplace. On the day the Time Warner-AOL deal was announced, the stock-swap was valued at $160 billion.

There had been rumblings for months on Wall Street and in Hollywood that one of the stock-rich Internet giants à la AOL, Amazon, or Yahoo! was preparing to make a bold run at one of the big brick-and-mortar media companies. Still, when it came, it was a shock to the media elite's system that the publishing house Henry Luce had built and the celluloid empire that Jack L. Warner and his brothers amassed would be owned by a dot-com, the biggest of the dot-coms with a market cap greater than that of General Motors.

Warner Bros.' Barry Meyer got a call at home the day before the big announcement from Time Warner president Dick Parsons, who gave him the news that the company had "done a transaction." Meyer guessed that Time Warner was buying NBC. The rumors about such a transaction had never ceased.

"No, three other letters," Parsons told Meyer. "A-O-L."

Jamie Kellner also called a few of his top lieutenants to prepare us for some big news. Something "really good" for all of us is going to happen, he told me, cryptically.

Kellner was excited by the potential for the union of new and old media. He felt AOL Chairman and CEO Steve Case and President Bob Pittman were like-minded entrepreneurs who would do great things with Time Warner's considerable assets. As it happened, Kellner and Pittman had known each other for many years. They'd moved in the same media-business circles, and Pittman had produced a show for Fox Broadcasting during Jamie's tenure. Meyer was won over by Time Warner Chairman Gerald Levin's enthusiasm for the merger and the fact that the company's competitors, particularly the Walt Disney Company, immediately began to put up a fight in Washington and elsewhere to block the deal or at least wring concessions out of Time Warner and AOL.

During the 12 months that it took to complete the transaction and secure regulatory approvals, Case, Levin, and Pittman did plenty of evangelizing to Wall Street, K Street, and Main Street about the benefits of the merger. Levin, who once described Time Warner's 1996 union with the Turner Broadcasting System as "manifest destiny," spoke in breathless terms about the arrival of the "Internet century." Those blue-sky pronouncements would haunt Levin, Case, and Pittman in time months after the merger was completed in January 2001.

Almost since the beginning of Valentine's tenure at UPN, there had been tension between the CEO and entertainment President Tom Nunan. Much of the uneasiness between the two stemmed from Valentine's interest in Nunan's job; all too often, Valentine seemed to prefer steering program development to his managerial role at the network. It put a strain on their relationship, especially when the two didn't see eye to eye on shows.

Nunan had worked hard to bring some prestige value to the UPN with the gritty, shaky-camera cop show *The Beat*. It was produced by Oscar-winning director Barry Levinson and Tom Fontana, who were behind the much-lauded NBC drama *Homicide: Life on the Street,* which Nunan had worked on during his time at NBC Studios. The principal cast of *The Beat* included budding movie star Mark Ruffalo and *CSI: Crime Scene Investigation* trouper Jorja Fox. It was unconventional, to say the least, and it was by no means a slam-dunk with critics, or with Valentine. UPN had made a sizable production commitment to the show, 13-episodes upfront, which was an extreme rarity for the network. *Beat* wound up with a far shorter episode run between March and May 2000.

To UPN insiders, the tug of war over *The Beat* epitomized the tension between Nunan and Valentine, who allowed Nunan to proceed with the show but wasn't shy about telling people how much he disliked it. It was more evidence that Valentine had been miscast in the role of CEO. What he really coveted was Nunan's job as head of programming.

"One of the difficulties when you become CEO is, you wind up in this really odd situation where you're not really allowed to be the guy who's in there scrunching up the script," Valentine concedes. "I had to delegate the things that I most enjoyed doing to somebody else. And that, for me, was just insanely painful and difficult."

Nunan's frustration mounted as he watched projects that he'd championed for UPN get away and become successes for other networks. One of his toughest losses involved a quirky comedy about a 13-year-old genius and his eccentric family that he bought from seasoned comedy writer Linwood Boomer. When it came time for Valentine and Nunan to make UPN's limited pilot pickup decisions in 1999, Nunan was still high on the Boomer script. Valentine did not share his enthusiasm. After UPN passed on shooting it as a pilot, the project quickly made its way to Fox, and there the show, by then called *Malcolm in the Middle,* became an instant commercial and creative success after its January 2000 premiere.

Another show that started at UPN only to be rejected and resurrected as a success for another network was *The Dead Zone,* based on the Stephen King novel, which migrated to USA Network. Again,

Nunan had had a hard time getting interest in a show from Valentine and again that show went on to greener pastures somewhere else.

Nunan was also drawn to some of the unscripted program pitches that were spurred around this time by ABC's success with its adaptation of the British quiz show *Who Wants to Be a Millionaire*. Nunan was a fan of the offbeat endurance race program *Eco-Challenge*, which aired annually as a multinight "event" on cable's Discovery Channel (it later moved to USA Network). The program challenged a group of hearty contestants to compete in an "expedition competition" in an exotic locale. The modes of racing in *Eco-Challenge* ranged from kayaking to horseback riding to mountain climbing. It made for great television, Nunan thought. He wanted to know how it was produced.

Nunan set up a meeting with the British producer, Mark Burnett, who was the *Eco-Challenge* mastermind. Burnett came in to pitch a new series concept to Nunan, dreamed up by another British producer friend of his, Charlie Parsons, for an unscripted show about a group of strangers dropped off in some remote spot and challenged to survive mostly on wits alone in the hopes of winning a $1 million prize. Burnett had been back and forth with ABC on a U.S. version of the project, but it clearly wasn't getting off the ground at that network.

Nunan kept trying to steer the conversation back to how Burnett managed to get all of that wild action footage seen on *Eco-Challenge*. Gradually, however, Burnett's vision for *Survivor* began to sink in. When Burnett described the show's hook—having the group members hold a "tribal council" vote at the end of each episode in order to eliminate one of the "castaways," Nunan was sold.

"You could feel the heavens part at that point," Nunan recalls. "You could just feel all of the psychological possibilities to the drama—taking people out of their comfort zones, the taboo thrill of a group getting to openly reject one of their own. It was such a simple, straightforward concept."

Survivor piqued Valentine's interest enough to allow Nunan to pursue it, but he didn't get far. UPN had the money to float only six episodes of the castaway show. Burnett, who would also take his *Survivor* pitch to us at the WB and every other network, was firm on getting a deal for 13 guaranteed episodes. Valentine begged Bill Siegel and others on the UPN operating committee for the additional $6 million or so. But it was a nonstarter with the operating committee that was still governing UPN. Operating committee members couldn't see the value in spending that kind of money on a summer flier. Valentine argued that summer was exactly the time that UPN should be trying something, anything to gain some traction while the competition was lighter against summer repeats on the Big Four nets.

By the time *Survivor* became a national sensation for CBS in the summer of 2000, Nunan felt as if his heart had been ripped out, stomped on, and shoved back in.

"I finally said to Dean, 'I don't want to do this anymore.' And I had a feeling that they didn't really want me doing it anymore anyway," Nunan says.

In mid-January 2000, the industry gathered in New Orleans for the annual NATPE programming convention, and rumors picked up that a buyout from Viacom to Chris-Craft was imminent. It was presumed that if Chris-Craft was selling the stations, Viacom would also take over UPN entirely because Chris-Craft would have no interest in holding onto its stake in the money-losing network if it no longer owned the stations. But no deal was announced that week, or even that month. In early February, Viacom pulled a stealth maneuver on Chris-Craft that hastened the end of the tortured UPN partnership. It was a final jab, or so Sumner Redstone and his lieutenants thought.

In an effort to kick-start the stalled station talks, Viacom on February 2, 2000 notified Chris-Craft that it had triggered the so-called buy/sell provision in the UPN operating agreement. The provision allowed either partner to name a price for the other's 50 percent interest in the network, after which Chris-Craft would have 45 days to either buy out Viacom's share at that price or sell its stake in the network to Viacom. The news was hand-delivered via formal letters from Viacom to Chris-Craft on that Wednesday morning. It was the corporate M&A version of a drive-by shooting. Viacom's price? A nominal $5 million, a fraction of the $800 million-plus the partners had sunk into the network since 1994.

"They never thought we'd exercise the buy-sell. Never saw it coming," a former senior Viacom executive says.

Chris-Craft filed a lawsuit against Viacom in New York Supreme Court five days later. Chris-Craft contended that Viacom's deal to buy CBS violated a clause in the UPN partnership agreement, clinched when Viacom paid its $160 million for 50 percent of UPN in late 1996. The clause barred the partners from launching or acquiring a competing broadcast network venture for five years, through January 15, 2001. Viacom countered that it had not breached the UPN contract because the acquisition of CBS Inc. had not been completed or approved by federal regulators. Plus, Viacom argued, the triggering of the buy/sell provision rendered Chris-Craft's complaint moot.*

Chris-Craft asked the judge assigned to its lawsuit to put a hold on the completion of the Viacom-CBS merger while the lawsuit was pending. After a brief hearing, New York Supreme Court Judge Herman Cahn issued his decision nearly three weeks later to throw out Chris-Craft's suit. Judge Cahn ordered the company to comply with the terms of the buy-sell provision Viacom had triggered.

With the 45-day window on the buy/sell provision coming to a close, Chris-Craft was backed into a tight corner. The company made a last-ditch effort to line up new partners to allow them to buy out Viacom's stake in UPN instead. Chris-Craft approached Barry Diller's USA Networks Inc. and Sony Corp., but no one was eager to jump into UPN as quickly as Chris-Craft demanded.

On March 20, Chris-Craft washed its hands of nearly seven years of toil and trouble in prime time. Viacom cut Chris-Craft a $5 million check, and Chris-Craft's tumultuous foray into network television

----

* _Daily Variety,_ February 4, 2000, "Viacom Wants All or Nothing of UPN."

came to an end on that Monday afternoon with a short, tame statement from company Chairman Herb Siegel.

"We believe that UPN and our shareholders will now best be served by ending any further uncertainty through our sale to Viacom," Siegel said. "We want to see UPN continue its recent ratings surge in the upcoming fall season and look forward to continuing our support of the network as its anchor affiliate group." *

Top Viacom and Paramount TV executives rejoiced at the news. The studio had finally cut its ties to the partner it blamed for stunting the network's growth during its formative years. Inside UPN, however, the takeover by Viacom didn't play nearly as well. The betting on the patios at UPN's West Los Angeles offices was that the network would fold once the Viacom-CBS merger was completed. Why would Viacom need a second network if it owned CBS? The WB's rapid growth during the previous two years only made UPN's performance look worse, the WWF notwithstanding.

Once Chris-Craft cashed Viacom's $5 million check, the infighting that had been so crippling gave way to a kind of operational stasis. UPN was now totally dependent on Viacom for its funding, and the Viacom executive suite had a new bottom-line oriented sheriff in the person of Mel Karmazin, who became Viacom's president and chief operating officer, the No. 2 to Sumner Redstone.

"UPN will become profitable, or it won't exist," Karmazin said in June 2000 at an investor conference in London.†

In the face of these changes, Kerry McCluggage championed a plan in the summer of 2000 for a marketing-catharsis initiative to help redefine the network's public image. The network would relaunch on January 1, 2001, as the Paramount Network—the moniker McCluggage had envisioned way back when. It made sense, in theory. The "U" in United Paramount Network was now history; Paramount was the 100 percent owner, plus rumors were heating up once again about Viacom coming to terms—through gritted teeth—on a deal to

---

*   *Daily Variety*, March 21, 2000.

†   *The Hollywood Reporter*, June 9, 2000.

buy the Chris-Craft station group. Plus, the name change would generate a fair amount of free media attention for the network.

But it was not to be. UPN's name might as well have been J-O-B, in the Biblical sense. Valentine unveiled the plan for the name change in July 2000 at the end of a fairly smooth (by UPN standards) Q&A session with reporters during UPN's portion of the Television Critics Association press junket. A new network logo and graphic featuring Paramount's familiar snow-capped mountain ringed with stars was distributed to the media. As predicted, the news generated a small flurry of stories about UPN looking for a "clean slate." Less than a month later, however, the plan for the name change was permanently derailed by a $5 billion parting shot from Chris-Craft against its former partner in UPN.

Despite Paramount's $5 million buyout of Chris-Craft's stake in UPN, there was still the issue of Chris-Craft's station holdings that needed to be resolved. After a lengthy period of on-again, off-again talks, in the dog days of August Viacom and Chris-Craft inched toward an agreement on a deal for Chris-Craft's 10 television stations.

By the accounts of multiple insiders, Viacom's Mel Karmazin finally reached the handshake point with the Chris-Craft team on Thursday, August 10. Preparations began for a press conference in New York to announce the deal as word spread on Wall Street.

At the eleventh hour, facilitated by communiqués through lawyers and bankers, News Corp. swooped in with an offer of $85 a share, which valued Chris-Craft at $5.3 billion, including the assumption of debt. In response to this new development, on Friday, August 11, a terse statement issued that morning by Viacom raised eyebrows by saying Viacom was no longer in talks with Chris-Craft on "any acquisition." Chris-Craft's stock had been spiking on rumors of an impending deal. After the Viacom statement hit the wires, Chris-Craft shares plunged $8.*

About five hours later, Chris-Craft countered with its own cryptic statement advising that it was in talks with another major media

---

*   *New York Times*, August 12, 2000.

company. It didn't take long for word to leak out, courtesy of the *Wall Street Journal*'s Web site, that the mystery suitor was Rupert Murdoch, despite his having professed to not being interested, at that price, just a few months earlier. Since Murdoch's original statement of disinterest, News Corp.'s stock price had rebounded, and now News Corp. could afford to pay more for the deal, which was sweeter for all the cash Chris-Craft was sitting on.

Kerry McCluggage had been on the phone with Sumner Redstone on and off for two days as the talks unfolded in New York. He couldn't believe the latest misfortune to befall UPN. He could not convince Redstone to engage in a bidding skirmish with News Corp.

"Who knows whether we would have won or not," McCluggage says. "To me, there was very little down side in participating in that bidding process because [the stations] clearly justified paying a higher price. Worst-case scenario, you make Fox pay a higher price. But Sumner just didn't want to engage Rupert in a bidding war."

After a dizzying 72 hours, this much was clear to all of those with a stake in UPN: the network's two most important affiliate stations, WWOR-TV in New York and KCOP-TV in Los Angeles, were now in the hands of Rupert Murdoch and his Fox empire.

The haplessness of UPN's situation was made clear shortly after News Corp. struck its deal to buy the Chris-Craft stations. Unsolicited, Fox Broadcasting's programming department sent over to UPN a small crate of "busted" shows—videotape dubs of pilots and specials produced by Fox's alternative programming department that were never going to make it on Fox. The crate was sent over for UPN's perusal in the hopes that Fox's new business partner would take some of them off their hands.

In a show of good faith to their new important affiliate station owner, UPN did buy a handful of the specials at hand-me-down prices. In Nunan's view, the crate full of two dozen-odd videotapes just rubbed in how little UPN had to work with.

"That one crate of tapes was so symbolic of the difference between us and them," Nunan says "We can't afford not to program everything we make, and they have the luxury of a whole box of re-jects."

Though the slew of industry-realigning ac-quisitions and mergers dominated the headlines and lunch conversations of nearly everyone in Hollywood, we couldn't let it distract us from our primary job of finding quality programming for the WB. Early in the summer, I ran into Peter Roth at the Warner Bros.' commissary. As always, Peter was buoyant and excited about the next big thing his staff was cooking up for us. He took his time telling me how they were developing the perfect property for the network and its *Buffy the Vampire Slayer* action-fantasy-loving demographic.

"So what is it?!" I said, curious. I felt totally comfortable with Peter. I didn't have to make any pretense toward niceties. My lunch was getting cold while he launched into his pitch.

"Superman . . . young Superman," Roth said. "It's Clark Kent in high school in his hometown of Smallville, just as he's realizing he has superpowers. Don't you think it's perfect?"

"Superman!" I replied incredulously. "*Super*-man! Don't you think Superman is over, Peter? Really? Can Superman possibly be hip again?"

Within a few weeks, I was eating my words.

Indeed, *Smallville* came to life in the summer of 2000 through a series of happy accidents. The show might never have happened if the Warner Bros.' film division hadn't been so protective of its Batman movie franchise.

Shortly after Peter Roth joined Warner Bros. in early 1999, he got a call from Mike Tollin and Brian Robbins, a pair of prominent television producers who had an exclusive, and lucrative, contract with the studio. The duo rang to ask Roth for help in persuading his counterparts on the feature film side to ease their grip on the rights to Batman so that they could develop a TV series based on the caped crusader. The film division was the gatekeeper of the character, which

Warner Bros. controlled through its ownership of DC Comics. Batman became an important movie franchise for the studio starting in 1989 with director Tim Burton's *Batman*, starring Michael Keaton.

Ten years later, Batman's star had cooled considerably, as evidenced by the ho-hum box office performance and critical drubbing that greeted 1997's *Batman & Robin*, featuring George Clooney behind the mask. Tollin and Robbins wanted to do a TV series focusing on the formative years of the Bruce Wayne character as he came to realize his gifts and obligations as a protector of the innocent. As Roth spoke on the phone with the producers, he realized in an instant that here was a succinct, instantly marketable, genius idea that was perfect for the WB demo.

Tollin and Robbins had made their names as highly efficient producers, writers, and directors of live-action programs for Nickelodeon (the sketch comedy *All That,* buddy comedy *Kenan and Kel*) and modestly budgeted movies (*Good Burger* in 1997, *Varsity Blues* in 1999) that connected with younger audiences. They had the right sensibilities to freshen up a dormant but still valuable character franchise for Warner Bros.

The film studio, nonetheless, was protective of its Batman properties. Executives there feared that a contemporary Batman TV series—even one far removed from the campy humor of the 1960s ABC series that starred Adam West and Burt Ward—would dilute the event nature of future Batman movies. After a while, Tollin and Robbins were ready to move on to other pursuits, but not Roth. The hunt for Batman reminded him of how much he loved superheroes, and how he could count on one hand the number of fantasy-action vehicles on the major broadcast networks at the time—one of them was *Buffy the Vampire Slayer.*

Undaunted, Roth set his sights on a revival of another iconic character in the DC Comics stable: Superman. Roth loved the Man of Steel. He had tried to develop a cartoon series around the Superboy character when he worked in children's programming at ABC in the 1970s. Tollin and Robbins also saw the promise in Superman, who at the time had an even lower profile than Batman at the studio. Warner Bros. had been stymied for years in trying to find suitable successors to the string of mostly successful Superman films that starred Christopher Reeve in the late 1970s and 80s. The Man of Steel's most recent reappearance since then had been as a romantic-comedy hunk from 1993 to 1997 in ABC's moderately successful *Lois & Clark: The New Adventures of Superman,* featuring Dean Cain as Clark Kent and future *Desperate Housewives* star Teri Hatcher as Lois Lane.

Tollin and Robbins adapted the same conceptual framework they'd had for the young Bruce Wayne story line to the adventures of young Clark Kent. The first order of business, even before finding their star, was to recruit the perfect writer to flesh out their vision. Tollin and Robbins settled on the highly regarded writing team of Miles Millar and Alfred Gough, who were known at the time for their movie credits, including *Lethal Weapon 4* and Jackie Chan's *Shanghai Noon.* Millar and Gough had delved into prime time during the 1999–2000 season with a short-lived action drama, *The Strip,* set in Las Vegas among casino security guards. The show happened to be produced by Warner Bros. Television for, of all networks, UPN.

Millar and Gough proved perfect for the young Superman project. They had the comic-book sensibilities needed for the assignment, and they had the skill as writers to do justice to a beloved piece of Americana. And they were brave enough to try. If *Smallville* clicked on the WB, the film studio would have a mile-wide opening to revive its once-thriving box office goldmine. If *Smallville* fizzled, the film studio's job would be twice as hard.

Millar, Gough, Tollin, and Robbins took their time working out the kinks—the story lines, the characters, the settings, and the tone for the pilot. They steadfastly adopted a "no tights, no flights" policy, refusing to depict Clark Kent in the traditional Superman imagery flying through the air in his blue tights and red cape. *Smallville* centered on Kent's emotional development as a young man, and one with incredible responsibility to bear. Executives at the DC Comics division were angry about those decisions at first. In their view, the TV studio was graciously granted access to the original superhero, and yet it was trying to downplay all of the elements that made him, well, super.

In time, the chatter in television industry circles about the project began to grow. Tollin and Robbins were hot producers at that moment and there was curiosity about what they saw in the Superman milieu. Roth was surprised at my lackluster reaction when we first discussed the project. So he turned his focus to selling the show to Fox, where newly appointed entertainment president Gail Berman, the same woman who had helped bring *Buffy* back to life as a TV show four years earlier, had a healthy appetite for fantasy-action fare. Berman liked what she heard and made a substantial commitment to Roth on the spot to snare the *Smallville* pilot. Berman's enthusiasm was music to Roth's ears because it gave him maximum leverage in bringing the formal series pitch to the WB, or any other prospective buyer for that matter.

Although I'd briefly made my feelings known about what I thought of the prospects for a young-Superman show, I'd not heard a formal pitch from a writer. Luckily, Peter felt an obligation to allow us to hear it, now that the premise was far more developed and the studio had writers to bring it to life. On our end, we owed our studio colleagues the courtesy of taking the meeting. By this time, Carolyn Bernstein, the Columbia TriStar TV executive who'd worked on *Dawson's Creek*, had joined the WB as head of drama development. I still had low expectations as Carolyn and I sat down in WB's main conference room with Roth, Tollin, Robbins, Millar, and Gough.

As Millar and Gough launched into their pitch, Carolyn and I were blown away. I had to apologize profusely, and sheepishly, to Peter for making such a snap judgment before. The pitch was captivating; it wasn't like any rendition of Superman we'd ever seen before. Miles and Al had thought through how to play it to avoid any whiff of cheesiness, and how to slowly unravel the Clark Kent story in a way that made a coming-of-age allegory that would resonate with our audience. The show would employ some but not all of the Superman mythos, and most of what was used was tweaked perfectly for the twenty-first century. Clark's best friend was a troubled fellow teenager named Lex Luthor who was outwardly charming but black-hearted on the inside. His primary love interest was a beautiful local girl named Lana Lang, not Lois Lane, and yet another close friend was the girl reporter for the high school newspaper, Chloe Sullivan. This Clark Kent wouldn't be caught dead in horn-rim glasses.

During the meeting, Roth sat off to the side, listening patiently and quietly as we made an offer to commission a pilot at a fee that he knew was generous by the WB's usual standard. He let us gush about the show and its potential for a few minutes before he responded.

"That's great. I'm glad you like it," he said without a hint of "I told you so" in his voice. But by his tone, we knew there was some complication.

"Fox wants it too. They've offered us even more," Roth said with a sigh.

We were taken aback. *Smallville* sounded like such a WB show. We didn't want to lose our reputation as the home of cutting edge youthful dramas. And the pitch we'd just heard was bulletproof.

I quickly conferred with Jamie Kellner and recommended we match Fox's offer. Jamie sparked to it right away. So we came back to Roth with a rarefied 13-episode commitment—the highest compliment a network can pay a series concept in its germinal stage. That meant Warner Bros. Television had to make the difficult call to steer *Smallville* to the WB. All things being equal, Roth knew in his bones that *Smallville* belonged on the WB. Although the show's ratings might be higher on Fox, it would have the longest life and receive the most TLC on the WB. That's what Roth surmised. He couldn't avoid taking some heat from Fox entertainment president Gail Berman, who was steamed about the situation for months afterward.

Once the show settled at the WB, the highest priority was finding the next-generation Clark Kent. The Warner Bros.' casting department mounted a nationwide search. Our Clark had to have a lot of vulnerability. We wanted the proverbial fresh face. The young man who wound up carrying *Smallville* on his strapping shoulders was a former model from New York. On the resume pasted onto the back of his head shot, Tom Welling had only a handful of guest starring roles on CBS's drama *Judging Amy*, but it was clear to Miles and Al and us that he had the handsome, unassuming charm and macho strength of a young Christopher Reeve or Tom Selleck.

Not unlike the girls of *Savannah*, Welling was cast as much for his muscular abdomen as for his acting chops, which improved markedly during the first few seasons. But he had enough skill, even during the pilot filming, to make a credible, conflicted Clark Kent, with the aid of a strong supporting cast that included a star from an earlier TV era, John Schneider of the Warner-Bros.-produced *Dukes of Hazzard*, and Michael Rosenbaum and Kristin Kreuk as Lex Luthor and Lana Lang. As we saw the group come together in preparation for the pilot, we were confident that our 13-episode commitment would prove to be a good bet.

For the 2000–01 season launch, the WB's focus was squarely on breaking through with a half-hour comedy series at long last. And we felt we had a couple of strong horses to bet on.

Nikki was a romantic comedy about a showgirl and a pro-wrestler who are young marrieds in Vegas. The Warner Bros. Television–produced show had seasoned executive producer Bruce Helford of *The Drew Carey Show* and *Roseanne* fame, and a star who was as hot at that moment as her figure was curvy: Nikki Cox, who was known to WB viewers for her stint on one of our inaugural shows, *Unhappily Ever After*.

Grosse Point was a much hipper, show-within-a-show vehicle about the off-screen antics of a group of young actors who worked on a *Beverly Hills, 90210*-esque teen soap. It was produced by the same writer, Darren Star (of HBO's *Sex and the City* fame), who created *90210* for Aaron Spelling. Embracing *Point* was risky for the WB because it was no secret that Star and Spelling didn't like each other much anymore. In the pilot, *Grosse Point* had unflattering scenes featuring characters who were thinly veiled versions of Spelling and his daughter, *90210* trouper Tori Spelling. Aaron Spelling, of course, was the producer behind two of our biggest hits, *7th Heaven* and *Charmed*. To Jamie's credit, he never panicked or pressured me to dump *Grosse Point*, even when Spelling personally called him to complain about *Point* and its depiction of the pseudo-Tori character.

By the time we got to the early September countdown-to-launch phase, we thought *Grosse Point* was a can't-miss show. The early response from critics was strong, and we'd all fallen in love with it, which in hindsight suggested a creeping sense of jadedness among the core WB team that none of us recognized at the time. Word of Spelling's angry reaction had leaked out to the tabloids and trades, generating all kinds of free publicity for the show.

Viewers, however, were less than enthralled with a show that was probably too hip, and too inside-showbiz for its own good. *Point* was gone by February. (Conspiracy theories sprang up that Spelling's outrage made us kill the show, but trust me, it was the low ratings.) *Nikki* limped along for an additional season—it seemed to be in a constant state of creative retooling, which is always a bad sign—but it never quite found its legs.

As is often the case, the new show that we didn't give as much marketing and promotional consideration to in the fall of 2000 was the one that stuck, and then some. The hour-long dramedy *Gilmore Girls* had been an under-the-radar project for us from the start. Of all people, I should have seen its true potential and pushed harder to give it more initial support. We even saddled the show with the kiss-of-death time slot, Thursday at 8 p.m. opposite NBC's *Friends*.

Gilmore Girls was born of an afterthought at the end of a pitch meeting that I had in fall 1999 with a promising young comedy writer, Amy Sherman-Palladino. She came to the ranch with her manager and producing partner, Gavin Polone (just as his career as a film and TV producer was taking off), for a routine get-to-know-you session that was highly entertaining because Amy is just that: vivacious, hilarious, whip smart, and incredibly savvy about pop culture.

Amy grew up steeped in show business, in the San Fernando Valley, the daughter of comedian Don Sherman and actress Maybin

Hewes. Her post-high school education came when she landed a job as a staff writer on ABC's *Roseanne*. She's known for wearing wild, fancy hats with feathers, bows, and razor-sharp edges, which nicely offset her penchant for torn fishnet stockings, tight T-shirts, and other punkette-chic fashions. With Amy, it's not an affectation of hipness; it's who she is.

During our first meeting, Amy pitched Jordan Levin and me a number of succinct concepts for half-hour comedies tailored for the WB demographic. I found her sensibility very appealing—she was edgy yet sentimental. As the conversation wound down, Amy mentioned, almost as an aside, that she'd long been kicking around an idea for a show about a young mother and her teenage daughter "who are more like best friends than mother and daughter."

As much as I'd been interested in her other ideas for comedies built around strong female characters, that pithy premise was immediately intriguing.

"*That's* great," I said. Amy looked a little surprised by my swift reaction.

We talked more about how she'd been wanting to write a smart teenage girl character who wasn't a bombshell, or a mousy loner yearning for a Prince Charming to come break her out of her shell. Amy had in mind a girl with real complexity—a kid who was fiercely independent and intellectually precious but naïve in matters of the heart.

As my own thoughts raced, I made a suggestion that I might not have voiced so quickly to another writer I'd just met, but after 45 minutes, Amy made us feel as if we'd been friends for a long time.

"Why don't you write it as an hour instead of a half-hour?"

I got a quizzical look from both Amy and Gavin. Amy had never written for a drama series; her background was strictly in sitcoms. Then and now, the typecasting of writers, producers, and directors is an unfortunate byproduct of the madness of pilot season. Creative people tend to stick to what they know best because the stakes are so high and there's little margin for error.

In characteristic Amy style, her first response was: "Does this mean you don't think I'm funny?" After I laughed, she said she was game.

Later I learned that after we said our good-byes in the lobby, Amy had a "Now what do I do?" moment with Gavin as they walked to the parking lot. Not only did she not have any experience in the hour-long form, she hadn't given the show much thought beyond the one-liner that had so piqued my interest. She didn't know exactly who the mother and daughter were, where they lived, what the mom did for a living, who the daughter hung out with after school—all the little details that breathe life into a skeletal pilot concept.

Polone wisely advised her to figure it out quickly because she could blow her opportunity. It was abundantly clear that I couldn't have been more enthusiastic about Amy and her idea.

Days after that meeting, Amy and her husband, writer-producer Dan Palladino, took a trip to the New York area. They spent a few days at a country inn outside Hartford, Connecticut, and by the time they were ready to check out, Amy had her show. She'd fallen hard for the inn's bucolic setting and the homey vibe of the tiny town—the kind of place where everybody knows everybody, and the locals go behind the counter to help themselves at the diner if the waitress is busy.

Amy decided her leading lady would be a young single mother who had retreated from her stuffy rich Connecticut family after she wound up pregnant at 16. Lorelai Gilmore, as she was christened by her creator, moved to another town and got a job as a housekeeper for the local inn. As the show opens, Lorelai is 32 and has worked her way up to being the manager of the inn. And her 16-year-old daughter, Rory, was every bit as emotionally and intellectually complex as Amy had promised us in the first pitch meeting.

The pilot story found Rory getting accepted to the prestigious private school Chilton, which would assure Rory of realizing her dream to attend an Ivy League college. Lorelai is proud of her braniac daughter but in a bind to come up with the tuition money. With extreme reluctance, she has to ask her parents for some help. Lorelai's insurance-magnate father, Richard, and tightly wound mother, Emily, agree to write the check but with one caveat, at Emily's behest: Lorelai and Rory have to commit to a weekly dinner date with them so that the foursome can get to know one another. As the setup episode for a family-based TV series, it doesn't get much deeper, richer, or tighter than that.

Amy's first draft of the pilot script was beautifully written, with lively, funny characters in the vivid, colorful surroundings of the fictional Stars Hollow, Connecticut. I adored it. There was very little I could add in the way of notes or suggestions to her script as we prepared for the Toronto pilot shoot in early 2000. Amy had a very specific vision that I wanted to respect, just as we had tried to do with our other writers.

But when Amy came in during the preproduction phase for a story meeting, a process in which writers pitch network executives the broad strokes of their ideas for where a show is headed in future episodes, she mentioned plans for a big blowout argument between Lorelai and Emily during the first of the Friday night dinner dates.

As I chewed over the idea, it seemed to me it really belonged in the pilot, to reinforce the characters of Lorelai and Emily and explain why they had become so estranged, and it reinforced to Rory what a personal sacrifice it was for her mother to ask her parents for the tuition money. Amy had intended to save that scene for the first episode following the pilot, but she didn't blink when I told her why I thought it belonged in the pilot.

Amy would have famously strained relations with other WB executives, most notably Jordan, during the run of *Gilmore Girls*. I always found her to be as collaborative as she was talented. When the pilot was finished and earning raves around our trailers, she thanked me profusely for prompting her to include that pivotal dinner scene.

"The show was all in the pilot," Sherman-Palladino says. "I walked away from that pilot knowing exactly what people's strong points were, what was going to gel, and what was not going to gel. Sometimes you're not that fortunate. You don't find your whole show in the pilot. But we did, and the dinner scene is what sold it. You saw all of those [family] dynamics playing out right there. It sold the whole show."

Amy's script was so strong it attracted top talent, including Tony winner Kelly Bishop as Emily and seasoned actor Edward Herrmann as Richard. Our leads were heaven-sent. Lauren Graham had done numerous sitcoms and sitcom pilots before she found her star-making vehicle playing the fast-talking, romance-challenged Lorelai.

In fact, Graham did the *Gilmore Girls* pilot under a "second-position" contract agreement while she was still legally committed to star in an NBC comedy series, *M.Y.O.B.* That show tanked in its short midseason run in spring 2000, but as we prepared for the May 2000 upfront there was a slim chance that NBC could have picked up *M.Y.O.B* and triggered Graham's contractual obligation. All of us involved had agreed that there would not be any quickie recasting over the summer if the worst-case-scenario came to pass. Without Lauren Graham, we had no show.

Alexis Bledel was discovered through a nationwide search for fresh faces to play Rory. She was 19 years old and had done a little modeling, but she had never set foot on a film or TV set until the *Gilmore* pilot. With that choice, we went with Amy's gut. Amy liked Alexis in large part because when they first met, she gave Amy some attitude and seemed genuinely blasé about whether she got the part. That's my Rory, Amy told us.

From the pilot on, no two actors on any WB show had better chemistry than Lauren and Alexis. They were so believable as mother and daughter that it was eerie at times.

"Lauren had done a lot of sitcoms by that time, so she was hyper-skilled, especially at the physical comedy," Sherman-Palladino says. "And Alexis had no trained skills but raw talent. Somehow that combination really fed off of each other from the beginning."

The primary elements of *Gilmore Girls* had fallen into place at the network before we brought in Warner Bros. Television as the studio to bankroll the production of the pilot. As a result, the show was something of an orphan at the studio because none of the executives there had been invested in it from the get-go. It made for rocky relations at times between Amy and Warner Bros.' TV executives, especially at the beginning.

Jordan also had some doubts about the subjects and story lines Amy wanted to tackle in the first half of the first season, scripts she and her team were working on before the show premiered on October 5, 2000. But Amy was no shrinking violet. In what became an oft-repeated anecdote at the network, a few weeks before the premiere, when the calls and notes from executives became too much for her, Amy blew up.

"Don't call me anymore, OK?" Amy famously instructed a Warner Bros.' TV executive who got her on the phone at the wrong moment one afternoon. "You're not my mother. I don't want to hear how disappointed in me you are, or how upset you are. If you want to fire me—fire me. But don't call me anymore!"

In hindsight, I wish I'd done more to keep people off her back during this crucial period. Not that she really needed my help. Amy's bluntness scared her detractors off, for a little while.

In the meantime, the first batch of reviews of *Gilmore Girls* came in. The critics uniformly raved about the writing, the acting, the sweet-but-not-syrupy tone, the unique look and feel, and what a wonderfully fresh take it was on a mother-daughter relationship.

The WB was far more sensitive to the power of good reviews and strong critical buzz than our Big Four competitors. It would be a long time before Amy would have to field notes and executive carping on her show again.

The ratings for *Gilmore* were good, not great, but we recognized that the deck was stacked against the show. It had to fend for itself against *Friends*, and then about halfway through its first season, CBS plopped *Survivor* into the same Thursday 8 p.m. time slot.

With limited marketing support on our part at first, it was a testament to the critics and the strong word-of-mouth buzz that the show drew any numbers at all. *Gilmore*'s ratings inched up throughout its first season, something Jamie Kellner would seize on by the time the show was preparing for its sophomore year.

For me, being involved with the birth of *Gilmore* was an emotionally gratifying experience on many levels—as an executive, as a woman, as a mother, as a champion of female writers, and as a connoisseur of great television. Somewhere around the two-thirds mile marker of season one, I knew it was a show that was in for a long and successful run on the WB and in syndication, because good mother-daughter stories never go out of style.

CHAPTER NINE

VAMPIRES AND VERTICAL INTEGRATION

If 2000 had been an eventful year for the WB Network and its parent company, 2001 was shaping up to be even more so, with more corporate turbulence hitting the WB ranch before the end of the first quarter.

The rescue mission that Barry Meyer and Bruce Rosenblum had undertaken in flying to New York to lobby Time Warner chief Gerald Levin in person to allow the studio to retain control of the WB had been cordial but unsuccessful. As of mid-2000, the WB became part of Robert Pittman's domain. At first the shift was subtle, though that would soon change. When Pittman came to the WB offices some time after the merger announcement to make a cheerleading speech to network staffers, he also went into a private meeting with senior executives and found himself peppered with questions about the company's television strategy.

"On one hand, we felt like now with AOL owning us we would become a more important strategic piece because the company was going to lean more toward younger demographics," Jordan Levin says. "But there was also anxiety about who were the new people running the company and would they continue to invest in broadcast television."

Pittman, by many accounts, was impressed with our rags-to-riches story and with Jamie Kellner. They knew each other from Pittman's days as a producer of *Totally Hidden Video*, Fox's spin on *Candid Camera*. We could tell that Jamie's star was on the rise. There was some gossip at the ranch and on the lot that he was in line for a bigger job overseeing television for the Warner Bros.' studio as well as running the WB.

In truth, Pittman had come to Jamie with a different offer that was hard to refuse: he wanted Jamie to relocate to Atlanta and take on the task of overhauling Ted Turner's empire, which would mean putting the WB under the Turner Broadcasting System umbrella. Ever since Time Warner bought the company, TBS had operated as a sovereign nation. Ted Turner ran it as his own empire—there wasn't much mixing with the other parts of Time Warner. Pittman wanted Jamie to go down South to shake up the status quo and integrate TBS's operations better with the rest of Time Warner. Pittman saw Jamie as the kind of business thinker who could help them figure out how to marry TBS's assets in smart and profitable ways with AOL's Internet platform.

The idea of relocating his family from their home in seaside Montecito, to the southern culture of Atlanta was daunting. The younger of his two children, Christopher, was still a pre-teen. But Pittman's offer came with a big carrot: if Kellner were to take the reins at TBS, AOL Time Warner would have to buy out the 11 percent stake he and a handful of WB insiders held in the network. There was no way Kellner could run a division for a company where he had an ownership interest in one of its operating units. Even in the anything-goes dot-com era, that kind of conflict of interest wouldn't pass muster. Kellner and Co. would have to be bought out by AOL Time Warner.

For Jamie, it was a gift from on high. As much as he embodied the WB and was emotionally and financially invested in its fortunes, he was also frustrated at not having a clear exit strategy from his venture. His ownership stake in the WB was clearly valuable, but first he had to find a willing buyer. All along, he figured it would be Warner Bros.; he just didn't know when.

"I never thought Jamie wanted to be there for 10 years," says a charter WB executive. "I just don't think he had a choice."

When Pittman came along with the TBS offer, suddenly Jamie had his way out.

Jamie didn't give anyone at the WB a hint that a big change was imminent during the first two months of 2001, but he did take a few key steps in preparation for his move up the ladder. In January, he promoted advertising sales head Jed Petrick to the new post of president and chief operating officer. He would need someone with a head for business to mind the store in his absence. He also deftly defused a problem with me when I came to him with some news that he wasn't prepared for.

A few weeks into the new year, I came to grips with a very hard decision. I went to see Jamie and told him we needed to make plans for naming my successor. After nearly seven years at the WB, I decided I would not renew my contract when it expired later that year. By then, I had two toddlers at home and another on the way. I was ready for a change.

I knew without asking that my replacement would be Jordan Levin, as it should have been. He'd earned it. He'd grown as an executive, and he'd worked tirelessly on our shows. He was as devoted to the WB as anyone could be. So when I sat down to finally tell Jamie of my decision, I didn't think there'd be much of a business issue about my leaving, just the emotional tug of parting from a network I helped build and a leader whom I greatly admired. For all of the strife about Acme and the WB's dot-com fortunes (or lack thereof), I was then and always will be profoundly grateful to him for giving me a unique opportunity at a young age.

I could tell immediately by the look on Jamie's face that there was a problem. He was generous with his praise for my contributions to the network. But he also told me very quickly in his stern yet fatherly way that I could "not leave" just then. I had to stick around for at least six more months or so and not let it be known that I was planning my exit. He told me "something" was up for the WB, and that it would be good for all of us. But he wouldn't tell me what that "something" was. He warned me that it might not happen if I announced my departure just then. And he said he really needed this mysterious thing to happen, for all of us.

It was maddening not to know what he was talking about, but

after a few minutes of processing his request for a six-month reprieve, I agreed. It had taken me almost a year to get up the nerve to formally tender my resignation, and now it turned out it was going to be a loooong goodbye. In that meeting, I asked Jamie to formally name Jordan co-entertainment president alongside me. That could only ease the transition at the end of the 2000–01 season. In hindsight, sharing the title with Jordan wasn't the best move for me, because it made me feel like a lame duck in my last months on the job. But it was the right move for the network, and by then it was only fair to give Jordan the recognition he'd earned.

About five weeks later, we learned that the "something" for Jamie was the new job as chairman and CEO of Turner Broadcasting System. There were gasps in the Tuesday staff meeting when it was announced to the staff. Even as I was preparing for my own departure, it was hard for me to fathom a WB without a smiling Jamie Kellner strolling the halls in his regular uniform of khaki pants, a preppy pastel dress shirt, and penny loafers. The idea of him picking up stakes and moving to Atlanta came as a jolt. Jamie tried to reassure everyone that, even with his move to Turner, he would still be the senior executive overseeing the WB. In AOL Time Warner's divisional hierarchy, the WB Network would now become part of the Turner Broadcasting System domain and report to Jamie, who would continue to report directly to co-president Pittman. So it was business as usual, as he tried to convince the shellshocked conference room.

We were even more spooked when we found out public relations head Brad Turell was going with him to Atlanta. Similarly, we were caught off guard when our research guru Jack Wakschlag, who read Nielsen numbers like tea leaves, had also been recruited to move to Turner. Then, lo and behold, Garth Ancier, the man Jamie swore he'd never hire again, was back in the picture. After a tough 18 months as NBC Entertainment president, Garth had been replaced, unceremoniously, by Jeff Zucker, the wunderkind producer of NBC's hugely profitable *Today* program, in December 2000. Not three months later, Ancier was on a plane to Atlanta to rejoin Jamie in the familiar role of serving as his programming guru.

In preparation for AOL Time Warner buying out the stakes that Jamie and the rest of us held in the WB, the company had the network's value appraised in early 2001 by an outside investment firm. Had the evaluation come even six months later, the market downturn would undoubtedly have dampened the estimate significantly. Nevertheless, at the start of 2001, the WB, which pulled in about $700 million in advertising revenue in that period, was determined to be worth about $1.1 billion. From our humble beginnings with *The Wayans Bros.* and *Muscle* at Chasen's just seven years ago, here we were: a billion-dollar business.

AOL Time Warner agreed to pay Kellner and the eight other partners $128 million in cash for our combined 11 percent stake in the network. Kellner received the lion's share, about $100 million. Next to him, Garth Ancier had the largest slice with a 2 percent interest that came out to $20 million. The remaining partners, myself included, had fractional shares that were valuable by the standards of everyday working people, but not impressive compared to the largess handed to executives by some media and entertainment companies in the 1990s.

There was a fair amount of resentment stirred up from the handful of charter WB executives who didn't get an ownership slice. And there were still more WB staffers who were aware of all the grumbling about who got what and thought it was all a little unseemly. The team spirit that the WB had always stressed suddenly sounded more like lip service, especially considering that we were fighting over the spoils of a business that wasn't exactly rolling in profits. It was the hangover of the go-go business climate in which the WB was born, and it was the natural familiarity-breeds-contempt dynamic among a group of bright, driven, competitive people who had worked long and hard together for years.

In addition to the tension that arose from the buyout packages, some of the WB staff couldn't help but wonder who would be next to head to Atlanta. Bob Bibb and Lew Goldstein? Others were openly speculating whether the WB was over. And as much as we loved working with Peter Roth and his team, we were worried about how much the studio would continue to support us with great shows now that the WB was part of a different division. There were a lot of questions and even more anxiety. We were unsure about what was coming next from inside our own company, and with our fearless leader on his way out, things began to feel downright chaotic. We were dealing with an unusual (by WB standards) amount of on-the-job stress, plus the usual end-of-season exhaustion that hits television executives every year in March and April.

Even as Jamie prepared to step into a much higher-profile job at Turner Broadcasting, he allowed himself to get caught up in an unusually bitter, unusually public fight with 20th Century Fox Television executives as the clock ticked down on the original *Buffy the Vampire Slayer* contract in spring 2001. Stranger still for an executive of his stature, Jamie took on the voluble creator of *Buffy*, Joss Whedon. In the annals of PR wars, no network television executive has ever won a fight with an aggrieved producer, at least in the court of public opinion. It was a rare yet major lapse in Kellner's typically pinpoint-accurate business sense.

"It should never have been so public," Brad Turell says.

Jamie was outraged at just how public the network's fight with the studio over *Buffy* had become. He stopped tempering his comments in industry forums like the January 2001 edition of the Television Critics Association press junket. At that event, Kellner reiterated his firm view that 20th Century Fox TV would make plenty of money from the show in syndication and worldwide licensing deals, not to mention a goldmine of spin-offs and ancillary product potential. He claimed that the WB would lose money on the show if it met 20th's asking price of $2 million per episode, up from a license fee of a little more than $1 million per episode. Plus, if the WB paid big bucks for *Buffy*, the producers of *Dawson's Creek, 7th Heaven,* and *Charmed* would be in his office with their hands out the next day, Kellner argued. Meanwhile, 20th maintained the WB was reaching to say it would "lose" money on the show at $2 million per episode. The WB countered that it was a start-up business, not one of the Big Four networks, and thus it had to live within its means to get to profitability. The WB's highest offer was around $1.8 million per episode.

As talk of the *Buffy* standoff dominated our executive Q&A session, Kellner didn't hide his exasperation. He predicted to a roomful of fast-scribbling journalists that the WB would wind up telling 20th executives something to the effect of: "We will take all the revenue we can generate with *Buffy,* and we'll give it to you in a giant wheelbarrow. And if that's not enough, then take it to somebody else. You've demonstrated that you're not the kind of partner we should be doing business with."*

Sandy Grushow by this time had been promoted to an über-executive job overseeing the Fox network and 20th television studio as chairman of Fox Television Entertainment Group. Grushow could hardly contain himself a few days later when he was asked about it during Fox's executive Q&A session. Grushow repeated his contention that the WB had not come "remotely" near a fair offer to renegotiate a deal for *Buffy.* And he made a pointed reference to the record-setting, $13 million-per-episode renewal deal for hit medical drama *ER* that Warner Bros. Television had wrangled from NBC a few years before.

"Jamie Kellner works for a company called AOL Time Warner. Time Warner, a couple of years ago, put a gun to the head of a little company called General Electric and extracted a $13 million-per-episode license fee for *ER* and changed the business in so doing," Grushow said, his face reddening. "And thirdly, they don't have wheelbarrows at the WB. They have Mercedes."

Advantage: Grushow. A few weeks later, it was Jamie's turn again, this time in a one-on-one interview with Lynette Rice of *Entertainment Weekly*. The magazine, more than any other media outlet on the planet, had adopted *Buffy* as its own, promoting and praising the show to an audience that hit the bull's eye of the WB's target demo. Kellner's remarks about the show and the deal imbroglio in the March

---

*   *Daily Variety*, January 8, 2001, "Buffy a Toughie for UPN."

23, 2001, issue of the magazine set off a bomb in the "Buffy-verse," as the show's fan base was known. Whedon took Jamie's remarks as a personal affront.

"It's not our No. 1 show," Kellner said. "It's not a show like *ER* that stands above the pack." He also pointed out the recent softening of the show's ratings, especially among teenagers. That point, in particular, was viewed as a low blow by the *Buffy* faithful.

"Our audience is a younger audience. . . . Maybe what we should be doing is to not stay with the same show for many years, and refresh our lineup."* The message was unmistakable: the WB was prepared to part with *Buffy* if need be.

Both sides knew there had to be a decision by the end of April, at the latest. The WB would need to know if it would have *Buffy* on deck for the 2001–02 season by the time it unveiled its schedule during the mid-May upfronts. The presumption in the industry was that 20th would move *Buffy* to Fox, its sibling network, which had passed on it six years earlier.

Although it was a WB show and not an astounding success on the level of *ER* or *Seinfeld,* such a move would still be a milestone for the industry. No major studio in the post-fin-syn era had moved a successful show produced for an outside network to one of the studio's corporate siblings in a dispute over money—as opposed to a network picking up another's cancellation. Executives at 20th were hypersensitive to the perception that the studio was being unreasonable or playing hardball with the WB by threatening to move *Buffy* to Fox in order to exact a higher price. The studio would be out of business in an instant with ABC, CBS, and NBC if they feared 20th was going to be yanking successful shows from the networks that groomed them in an effort to aid Fox.

"I didn't want to move the show. I certainly didn't cherish the idea of being characterized as somebody who was self-dealing because there was some discussion [in industry circles] about the show coming to Fox, which never was seriously considered," Grushow says.

---

* *Entertainment Weekly,* March 23, 2001, "Slayer' It Ain't So."

"Nor did I wish to be perceived as a guy who would haphazardly dam- age a network by moving a show for no good reason."

Whedon was deeply hurt by Kellner's comments about the show that had done so much for the network. *Buffy*'s puppet master had mostly stayed out of the fray as it simmered on the industry radar for two years. But after Kellner's remarks ran in *Entertainment Weekly*, Whedon adjusted his filter and let it be known, in his own colorful terms, that he thought the WB's leader was being cheap, ungrateful, and shortsighted. Here he had created the greatest cult favorite series of the 1990s, adding luster and hip cachet to the frog network, and this is how he was rewarded? Whedon became resigned to the idea that *Buffy* was going to move to another network. He'd been comfort- able at the WB. He liked the network's youthful thrust and the sur- roundings it provided his show. But more than anything, he was fond of all of us who had fought so hard to support him early on. Before the *Entertainment Weekly* article, Whedon cringed at the suggestion of the show moving; afterward, his pride as an artist was wounded by the dismissive suggestion that the WB could easily "freshen" its lineup with a better show than *Buffy*. He gave 20th his wholehearted bless- ing to shop the show to a new buyer.

"Once Joss said 'Fuck Jamie,' it got easier for us," says an execu- tive who was intimately involved in the *Buffy* negotiations.

Executives at 20th flirted with ABC and NBC about picking up the show—for about five seconds. Studio presidents Gary New- man and Dana Walden knew the mentality of their industry col- leagues. No executive at a Big Four network would pick up a WB or UPN show, not unless it was a huge hit by their higher standards. The only real offer forthcoming was, as the 20th camp had predicted, from UPN. But it still came as something of a surprise because it was un- certain whether UPN would be able to muster Viacom's support to come up with the $102 million-plus that 20th sought for a two-season deal.

The caution at 20th was well warranted. UPN had seemed per- petually on the verge of shutdown in the months that followed the Viacom–CBS merger. Industry insiders also knew UPN was part of a larger power struggle then unfolding between Viacom Chairman and CEO Sumner Redstone and Mel Karmazin, Viacom's president and COO. Karmazin wanted to shift the network under CBS's successful team, led by CBS Chairman Leslie Moonves. Redstone wanted to leave UPN where it was and not roil his longtime lieutenants, Jonathan Dolgen and Kerry McCluggage.

When the *Buffy* opportunity arose, Valentine laid out the numbers to McCluggage and Dolgen—what the show would cost and what advertising revenue the network could reasonably expect from it—and they were immediately receptive. UPN needed some kind of jump-start, badly, and *Buffy* just might be it.

After all the posturing, the decisive round in the battle for *Buffy* came down to a series of meetings and phone calls in March and April 2001. Whedon had an important meet-and-greet session with Dean Valentine and Kerry McCluggage on the Paramount lot, and both sides turned on the charm as if they were on a first date. By the end, Valentine had convinced Whedon that he was a genuine fan of the show and a genuine eccentric himself. Whedon came away with the assurance that UPN would pamper *Buffy* with promotion and marketing dollars in the same way the WB had done in the beginning.

As 20th and UPN representatives began to negotiate the deal, 20th executives made a point of stating upfront and in no uncertain terms to UPN execs that they intended to give the WB the chance to match any deal UPN agreed to, even though 20th had no legal obligation to do so. In truth, executives from 20th and the WB were in constant communication during this period. WB staffers couldn't believe Jamie's obstinacy. We couldn't believe he would actually let *Buffy* go. The situation was made even more awkward by the fact that the *Buffy* spin-off *Angel* still had another season to go on its WB contract. The shows were now likely to air on two different networks, at least for the upcoming 2001–02 season.

Jamie was resolute, despite our pleading for him to reconsider the situation. If anything, he seemed to dig in deeper the more panicky people around him became. The WB might even agree to a break-even deal, but not a loss-leader deal with 20th, Jamie explained to everyone who asked. Barry Meyer and Bruce Rosenblum sat on the sidelines at the studio, unable to intervene now that Jamie no longer reported to Meyer. Bob Daly, who by then had retired from Warner Bros. and was serving as CEO of the Los Angeles Dodgers in partnership with team owner News Corp., made a few calls at the behest of News Corp. President Peter Chernin to see if he could broker a *Buffy* compromise, to no avail. Jamie had surprised the principals in the *Buffy* battle by cutting short a lunch date with Chernin a few weeks earlier when the subject of the show's renewal came up.

Behind the scenes, the WB gradually inched up its offer until it came within a hair—$1.8 million and change—of the $2 million-per-episode figure that Grushow had been so quick to throw around in public. In fact, the WB at one point quietly offered the $2.1 million license fee with the huge caveat that 20th would have to allow one of the Turner cable networks to carry a repeat of each episode shortly after its premiere on the WB. But 20th would not agree to any such arrangement without other sizable guarantees to back it up, and so the offer was tabled.

By this time, 20th had a handshake deal with UPN for a two-season pickup at a per-episode license fee of $2.33 million. The deal also included a commitment to pick up *Angel* should the WB drop it after the 2001–02 season.

Late in the afternoon on Friday, April 20, Grushow sat at his desk in his dark-wood-paneled office on the 20th Century Fox lot and had his assistant place a call to Jamie Kellner's office. Unlike most times when he was on the verge of closing a $100 million-plus deal for the studio, Grushow felt no giddiness, no excitement, no rush to celebrate a job well done. Instead, he felt unease, as if he were about to do something unsavory to a friend, when in fact he knew he was only doing the right thing for Fox and its shareholders in seeking fair market value for a hit show.

Grushow may have been guilty of baiting Kellner with his early public comments on the *Buffy* deal, but he did so banking on the strength of their relationship to allow for a little professional jousting.

Despite the innate competitiveness of both men, Grushow genuinely considered Kellner a close friend and compatriot from the wars of the early Fox days. He got no pleasure from placing this call.

When Kellner came on the line, Grushow didn't need any pre-amble. He detailed the offer UPN had agreed to. He offered to cut a two-season deal with the WB at a slightly discounted fee of $2.25 million per episode. Kellner didn't skip a beat. In his best Jack Webb, just-the-facts delivery, he declined Grushow's offer and the call ended. UPN's deal for *Buffy* was sealed in principle the same day.

The publicity departments of the WB and 20th went into crisis-spin mode as they dealt with the deluge of media inquiries, even over the weekend, about what had become a sexy story for the business press—vampires and vertical integration, AOL Time Warner versus News Corp., publicly bickering executives with long histories. It had all the elements. Brad Turell had very capable help in his effort to spin the story in a favorable way for the WB. PR executive Paul McGuire had left UPN in frustration a few months earlier. He joined our team as Brad's successor weeks before the *Buffy* deal went down.

"The crazy part is that [the WB] wound up losing the show on a difference of a few million bucks a year, based on where they came up to" at the end, said an executive who was closely involved in the deal. "For a big company like Time Warner? It's laughable."

But no one was laughing at Fox or 20th after the *Buffy* sale was completed. They were glad to have a $102 million deal in hand, but there was no high-fiving in the hallways of 20th's offices on the ground floor of a nondescript building on the storied Fox lot in Century City. It was never hailed as a big victory or a sign of the studio flexing its muscle. Quite the opposite, say insiders.

"We would have preferred to extend the license with the WB," Newman says. "It felt like a failure of the system."

Afterward, a conspiracy theory sprang up at the WB that the UPN-News Corp. station affiliation deal was the real driver behind UPN securing *Buffy*. The thinking was that UPN needed the stations so it was more than willing to outbid the WB for the show. News

Corp. had an incentive to help give UPN a pulse outside of wrestling now that it owned the network's most important station group. There was talk of News Corp. getting a minority stake in UPN in exchange for a long-term station affiliation agreement.

In reality, sources in both camps insist that the affiliation pact had little bearing on the *Buffy* deal, other than to remind both sides that they now had a certain amount of regular business to do together for the foreseeable future. UPN would have made a big play for *Buffy* when it came on the market, regardless of any other pending business between Viacom and News Corp. A hit show levels the playing field. A hit show conquers all hate, prejudice, and bad blood among executives from deals gone by.

"As soon as I heard it was coming up for bid, I was on the phone," says Dean Valentine.

The psychological drama of the test of wills playing out between Kellner and his former Fox colleagues didn't go unnoticed in industry circles. Many wrote off Kellner's intransigence on the license fee to an ego clash between him and Grushow—two strong-willed executives with a long history. But Kellner's close associates say it was less about a rivalry with Grushow per se than it was about "Jamie Kellner versus the death-star Fox empire."

"Jamie was still mad. All those years later, with the WB a hit and him getting the big corporate [TBS chairman] job—he still had a lot of anger towards Fox," says a former Fox colleague of Kellner's. "He was not about to let Fox push him around on *Buffy*."

To many in the industry, Kellner had committed the cardinal sin of letting his emotions get in the way of business, letting it get personal with his former colleagues. To others, Kellner had sacrificed not just a show but a night for the network. The *Buffy* spin-off *Angel*, which came along in 1999, had been successful but only when it aired in tandem with *Buffy*; it was not a self-starter.

"You don't give up a show, and you don't ever give up a night," says Bob Daly, who handled many a tough series renegotiation during his years at CBS and Warner Bros. "Not if you can help it."

. . .

The loss of *Buffy* was a shock to the WB's system. We could not believe it had actually happened, and in hindsight it's clear that the deal signaled the end of the WB's ascent. In a matter of weeks, *Buffy* would be finished on the WB and relocate to enemy territory. It was the most painful thing imaginable having to read Dean Valentine crowing in the press about stealing our show! It was sad, and wrong, and it made me angry. And it all came down in late April, just as we were in the thick of preparing to go to New York in a few weeks for the upfront schedule presentation.

The process of screening and selecting pilots is grueling enough, and then setting the schedule, time period by time period, takes every last ounce of fight right out of you. But what *really* gets to you in the first week of May are all the little details: arguing over show titles, figuring out marketing taglines, deciding which cast members should be flown to New York for the event, selecting clips from the new shows to use in the teaser trailers for the event, and on and on. With *Buffy* gone, we were forced to revamp our Tuesday night plans, though Jamie Kellner and Rusty Mintz had already decided weeks ago that we'd fill *Buffy's* void in the 8 p.m. slot with *Gilmore Girls*. I thought that was a lot to ask of the show in its second season. (Turns out it wasn't.)

Jamie was maddeningly dispassionate about the whole thing. It was, he kept telling us, a question of principle. I wish I could say we admired his commitment to his own beliefs, but I can't. We were so upset. We didn't have to hide our anguish around him, but the subject was no longer open for debate either. Jamie never let you forget that he was the boss.

It was excruciatingly awkward, but not two weeks after the *Buffy* deal went down, 20th hosted a fifth-season finale party for the show at the funky Hotel Figueroa in downtown Los Angeles, which is not exactly a hot locale for Hollywood wrap parties, but it was perfectly Joss Whedon. The atmosphere was dark and late-spring hazy, with lanterns lighting an outside patio right off Figueroa Street, one of the busiest in downtown Los Angeles. There was a whole lot of drinking going on—tequila in particular was flowing like water. It was definitely not the happy, celebratory mood we should have been in after another season well done.

I didn't stay long, but I was there long enough to observe a sweet moment between Jordan Levin and Joss Whedon that took a tiny little bit of the sting away for me. I watched Jordan walk up behind Joss, who as always was surrounded by a hive of activity, and wait for him to turn around. It took a few minutes but Joss must've felt the eyes burning through the back of his neck. He finally turned around and saw Jordan, and, without saying a word, the two made their way over to a table. Jordan put a bottle of tequila and two glasses on the table in theatrical fashion, and the two knocked back good-size shots. And then they gave each other a long bear hug with plenty of back-slapping. After a while, Jordan sidled away, still without saying a word.

Emotional trauma aside, another huge concern for us was how the *Buffy* blowup would affect our standing with other studios. It couldn't have come at a worse time. It sent a signal that the WB wasn't ready to join the big leagues as the fifth network because we weren't prepared to pony up more for a contract renewal on a hit show, like the Big Four routinely do. Or used to. The *ER* deal and the *Buffy* battle pushed the major networks and studios to create a new extended-term business template, in which the networks pay more for the show upfront in exchange for more time on the initial contract to avoid the possibility of a license-fee standoff after five years. We certainly wished we'd had such a deal in place in 1997 when *Buffy* went on the air.

On top of the intrigue at work, I had my hands full at home with two toddlers and an infant. I'm not surprised that I cracked when I did, at the end of my last WB upfront presentation in New York on Tuesday, May 15, 2001.

Pent-up emotional turmoil came welling up as I was coming offstage at the Sheraton Hotel ballroom in Manhattan. I'd barely made it through my speech about that season's new shows—a good crop that included the comedy *Reba*, which came from 20th Century Fox TV in a deal struck before the *Buffy* blow-up; and *Smallville*. I wasn't aware of being particularly depressed or emotional that day, just exhausted as usual for that time of year. But when I exhaled after completing my speech in front of hundreds of media buyers—under hot stage lighting, I broke down in a way I never have before or since.

I felt the strangest sensation, a kind of physical rush, come over me, and I began hyperventilating. A bunch of people rushed around to help me, but that only made me feel penned in and more embarrassed. I'll never forget the kindness Jordan showed me by immediately shushing the crowd away and hustling me off into a quieter space. I was able to collect myself after a bit, but I was feeling fairly wrecked. After seven years of pushing, fighting, hustling, hoping, praying for, and cheering along our network baby it was finally time for me to go. It had been an unforgettable ride, but it was time to get off.

"I'm done," I told Jordan as I gradually calmed down. "I'm *done*."

That day was, without question, one of the longest and toughest of my life. All I wanted to do after I caught my breath backstage at the hotel was to go home. Jamie was established in Atlanta, and I had stayed five months longer than I intended at his request.

I needed a change of pace, but I didn't want to stop working entirely, or leave the industry I love. I quickly worked out a deal to develop shows as a producer for Warner Bros. Television.

For a few weeks after the upfront, my soon-to-be-former WB colleagues were incredibly kind and respectful in their dealings with me. As I went through the final steps of clearing out my office and approving the press release announcing my resignation, Jamie and Jordan asked me if I wanted them to "do anything" for me, as in a good-bye party. I thought they'd never ask. By then, I had given it some thought. I knew exactly what I wanted—something that would remind me of the incredible camaraderie we'd shared in the early years of building the network.

"I want a dinner . . . and I want a froggy . . . and I want everyone to be there . . . ," I blurted, sounding like a kindergartner describing what she wants at her birthday party. Jamie and Jordan took my wish-list to heart and delivered the perfect evening. When I stepped onto the tree-lined patio at Orso, a well-loved trattoria on Los Angeles' Third Street restaurant row, I knew it would be a gathering to remember. The central nervous system of the WB Network was collected around a long row of mismatched tables pushed together to accommodate our party of nearly two dozen, including Jamie and Jordan, Garth Ancier, Bruce Rosenblum, Bob Bibb, Lew Goldstein, Brad Turell, Jed Petrick, Rusty Mintz, Kathleen Letterie, and other close associates. There were no spouses. Just shoptalk and war stories.

The restaurant was open to other diners that night, but I didn't even see them. Wine, conversation, and fantastic food were moving around the table all night. We were all off duty. I was saying good-bye to the team for good. It was a monumental moment for me. I was 36. I expected the WB would go on forever, even without me.

We toasted hard work, dumb luck, and success. We were noisy and boisterous, but in a friendly rather than rowdy way. We sat out on the patio yakking so long that leaves, pods, and twigs dropping from the trees overhead began to pile up on the white tablecloths that connected our tables. It was light-sweater warm late into the night.

Best of all, I got my frog.

Way back in the launch days, our marketing department had whipped up a bunch of fancy, large Michigan J. Frog busts to give out to affiliate station managers as prizes and incentives in contests and promotions and such. I'd always wanted one. I fell for Michigan J. as our 'toon mascot the first time Bob and Lew showed him to me on paper.

When Jamie and the others presented me with the statue as the night wound down, I felt an uneasy sense of closure, a little bit like Dorothy at the end of *The Wizard of Oz*—glad to be getting her wish fulfilled but still conflicted about leaving her friends in Oz.

My froggy has a special plaque affixed to the base of the pedestal with the inscription:

Michigan J. Frog is awarded to Susanne Daniels. From all of us at the WB, thank you.

At UPN, the excitement over landing *Buffy* was muted by lingering unease about the future. The network's rank and file had been as pleasantly surprised as anyone else that Viacom was willing to shell out a big two-season commitment for *Buffy*. That was a good thing, but there was more upheaval on the horizon.

By the close of the 2000–01 season, it was generally known at the network that Tom Nunan was on his way out as entertainment president. Nunan had been attempting to help line up his successor, but after the season ended in May and there was no new entertainment president announcement, insiders began to realize that the Viacom brass weren't going to let Valentine pick Nunan's successor because he was heading for the exit too—as fast as he could get there as the end of his five-year employment contract approached.

Yet there was one big hitch. Even before the Chris-Craft–Viacom split, Valentine had seen UPN's owners to settle the issue of how to calculate the bonus due him at the end of the five-year employment contract he had signed in 1997 after moving from Disney. Valentine's contract called for him to be paid a handsome base salary, starting at $1.75 million in the first year and rising to $2.25 million in the last. In Valentine's view, the contract clause on how to calculate his bonus payment was vague and subject to interpretation.

Valentine had sought for all sides to come to an agreement on the matter for more than a year. Once they had the *Buffy* deal in hand and things were looking brighter for UPN, at least in the near term, Valentine pressed the issue with Kerry McCluggage and Jonathan Dolgen. He made it clear to them that he had no intention of signing a new contract, and he was savvy enough to know that they probably wanted to make a change anyway. The basic disagreement on the bonus boiled down to the question of how the network defined "improved" ratings and profitability. Valentine claimed that he had lifted ratings and improved the network's financial picture by stemming the losses he inherited upon arriving in 1997. Viacom's contention was that the network had yet to turn a profit, so he wasn't owed anything. After a long impasse among lawyers for both sides, Valentine felt he had no choice but to file a $22 million lawsuit against UPN in Los Angeles Superior Court on September 6, 2001.

"It was just another episode in the long, sad saga of the United Paramount Network," Valentine says. "As a guy who's never been sued and who had never sued anybody in my entire life, I found it extraordinarily embarrassing and personally painful to go through . . . I kept begging them not to put me in the awkward position of having to file suit."

Valentine had no illusions about what the town's reaction would be to the suit once the word got out. He and the network would once again be the butt of jokes and the subject of snarky cocktail party chatter; media outlets got wind of the suit hours after it was filed.

A few weeks later, Valentine appeared at the annual preseason Hollywood Radio and Television Society luncheon ritual, featuring the network entertainment presidents and their prognostications on the season to come. With Nunan gone, Valentine represented UPN on the HRTS stage that year. At a time when Valentine should have been in his element as a quick-witted raconteur, he was dogged by the one topic that he was sick of hearing dumb jokes about.

The session was moderated by sharp-tongued comedian Bill Maher, then host of ABC's late-night talk show *Politically Incorrect*. As the Q&A got underway, Maher went right for the material he knew would kill in front of the industry-only crowd at the Regent Beverly Wilshire Hotel in Beverly Hills.

"So Dean, you're suing the network. How's that working out for you?" Maher opened.

The lawsuit hastened the end of Valentine's days at the network by essentially pushing the network into full-scale paralysis. The chill of litigation made it hard, if not impossible, for Valentine to communicate with his bosses. Though it was fall of 2001 and pitch season for the upcoming 2002–03 season, there wasn't much development activity in progress because after the *Buffy* deal, the network didn't have much left in the till to buy new scripts. Valentine focused his staff's attention on one laserlike target: mounting a massive promotional campaign for *Buffy the Vampire Slayer* that fall, alerting the fan base to the network switch. In most markets around the country, outside of the nation's 20 or so largest cities, that meant instructing people to switch from one obscure UHF station (WB channel 63) to another (UPN 56). It was a considerable undertaking. UPN wisely kept the show in the same Tuesday 8 p.m. time slot that it had been in on the WB.

Buffy opened solidly for UPN on October 2, 2001, with a two-hour episode that piled on all the show's bells and whistles. The show performed respectably overall in its first season on UPN, but the following season the audience drop-off was pronounced. The fears of 20th Century Fox TV were realized, even as studio executives outwardly put their best face on the situation, which involved their significant investment. The move from the WB had taken its toll. *Gilmore Girls* had no trouble beating *Buffy* in head to head competition.

The fall of 2001 also saw UPN raise the curtain on another *Star Trek* drama, this time designed as a prequel set 100 years before the original series, just as the Federation of Planets was being formed. Paramount Television executives promised that in contrast to *Voyager,* the new *Enterprise* would mark a return to a more action-oriented adventure drama with a heroic captain in the William Shatner mold fighting weird-looking aliens and romancing exotic beauties in every port in the galaxy. The role went to Scott Bakula, star of the 1980s sci-fi hit *Quantum Leap.*

Valentine did his best to talk Paramount out of rushing a new *Star Trek* series on the air so soon after the series finale of *Star Trek: Voyager,* which limped through its final season in 2000–01 with weak ratings and little heat, even with the *Trek* faithful. Valentine noted how clear it was that audience fatigue had set in to the TV shows and even to Paramount's feature film franchise, with 1998's *Star Trek: Insurrection* pulling in a modest $70 million at the domestic box office. (The box office receipts fell even further with 2002's *Star Trek:*

Nemesis, which took in only about $43 million domestically.) Kerry McCluggage was adamant, though the studio did consider pitching *Enterprise* to other networks or going back to syndication.

In the end, however, the decision was made to keep it on UPN to ensure that the studio retained maximum control of the show, rather than risk an embarrassing quick cancellation if it did not perform well. The conflict about the project within Paramount was clear, beginning with the curious decision to drop the *Star Trek:* branding common to the three previous spin-offs and call the show simply *Enterprise.* It was explained as an effort to gain more sampling for the show among non–sci-fi fans—as if the iconography, starships, and futuristic jargon wouldn't be a dead giveaway to any viewer who hadn't been in a cave for the past 40 years.

At first, McCluggage was vindicated. Amid the national trauma immediately following September 11, 2001, the two-hour opener of *Enterprise* on September 26 brought in 12.5 million viewers, making it UPN's second-most-watched night ever—only behind the *Voyager* premiere the night the network launched. But the ratings took a dive in subsequent weeks and never recovered. Moreover, the show and Bakula as Capt. Jeffrey Archer (a pivotal character in *Star Trek* lore) never resonated with hard-core fans in the way Paramount had planned; the studio had wrapped the prequel in stories and characters from the sacrosanct Gene Roddenberry-produced 1966–69 NBC series.

For Valentine, the successful relaunch of *Buffy* and the surprising initial pop from *Enterprise* signaled that it was the right time for him to make as graceful an exit as he could, under the circumstances. As the year wound down, the lawyers were making progress on a settlement of Valentine's lawsuit. There was also growing chatter in media circles about Karmazin using it as a club in his internal struggles with Redstone. Karmazin was appalled at the seven-year flood of red ink UPN had produced under Paramount's management—with no significant program successes in syndication to offset the investment. He saw UPN as a sign of weak fiscal discipline on Redstone's part, according to CBS insiders of the era.

With UPN's losses for 2002 set to grow because of the *Buffy* price tag, there was no rational argument against combining some of UPN's operations with CBS to save tens of millions of dollars each year. Viacom made it official in early December: Leslie Moonves was taking on oversight of UPN. Karmazin had won this round. Kerry Mc-Cluggage tendered his resignation the same day.

By the time the news became official, it was anticlimactic for the executive who had run Paramount Television over the past 10 years of rapid-fire changes within the studio and the industry at large. Mc-Cluggage had been well aware for months that Karmazin wanted Moonves to take over UPN. McCluggage had numerous conversations with his direct boss, Jonathan Dolgen, as well as Redstone and Karmazin, about the UPN situation in the months before the switch was formally decreed.

"Moving UPN over to CBS was clearly a breach of my contract, which they were aware of," McCluggage says. "At some point within 18 months to two years, I probably would have finished up at Paramount. But I wanted to finish the job of getting UPN on track. I wanted to get it to the point where it was breakeven or profitable. And then, in all likelihood I would have moved on" from Paramount, McCluggage says.

Valentine was not particularly concerned about the McCluggage-to-Moonves regime change. He was on the verge of settling his lawsuit. He was already packing up his art collection (he considered options for removing the conference room's exterior wall featuring the Barry McGee mural but gave up the idea as unworkable) and looking forward to an extended break. At the time, he had a toddler daughter at home and a son on the way. He left UPN with a promise to his family to "hang out with them, and look at the world again, and think about what was happening and what I wanted to do." In the end, Valentine did settle with UPN on his bonus package. The size of Valentine's settlement was the subject of much speculation; industry gossip at the time pegged it at around $20 million. Other sources contend that $20 million figure included the base salary he earned each year under the terms of the contract, which climbed from $1.75

million in his first year to $2.25 million during his last year. Both sides continued to stick to the letter of their confidentiality agreement about the settlement details. Even more than the spectacle of the lawsuit itself, it was the details of Valentine's salary agreement contained in the complaint that caught the attention of senior WB executives. It was hard evidence that pay scales at UPN were higher than they were at the network's more successful rival.

On Wednesday, October 17, 2001, Peter Roth had a 6 a.m. phone call with Jordan Levin. The night before they had premiered the series *Smallville,* and the pair spoke to digest the overnight rating returns, which were very strong. It was barely a month after the September 11 terrorist attacks. Nerves were on edge. The WB had poured most of its fall season launch marketing budget into getting *Smallville* off in style. In the network's first season after *Buffy,* the heat was on Jordan to prove that the WB still had it.

After all the stress, tension, and excitement, their labors boiled down to a Nielsen rating that translated into 8.4 million viewers, the highest debut for any WB show in the network's history. Young Superman beat the WB mark set nearly four years before with the premiere of *Dawson's Creek.*

"We were screaming at one another. Just screaming with delight and joy," Roth recalls. "There was so much pressure."

Because of the special effects, the pilot had come in at a cost of about $8 million—expensive by any network's standards. For the WB, it was a record breaker. But by all accounts, Warner Bros. Television never wavered in its faith that *Smallville* was worth the investment. The stakes were high, just like a good Superman comic adventure.

The emergence of *Smallville* as the WB's next big hit provided an oasis of calm during an otherwise turbulent period for the network. As I watched it blossom from my unfamiliar spot on the sidelines, I was relieved that I'd dodged a speeding bullet of suffering the blame for letting the show get away to Fox.

The success of *Smallville* was fabulous, but it also brought a new series of conflicts to the forefront. In Atlanta, Jamie Kellner was seeking to beef up TNT and TBS by having them run repeats of WB shows a day or two after the episode premiered on our network.

Right around the time Jamie took over Turner, some studios saw those repeats on cable as a way to help them cover more production costs by collecting a little extra license fee money (usually $75,000 to $120,000) from a cable network happy to get a nearly new, highly promotable program. ABC had *Alias* encores, among other shows, running on its ABC Family cable network. Fox had the *24* clock ticking on FX. Universal Television had its *Law & Order: SVU* and *Law & Order: Criminal Intent* running on its sibling USA Network.

Jamie believed repurposing episodes of WB hits on TNT or TBS a few days after their airing on the WB could help the networks and the programs by generating more advertising revenue, and greater exposure for the show, and better image-branding for the cable networks. After *Smallville* opened big, he sought to repeat that show on TNT within a week of each episode's telecast on the WB.

But Warner Bros. Television wasn't having any of it. Barry Meyer and Bruce Rosenblum were dubious about what all those extra repeats would do to the show's long-term syndication value. They were concerned that a show might wear out its welcome too quickly with viewers to have a long life in reruns. Worse, in their view, if those repeats drew low ratings, Warner Bros.' syndication sales guys would have an impossible time getting top dollar when they went out to sell the long-term rerun rights to the show if it lasted long enough to deliver 80 to 100 episodes. Barry and Bruce would not grant Jamie the rights to repeat Warner Bros'. shows on the Turner networks.

The studio's stance perturbed Kellner to no end. Eventually he managed to cut a deal with Spelling Television to do repeats of *Charmed,* which did pull in good ratings for TNT, but he never managed to get the bulk of the WB's shows for repurposing on TNT and TBS. This conflict with Warner Bros. caused him to respond in a particularly bold fashion. Kellner was no longer just the CEO of the WB; he was the head honcho of one of the largest divisions of AOL Time Warner, and he had significant resources at his disposal.

In October 2001, as Jamie was getting nowhere with Warner Bros., TBS orchestrated a stealth announcement that struck his colleagues back home in Los Angeles as a thoroughly Kellner-ish maneuver. If Warner Bros. wouldn't let him use their shows to help amortize costs and beef up the WB and TNT, then he'd start his own studio to make shows that he could control. It was dubbed Turner Television, and he sprang it on Warner Bros. and the rest of the television industry that fall with a front-page story planted with *Daily Variety*'s Josef Adalian.

Kellner's tactic reflected the maverick mentality that had developed within the WB toward Warner Bros., despite the mutual respect and friendship that existed between him and Barry Meyer. There was plenty of goodwill among the WB staff toward Meyer and Bob Daly for the support they'd shown the fledgling enterprise in its lean years. Still, Warner Bros. was often viewed as a corporate master to be tolerated or humored, or sidestepped if possible. Even after Peter Roth brought harmony to the creative relationship between Warner Bros. TV and the WB, Warner Bros. wielded the ultimate veto power as the net's majority owner until it shifted to Robert Pittman's control following the AOL merger. After that, there was awkwardness at times when the WB and Warner Bros. TV would inevitably encounter conflicts.

"There's a natural push and pull between any studio and a network," says Bruce Rosenblum. "It was easier for us to manage the relationships between the studio and the network when they both reported to us."

The introduction of Turner Television was sure to add to the confusion. It all seemed very hastily thrown together. Jamie expected me to play a key part in running Turner Television. Only he hadn't bothered to tell me that before the news broke.

The first of many calls I got that morning came from Joss Whedon's agent, Chris Harbert.

"Congratulations," he said, "Why didn't you tell me about this?"

"Huh?"

"On your new Turner job. I can't believe you didn't mention it to me once. What's the plan?"

"What are you talking about," I said with exasperation. I was sitting in my downscaled office in the WB trailer, which was a bit awkward. I had formally started my producing deal with Warner Bros. Television, but I stayed at the WB's offices until a spot was found for me on the main lot.

As I listened with one ear to Chris I could hear my e-mail alert sound ringing steadily in the background. I couldn't figure out what Chris was getting at.

"Uh, Susanne, I think you might want to read *Variety* today," Harbert said. "There's a story about you running a new studio at Turner."

I made a beeline for the hallway and snatched the first copy of *Daily Variety* I could find. It was true. There was a page-one story about me, complete with a picture, reporting that I was going to run a newly created production division that would be housed at Turner and report to Jamie. I found out later that Brad Turell issued a formal press release on my "appointment" that morning.

After the reality of my predicament sank in, I had two reactions:

No. 1: Flattering, but I don't want the job.

No. 2: Jamie Kellner is a cowboy. It takes a cowboy to do what he's just done.

I didn't know the scope of his plans for Turner Television, but I realized in an instant why he'd planted the story. Jamie wanted to tweak Warner Bros. over all the business fights he'd been having with them. And, he genuinely wanted a facility for producing shows where he wouldn't have to negotiate the licensing and repeat terms with Barry Meyer and Bruce Rosenblum. But his decision to make me the poster girl for the new entity created all kinds of problems, just as I was starting my producing deal with Warner Bros. TV.

Still, I went through the motions of demanding an answer from Brad Turell by phone from Atlanta. Brad told me what I already knew—that Jamie felt he was getting a raw deal from Warner Bros. Television. I made it clear that I had no intention of running a new studio. I might've taken more time to consider the opportunity, but I was overwhelmed by the surprise. And my phone was ringing off the hook.

Rosenblum and Peter Roth were among the first to call. They felt betrayed. I sputtered on the phone with both of them, trying to convince them that I sincerely had no clue until, like everyone else, I read about it in the paper. Bruce and Barry knew Jamie had been threatening to launch his own studio if they couldn't resolve their issues. But they had no idea Jamie was planning to have me run it. I tried to no avail to convince Peter and Bruce that I had no intention of taking the job. I told Brad that I was going to call key people and tell them I had nothing to do with the story or the studio. I spent the next few days on the phone trying to sort the mess out.

Upset as I was, I did not call Jamie on the carpet. He would have shrugged off my irritation in a nonchalant way that would have only aggravated me more. Jamie eventually recruited an existing WB executive, John Litvack, to spearhead the launch of Turner Television. Litvack had the production experience to do the job, but in hindsight, it wasn't the best move because it distracted Litvack from his primary responsibility of maintaining quality control on the WB's series—a key job at any network.

Litvack, who'd joined the WB from Disney in 1997, was well-liked within the network for his expertise and skill. His mandate as head of current programming was to make good shows great, and to make bad episodes tolerable against a punishing deadline. The job essentially involved troubleshooting to make sure episodes were delivered on time and in respectable condition. He didn't give up his WB job when Turner Television came along, though he by necessity had to delegate more of his network responsibilities to less experienced staffers.

Litvack had logged time in the trenches as a writer-producer, on *Hill Street Blues*, among other shows, and that earned him the respect of our show runners, particularly Joss Whedon, J. J. Abrams, and the crew on *Dawson's Creek*. They'd listen to him because they knew he'd once walked in their shoes. Litvack's bluntness and caustic nature took some getting used to, but he added an important component of experience to our young staff. And as Jamie's peer, in age and range of experience, he could talk to him in a way that many of us who owed so much of our careers to Jamie could not. With his ivory-white hair and longish beard, Litvack was affectionately known around the ranch as "Santa."

Perhaps if I'd been able to see the struggles that were in store for me as a free-agent producer, I would have done it Jamie's way and taken the Turner Television job. I wouldn't have worried so much about my obligation to demonstrate loyalty to the people at Warner Bros. who were paying for my production deal.

As the year came to an end, nothing could disguise the upheaval that had transpired within the once-idyllic confines of the WB's trailers. It had been a rocky 12 months marked by a whirlwind of change: Jamie Kellner relocating to Atlanta; me moving on and Jordan becoming entertainment president; former advertising sales head Jed Petrick taking on a more senior management role; Garth Ancier coming back into the picture alongside Kellner at TBS. Not to mention that by year's end, it was also evident there was real trouble afoot with the broader corporate merger of AOL and Time Warner. That much became clear when AOL's stock price sank even before the merger transaction was completed in January 2001. The long-awaited correction to the era of irrational exuberance came in like a hurricane.

But as the holiday season came around, morale at the WB received a lift from a most unexpected gesture. In December, Kellner and Ancier were in town and were spending a few days in their WB offices. The trailers were trimmed with holiday decorations, some of them WB-ified with Michigan J. Frog and other motifs. A few of the

WB's senior executives knew the real reason Jamie and Garth were there, but for most of the network's roughly 275 employees, the pair's mission came as a heavenly bolt out of the blue.

Kellner and Ancier began calling staffers one by one into the company conference room and handing them checks—big, fat bonus checks meant to show gratitude and recognition for the hard work everyone had put in to build the network. The checks came complete with letters signed by Jamie and Garth. Kellner put in $4 million, Ancier chipped in $1 million, and the pot was divvied up among the staff.

The bonuses were calculated in large part on a sliding scale based on seniority. Some of the longest-serving people walked away with six-figure bonuses; at least one of the checks handed out had seven figures on it.

Despite all the turbulence that year, Jamie Kellner remained a patriarchal figure to most at the WB. The surprise bonuses only reinforced his revered status. To those of us who knew him well, it was particularly impressive because we knew him to be frugal by nature. But Kellner and Ancier got a kick out of bestowing the checks on the network's rank and file. There were tears; and there was rejoicing, whooping, and hollering. For many of the network's young employees, it was the largest lump sum they'd ever received.

"I remember thinking, 'This is something Rupert Murdoch wouldn't do,' " says one WB alum who choked up that day.

CHAPTER TEN

A NEW ENTERPRISE

Three months after the September 11, 2001, terrorist attacks, Dawn Ostroff was in her midtown Manhattan office at Lifetime Television when she got a call out of the blue from the West Coast. It was Leslie Moonves.

Ostroff, who was head of programming for the female-focused cable channel, had worked for the CBS chieftain as a secretary nearly 20 years earlier when he was a TV movie development executive at 20th Century Fox; it was in the 1980s just before Rupert Murdoch bought the studio. Moonves had been impressed from the beginning by the bright, ambitious, and driven young woman from Brooklyn who read every script she could get her hands on and was persistent in telling him what she thought of the material. Moonves kept in touch with Ostroff over the years, and as his career ignited, first at Lorimar Television, then at Warner Bros. Television, and finally at CBS, Moonves kept Ostroff in the back of his mind as a good candidate to fill a creative development job when the right opportunity arose. Ostroff was flattered by his interest and more than happy to keep in contact with him. He'd reached out to her most recently in January 2001, on the day when *Daily Variety* and *The Hollywood Reporter* carried page-one stories about Lifetime's rise to No. 1 in prime time among all basic cable networks. He'd been the first to call to congratulate her that morning—and he was calling from the West Coast, no less.

Eleven months later, Moonves finally found the opening he'd been waiting for when UPN moved from Paramount to CBS under the Viacom corporate hierarchy. UPN needed a spitfire programming executive who would be game enough to parachute in and try to resuscitate a nearly dead horse. The network had been rudderless for the previous six months, between Dean Valentine's lawsuit and the lack of a successor for Tom Nunan.

The biggest immediate problem was that there had been precious little development of new programs for the upcoming 2002–03 television season. That meant UPN was squandering its chance to capitalize on its high-priced *Buffy the Vampire Slayer* acquisition by using it as a launching pad for a new 9 p.m. show to complete the night, as the WB had done with the *Buffy* spin-off *Angel*.

Moonves had watched what Ostroff accomplished at Lifetime. She'd been a pivotal member of the management team that pushed it to become the top-rated basic cable channel after years of lagging behind its established rivals with a blend of series, original movies, and unscripted shows that connected with Lifetime's target audience. As he evaluated the damage at UPN, Moonves knew it was the mission he'd been keeping Ostroff in mind for all these years. His timing was good. Ostroff was getting restless at Lifetime. By the end of 2001, she'd been at the channel for more than five years. Much as she enjoyed her colleagues and her surroundings, Ostroff was beginning to think about her next career move. The issue was forced when the time came to renew her employment contract, and she wasn't sure if she wanted to sign up for another long hitch. She'd received entreaties from other companies during the previous few years. She knew there were interesting options out there if she sought them.

Then on that unforgettable Tuesday morning in September, the Twin Towers fell. Ostroff's husband, Mark Ostroff, was a partner in a Wall Street asset management firm, and while he wasn't in the towers, he easily could have been. The premeditated savagery of the September 11 terrorist attacks on New York and the Pentagon left her spooked. She had a baby boy at home, her firstborn. And though a native, Ostroff could not shake the feeling of being trapped, living on an island that seemed to have a bull's eye painted on it. In addition to her son, Ostroff's blended family included her husband's two older children, and she was finding it harder to raise them all comfortably in the big city. Ostroff had lived in Los Angeles and its environs for 15 years in the 1980s and 1990s. She was fond of its wide-open spaces and pleasant weather. But her husband's work had long made the cross-country move a difficult proposition for the family.

Nevertheless, the opportunity to run a broadcast network, even a broken-down broadcast network, was something completely different from offers that had come her way in the past. Ostroff was aware that UPN was in bad shape and had been for some time. But she didn't hesitate much, not with the offer coming from Moonves at a time when CBS was clearly on the rise. After mulling over the UPN opportunity during the holidays, Ostroff flew to Los Angeles for a meeting with Moonves in early January 2002. He greeted her in his expansive office on the famed CBS Television City studio lot. Ostroff was struck by how tan he was for the middle of winter, even by L.A. standards.

Moonves confidently outlined his plan to merge UPN's operations with CBS's, giving the struggling network the benefit of big-league executive talent and other resources. Plus, he reasoned that he could better amortize the costs borne by CBS on back-office functions like finance, legal, affiliate relations, and research by spreading them across two networks. What he really needed was a sharp programming executive to pull UPN out of its trench. As Moonves sat with Ostroff discussing the possibilities and the problems, he admired her feistiness and her eagerness to take on a rehabilitation project when she could have coasted on her success at Lifetime.

Petite and vivacious, blond and blue-eyed with a girlish voice that belies a fiercely competitive spirit, Ostroff proved an easy fit into Moonves's inner circle at CBS. She returned to New York after the first meeting in his office and began preparing for the move. Six weeks later, she settled into her office at UPN's West Los Angeles headquarters.

"UPN was the kind of opportunity that absolutely got me right away. I always love a challenge," Ostroff says. "For me, it's much more fun to push a boulder up a mountain than it is to be sitting on top of the mountain. And UPN was definitely a boulder that needed to be pushed up—in a big way."

• • •

The twenty-four months that Jamie Kellner spent as chairman and CEO of Turner Broadcasting System in Atlanta were, by all accounts, hard ones for both him and the network he left behind in Burbank. The WB felt like a child torn between two parents in a messy divorce, and there was a clear leadership vacuum.

Kellner seemed very unhappy about having to make such a personal sacrifice—trading Southern California for Atlanta—in order to pave the way for his exit strategy from the WB. It became generally known that Kellner intended to make it a short stay while he revamped divisions, including implementing layoffs as part of AOL Time Warner's broader cost-cutting crusade. TBS's thousands of employees "didn't want him there, and he didn't want to be there," recalls one high-ranking WB alum.

Kellner didn't mix much with the TBS rank and file during his stay in Atlanta, instead surrounding himself with the older compatriots that he had brought with him like Brad Turell and Garth Ancier. Turell told his old and new colleagues that his role would be much more than just corporate communications for TBS; he would serve as Jamie's "chief of staff" in overseeing a far-flung empire. The Time Warner corporate press release announcing Turell's appointment was particularly gushy about the depth of his long professional relationship and friendship with Kellner.

The end result of these movements was that Kellner was seen by many TBS veterans as a Hollywood guy who was dispatched to tell the ignorant Southerners how to do their jobs, even though Jamie was anything but a Hollywood guy.

Back home in Burbank, Jed Petrick finally relocated with some trepidation from New York to the West Coast to take a more hands-on role in the management of the network as president and chief operating officer. In addition, Garth was back in the picture at the WB in an advisory role.

Petrick still reported to Kellner, and he and Jordan Levin logged plenty of time on the phone with him in Atlanta. The three of them emphasized to outsiders that everything was business as usual for the WB, but it was not the same. Kellner was not the same cool, calm leader the WB staff had known for years. He was uncharacteristically short-tempered and more aloof than usual, even with close associates. Worst of all, he seemed willing to do things with his new authority that were not in the WB's best interest.

One development that rankled many at the WB was the decision that it would fork over significant money to help Turner's TNT and TBS pay for big-money movie rights deals with major Hollywood studios. The WB shared in the right to run the movies, but strategically the deals made no sense for a still-young network. It takes a lot of marketing muscle to bring a large audience into a one-time-only telecast. When you spend money on the launch of a series, you hope it pays dividends week after week. Not so with a big theatrical movie telecast where a network pays big bucks for the rights to run the movie once, maybe twice. The WB didn't have any advertising and promotion dollars to spare at a time when it needed to seed the next generation of signature WB shows.

The most profligate example was the $75 million the WB committed in January 2002 for the broadcast premiere rights to director Peter Jackson's *Lord of the Rings* film trilogy, which hailed from a Time Warner sibling, New Line Cinema. Turner's portion of the deal actually shot the total price tag up to about $160 million.* The deal gave the WB the rights to air the three blockbuster movies over a 10-year term, with the payments spread out as well, but it was still a big bill for the WB to swallow. To make matters worse, the *Lord of the Rings* movies bombed in their airings on the WB. The network didn't do as well with these high-priced movies as it did on a good night with *Charmed* or *Smallville*.

Inside TBS, meanwhile, the feeling was that Kellner favored the WB at the expense of TNT, TBS Superstation, CNN et al. At one point, Jamie's biggest detractors in Atlanta initiated an internal investigation

---

* "WB, TBS Use Synergy for $160 Mil *Rings*' Circus." *The Hollywood Reporter*, February 1, 2002.

into how he was allocating resources to TBS units, according to multiple sources with knowledge of the situation. It never came to anything in the long run, but the message it sent to Jamie was unmistakable.

Dawn Ostroff walked into her new job at UPN on February 11, 2002, with every intention of focusing first on building a new team and rebuilding morale among a staff battered and bruised by the whirlwind of the previous seven years. From talking to Moonves and others, she had some idea of what was in store for her, and luckily for her it was not new territory. She knew how hard it was to turn a network around when the industry's perception of it was mostly negative. That had been the situation at Lifetime when she arrived in the fall of 1996.

After a few weeks, Ostroff was floored by the magnitude of UPN's problems. The network wasn't the last stop on the list when agents and producers were shopping a hot new series concept; it wasn't even on the list. As Ostroff learned, its reputation for having a pauper's programming budget meant that few people were willing to bring their projects to the network because they knew they'd have to produce them on a shoestring budget. In the industry, UPN was thought to be cursed, partly as a result of all the turnover and upheaval. With only a few exceptions, UPN programs from the 1999–2001 period were forgettable at best, vulgar at worst.

The only consistent ray of promise for UPN's original scripted programming was its Monday urban comedy block. In fall 2000, the female ensemble show *Girlfriends* emerged with favorable notices and more than a few commentators calling it an African American spin on *Sex and the City*. But that wasn't enough to offset the scorn from critics and low ratings generated by most UPN offerings.

One such show was *Chains of Love*, which was based on a Dutch property and came about amid the post-*Who Wants to be a Millionaire* craze for out-there foreign TV formats. The dating-game reality show involved four men being chained to a woman for a few days while she decides which one she wants to date. She unlocks them one by one until only her intended is left. Surprisingly, Garth Ancier while at NBC originally picked up the show for the U.S. as a desperation move after NBC President and CEO Bob Wright roundly criticized him for allowing NBC to miss out on the reality boom. Reality craze or no, *Chains* proved too outré for NBC. UPN swooped in to grab the half-finished project when NBC dumped it. But even with the copious advance attention the show had received as an example of reality TV run amok, *Chains* was a ratings dud when it premiered in 2001.

"You couldn't kick this network any more," Ostroff says. "It was dead as could be. Just dead as could be."

Despite her best intentions, Ostroff found she had no spare time to get to know the staff or the morale problems she inherited at UPN. The clock was ticking the moment she entered the UPN building because the rest of the industry was nearly halfway through pilot season. Ostroff faced a mad dash to rush into production a few comedy and drama pilots if she were to have any hope of making progress in the 2002–03 television season. She needed at least two or three pilot prospects by mid-May, in time for UPN's upfront schedule presentation to advertisers in New York. Her innate competitiveness fueled her drive to find the right stuff to impress her boss and her industry peers.

As an experienced development executive, Ostroff knew she had to hurry and comb through stacks and stacks of other networks' rejected pilot scripts in the hopes of gleaning a pearl or two. In her first weeks at UPN, Ostroff was preoccupied with reading "everything I could get my hands on," mostly through agents she knew who also had an interest in breathing new life into projects thought to be dead. Ostroff combated the bad ol' UPN image by constantly reminding people that Leslie Moonves was now overseeing the network, and he was a guy known for winning more than losing. Little by little, Ostroff convinced television's creative community that UPN was off to a fresh start, with a little money to spend for a change.

"Once they realized (UPN) wasn't going away, the only thing everyone could do was rally around it and hope for something," Ostroff says.

Ostroff still shudders at the memory of the indignity of her first Television Critics Association appearance as head of UPN in July 2002.

"The reporters actually said, 'What's the point? Why don't you just shut the damn place down?' " Ostroff recalls. "We were so far in the negative that it took me two years to get us to the neutral zone, where people would even consider that maybe it was possible we could have a hit."

Next to the lack of signature programs, the second-biggest problem UPN faced, in Ostroff's view, was schizophrenia. The network's program lineup had no common threads, no network identity à la the WB or NBC in its "Must-See TV" heyday. UPN chased after a different audience target on each of its five nights: Monday was geared to black and Hispanic audiences with *Girlfriends, The Parkers,* and other comedies; Tuesday with *Buffy* went after the WB's business with young hip viewers ages 18 to 34; Wednesday was a mishmash of male-oriented sci-fi dramas including *Enterprise,* the shortest-lived of the four *Star Trek* spin-off series Paramount has produced since 1987; Thursday brought in the wrestling audience, an animal unto itself; and Friday was a showcase for C-grade movies and direct-to-video titles, plus occasional theatrical releases.

Ostroff's mission was to develop some hits and improve the network's "flow" of audience from night to night. To do that, she needed shows that could bridge the gap between the various UPN audiences. Coming out of the niche-oriented world of cable programming, Ostroff was particularly sensitive to UPN's need to develop an overarching "brand" to allow it to appeal to a narrowly targeted audience in the cluttered television landscape.

"It was really like a multiple personality disorder where nobody knew who (UPN) was because we were something different every night," says Ostroff. "The WB had built a brand. People heard 'the WB' and they knew what it stood for."

• • •

One day after Dawn Ostroff was forced to
defend UPN's very existence, Jamie Kellner and Brad Turell were back
on the West Coast to speak at the WB's portion of the July 2002 network press junket. Brad opened the WB's sessions with a pitch to the
assembled reporters and critics. He made an impassioned statement
that journalists should finally grant the WB the "fifth network" mantle
it had sought since 1995 and begin referring to the "Big Five" networks in their stories. It was no secret in this crowd that Jamie disliked diminutive labels such as netlet and baby network, which were
affixed to the WB from the start. Turell appealed to the writers' hu-
manity. He appealed to them as grown-ups.

"For us, it's a little like when you reach a certain age and level of
maturity, and you earn the right to be called an adult," Turell said.

In truth, he had a case. By then, the WB was a known commodity in a good portion of America's 100 million-plus television households, particularly those with teenagers and young adults under their
roofs. Its best shows had left a mark on pop culture. It was a proven
innovator in programming, marketing, and distribution. UPN couldn't
come close to the WB's track record; and when Turell pressed his
case, UPN was on its third management regime in seven years.

But the nation's TV critics, columnists, and reporters are a surly
lot, especially when they gather in large numbers in smoggy midsum-
mer Pasadena heat. Those who didn't ignore Turell's semantic suggestion wound up challenging or needling him. Later that morning,
during his Q&A session with reporters, Kellner poked fun at Turell
for the pitch that didn't fly, calling it "Brad's bar mitzvah." Not that
Kellner disagreed with him.

"I think it's appropriate," Kellner told reporters. "It's seeking
your support, seeking your respect for the work that we've done."*

As evidenced by their leaders, WB executives were feeling cocky
that year, for sure, and for good reason. The network had banked

---

* *The Hollywood Reporter,* July 15, 2002, "WB lays claim to 5 status."

more than $725 million in advertising sales in 2001. UPN barely reached one-third the WB's take. The WB was rewarded for the successful launch of *Smallville,* ensuring the network a strong season post-*Buffy the Vampire Slayer.*

The icing on the 2001–02 television season was the WB's long-awaited traction with a comedy, with Friday night newcomer *Reba.* The domestic sitcom played like a Reba McEntire country and western song; McEntire starred as the matriarch of a blue-collar household that included a cheating husband and a pregnant oldest daughter. *Reba* felt far afield from the WB's young-female wheelhouse; it was easy to imagine the show running on ABC or CBS, in violation of the WB's mantra of only offering shows that could not be found on another broadcast network. But the WB brass seized on *Reba's* credible ratings and called it a hit so often that the label eventually stuck.

While the WB's future seemed to be nothing but rosy, the behind-the-scenes turmoil was beginning to affect strategic management decisions. It preoccupied Jed and Jordan and other executives at a time when the network's best minds needed to work together to plot a growth strategy for the WB's next five years. The network at this time was moving in the right direction, but it was not yet generating significant profits for Time Warner. That was one of the major reasons why Jamie was so adamant in not taking a financial hit on the *Buffy the Vampire Slayer* renewal deal.

In hindsight, some insiders regret that lack of strategic planning and research and development initiatives that would have helped the WB's stewards understand its audience and industry trends. There should have been some preparation for the inevitable cooling off of our heat with the notoriously fickle demographics of teens and young adults. Garth Ancier had wisely pushed us to look for ways to broaden our appeal slightly without alienating our youthful core viewer; *Reba* was one such example.

It is network television's law of gravity that all hot streaks come to an end at some point. Despite this certainty, there was little entrepreneurial introspection within the network, in part because it hadn't been ingrained in the go-with-your-gut strategy that Jamie cultivated. The WB had always succeeded through trial and error; *Savannah*— No. *7th Heaven*—Yes. *Muscle*—No. *Buffy the Vampire Slayer*—Yes. The WB's initiatives had rarely been influenced much by focus group testing or other market research tools. By 2002, after a string of successes, hubris was clouding some of the decision making at the network.

"There was such an inflated sense of what the WB was and what it 'meant' to its audience," observes a former insider. There was talk of trying to launch a radio program service and all manner of other WB licensed products.

By the summer of 2002, however, there were plenty of signs of trouble on the horizon. At the highest level, Robert Pittman made a hasty forced exit as AOL Time Warner's chief operating officer as the stock price sank and earnings reports failed to measure up to Pittman's lofty projections. The WB's ratings with young women and teenagers were clearly trending down. Even *Dawson's Creek* hit a ratings slump, as all shows inevitably do.

Within the WB, however, a smug sense of superiority had taken root. The feeling was that no matter what happened, the WB would always be miles ahead of its ostensible archrival. The sentiment grew among WB staffers that it was just a matter of time before UPN went away, for good.

Jordan Levin had a lot of ego at stake as he and the WB's programming team focused on developing shows for the 2002–03 season. It seemed to some that he wanted to prove beyond all doubt that he could develop hits on his own.

Having safely maneuvered through the network's first season without *Buffy*, Jordan sought to capture *Smallville*'s lightning in a bottle again by adapting a lesser-known, more contemporary DC Comics property, *Birds of Prey*. On paper, *Prey* seemed perfectly suited for the WB treatment. The graphic novel was a spin-off of Batman revolving around a trio of young female crime fighters in tight leather outfits. The lead leatherette, known alternately as Helena or the Huntress, is the spawn of Batman and Catwoman.

Mike Tollin and Brian Robbins, the producers who turned to *Smallville* after being stymied in their pursuit of Batman, were in the picture as executive producers of *Birds of Prey*. It was a challenging show from the start, requiring special effects and elaborate fantasy elements. But by this time, Warner Bros. Television was accustomed to spending whatever it took to keep *Smallville* on the right side of that thin line separating corny from captivating visual effects. *Birds of Prey* benefited from Warner Bros.' willingness to invest more in big properties that had the potential to deliver ancillary payoffs through films, animation, music, licensing, and merchandising, and other divisions throughout the conglomerate then known as AOL Time Warner.

WB expected *Prey*, with its connection to the Batman mythos, to be a star-making vehicle. The lead roles went to three virtual unknowns: Ashley Scott, Dina Meyer, and Rachel Skarsten. The writing wasn't stellar, but the girls were sexy and curvy in their black leather and bare midriffs. The pilot episode, directed by Robbins, had its moments of slick comic book action and sexy humor. In truth, many at the WB knew the show was in for a hard time. It had obvious big flaws, primarily a ridiculously complicated universe and backstories for its three main characters, who came across as flat and devoid of emotional connection with the audience.

(I never cared for *Prey* and its dark tone, but I was biased that year. I'd developed a two-hour pilot based on *The Lone Ranger* that was passed on; it eventually aired as a movie on the WB. The actor I cast as the masked man, Chad Michael Murray, went on to star in a later WB series, *One Tree Hill*.)

But the problems in the *Prey* pilot were papered over and most of the WB's fall 2002 marketing budget was plowed into the show. Images of the stars in *Charlie's Angels*-like poses were plastered all over New York and Los Angeles and other major cities in the weeks leading up to the series premiere. "Batman's little girl is all grown up," read the tagline on the handbills featuring Ashley Scott in the role of

Helena perched atop a gargoyle with the nighttime Gotham City skyline behind her.

As always, when premiere night came on Oct. 9, 2002, WB executives held their breath and crossed their fingers. The Nielsen returns the following morning were, in fact, impressive. The WB's marketing department had done its job spectacularly well once again. The target audience's appetite had been whetted. They showed up 7.5 million strong for *Prey*'s maiden voyage in the Wednesday 9 p.m. time slot behind *Dawson's Creek*. The reviews had been mixed, more negative than positive, but that didn't bother many at the network after the first ratings bulletins came in.

Jordan, however, soon became aware that there were big problems behind the scenes. The show had essentially collapsed from the lack of a solid foundation. The movie screenwriter who had penned the pilot, Laeta Kalogridis, was a TV neophyte who'd never worked on a series staff before, let alone served as an executive producer. The plan all along had been to bring in a seasoned show runner to help Tollin and Robbins bring Kalogridis up to speed. But that match hadn't been made by the time *Prey* premiered. Tollin and Robbins were both juggling numerous other projects. Executives at Warner Bros. Television hadn't kept close tabs on *Prey* after the pilot was picked up for a series, in part because of Tollin and Robbins' track record on *Smallville*. The difference there was that *Smallville* executive producers Miles Millar and Al Gough didn't need reinforcements. They were already experienced show runners and writers.

All told, *Prey* was doomed before it began. The show was falling apart at the time when it most needed to have its act together with fresh episodes to give the viewers reasons to keep watching. *Prey* couldn't do that because its basic infrastructure—the orderly production of scripts, casting, set building, location scouting, music licensing, and on and on—had never gelled.

As Jordan came to grips with the depth of his problem, he couldn't believe he hadn't seen it coming. He'd been so preoccupied with corporate politics and other issues that he hadn't noticed the giant red flag waving around his big show for the fall. There was much finger-pointing about the mess among Levin and others at the network, Tollin and Robbins, and Warner Bros. Television. After a few airings, *Prey*'s ratings had fallen by more than half. By the end of November, WB was forced to acknowledge that *Prey* was finished, though new episodes continued to air through January. Levin publicly blamed the show's flameout on a "failure of execution."

"We didn't have the right team," Levin says in retrospect. "We didn't work together enough to make sure we had the right team."

The high-profile flop of *Prey* overshadowed the arrival that fall of what proved to be the last signature WB drama series. *Everwood*, produced by Warner Bros. Television, was a family drama about a widower with two children who trades the fast-track life of a New York City neurosurgeon for a small-town practice in Colorado after his wife dies. It was a little bit *Ben Casey,* a little bit *Northern Exposure,* a little bit *Family Affair.* Most of all, it was pure WB—a passion project from an extraordinarily talented young writer-producer, Greg Berlanti, with a strong creative vision for his show. As was the case with *7th Heaven* in 1996, the WB stood out from the pack in fall 2002 by serving up a small-town family melodrama amid a sea of cops, docs, cadavers, and lawyers on the Big Four networks.

All of 30 when *Everwood* premiered, Berlanti was a known commodity at the WB; he'd cut his teeth working on *Dawson's Creek* and was considered a key factor in that show's longevity. The pilot was smartly written and smartly cast with a recognizable lead in Treat Williams and Gregory Smith, a can't-miss-handsome newcomer with acting chops beyond his years, in the role of the teenage son. Williams, an industry pro with a long resume, marveled at how Berlanti, then 30 years old, single, and childless, could tap into the soul of a forty-something overachiever who's agonizing over the death of his wife and how to start life anew with his children.

Everwood was never a ratings magnet on its own, but it was a good companion to *7th Heaven* in its first two seasons airing in the Monday 9 p.m. slot. By the end of its first season, *Everwood* was ranking high on critics' lists of the best shows on TV.

Within the WB, the natural inclination was to focus on *Ever-*

wood's success rather than question the reasons for *Prey*'s collapse. Though there are always shows that open strong and fade quickly, *Prey* was the first time that the WB let a potential hit slip through its fingers because of chaos behind the scenes.

As public a disappointment as *Prey* was, it was not enough to raise alarm bells with Jamie or other senior executives. The WB was still well stocked with older hits and its hard-earned cachet as the hip new network on the block easily withstood the *Prey* debacle.

The WB still had fresh success stories in *Smallville* and *Reba* and good prestige-buzz in *Everwood*. No network has a .500 batting average with its shows, and for a long time it seemed the WB could do no wrong with its drama series. But as every good development executive knows, after you've made a costly mistake on a show, it's what you learn from that misfire that makes all the difference.

CHAPTER ELEVEN

AMERICA'S NEXT TOP NETWORK

As UPN began to get its act together, the WB faced still more behind-the-scenes upheaval in the first few months of 2003. On February 18, a press release was issued by Time Warner's corporate communications department stating that Jamie Kellner had resigned his post at Turner Broadcasting System and would return to the West Coast and begin the management transition process at the WB. Jamie planned to retire from the WB for good in May 2004, at the close of the network's tenth season.

With Jamie's return to his former role as WB chairman and CEO, oversight of the network shifted out of TBS and back to Warner Bros. under Barry Meyer and Bruce Rosenblum. By this time, Rosenblum was the executive vice president of the studio overseeing all television operations, the same role Meyer had filled for Bob Daly at the time the WB was founded in 1993. Jamie would once again report to Meyer, as would his successor at the WB.

The news that Jamie was leaving TBS was not a surprise to Jordan Levin, Jed Petrick, and other top executives at the WB; a large group of them had learned of Jamie's plan to depart TBS during a Time Warner executive retreat in New York a week before. Jordan had also received another significant piece of news at the retreat: once Jamie left the WB in 2004, he was to be promoted to CEO of the network.

Jeffrey Bewkes, the former HBO chief executive who became Time Warner co-president after Robert Pittman's departure in July 2002, had informed Jordan of his impending rise to CEO at the WB in a matter-of-fact way during a cocktail party held as part of the retreat at the Ritz-Carlton hotel in Battery Park. It was the kind of corporate event where Levin couldn't help but notice that he was the youngest person in the room.

At age 35, Jordan was a creature of the WB through and through. In many ways, he was the same as he was when he joined the network in the summer of 1994. He'd stepped in to greater and greater responsibility during his tenure at the network, and he won more battles than he lost. He wore his ambition on his sleeve, which some found grating, and by many accounts he was not equipped for the role of CEO at the time he was handed the reins of the WB. Yet even his biggest detractors acknowledge he lived for nothing, short of his wife and children, like he lived for the WB.

After I left the WB, Jordan dropped the "co-" from his entertainment president title, but nothing else about his status at the network had formally changed. He had expected Jamie or someone to approach him with "a new deal," in industry parlance, or a new long-term employment contract with perks in recognition of the expanded responsibilities he'd assumed. With all of the moving and shaking within Time Warner and TBS at the time, management planning for the WB was low on the list of corporate priorities. When Jordan inquired about his status, he was assured that he would be "taken care of" down the road. Jordan had every confidence that Jamie would be good to his word, but after 18 months had gone by, he couldn't help but feel ignored.

On the heels of a day of corporate cheerleading and strategizing, complete with a motivational speech from Retired General Norman Schwarzkopf, a small group of executives milled around a mini cocktail bar set up in the lobby outside the ballroom where the presentations were made. Bewkes, who has the air of a Wall Street strategist and an affable charm, approached Jordan with a bottle of burgundy in hand. He was not surprised by the overture. Jamie had been told that Bewkes wanted to get to know him better during their stay in New York. Jordan figured that it was so Bewkes would endorse giving him a new long-term deal to remain as the WB's entertainment president.

"Congratulations," Bewkes told Jordan in his characteristically low-key style. "You're going to take over for Jamie as CEO."

Bewkes spelled out Jamie's plan to resign from TBS and return to Burbank to serve out the remainder of his employment contract with Time Warner in his old role as WB chairman and CEO.

A surge of adrenaline swirled through Jordan as he processed what Bewkes was saying. For a few frozen seconds, he felt as though he was replaying a slow-motion video of what Bewkes had just told him in his brain. Bewkes and Jamie were smiling at him, calmly and paternally, as Jordan sat down on a divan to collect himself. He was instantly concerned about what Jamie's eventual departure would mean for the WB within the Time Warner chain of command. He was glad to hear the plan was for the network to shift back into the Warner Bros.' fold.

Jamie spent much of his immediate post-TBS time at home with his family on the Santa Barbara coast, though he maintained daily communications with his department heads and was a presence at company functions and pilot-screening sessions. To his closest associates, it seemed as if Jamie needed a soft landing after a grueling two years at TBS. "I'm really looking forward to scaling it all back and watching my son grow up," Jamie told reporters on a conference call the day his resignation was announced.

During his time at TBS, his oversight of CNN had been particularly difficult, coming as Fox News Channel ascended. Jamie pursued but could not seal a deal with Disney to merge ABC News and its high-profile on-air talent into CNN. Jamie and Garth spearheaded a radical makeover of CNN's sibling Headline News channel, making the screen take on the look of a Web page, with multiple graphic elements grouped around a smaller window for the live anchor. It drew mixed reviews at first, but elements of the design have since been adopted by other TV news outlets.

Jamie was also instrumental in encouraging the Cartoon Network to expand its *Adult Swim* late-night block of irreverent, adult-themed cartoon series, which has grown into a ratings powerhouse that surpasses the late-night programming on NBC, CBS, and ABC in the coveted young-male demographics.

Among Jamie's most memorable experiences during his run at Turner came via an interview he gave in April 2002 to a cable industry trade publication about the rise of TiVo and other digital video recorders that allow viewers to skip through commercials. Jamie had been sounding the alarm about the new ad-skipping devices for some time. His blunt assertion that "any time you skip a commercial . . . you're actually stealing the programming" was widely picked up by other media, given his lofty status at AOL Time Warner, and criticized by commentators as a sign of the entertainment industry once again fighting technological innovation.* Jamie never wavered on the sentiment he expressed, but the force of the mostly negative reaction was disconcerting to him, close associates say.

One initiative of Jamie's that was scrapped entirely after his departure from Turner was the Turner Television production banner. The unit born out of Jamie's frustration at Warner Bros. over their various business conflicts on programming deals had proven to be a bustling development lab for the WB in 2002 thanks to the talents of John Litvack. During its brief existence, Turner Television produced about a half dozen pilots. A few of them became WB series, including the Latino family comedy *Greetings from Tucson,* which was well received but low-rated, and a short-lived drama *The O'Keefes.*

Litvack was unabashed in bragging about how much more efficiently and cheaply his tiny unit with a handful of support staffers could produce pilots, compared to a big studio like Warner Bros. Television. But after Jamie left, Warner Bros. had no incentive to keep the separate operation alive. Nor did Jamie's successor at Turner have any need to keep it around.

In addition to a desire to slow down and spend time with his family, there was another big reason why Jamie was eager to restart his life in Southern California. Around the same time as his resigna-

---

*   *Cable World*, April 29, 2002, "Content's King."

tion, Jamie and the other WB stakeholders received our buyout payments under the terms of the deal struck in early 2001, just as the AOL-Time Warner merger was closing. According to sources, when the buyout agreement was finalized, Jamie expected to be paid out at least in part in AOL Time Warner stock. But AOL Time Warner executives told him that the stock was too valuable at that moment, and that he and the partners would have to take cash instead.

For Jamie and the rest of the partners, it was the dumb-lucky moment to beat all others. Two years later, when it came time to collect, we had $128 million in cold cash waiting for us. (By then, Time Warner had dropped AOL from its name and forced the resignations of the architects of the merger, CEO Gerald Levin and Chairman Steve Case.) None of us fortunate enough to have a stake in the WB appreciated the significance of this until the money was in our bank accounts.

Within weeks of Jamie's relocation to Atlanta in 2001, AOL Time Warner's stock price would begin its precipitous decline. The month the merger closed, in January 2001, AOL Time Warner's average closing price was $52.56—a long way from AOL's $71.25 per-share price 12 months earlier when the merger pact was announced. By January 2002, AOL Time Warner stock was down to around $26; by December of that year, it had sunk to about $13.

Amid all of this corporate drama, the problems of the WB were but a blip on Time Warner's radar. But Jordan's executive survival instincts told him he was in for a rocky time of it as CEO for the simple reason that he had been chosen without any consultation with Warner Bros.' Barry Meyer, who was to be his boss once Jamie formally bowed out the following year. Jordan knew it would be a difficult transition, given the recent strain on relations between the WB and its once-and-future parent studio. At Meyer's urging, it was decided that Garth would also return to the WB in the role as chairman, and that Jordan and Garth would both report to Meyer. Jed Petrick would remain in his post as president and chief operating officer, reporting to Jordan.

Levin didn't know how abrupt Kellner's departure from Atlanta would be until he got a call on his cell phone about a week after the corporate retreat where he'd learned his fate. He was told by his office that the announcement of Kellner's resignation from Turner was about to be released. A process he presumed would take at least a few weeks was triggered just days after he was informed of his pending promotion to CEO. Levin learned about Jamie's announcement while he was on vacation in Park City, Utah, with his family. He was standing on the snowy deck of a ski lodge when he got the call. He was told in unvarnished terms to keep quiet about the succession plan within the WB, which he took as more evidence that his new masters were not entirely thrilled with naming him to lead the network. It would be another six months before Jordan was formally anointed the crown prince of the WB.

When Dawn Ostroff was scrambling to come up with programming in her first months on the job at UPN in early 2002, the most intriguing thing she uncovered was a soapy drama revolving around two brothers struggling to run a successful rap music company and hold their families together. It was dubbed *Platinum* and had previously been under consideration at HBO. Ostroff thought it had great potential and, just as important, it hailed from interesting creative auspices. The show was conceived by two bubbling-under feature-film talents, Sofia Coppola and John Ridley.

Ridley at the time was a rising young screenwriter known for penning the slick 1999 George Clooney caper feature *Three Kings*. Coppola was on the cusp of seeing her mainstream movie career take flight later that year with the Oscar-winning *Lost in Translation*. These weren't the kind of people who had done much business with UPN during the previous few years. Ostroff got them to come to the network with her enthusiasm for the script and her belief that *Platinum* had the makings of a kind of hip-hop *Sopranos*. It was the story of two strong-willed, very different brothers, who were conflicted in their own way by the harsh realities of the family business. It had built-in opportunities for flashy, highly promotable guest star appearances and a pulsating soundtrack that propelled the action along. Ostroff had the luxury of being able to spend a little more for quality, in contrast to her predecessors.

As envisioned for HBO, *Platinum* was a sprawling, ambitious production with a large cast and plenty of expansive sets and location work. It didn't downscale all that much in the switch to UPN for a six-episode order. The key was finding two strong young actors for the lead roles of Jackson and Grady Rhames, and they found them in Jason George and Sticky Fingaz (aka rapper-actor Kirk Jones). The show had the shaky-camera look of a hip-hop video blended with sharp dialogue and the commercial sensibilities of an Aaron Spelling soap. Ray Richmond, reviewing for *The Hollywood Reporter,* called it "sharply produced, hypnotically shot akin to *Dynasty* for the hip-hop crowd, a def jam of backstabbing, power trips, dirty tricks, threats, counterthreats, general thuggery, and, of course, sex." Ostroff thought it could be a kind of bridge program that would appeal to UPN's core African American audience, the rap- and hip-hop-loving *Buffy the Vampire Slayer* demographic, and young adults in general.

When the ambitious series was finally ready to air, Ostroff orchestrated a big promotional push for *Platinum*'s April 2003 premiere. UPN cut a deal with MTV, its cable cousin under the Viacom umbrella, for MTV to carry repeats of *Platinum* episodes one week after their premiere. (*Platinum* was produced by Viacom Productions, a small unit within Paramount Television Group.) The music biz theme and high number of rappers and artists who had supporting roles and guest shots in the first few episodes made for a perfect tie-in with MTV, which also carried videos fashioned from the show in heavy rotation around the time of its debut.

As is so often the case in prime-time television, for all of the advance planning and care, for all of the brainstorming and creative thinking that went into it, *Platinum* was over and done with in a matter of weeks. Despite the "no kidding, it's good" reviews, solid promotion, and additional exposure on MTV, the show had no pulse in the Nielsen ratings. At that stage in UPN's history, Ostroff and Moonves couldn't justify continuing with a show that expensive. Ratings are the real currency of the television business, and with ratings that low, the advertising revenue just wasn't there to support such a high-end, expensive production

Ostroff remained unfazed. She'd have been happier if the show had lasted, of course, but the network still notched an important victory with *Platinum*, particularly in industry circles.

"It's one of the shows I'm most proud of in my career," Ostroff says. "It was the first time people said, 'OK, maybe [UPN] can at least develop something good.' It wasn't a hit, but at least they had respect for the material. That helped us."

Another helping hand for UPN came from an unlikely source who "walked in the door one day," as Ostroff recalls, around the same time that *Platinum* was coming together at the network.

Supermodel Tyra Banks had been looking to segue into a second career in television for some time, ever since she made a string of guest appearances in 1993 on the Will Smith NBC comedy series *The Fresh Prince of Bel-Air*. As Banks studied the prime-time landscape, it didn't take her long to see an opening in the reality-crazed landscape for an *American Idol*-esque elimination competition series, only with aspiring models instead of wannabe warblers. Banks teamed with veteran producer Ken Mok to pitch her vision of *America's Next Top Model* to various networks. Banks' supermodel status got her in the door, but her show got a cool reception until she came to UPN. Ostroff sparked to the idea immediately. If done well, Ostroff thought, *Top Model* could tap into young America's well-documented obsession with fashion, celebrity models, and looking fabulous. Banks' fame would give the show credibility as a talent-scouting contest. As an on-air personality, Banks was a slam dunk for UPN's core audience of African American urban youths.

"I figured the girls would want to watch for the models and the clothes and the wish-fulfillment part of it, and guys would watch just to see all the beautiful girls," Ostroff says. "Tyra just totally wowed me. When she pitched the show to me I got it 100 percent. I walked out of the room with her and said, 'You know, I get this. I really want to do this.' "

On May 20, 2003, *America's Next Top Model* premiered the

same night that *Buffy the Vampire Slayer* wrapped its seven-season run after two years on UPN. The symbolism was not lost on Ostroff: the pairing of those particular programs—the last of *Buffy* and the first salvo from a new show that she had developed and believed in whole-heartedly—signaled UPN's shift from a network so desperate it had to dig deep to buy a hit from its arch rival.

Given *Buffy*'s international renown, the lukewarm audience turnout for the final installment of *Buffy* was disappointing, but not so surprising. The show had taken its blows from critics and many fans as having gone downhill creatively after the move to UPN.

In sharp contrast, the numbers for *Top Model* were anything but disappointing. The show performed well by UPN or WB standards in its initial off-season summer run (premiering on the penultimate night of the 2002–03 season). Ostroff was encouraged, but cautious. It wasn't until the second edition of *Top Model* returned to UPN's lineup in January 2004 as a hit that Ostroff's team allowed themselves a victory dance. *Top Model* had entered the more competitive environment of regular-season play and drew a larger audience than its first time out. Its success was even sweeter for Ostroff and her boss, Leslie Moonves, because with *Top Model*, UPN had scored in an area the WB had never truly been able to crack: the reality-competition show. Despite the WB's track record with young adults, those same viewers were flocking to the high concept, quasi-unscripted shows (e.g., CBS's *Survivor,* Fox's *Joe Millionaire,* ABC's *The Bachelor,* and NBC's *The Apprentice*) on every network but the WB.

"To Leslie's credit, I was so passionate about it that he just said 'OK, you believe in it so much, try it.' That kind of support from a leader is really all you need," Ostroff says. "By giving us the freedom to fail, we were able to succeed."

On top of the usual pilot-development frenzy that consumes programming executives in the winter and early spring, Jordan Levin had a big challenge on his hands with *Dawson's Creek* in the second half of the 2002–03 season. The show that defined the WB was creeping toward long-in-the-tooth status. The core cast members—Katie Holmes, James Van Der Beek, Michelle Williams, and Joshua Jackson—had grown up and were focused on their movie careers. They were ready, in varying degrees, to give up the rigors of series television.

What's more, the show had hit the inevitable ratings slump. Jordan cared too much about *Dawson's Creek* and its legacy, to let the show slide into a serious jump-the-shark territory. He knew it was time to figure out a classy exit for *Dawson's*.

The obvious solution was to recruit creator Kevin Williamson to determine how the show should bow out. But that wasn't as easy as it sounded. Williamson had left the show at the end of its second season in the spring of 1999, after facing a near-nervous breakdown from trying to juggle too much film and TV work all at the same time. Kevin hadn't even watched the show since he left. He'd been busy with his movie career and other new projects, including an unhappy experience with the WB on a short-lived drama series, *Glory Days*, in 2001.

But Jordan had gotten to know Kevin well during the formative years of *Dawson's*, and he knew how to approach him—through a fellow writer. Greg Berlanti was the wunderkind show runner credited with keeping *Dawson's* from sliding into mediocrity after Kevin departed.

At the time, Berlanti was consumed with finishing up the first season of *Everwood*, but even with a new show on his plate he had kept in contact with the *Dawson's* team. To bring it to a worthy conclusion, Jordan and Greg knew they had to hustle. It was then mid-March, which was very late in the game to be plotting a series finale to air in May. Over a series of conversations, they brainstormed a simple premise for a two-hour finale that they would pitch to Williamson and beg him to write, or at least guide, so that the show's conclusion would reflect his vision.

Williamson at that time was spending his days in downtown Los Angeles working with director Wes Craven on the location shoot of a horror movie called *Cursed*, which was living up to its title. Kevin at first begged off Greg's dinner invitation, citing the troubled movie shoot. But Greg and Jordan were persistent, offering to meet him for lunch at a downtown L.A. spot to make it easy for Kevin.

After Jordan and Greg laid out their pitch, Williamson was gracious but cool to the idea, in part because the script would have to be turned around super-fast. He confessed he hadn't kept up with the show. But Williamson had a soft spot for Greg, who had impressed him from the outset when Berlanti joined the show as a staff writer, and also for Jordan, who had given him respect and support long before Kevin was an above-the-title player in movies.

"Can I do it any way I want?" Williamson asked, in a tone that made Greg and Jordan realize he was warming up to the idea.

"That's why we want you to do it," Jordan replied.

Somehow, Williamson found the time during the ensuing two weeks to pen the two-hour episode in collaboration with Greg and long-serving *Dawson's* scribe Maggie Friedman. Together, the group crafted a clever story that scored with the show's ardent fans and reflected the blend of humor, soap, teen angst, and relationship drama that made the show stand out at the beginning.

The plot incorporated a device that allowed the episode to be packed with wink-wink references to itself and pop culture that cheered the fans. Five years into the future, our hero Dawson is working in Los Angeles as the producer of—what else?—a teen TV drama series dubbed *The Creek,* and, in fact, we see him struggling to come up with the story for a season finale episode that resolves the unrequited-love question mirroring *Dawson's* own first-season closer. A family wedding brings Dawson back to Capeside, where he encounters the old gang, including his on-again, off-again soul mate Joey, who's now a successful book editor in New York but back in town for the wedding. As soon as she's back home, Joey realizes she's still emotionally torn by her love for Dawson and Pacey, a triangle that got quite a workout during the show's six seasons.

Through a number of other twists and turns, *Dawson's* devotees were given the chance to cry over the death of rebellious Jen, who was felled by a heretofore undiagnosed heart condition, and swoon over the surprising but satisfying twist at the end that saw Joey choose not Dawson but Pacey to join her in New York.

"The first hour is a little stumbly, because we had to write it so fast. It started shooting two days after we turned it in," Williamson says. "But the second hour really works. It comes home."

And with that homecoming, the show that turbo-charged the WB came to an end in style. The finale yielded some of the WB's highest-ever ratings among teenagers and females in the 12–24 age range.

By the fall of 2003, Dawn Ostroff was starting to feel like she was getting somewhere. UPN no longer seemed to be on a 24/7 red alert. Ostroff could sense it in ways that were mostly intangible and anecdotal from friends and coworkers in the industry. It was also indisputable that the WB was taking a beating in the ratings after losing *Dawson's Creek* and *Buffy the Vampire Slayer* and striking out two years in a row with its "next big thing": *Birds of Prey* in 2002 and *Tarzan* in 2003.

Tarzan began as another effort to WB-ify a well-known fantasy-adventure property. It was seen as a hot prospect for the network—so much so it had attracted the interest of producer Laura Ziskin, who was red-hot at the time in Hollywood coming off the success of her 2002 revival of *Spider-Man* on the big screen. The original concept for the Warner Bros. Television-produced show had been to stick to the basic fish-out-of-water tenets of Edgar Rice Burroughs' ape-man creation, leaning heavily on his tender romance with Jane, of course. After a lengthy search, the network and studio settled on Travis Fimmel, a hunky, blond Australian model with minimal acting experience, to play the modern-day vine-swinger.

In the hurly burly of life at the WB in 2002 and 2003, when Jamie was managing from afar and none of his lieutenants had clear authority beyond their respective domains, programming decisions, especially greenlighting decisions, were settled much more by committee than they ever had been before. Even Jamie had pushed the

WB to develop a few more traditional shows built around sturdy prime-time formats à la cop shows, legal case-of-the-week dramas, and medical themes because he hoped to amortize the WB's costs by running some of the network's shows on Turner's TBS and TNT as well. The older audience drawn by those well-established cable networks wasn't drawn to the teen angst of *Felicity* or *Dawson's Creek*.

In this environment, to Jordan's dismay, the concept for *Tarzan* morphed into a more farfetched premise in which Jane was a New York Police Department detective and Tarzan helps her solve crimes. Despite a marketing blitz by the network (in his tepid review of the show *Variety*'s Brian Lowry noted "you can't throw a banana without hitting a billboard of him"),* *Tarzan* was a flop that barely lasted a month.

While *Tarzan* was tanking, Dawn Ostroff was reaping the benefits of an attention-getting coup that she'd pulled off by luring an A-list movie star couple to produce a comedy series for the network for the 2003–04 season. Will Smith, one of Hollywood's most bankable stars and his wife, actress Jada Pinkett Smith, sought UPN out for their idea of creating and producing a comedy series about the trials and tribulations of blended families. They were inspired by their own experience with an extended family that included their young son and daughter, Smith's two children from his previous marriage, and his ex-wife. The premise immediately struck a chord with Ostroff, who has dealt with the same issues in her own life. She knew the blended-family experience could be fertile ground for comedy and relatable characters.

Ostroff's excitement was sincere. Will Smith knew television comedy, having gotten his start as an actor on the highly successful 1990s NBC sitcom, *The Fresh Prince of Bel-Air*. Ostroff was impressed that the Smiths had spent money out of their own pocket to hire a seasoned comedy writer, Betsy Borns, to flesh out their ideas and co-write a pilot script with Jada. If done well, the show would ring true to viewers just as it had to her, Ostroff believed. And she knew the

---

*   *Daily Variety*, October 1, 2003.

Smiths' association with the show, loosely inspired by their home life, would draw a ton of media attention—some positive ink on UPN for a change. Ostroff was sold on the show, eventually titled *All of Us,* before the first meeting ended.

As numerous TV critics would observe, *All of Us* was not *The Cosby Show,* but it was a cut above the garden-variety UPN sitcom. Will and Jada were committed to being more than just name-only producers. Jada Pinkett Smith cowrote the pilot script with Betsy Borns, and both Will and Jada maintained a semiregular presence on the set, reviewed scripts, and contributed to the writing process— particularly during the first season. The presence of the Smiths and their young children lent a homey feeling to the *All of Us* set. It was not coincidental that the show's lead actor was Duane Martin, who happened to be the person who introduced Will to his future wife in the mid-1990s.

Signing up *All of Us* proved a testament to how far Ostroff had brought the network in the past year. That a marquee name like Will Smith and his representatives would even pitch a show to UPN, let alone agree to do business with them, was a pleasant change from the hostile environment she'd stepped into ten months earlier. Much of the turn in industry perception of UPN had to do with the fact that UPN now had money to spend. But most of the credit belonged to Ostroff. By this time, she had some of her own lieutenants in place in programming, marketing, and business functions, plus UPN was now able to lean on CBS for support. The benefits of that older brother-kid sister relationship, especially early on in Ostroff's run, were enormous. Top CBS executives had a mandate from Leslie Moonves to take their UPN counterparts under their wings. But they also had hearts. UPN was so bad off at the time that the CBS executives couldn't help but take pity on them.

"The CBS executives were *so* in our corner. All of these people had other jobs, and yet anytime we called them or needed them for anything, it was never an imposition," Ostroff says. "It was always [done] with a smile. They were rooting for us."

For its fall 2003 lineup, UPN got another vote of confidence from a surprising source: Warner Bros. Television. The studio was in the midst of a push to reclaim the mantle it had lost in the late 1990s to News Corp.'s 20th Century Fox TV as the industry's top supplier of prime-time series to the broadcast networks. And that meant it could no longer afford to mostly ignore UPN, especially now that the network was in business with notable creative talent like Will Smith and Jada Pinkett Smith.

Ostroff was more than happy to have a five-star studio like Warner Bros. handling her shows. UPN had stopped relying on its Paramount Television for the bulk of its programming—from the minute Leslie Moonves took over in 2002. But it was still a struggle to find production partners willing to gamble on projects for UPN. In addition to *All of Us*, Warner Bros. Television took on three additional sitcoms for UPN that year. Two of them died quick deaths—*The Mullets* and the hipsters-turned-parents domestic comedy *Rock Me Baby*. But *All of Us* and *Eve,* a workplace vehicle about a fashion designer played by the rapper Eve, were serviceable shows. *All of Us* was never a true hit for UPN, but it paid huge dividends by burnishing the network's image within Hollywood's creative community.

Despite these programming advances, UPN still had issues on the affiliate front. In the aftermath of News Corp.'s acquisition of the Chris-Craft stations, Rupert Murdoch and Peter Chernin had bought themselves tremendous sway over the future of UPN. In the duopoly ownership era, the Fox Television Stations Group was also allowed to be the home of UPN's most important affiliate stations, WWOR-TV New York and KCOP-TV Los Angeles, plus its outlets in San Francisco, Washington, Houston, Baltimore, Minneapolis, and Phoenix. News Corp. further increased its grip on UPN by spending $425 million in 2002 to buy the network's affiliate station in Chicago, WPWR-TV.

Because of the impossibility of lining up comparable affiliate stations in New York, Los Angeles, and Chicago, News Corp. had the clout to sign short-term, two- and three-year affiliation deals to keep Viacom at its mercy. News Corp. even lobbed a $108 million lawsuit at UPN in 2003 when it discovered some advantageous fine print in its UPN station affiliation contracts indicating that Viacom owed the erstwhile Chris-Craft stations significant retroactive payments.

Despite the uneasy relations and lawsuit, Moonves and Fox's top brass were able to hammer out a new affiliation agreement that took effect September 1, 2003. Moonves gleefully unveiled the deal in late September 2003 to the business press, which had been speculating about UPN's imminent demise, as News Corp. toyed with Viacom over whether it would renew the UPN affiliations in the crucial New York and Los Angeles markets. The three-year term of the UPN affiliation agreement would prove to be pivotal for the network before the contract was up.

As Garth Ancier and Jordan Levin offi-cially moved into their respective new roles as co-chairman and co-CEO in September 2003, the mood at the WB was uneasy. (Both executives carried the qualifying "co-" with their new titles for the next eight months while Jamie Kellner remained at the network.) At the outset, Garth felt like a chairman without a country, as if he were expected to serve as "the wise old man in the corner," as he put it. It was a far cry from the days of us sitting around a conference room talking about television shows. Jed Petrick, who was given the title of president and chief operating officer, would also play a role in the transition.

By September, Warner Bros. had gone public with its succession plan for Kellner, and the news was anticlimactic for most network insiders. Warner Bros.' publicity executives went out of their way to position the succession team as the triumvirate of Jordan, Garth, and Jed.

Nevertheless, there was chatter in the halls at the WB that Jordan would never last in the post-Kellner era with Warner Bros.' more buttoned-down corporate culture. But Jed dismissed it as gossip from a few detractors. Jed figured Jordan had Jamie's support, and that would be enough to keep him in place for the foreseeable future. The dynamic made for an awkward few months after Jordan was anointed.

"There were three people, but there wasn't three people's worth of work," says one WB insider.

Jamie had run WB using a classic spoke-in-wheel management philosophy. He was the wheel, the various department heads were the spokes, and there was little to no hierarchy in between, save for sometimes at the corporate level. Jamie was the kingmaker who bestowed authority, favors, commendations—even slivers of ownership in the network—to his favorite employees. There was an esprit de corps among most of his senior staff, who had been together since the WB's early bricklaying days. But by many accounts, there was also a slow-boiling resentment for the haves—those who received slivers of ownership in the network from Jamie—by those who had not, despite their lengthy tenures.

As 2004 began and Jamie prepared to remove himself from the network, the newly formed transition team hit a bump in the road when Jed resigned in January. He was nine months shy of his tenth anniversary at the network. Even with the publicity push that followed the succession announcement, Jed saw that the situation was intractable. Garth and Jordan were both relatively young, with far deeper Hollywood ties than an ad sales veteran from New York could hope to foster after living on the West Coast for only a few years.

Jed had been a reticent leader at times after he relocated to Burbank, which only made it harder for him to exert any authority once Jordan and Garth were appointed as his superiors. But it was undeniable that Jed's hustling as head of advertising sales for the first six years of his tenure helped keep the network's lights on, particularly in the 1998–2001 period when *Pokemon*, the Japanese craze he discovered before anyone in the U.S. knew how to pronounce it, became a money-minting hit for Kids' WB! Petrick had always been well liked within the WB and respected as an indefatigable champion of Jamie Kellner's vision.

With Jed's departure, other realities became increasingly apparent for the WB staff. WB executives learned that even though Jordan's authority had been clearly delineated, the absence of any hierarchy made it tough for him to claim CEO authority. Trying to lead among executives who had long been his peers, Jordan was confronted with the reality that much of the staff was used to one way of leadership: the Kellner way. Most if not all of the WB's department heads were accustomed to working with great autonomy, and that led to an unavoidable tension between the new management and people who preferred doing things their way.

Jordan also faced another problem that was a byproduct of his youth and lack of heavy-duty managerial experience. Jordan, like other youthful WB staffers, was known for his penchant for partying, for bonding in after-hours revelry with the WB's young stars and creative talent. It was the kind of thing that seemed to many at the network to be appropriately charming for a creative executive but wholly inappropriate for the head of the network. Much was made within WB trailers of gossip about Jordan's taste for the high-life and costly executive perks, something he contends was blown hugely out of proportion by his rivals and detractors at the network and Warner Bros. There were instances of eyebrow-raising behavior and remarks at company-wide meetings that were off-putting to many, even in the WB's hang-loose start-up network environment.

By multiple accounts, Jordan made a public show of firing an assistant in a fit of pique one day when the woman ordered the wrong-size luxury car to take him and other executives to the airport so they could fly to New York for the May 2004 upfront. It was later explained that the assistant was unreliable, but the on the spot firing still didn't sit well with Jordan's colleagues.

Eyes rolled and tongues clucked in the WB trailers when Jordan was described as being "a man with the heart of a 17-year-old girl" in a flattering *New York Times* profile that ran two months before he was officially crowned CEO-in-waiting. The article also cited Jordan's "reputation for downing tequila shots with his stars into the early-morning hours," though it duly noted that he had a firm home anchor in his three young children and marriage to his college sweetheart, Helen.*

- - - - - - - - - - - - - - - - -
*   *New York Times*, "A Must for a TV Chief: Think Like a Teenager," July 14, 2003.

All of the chatter about Jordan—good, bad, and just plain gossipy—made its way down the street to Barry Meyer and Bruce Rosenblum on the main Warner Bros. lot.

Rumors and speculation aside, Jordan was also forced to confront the realities of the WB's programming challenges. The 2002–03 and 2003–04 seasons had come and gone without a sizable new hit, save for *Everwood*. In both years, the shows that the network had banked on, *Birds of Prey* and *Tarzan*, had fallen flat, and the more closely insiders looked at the facts, the more it seemed that these shows had failed for all the wrong reasons, reasons that pointed to larger structural problems at the network.

"Once shows started working for us, there was this overarching, ongoing discussion about what the WB brand was. So rather than the WB brand evolving on its own, the discussion oftentimes became restrictive because it pushed us into replicating what we were doing," Levin says. "The thinking was, *Smallville* works; let's do *Birds of Prey*. . . . This was not what we had done in the past."

As he prepared to assume the sole CEO mantle in the spring of 2004, the question that continued to haunt Jordan and the company was just what kind of legacy he would be taking over. While the WB still had strong ratings on its core group of shows like *Gilmore Girls*, *7th Heaven*, *Smallville*, and *Everwood*, too many shows were stalling out of the gate. The network was still beating UPN in the overall ratings race, but not by nearly as much as they once were. All of the corporate shakeups—both at the WB and at Time Warner—had come at the high cost of distracting the core WB team's focus from their most important tasks.

Part of the programming quandry for the WB was fueled by the problem of reality television. Although just about every network had managed to spark interest through one reality program or another, the WB's lack of traction in the area of unscripted programs was glaring. The mania sparked by *Who Wants to be a Millionaire* and *Survivor* and *American Idol* had given way to a cottage industry and a significant shift in the prime-time business paradigm that had quickly been embraced by the Big Four networks. The major networks now routinely employed lower-cost, unscripted reality programs to help them cut down on the volume of regular-season repeats of high-priced scripted series.

As has often been noted in industry circles during the past decade, reality programming can quickly become a form of crack cocaine for television executives. But far from overdosing, the WB had missed out on the programming boom that was scoring particularly well with the WB's sweet spot, younger viewers. Even worse, the WB's drought in the cutting-edge department came as UPN notched a big win with the unscripted catwalk competition series, *America's Next Top Model*.

Complicating the development of reality projects for Jordan and his team was the fact that unscripted shows tend to be all or nothing development propositions. Because of the nature of the beast—the set up, the competition, the pranks, and the surprises—it's often inefficient to produce a pilot for an unscripted show, especially one with a competitive angle. By the time all the prep work is done, it's much more efficient if producers and participants plow through to generate enough material for a contained multi-episode arc culminating in a big finale.

As a result, Jordan had to secure higher levels of approval at Warner Bros. to commit more money upfront before he could roll the dice on a project. According to WB insiders, the network's attempts at reality programming became development by committee—a large committee—and it was virtually impossible to get consensus among the WB's key constituencies on a show, especially those with a daring premise. Suddenly the WB development team found itself fighting the same problem that crippled UPN in the era of Chris-Craft/Viacom joint ownership.

"It's hard for a roomful of people who didn't hear the original pitch to envision what a reality series will be without any tape to watch," Levin says. "It became very difficult to push through ideas that were different. It was much easier to push through ideas that were a version of some existing reality show."

As such, the WB's reality shows were derivative of other hits:

The Surreal Life, a C-list celebrity spin on the housebound antics of *Big Brother*; *The Starlet,* which was the WB's answer to NBC's *The Apprentice* with Faye Dunaway presiding over wannabe actresses; and others. Late in its life, the WB hit with a well-crafted competition series *Beauty and the Geek,* which challenged nerdy guys to impress beautiful young women. The show generated credible ratings and made money for the network because it cost considerably less for the WB to license than a comedy or drama series.

On the morning of Tuesday, May 18, 2004, the WB's upfront presentation was the network's grandest production yet. The 2004 extravaganza was held in Madison Square Garden, where Garth, Jordan, and others took the stage after a rousing performance from Lenny Kravitz that woke the media buyers up at 10:30 on a Tuesday morning. It was Jamie Kellner's last official day on the job.

Jamie was firm with his executives that there was to be no fanfare or hoopla over what he termed his "retirement" from the WB. By then, the cabinet knew Jamie well enough to know it wasn't false modesty; he really didn't want it. So his lieutenants complied, for the most part. The Garden, a real rock-star setting, was so invigorating, and the executives were so pumped that Ancier couldn't resist the urge to call for a round of applause to salute Kellner for a "truly Hall of Fame career."

About a week later, Garth got a call in his office at the WB from Rosenblum. He wanted him to "come across the street" for a meeting in Rosenblum's office on the main Warner Bros.' lot. When Garth arrived minutes later, Rosenblum told him that he, Meyer, and Jamie Kellner had decided that it was time for Jordan to go. Garth wasn't surprised. He knew Jordan's behavior hadn't gone over well with the more traditional culture at Warner Bros. Jamie had no formal authority at the WB by then, but he had been consulted and concurred with the decision to make a change.

"We just didn't think he was the right person for the job," Meyer says.

Rosenblum told Garth that he was to be named chairman and CEO, and because of that, he had to line up a new head of programming—quickly. Garth began having discreet discussions with candidates for the job the same day. Of course, he had to keep it all secret from Jordan, whose office was next door to his.

"That was tough," Ancier says.

At the top of Garth's wish list were Warner Bros. Television president Peter Roth, who like Ancier had also worked as head of programming at Fox; *Six Feet Under* producer and former Warner Bros.' TV executive David Janollari; and as a long, long shot, Susan Lyne, who had been abruptly squeezed out of her job as entertainment president at ABC two months earlier. Janollari was a natural choice. He was closer in age to the WB's target demographic than Roth or Lyne, and he was well liked by Meyer and Rosenblum for having played a big part in the development of *Friends* and other hits during his tenure at Warner Bros. Television. Janollari had impeccable credentials in the creative community.

Garth and Janollari began having meetings at Garth's Beverly Hills home to bring Janollari up to speed on the WB's new shows for the fall season and a range of other issues. The subterfuge with Jordan in the office was beyond uncomfortable for Garth. Adding to the tensions, the post-upfront advertising sales market for the WB and the other broadcast networks took a far-bigger-than-expected drop that year; it was the correction Madison Avenue had promised for so long after years of go-go spending on national television advertising. And the WB was coming to market after two years of ratings declines and nothing that looked like a sure-fire hit on the horizon.

Jordan was aware of what a precarious situation he was in. He'd been picking up on the hints and signs for a long time. He felt the strain with Garth as both were trying to exert authority. Garth and Jordan sought to be respectful of each other, yet it was clear they were competing for control of the network. Jordan knew when he stepped off the stage at Madison Square Garden that it was the last upfront presentation he would give for the WB.

"At that point in time, I knew that I wasn't the answer for them, and that was really draining. I was getting away from what I loved and where I wanted to lead the network. There were just different visions" for the WB, Levin says.

The situation was equally awkward for Garth. The two had a long history that stretched back to Jordan's days as an executive-in-training at the Walt Disney Co. when Garth came in as head of Disney's television department after leaving Fox. But as they jockeyed for power, even the easygoing Garth had been put off by some of Jordan's behavior.

By multiple accounts, one of the last straws for Warner Bros. came in a local TV report on the network and its new drama series *Summerland* that aired shortly after the upfront on the WB's Tribune-owned Los Angeles affiliate, KTLA-TV. Jordan was seen live from the site of a WB affiliate meeting on the Warner Bros.' lot holding a beer bottle. *Summerland* star Lori Loughlin, known to viewers for her long run on the ABC comedy *Full House,* was at Jordan's side, giggling about how he was "not like other network presidents" and was making them pound down shots of tequila.

Jordan got a phone call from Bruce Rosenblum the next day. It wasn't a laudatory conversation. Jordan was increasingly anxious about the possibility of getting fired. But with the summer prelaunch period approaching, many at the network, including Jordan, figured his job was secure for at least the rest of the year, once he'd made it through pilot season and the upfront presentation. If Warner Bros. had decided to fire him, why would they let him stick around to pick the pilots and set the schedule for the 2004–05 season?

By the second week of June, Jordan sensed that something was brewing. His first big clue that his firing was imminent came from an unlikely source: Jimmy Kimmel. The ABC late-night host was a friend of his, and he sent him a pat-on-the-back e-mail that began, "No matter what happens, you're one of the best guys ever to wear a suit in this town." Jordan thought Kimmel's e-mail was curious. When he returned to his office the next day, he received more calls and e-mails from his core team and outside associates who called "just to check in" and see how he was doing. Some were candid enough to tell him that the rumor was flying around the industry's e-mail servers that he was about to be let go. Jordan gritted his teeth, pasted on a grin, and tried to keep working.

Unable to concentrate, he was intent on sorting out in his head what was going on behind his back. He correctly presumed Garth would become chairman and CEO and that they would bring in someone new to run programming. Jordan had held on to the reins as the WB's head of programming even with his ascent to chief executive.

Getting his work done had suddenly become impossible because he couldn't get any of the other WB department heads on the phone. By noon on Friday, the WB's senior executives seemed to have vanished. No one was in the office. Late in the afternoon, Jordan made his way to a recreation center in Pacific Palisades to catch his son's Little League game. He hadn't been on the field long when his cell phone chirped. Amid the noise of the game, the pounding of his heart and the shaky wireless connection, he remembers hearing only one thing clearly during the brief conversation: David Janollari. It makes perfect sense, he thought.

Jordan knew Ancier thought highly of Janollari as a producer, particularly the Emmy-winning HBO drama *Six Feet Under* that Janollari and his producing partner Robert Greenblatt had shepherded with *American Beauty* screenwriter Alan Ball through their Greenblatt Janollari Studio banner. And the timing was good for Janollari. His producing partnership had ended months before when Greenblatt took the job of head of programming at the pay cable channel Showtime.

Undeterred, Jordan stuck with his plan to attend a birthday gathering that night for Ernie Del, a prominent entertainment lawyer in Hollywood, who happened to represent both Jordan and Janollari. He knew he'd see plenty of friends and industry colleagues at the party which was being held at movie producer Mike Medavoy's mansion in the ultrarich Beverly Park gated-community above Beverly

Hills. Jordan didn't know for sure he'd find himself face to face with Janollari, but he wasn't too surprised when it happened. Fueled by a mix of adrenaline and melancholy, Jordan sought to demonstrate to himself and to his peers that he was not devastated by the looming end of his time at the WB. He walked up to Janollari and in a long, characteristically impassioned burst tried to express to his impending successor that he bore him no ill will and did not blame him for the situation.

Janollari looked as if he didn't quite know what to say, but was sensitive enough to realize that Jordan had to get it off his chest somehow.

"Don't worry about me," he told Janollari. "You've got enough to worry about. Just know that you'll have a great team of people supporting you from below. You've got a lot of people you can lean on and rely on at the WB."

Jordan didn't stick around the party much longer. The next morning, he called his lawyer.

On Monday morning, June 14, 2004, Jordan went to his office as usual, and before 10 a.m. he got the call to go see Barry Meyer in his office on the main lot. As he drove the short hop to the entrance closest to the ranch, he felt a sense of relief. He was numb at the prospect of packing up and leaving the network he'd nurtured for 10 years. But the big what-if that he'd fretted about for months had finally arrived, so at least he could stop worrying about when the time would come. Including the day of his termination, Jordan served a total of 26 days as the WB's solo chief executive following Kellner's retirement.

Meyer didn't belabor his explanation for the changes they were making, but on the spot he made a call to help put him in the running for a prominent executive post at another studio. Jordan, for his part, wasn't sure he was prepared to jump immediately back into the executive fray. The meeting ended with a bear hug. "It didn't end badly," Levin says. "It just ended."

From Meyer's office, he was sent to meet with Barbara Brogliatti, Warner Bros.' longtime head of corporate communications, who was known for her firm but fair hand in her dealings with journalists and executives alike. Brogliatti walked Jordan through a plan to emphasize to the media and WB staffers that his leaving was part of a corporate restructuring, and that he had been asked to stay on as head of programming but declined. And while Brogliatti went over the spin, Meyer and Bruce Rosenblum headed to the WB, where the two of them and Garth broke the news of Jordan's departure to the employees in the main conference room. Senior executives who were not surprised nonetheless felt the nostalgic tug of saying goodbye to someone who'd been at the WB so long he'd become synonymous with its youthful, playful image.

When Jordan returned to the network to clean out his office, a number of staffers ran out to meet him as he parked in his reserved spot on the black asphalt parking lot that was always blazing hot. Warner Bros. wanted someone to move the WB into areas where he didn't want to go, he told his ex-colleagues repeatedly. Friends and associates say Jordan appeared understandably shell-shocked that morning, and ultimately had a hard time letting go of his ties at the network. Jordan says he was mostly saddened at the fade out of the original WB culture and the feisty spirit the network enjoyed during its first five years.

"The thing that was upsetting to me was to see how upset everyone else was" after his departure was announced, Levin says, "and to know that what had existed there was inevitably going to change."

With the WB swept up in Jordan Levin's ouster, UPN was also in the midst of what felt like a transformative moment. Things were looking up for the perennial underdog network. After continued clashes with Sumner Redstone led to an exit by Mel Karmazin, Leslie Moonves was promoted to co-president and co-chief operating officer of Viacom, alongside MTV Networks kingpin Tom Freston. Moonves and Freston's promotions would set into motion a top-to-bottom corporate restructuring within Viacom that would ultimately have a profound impact on UPN as well as the WB.

But in the summer of 2004, the only thing that was certain was the fact that UPN had two new shows on deck for the 2004–05 season that were making all the critics' picks lists. That alone was enough to generate buzz-building media stories about the network's turnaround under Ostroff and Moonves. Ostroff couldn't have bought better promotion for the network, though she tried to be careful about walking the fine line between sounding hopeful and sounding as if the network was beating its chest.

Kevin Hill was a heart-tugging drama about an ambitious, single lawyer who finds himself adopting an infant baby girl. It had a charismatic star in stage actor Taye Diggs, known for his work on Broadway, and it had high-end production backers in Walt Disney Co.'s Touchstone Television unit and Mel Gibson's Icon Productions. On the other hand, *Veronica Mars*, produced by Warner Bros. Television, was a light detective drama envisioned as a fresh spin on Nancy Drew set to the pulsating sounds of pop-flavored alternative rock hits. *Mars* boasted an It-girl star in Kristen Bell and better-than-average scripts thanks to series creator and executive producer Rob Thomas' deft touch with teen angst. Joel Silver, Warner Bros.-based producer of blockbuster movie franchises like *Lethal Weapon* and *The Matrix,* was closely involved in the project as an executive producer. *Mars* had all the clinical conditions for success: good buzz, hot star, talented showrunner, and an experienced movie producer standing behind them all.

But television is not a clinical science, and when fall rolled around neither *Kevin Hill* nor *Veronica Mars* brought people to the set for UPN, in spite of all the heat. In the case of *Hill*, UPN gave the show its best time slot behind *America's Next Top Model* but *Hill* had a terrible time holding on to all the young female viewers that *Model* drew. They had figured the mix of the handsome Diggs and the adorable infant would be a magnet for *Model* fans. But the numbers for *Kevin Hill* were so low they were impossible for UPN's publicists to spin as anything other than the *Model* audience bailing out before the first commercial break. *Mars* wasn't any better on Wednesday night paired with the 8–9 p.m. comedies *All of Us* and *Eve.*

Nevertheless, it was moments like these where Ostroff proved her strength as a leader. She never stopped reminding her staff that no network can be turned around overnight, and that the hardest part was finding good shows, which they had done. Though she was privately disappointed, she never let up on her if-you-build-it-they-will-watch outlook for UPN. It was the characteristic that convinced Moonves that she was a natural-born leader.

Privately, however, Moonves and others were looking at UPN and wondering what it would take to make "this thing really explode." Ostroff had done a good job of stabilizing the network and improving the quality of its shows, but UPN had miles to go before it reached the promised land of profitability, or even breakeven territory. They had done what they could to pare down the losses with the consolidation in CBS and other cost-cutting. Now it was up to the prime-time gods to gift the network with a big runaway hit to draw crowds. They'd hoped it might be *Veronica Mars* or *Kevin Hill* right out of the gate.

One afternoon that fall, Moonves got a call from Warner Bros.' Barry Meyer. Meyer and Bruce Rosenblum wanted to get together with Moonves to discuss the possibility of pulling off the long-overdue union of the WB and UPN. Though it would have been jaw-dropping to outsiders, after more than a decade of the WB-versus-UPN jousting in the industry, Meyer's overture to Moonves did not come completely out of the blue. Ever since he had taken on oversight of UPN, Moonves and his trusted No. 2, CBS Paramount Television Entertainment Group president Nancy Tellem, had engaged in a few informal "what if?" conversations with Meyer and Rosenblum about the possibility of a deal that could ease the financial pressure on both Viacom and Warner Bros. Despite UPN's momentum and the WB's success—and its moment of eking out a small profit on paper in 2002 and 2003—both networks were still losing money. Lots of money.

As informal as those merger conversations were, there was a serious undertone to them because of the history among the foursome involved. Rosenblum, Moonves, and Tellem had come up together as executives in the 1980s and early 1990s at independent production powerhouse Lorimar. Meyer was Warner Bros.' executive overseeing television in 1989 when the studio bought out what was then Lorimar

Telepictures Productions, which brought Moonves and Tellem into the fold. All three were hard-working, highly ambitious people who had bonded by achieving great success together.

But Moonves didn't care for the broad strokes of the deal Meyer outlined to him over the phone. Warner Bros. proposed that CBS shut down UPN entirely and become a minority partner in the WB, contributing key stations that CBS now owned and operated as UPN affiliates.

Moonves knew instinctively that Meyer was overplaying his hand. UPN was making too much progress for him to pull the rug out from Ostroff right then, especially if there'd be nothing to show for her efforts. Moonves knew Warner Bros. wasn't coming to him with the WB in a position of great strength—far from it. Even if its shows hadn't been clicking with audiences, UPN won at least half the battle with all of its positive press. The WB had clearly lost its edge, and Moonves, according to multiple accounts, could sense that Warner Bros. was eager to find a partner to take some of the WB off of its hands. He wasn't up for a deal that would leave Viacom with a minority interest and no trace of UPN or its management team, namely Ostroff.

So he told Meyer and Rosenblum thanks but no thanks, in friendly but unvarnished terms. His reaction didn't surprise the Warner Bros.' executives. They knew Moonves too well.

CHAPTER TWELVE

PROJECT 'S'

As Dawn Ostroff was preparing for the May 2005 upfront presentation, her confidence and optimism were higher than they had been in the three years since she joined UPN. She had been able to salvage one of her two pet shows from the 2004–05 season, giving *Veronica Mars* a reprieve for a second try at finding an audience. And she was as excited as a development executive can be to show off her big gun for the fall of 2005, the sweet-natured coming-of-age comedy *Everybody Hates Chris*.

Produced by comedian-actor Chris Rock, it was loosely based on his own experience growing up in Brooklyn's rough and tumble Bedford-Stuyvesant neighborhood in the era of Reaganomics and the crack cocaine epidemic. In Hollywood shorthand, *Chris* was tagged as a "black *Wonder Years*," complete with Rock providing the voice-over narration for the early 1980s period piece.

Chris had been a reclamation project for Ostroff. The show was originally developed at Fox, which passed on the completed pilot script penned by Rock and his longtime writing-producing partner Ali LeRoi. Ostroff was sent the script by LeRoi's agent as a writing sample, to see if she had any interest in developing something else with LeRoi. As she read it, Ostroff couldn't believe that Fox was not going to take a stab producing a pilot from the script that made her laugh out loud more than once.

The script had little of the visceral rage and bitter socioeconomic commentary usually voiced in Rock's standup routines and HBO specials. It was funny, and sweet, and even emotional in parts as it depicted a family struggling to climb a few more rungs above the poverty line. The family wasn't dysfunctional, just broke and exhausted from their daily labors to make ends meet. As was the case in Rock's real-life childhood, the mere fact that the family boasted a mother and a father was enough to make them stand out in the neighborhood. Ostroff felt this funny but non-sugary look at life in a working-class black family in Brooklyn would have the kind of resonance with viewers that ABC's *Roseanne* had in reflecting the plight of blue-collar middle-class families in the late 1980s.

Ostroff learned that Fox's option on the script would expire in December, after which the rights would revert to Rock and LeRoi. She'd been in the business long enough to know that she didn't want to telegraph her interest to Fox, lest the network decide to take a second look at it. She did, however, begin a campaign to convince Rock and LeRoi that UPN was the only network that would do the show justice.

The more she re-read the script and imagined what the show might look like, she revved herself up to make sure it happened at UPN. She courted Rock with daily e-mails and calls to his cell phone. She learned that Rock had been put off by Fox's questioning of Rock about his willingness to do guest appearances. Ostroff made sure she emphasized how important it was to have his vision guiding the show on an ongoing basis, whether or not he ever appeared on camera (other than his narration).

Ostroff's doggedness impressed her friends and industry colleagues, including Leslie Moonves, himself a noted talent schmoozer.

"She just chased him until she got it," Moonves says. "It was phenomenal."

The casting of the show was superb, particularly young Tyler James Williams in the title role and Tichina Arnold and Terry Crews as his overworked mother and father. Rock would prove to be heavily involved in the day-to-day production, much more than Ostroff expected. As showrunner and head writer, LeRoi showed a natural talent for comedy far beyond his limited experience as a showrunner of a sitcom.

At the upfront presentation that year, UPN demonstrated its

faith in *Chris* by boldly placing it in the Thursday 8 p.m. time slot that was once home to NBC's powerhouse hit *Friends*. *Friends* was gone by the time *Chris* arrived in the fall of 2005, but the presence of CBS' *Survivor*, Fox's *The O.C.*, and NBC's *Friends* spinoff, *Joey,* made it a tough time slot for a new show. UPN decided to uproot World Wrestling Entertainment from its six-year residency in the Thursday 8–10 p.m. block to make way for scripted comedies. UPN was looking to grab a piece of the advertising action that flows freely into Thursday night from movie studios and other distributors who want to open a movie on a Friday.

It was a risky strategy, but it got the network another round of favorable press. Not only was UPN confident in its program, it was willing to go head to head with the toughest night of television, and in industry circles the quiet chatter about Ostroff and her network began to grow louder.

As many critics would gush, *Chris* was universal enough in its familial themes to have played on any network. The *New York Times* gave it a rave, with critic Alessandra Stanley calling it "charming" and zeroing in on its distinctiveness. *Chris* didn't tell its audience that the family was poor; it depicted how poor families cope. *"Everybody Hates Chris* is the first show in a long time centered on a teenager whose main problem is not adolescent angst, but real life. And Mr. Rock makes it funny, not maudlin or mean," Stanley wrote.

David Janollari, a savvy television vet-eran known for the strength of his taste in material, came to the WB at an inopportune moment. Not only was UPN on a roll, but in the months after Janollari succeeded Jordan Levin as programming chief in June 2004, the WB went on a stealth crusade to slash overhead and administrative costs by nearly half, from $90 million in the 2003–04 period to around $55 million in 2005–06. Janollari came into the job with no illusions about the depth of the WB's problems.

Garth Ancier and John Maatta, the network's loyal general counsel and now chief operating officer, who had been the first WB employee hired by Jamie Kellner in 1994, spent most of 2005 at the WB cutting staff and marketing and advertising expenditures. Inside and outside the network, the downsizing was kept under wraps to a surprising degree; they accomplished a lot through attrition and "reorganizations" to make staff reductions look like organic change rather than the harsh reality that the network was actually facing. But times were tough, both for the WB and for its parent company, Time Warner.

Under the direction of chairman and CEO Richard Parsons, the world's largest media conglomerate had done an admirable job of cleaning up the world's largest mess left by the fallout from the AOL merger. In 2005, Time Warner was fined $510 million stemming from Justice Department and Securities and Exchange Commission investigations into AOL's accounting practices. By then the stock had long-since stabilized from its nadir of about $10 in July 2002. Yet the market valuation of the company was still far out of line with the value of Time Warner's hard assets alone. With so much wealth so unforgivingly discounted by financial markets, the company was becoming over-ripe for a hostile takeover by another firm, or by private equity concerns looking to sell it off in pieces, or any number of other scenarios unwelcome to Parsons and his top lieutenants.

To appease the markets and help keep its own sprawl in check, Time Warner embarked on an austerity program that included some asset sales and plans for staff reductions at all levels. It was no surprise that the money-losing WB would come under scrutiny amid such a cost-cutting frenzy. Garth could see it coming, and he knew there were other urgent problems to solve. The big one was its long-term future with Tribune Broadcasting.

After the heady growth years of 1998–2001, the ties had frayed some between Tribune and WB executives. The network's downturn in prime time had taken a toll on Tribune's stations, just as its surge had been a bonanza for the local outlets. Garth and others knew that Tribune was still making more money off WB programming than the network by virtue of its local station advertising sales. Garth was pushing for Tribune to become a 50/50 partner with Warner Bros. in the WB to help shoulder some of the losses and take the joint venture's red ink off Time Warner's books. Tribune Co. by then was headed by Dennis FitzSimons, the former Tribune Broadcasting executive who'd been instrumental in championing the station group's involvement with the WB. But increasing its stake from its existing 25 percent was a non-starter for Tribune. It had plenty of its own troubles on the horizon with bringing its core newspaper and television station holdings into the digital age.

As a result of all the negotiations and the depth of the differing agendas, the WB and Tribune for the past several years had resorted to a series of 12-month affiliation pacts to keep the network afloat in key markets while the two sides tried to settle on a long-term solution. The WB executives were so frustrated they would have switched to replacement outlets in Tribune markets if they could have. (But that was impossible to do. There were no comparable stations available in markets like New York, Los Angeles, Chicago, and Philadelphia.)

During this period, Garth and Janollari were hardly sitting still on the programming front. For most of his first year in the job, Janollari faced the difficult task of having to embrace the shows on the slate assembled by his predecessor. One of those newcomers for the fall of 2004 was a high-minded drama from *Everwood* and *Dawson's Creek* producer Greg Berlanti that depicted the boyhood years of two brothers, with the hook being that one of them—we don't know which—will grow up to be president of the United States in 2041.

Jack and Bobby was creative in its storytelling approach. It blended the contemporary drama of two brothers, Jack and Bobby McCallister, growing up with a domineering, independent-minded single mother pushing them to succeed with segments done in a PBS documentary-style from far in the future examining the legacy of "President McCallister" in a way that offered bits and pieces of both boys' backstory, without revealing which one winds up in the Oval Office.

The show had a strong pedigree, coming from Berlanti and Emmy-winning director-producer Thomas Schlamme, of NBC's *The West Wing* fame. It had two good-looking young stars and a recognizable supporting player in Christine Lahti as the mother. It was the network's prime focus that fall. In general, the critics' response to *Jack and Bobby* was good, not great. Berlanti got a lot of credit for taking an innovative approach but there was hesitation raised in many reviews about whether the mix of flash-forward and contemporary sequences would enhance or distract from the characterizations of the two brothers.

The timing of *Jack and Bobby*'s debut, coming about six weeks before a presidential election, was well thought out. All the ingredients for the show to be a prestige player were there—except for the fact that it didn't connect with WB viewers in a meaningful way. The WB's target demographic of young adults in the 18-34 age range shunned *Jack and Bobby* just as much as that age group still tends to shun going to the polls on Election Day.

Janollari, however, was won over before *Jack and Bobby* premiered. During his time as a producer he'd been impressed by Berlanti's work for the WB. As an executive, he appreciated what Greg was trying to do with the show. Janollari pushed through the decision to pick up the show for a full 22-episode season after only two airings, even after ratings for the second episode took a dive from the modest turnout for the premiere episode.

Nonetheless, *Jack and Bobby* was not the biggest headache Janollari and Garth had that season. Some of the network's new offerings were falling apart before they made it on the air, and some of those that did make it were trashed by critics. One new drama in particular, *The Mountain*, starring Oliver Hudson as the scion of a family that runs a ski resort, took a drubbing from reviewers who began to observe that the WB of late had been suffering under the weight of new shows that were little more than derivative spins on the network's past glories.

The pressure could not have been turned up much higher on Janollari as the WB endured a miserable fall launch period in 2004. He stepped up his scramble to develop some new hits for the 2005–06 season, and he held out hope that *Jack and Bobby* would show some sign of life by the end of its first season. During the annual Television Critics Assn. press junket during the summer of 2005, Janollari earnestly told reporters that having to ax *Jack and Bobby* after one season was "the most heartbreaking experience I've been through in my entire career."

With this difficult stretch behind them, Garth and Janollari took up the cause of broadening the network's appeal for its 2005–06 season. Garth wasn't looking to attract a much older audience to the WB, he was just trying to make sure it wasn't tagged as a teenage-girl network so thoroughly that it would turn off potential twenty- and thirtysomething viewers. He was convinced that having too many teenagers in its marketing campaigns was starting to backfire on them. He sought to make subtle but significant changes in the network's approach to programming, casting, marketing and the way it presented itself to the industry.

As part of this grown-up makeover Garth took one more decisive step that he'd waited a decade to accomplish. He killed the frog.

The WB announced it was dropping Michigan J. Frog as its on-air mascot in July 2005. The news generated a thousand cheeky headlines, but by Garth's design it also sent the message that the WB wasn't a teens-only zone. In the 2004–05 season the median age of the network's viewers was in the 30-ish age range.

"I thought (Michigan J. Frog) was something that made the network seem too kiddie, too juvenile. It wasn't that I wanted the network to be older; I just wanted to get away from the perception that it was a teenage-girl network," Ancier says.

I couldn't believe the news when I read the obits for Michigan J. Frog the next day. As much as I adore Garth, I thought it was a bad move. You kill the frog, you kill the network.

Everybody Hates Chris lived up to its promise in its September 22, 2005 premiere. UPN's hotshot beat *Joey* and *The O.C.* to rank second in the Thursday 8 p.m. time slot behind *Survivor*. For UPN, it was a feat bigger than anything since its opening night with *Star Trek: Voyager*. Ostroff was giddy the following morning as she scrolled through entertainment news Web sites with bulletins about UPN's triumph. They were headlines she'd never thought she'd see, outside of her dreams.

In a role-reversal from the days of *Charmed* and *Felicity* versus *The Secret Diary of Desmond Pfeiffer*, the news of UPN's success came at a rotten time for its rival. By the fall of 2005, Warner Bros. was preparing to lay off 400 people, or about 5 percent of its worldwide staff of 8,000, despite having a strong summer at the box office. A few dozen layoffs were in store for the WB by year's end, and the volume of cuts would have to come at a high level that would make them impossible to mask in the industry.

While Garth braced for unleashing this internal bombshell, the WB limped through another weak fall launch. Giving the boot to Michigan J. Frog and pursuing an older demographic had done little to change things. The spooky ghost-chasers drama *Supernatural* would eventually qualify as a moderate success, but it was not enough to overshadow its flameouts—not by a long shot. The WB's fate was further complicated by the fact that Janollari had ordered a higher-than-usual volume of new shows that year, partly in response to the WB's crying need to replenish its lineup, and partly because it is a typical reaction of new programming executives to over-indulge in their first year at the helm.

Garth and Warner Bros. were supportive of Janollari in the effort to give him enough berths to find the next *Friends* or *Dawson's Creek* and restore some of the WB's luster. The problem with over-ordering is that there are only so many hours to go around on the schedule, and all of those new shows require marketing dollars put behind them to get the word out.

The biggest bomb on the WB that season was a poorly executed legal buddy-drama that encapsulated the WB's efforts to draw a broader audience. *Just Legal* starred Gen-Y favorite Jay Baruchel and 80s icon Don Johnson in a show about an 18-year-old prodigy law school grad who teams with a boozy ambulance chaser to aid the wrongfully accused. The WB gave the Warner Bros. Television show, from the Jerry Bruckheimer stable, its best time slot following *7th Heaven* on Mondays, but it was no use. Badly written and miscast,

Just Legal couldn't hang on to half of *Heaven*'s lead-in ratings. The meager audience that it did draw was Jurassic (age 50 and up) by WB standards. *Just Legal* was gone after three airings.

The toughest blow for Janollari came with an hour-long dramedy called *Related* that revolved around the lives and loves of four very different sisters. Janollari had leaned on his relationship with producer Marta Kauffman, co-creator of *Friends*, to come aboard the show to give it a smart-funny spin. A dozen years before, Janollari had been the major factor in bringing Kauffman and *Friends* co-creator David Crane to Warner Bros. Television. He never expected *Related* to be the instant hit that *Friends* was, but he didn't expect its potential to be sapped from the start by the malaise that seemed to put a cloud over the entire schedule.

Janollari and Garth worked hard that fall to keep their heads above water and plot new scheduling moves and strategies to salvage what was left of the 2005–06 season. After *Related* did a fast fade in the Wednesday 9 p.m. slot, it was rerouted in late October to Monday 9 p.m. behind *7th Heaven*, the time slot that had belonged to *Just Legal* at the start of the season. *Related*'s ratings improved only marginally with the bigger lead-in audience from *Heaven*. Janollari was encouraged by the uptick, however, and went out of his way to assure Kauffman and her team that the network was behind her show and planned to double-down on marketing and promotional efforts. Janollari had every intention of keeping his word. He had no inkling of what an impossible task that would become in a matter of weeks.

Garth, meanwhile, had bigger worries on his mind. He knew the network's situation was dicey within the company; Time Warner co-president Jeff Bewkes seemed to be saying as much in coded terms in his remarks at investor conferences and elsewhere.

In his desperation that fall, Garth reached out to Robert Iger, then newly appointed to the job as chief executive of the Walt Disney Co. Garth proposed that ABC do with the WB what CBS had done with UPN. By annexing some of the WB's operations, ABC could gain economies of scale for its existing infrastructure and share in the upside of improved performance at the WB. Controlling the advertising sales for ABC and the WB would also give Disney more clout on Madison Avenue.

Iger listened respectfully to Garth's pitch. Disney at the time was unabashedly turning its ailing ABC Family cable channel into a cable version of the WB by buying up the rerun rights to its shows, including *7th Heaven, Gilmore Girls, Smallville,* and *Everwood.* Iger admitted as much to Garth. So it was not for lack of interest in the WB itself that Iger responded as definitively as he did. It was business, pure and simple, and Iger's quick decision to pass spoke volumes about the state of the broadcasting business.

It was also a surprisingly fast reversal of fortune for a network that had reveled in its uniqueness.

"It was sad at the end," Jamie Kellner observes in retrospect. "The whole place was mired in politics."

Barry Meyer didn't plan on rerouting the course of history for the WB Network and UPN when he and his wife, Wendy, arrived at the Beverly Hills home of Israeli media mogul Haim Saban for a dinner party in November 2005. But by the end of the night, he and Leslie Moonves had set in motion a deal that would rock the industry in another few months and help each other out, CEO to CEO, at the same time.

The party was a smallish affair at Saban's chateau-style home, and Barry and Wendy Meyer arrived just as the poolside cocktail reception was filling with guests. Barry got himself a glass of chardonnay and began mingling among the mostly familiar faces at the party. One of the couples on the guest list was CBS Corp. chief Leslie Moonves and his wife, Julie Chen, co-anchor of CBS' *The Early Show* morning news program.

Eventually, the Meyers found themselves standing in a small group that included Moonves and Chen. Moonves was sipping at his glass of wine as he and his former Warner Bros.' boss drifted into friendly chitchat. When Meyer looked around and saw his wife deep in conversation with Chen and hostess Cheryl Saban, he turned to

Moonves and motioned toward a pair of deck chairs. The two sat and chatted a bit more about changes in the industry at large, and then in a determined way, Meyer changed the subject with a deliberately vague suggestion.

"We should think about this," Meyer said.

He didn't say UPN or the WB. He didn't need to. Moonves knew exactly what "this" was, and he was open to the discussion. At the time, he was barely six weeks away from officially flying solo at the helm of a newly configured CBS Corp. Moonves' current boss, Viacom chairman Sumner Redstone, had once again bucked convention and was pursuing a de-consolidation plan for his media empire.

Five years after Viacom swallowed up CBS Inc., Redstone was putting the finishing touches on a plan to spin off CBS Corp. as a separate entity from Viacom's powerhouse cable holdings, including MTV, VH1, Nickelodeon, Comedy Central, and Spike TV, and its movie studio Paramount Pictures, though CBS would keep Paramount's TV production and distribution operations in the divorce. Redstone's bet was that the separation would boost the stock price of both companies by allowing them to perform better within their respective sectors in the eyes of Wall Street.

Although Moonves and Dawn Ostroff had made great strides, UPN was still far, far away from turning a profit, or even reaching the break-even point. As he prepared to go it alone at CBS Corp. in a business climate focused on quarterly earnings, Moonves welcomed any reasonable offer that could help him manage those losses. A joint venture with an outside partner would allow him to bury the smaller 50 percent share of CW's red ink in the "investment" column of CBS Corp.'s books.

"I know where you are with Fox, and I know where we are with Tribune," Meyer continued. "If we don't take advantage of this now, the shareholders in both of our companies will look at us five years from now and think we were just really, really dumb."

"Look," Moonves responded with the leading-man diction he had learned in his early days as an actor. "I'm interested, but only in a real partnership."

"Absolutely," Meyer said, with a knowing nod.

The following Monday morning, Meyer told Bruce Rosenblum of his poolside conversation with Moonves. Meyer and Moonves hadn't gone into any more detail during the Sabans' party about how such a partnership might be structured. Both of them had dropped the topic before the cocktail hour was over, out of an unspoken fear of jinxing the possibility of actually getting a deal done.

Meyer asked Rosenblum to follow up that day with Nancy Tellem. "See if there's real interest," Meyer told Rosenblum.

By day's end Rosenblum was excited to be able to report that there was sincere interest on CBS' part. And because of the level of friendship among the four principals—Meyer, Moonves, Rosenblum, and Tellem—they eschewed the typical posturing and jockeying and were able to quickly get down to the nitty-gritty of what it would take for both sides to get a deal done. And they trusted one another to do it in top-secret, need-to-know only fashion to keep any of their discussions from leaking out to the news media. The conceptual framework of a 50/50 partnership agreement to create a single successor to UPN and the WB came together in a matter of days.

"I could be in a partnership with Barry Meyer all day and all night, because I can put my head on the pillow at night and trust that he and I can solve problems. We may not always agree, but I know that he and I can talk it out," Moonves says. "We knew that's why we had a real shot at doing the CW."

For Rosenblum, the process of thinking through a WB-UPN merger was something of a déjà vu of his days in the tiny conference room with Jamie Kellner in the summer of 1993, hammering out the foundation of a new broadcast network. He was ably matched by his CBS counterpart, Nancy Tellem. A lawyer by training, Tellem is among the highest-ranking female executives in the entertainment industry. She's known as a sharp, tough dealmaker who is respected for her integrity and sense of fairness.

As Rosenblum and Tellem made speedy progress in crafting the broad outline of a merger agreement, Meyer and Moonves and their wives met for dinner again a few weeks later, this time at one of

Moonves' favorite Italian haunts in Beverly Hills. The chatter at the table was strictly social, off-duty stuff. Nobody brought up any business issues, until the very end.

"I know Bruce and Nancy have been talking about this," Meyer observed, with the accent on *this*. "If you're not serious, let's stop right now. . . . Are you really serious?" he asked.

Meyer was sure he knew what Moonves' answer would be, but he wanted to be absolutely certain.

"I'm dead serious," Moonves assured him, right on cue.

"Dead men walking" was how WB insiders described the mood inside the network in the second half of 2005. People were finally noticing the staff shrinkage and the steep cuts in spending on marketing and advertising. With the network's new season off to a weak start, again, WB veterans were losing faith in Janollari's ability to pull out of its deepening rut. During the summer, word spread that Warner Bros. would be lowering the layoff boom later that year as part of the corporation-wide cost-cutting binge. It was clear to WB staffers that the job cuts wouldn't stop at the main studio gates.

"We were just waiting for Black Friday," says a WB alum. "We knew it was coming."

There was little communication or discussion of the network's precarious situation. Staffers were left to speculate among themselves in the hallways about who was likely to go next. It was unnerving, and in the eyes of many, unnecessarily drawn out.

When the layoffs of about 40 staffers finally hit in December, the WB took some cover from Warner Bros.' broader cost-cutting mandate. But it was understood among network insiders that the WB's woes were so great that it would have had to make deep cuts even if there had been no corporate directive.

Garth Ancier and John Maatta were brought into the circle of executives who knew about the CW conversations in the second week of December, shortly after the layoffs hit. The two WB veterans were understandably more skeptical than the others about a deal coming together because they'd heard it all before, once at the beginning just before WB and UPN came onto the scene in 1995, and once at the behest of overzealous investment bankers during the WB's late-90s zenith. Such talk never progressed beyond the conceptual stage because it was such an overwhelmingly complicated thing to pull off, even in the friendliest of scenarios.

At the time, Garth and Maatta were also distracted by the fallout from the corporate bloodletting. Black Friday finally came for the WB on December 9, 2005. Rumors had been building earlier in the week that pink slips were on the way. It was impossible to keep quiet; the cuts went too high up into the executive ranks. PR chief Brad Turell, who'd returned to his old job at the WB after the sojourn in Atlanta, used all of his clout and most of his favors with journalists to get news outlets to sit on the story until after the employees were formally notified that Friday. Brad was savvy enough to know that advance stories on the layoffs would inevitably yield follow-ups. "It's bad enough these people have to get laid off. Do they really need to read two stories about it?" Brad told more than one journalist that week in a half-pleading, half-bullying tone. It worked.

By the time Garth began calling people into private meetings that Friday, staffers already had educated guesses about who among them was earmarked for a severance package, which were generous even by Hollywood standards. The trauma of the layoffs shredded what was left of the frayed morale inside the WB's trailers. The misery index was only magnified by the timing of the cuts, coming just weeks before the December holidays. And the fact that the downsizing claimed even some of those at the senior vice president and executive vice president level was enough to make the remaining staffers nervous about the network's long-term health.

The sidelined employees included two who'd been with the WB since the prelaunch days in 1994: Rusty Mintz, our zealous and charming head of program scheduling, and our brilliant casting chief Kathleen Letterie. Mintz was part of WB lore as the ratings geek who waited up in the middle of the night for the first night's numbers. He was the keeper of the gong, the emcee of the weekly Tuesday staff meeting. Letterie was the one who "found" *Buffy the Vampire Slayer* star Sarah Michelle Gellar, *Dawson's Creek*'s Katie Holmes and James Van Der Beek, and many other WB stars. If the WB could let them go, nobody was sacred. The last vestiges of the WB's halcyon days were gone.

Because of the financial reward he'd reaped from the network just three years earlier, Garth was in an awkward situation. He sent out a memo to the staff after the pinkslips were handed down citing the "tough decisions" that were "painful and heartbreaking." Brad spent the day on the phone scoffing at the questions from journalists about whether the network was in danger of being shut down. Yet the defensive tone of Garth's memo was unmistakable.

Days later, Bruce Rosenblum and Maatta began assembling a task force to work on the initiative that became known as Project S, so named for the last letter in CBS. Executives were sworn to absolute secrecy. They didn't write CBS or UPN in memos or discuss any aspect of the talks in front of their assistants in an effort to keep everything secret. In addition to Garth and Maatta, the WB insiders who were in on the planning included finance chief Mitch Nedick and distribution head Ken Werner, a former Walt Disney Co. television executive who'd been with the WB since 1997.

Rosenblum and Tellem and their close circle of support staffers had begun to make progress on a joint-venture agreement by the middle of December, but the momentum dissipated during the holidays. They would resume at a furious pace in the first week of January 2006, and from then on it was a race against the clock to get an agreement signed. Time was of the essence, the CW architects concluded.

Though the close relationships between Moonves, Meyer, Tellem, and Rosenblum were a critical ingredient to the advancement of the talks, more than anything else, what made the stars align for a UPN-WB merger at long last was the status of both networks' affiliation agreements with their most important station group partners. Fortuitously, by the time they began their 12th years on the air, both networks had key affiliation pacts set to expire within days of each other in August and September 2006.

The WB had been struggling to find common ground on a new deal with Tribune for more than two years. Moonves was bracing for talks with Rupert Murdoch's News Corp. on a new affiliation deal for the former Chris-Craft stations. He knew News Corp.'s station executives would try to extract a small fortune and other forms of compensation for a multi-year renewal deal. In the past, discussions about uniting the networks had stalled because the two sides had been unable to overcome the single-biggest hurdle: whether Tribune or Chris-Craft stations would get to keep the affiliation with the successor network in top markets.

Now with both affiliation pacts expiring at the same time, CBS and Warner Bros. were free to plot their future unencumbered by the station issues that had been insurmountable in the past. However, Tribune's cooperation was vital if CBS wanted to bid adieu to News Corp. and its UPN affiliated stations. WB executives knew from their many discussions with Tribune that what that company wanted most was to be off the hook for shouldering any of the WB's losses. Meyer and Rosenblum had a hunch they'd be willing to give up their ownership stake in the WB in exchange for a long-term affiliation contract. That hunch was right, as they confirmed when they had the first conversation with Dennis about it over dinner in Los Angeles in early January. Meyer and Rosenblum were relieved to hear from FitzSimons that Tribune had seen the writing on the wall for the WB and was enthusiastic about plans for the new joint venture.

FitzSimons, who was bracing for what he knew would be a tough year ahead for Tribune and its core newspaper and television operations, was happy to hear that Warner Bros. was considering some bold steps that could help Tribune on Wall Street. Given the state of both networks, a merger was long overdue, FitzSimons told them.

"The WB had become kind of a cloud hanging over our horizon because people were starting to believe Time Warner would shut it down," FitzSimons says. "As it happens, many times in business, the pain had to get worse for everybody before everybody recognized what the right thing to do was."

Warner Bros.' executives left the dinner in good spirits because while nothing had been committed on paper, it was clear Tribune was willing to work with the new network and compromise with CBS on affiliation deals in top markets. If the merger was to succeed and the companies were going to receive some return on their investments, it would require a bit of sacrifice from each side.

With Tribune on board in principle, the other big concern involved the production side. The WB and UPN were born of two studios' desire to make sure they could still profit from producing prime-time television series. How would the partners avoid squabbling and competing for the network's most promising projects? The answer proved as simple as the straight-down-the-middle, 50/50 structure of the joint venture. Warner Bros. Television and CBS Paramount Network Television would jointly own every show that either one produced for the new entity. That would mean splitting the profits in success and absorbing losses in failure, no matter which studio was responsible for generating the project. Both studios would automatically have an equal stake in any new shows either one of them produced for the merged network. The hope was that with the successes and the failures evenly split on all shows, it would mitigate some of the inevitable intramural competition between the rival studios.

The talks between CBS and Warner Bros. were conducted stealthily through phone calls, e-mails, and shuttle diplomacy missions between Warner Bros.' Burbank lot and CBS Television City in Los Angeles' Fairfax district. The bonds between the foursome were as strong as their collective dealmaking savvy. Meyer, Moonves, Rosenblum, and Tellem leaned hard on that friendship in trying to look ahead and anticipate potential problems that might crop up down the road. As friends, they made a pact to not sweat the small stuff for the sake of the greater good.

"Where the relationship between the four of us really came in more than anywhere else is that we sat down together and said, 'We're not going to let the little partisan issues that come up get in the way of the four of us executing the big idea,' " Meyer says. "We have to keep the focus on the fact that this new network is a really, really good idea, and it's a big idea. And there were times when things came up and we all stopped and said, 'The big idea, remember? It's all about the big idea.' "

For Moonves, there was an undeniable sense of closure about the prospect of fusing UPN and the WB stretching back a dozen years. It was a testament to the strength of his relationships with Barry Meyer and Bob Daly that he didn't bear a deep grudge for the decision made to keep him in the dark about the WB at the network's inception. Moonves had always felt undeservedly snubbed, and resentful that Jamie Kellner had been granted a lucrative piece of the WB, when he hadn't received anything comparable after delivering not one but two billion-dollar assets in *Friends* and *ER*.

In the end, the complex undertaking of the deal proposition came down to a few sheets of paper. It was 50/50 straight down the line. No money changed hands between CBS and Warner Bros. Both companies absorbed the costs of shutting down their respective networks, and they agreed to jointly shoulder the burden of financing and losses going forward. CBS Corp. wound up eating $24 million on the shutdown of UPN.*; Time Warner took a $15 million to $20 million write-off on WB shutdown costs, on top of $4 million in restructuring costs from the December 2005 layoffs, according to Securities and Exchange Commission filings.

By the second week of January the agreement was falling into place. Warner Bros. retained Los Angeles-based law firm O'Melveny & Myers as its outside counsel; CBS brought in New York-based powerhouse Weil, Gotshal and Manges. As the negotiations progressed it became clear to Ancier and others at WB that Moonves was calling most, if not all, of the shots, and that he did not intend to bring the WB's top

---

*   "Radio Gives CBS Static." *The Hollywood Reporter*, August 4, 2006.

programmers into the new tent. Moonves did want a number of the WB's senior business executives, starting with John Maatta, who had been the WB's employee No. 1 and also went back with Moonves to the Lorimar days. Maatta would make the segue from the WB to CW in his same capacity as chief operating officer. The same was true for the WB's business affairs chief Michael Ross and finance guru Mitch Nedick, another charter WB executive. It was not to be for Ancier and Janollari.

At this point, the union of UPN and the WB made too much sense for the three main players—CBS, Warner Bros., and Tribune—for the merger to be scuttled once again. The CW would be built of the strongest parts of the WB and UPN, from shows to stations to executives. Jamie Kellner blessed the deal via proxy through Ancier and Maatta and through his own communications with Meyer. Meyer and Kellner's former colleagues at the WB went out of their way to respect his feelings even though he no longer had any formal authority at the network. Kellner recognized the direness of the WB's situation, and he saw it as the only way Warner Bros. would salvage any of what he and his kitchen cabinet had spent the past decade building. Kellner also voted with his pocketbook by signing new CW affiliation deals for seven of the eight television stations he continued to own through Acme Communications.

CBS and Warner Bros.' challenge with the revamped combination of the WB and UPN was to prove that the merger would result in a network that was more than the sum of its parts, and that it would succeed on its own merits rather than because a competitor had gone away. CBS (and its Viacom predecessor) and Warner Bros. had sunk more than $1 billion apiece into their networks. They owed it to their shareholders to take another stab at squeezing some long-term value out of those 12 years of heavy capital investment.

Still, there was no escaping the fact that the world had changed in the decade since the WB and UPN dawned. The younger end of CW's target audience of 18-to-34-year-olds have grown up in a 500-channel, online, on-demand, and increasingly customized multi-media world. Being the fifth network was a meaningless marketing slogan to these multitaskers.

Once they had agreed in broad strokes on the deal between CBS and Warner Bros., their focus shifted to securing an agreement with Tribune. Tribune had to be on board with its strong stations in big markets or the new venture was sunk. After the initial pitch had been warmly received at dinner with Tribune executives in early January, a contingent of executives from Warner Bros. and CBS, including Bruce Rosenblum and John Maatta, made a diplomatic mission to Chicago, in the middle of a cold snap, to spend a week pounding out a 10-year affiliation agreement with Tribune. Tribune would exchange its ownership interest in the WB for the long-term affiliation deal for 16 of its stations.

There were station sacrifices for both Tribune and CBS, which inherited 19 UPN-affiliated stations in medium-size markets from Paramount Stations Group as part of its merger with Viacom. In another sign that the merger was meant to be, CBS' and Tribune's station holdings overlapped in only a few markets, making it much easier to divvy up the station affiliation assignments. Tribune would keep the biggest markets of New York, Los Angeles, and Chicago, where CBS had no UPN outlets anyway.

In places where there was overlap, both sides made concessions for the sake of the larger goal. CBS gave up the affiliations for its stations in big markets like Boston, Dallas, and Miami; Tribune did the same in Atlanta, Seattle, and Philadelphia, the fourth-largest market. And Jamie Kellner's legacy lingered in the fact that the business plan for the new network did include reverse compensation.

On January 16, 2006, the WB held its portion of the winter Television Critics Association press junket. Garth Ancier and David Janollari took the stage for the opening executive Q&A session and gave no hint of the monumental news to come—because only one of them knew it was happening. Janollari was still in the dark about the developments, but that did not make the Q&A any easier. Janollari was on the ropes during the 45-minute session with a slew of questions about the message sent by the WB's reality show *Beauty and the Geek*, which had been a success the previous summer and was getting a big push for its second edition coming up in the spring. And the grilling over *Geek* was a warm-up for a barrage aimed at Ancier and Janollari about the WB's recent decision to end *7th Heaven* after 10 years.

Ancier made the mistake of being very matter-of-fact in telling the crowd how *7th Heaven* had become too expensive for the network. A show that's been on the air for that long, especially with its large cast, carries a big nut just in actor salaries alone. But the journalists were relentless. The stars of the show and *7th Heaven* creator Brenda Hampton hadn't been shy about publicly criticizing the network's decision to pull the plug. Couldn't the WB afford to take a hit on a show that had worked so hard for the network? The true answer was no, but Garth wasn't about to reveal just how much budget cutting they'd had to do during the past year, before and after the large-scale layoffs implemented the previous month. He coolly explained that the WB couldn't afford to carry a loss leader.

After the executive Q&A, a clutch of WB executives gathered around Ancier and Janollari in a corner of the hotel ballroom to analyze what had undoubtedly been a tough session, in parts. You have no idea how tough it's going to be, Ancier thought as he observed his colleagues in the huddle.

At the press junket, two old WB hands, Bob Bibb and Lew Goldstein, were pulled out of the crowd by Bruce Rosenblum and escorted to a private room next to the ballroom in the hotel where the junket was held. The WB's marketing gurus noticed as they followed Rosenblum that he looked pale and tired, as if he'd been working long nights and early mornings. Safely tucked away in the room, Rosenblum filled them in on the CW negotiations. Bibb and Goldstein had wildly mixed feelings about the deal. True to form, their feelings were mixed in just about the same way. Like most of the charter WB team, Bibb and Goldstein had long assumed that the WB would one day swallow up the inferior UPN. Even after three seasons of ratings struggle and another tough fall season launch that year, WB executives could not fathom handing over the keys to *Smallville, Gilmore Girls, Everwood,* and *Charmed* to the enemy.

But Bibb and Goldstein were nothing if not consummate pros. The duo got to work creating a sizzle reel for the new network that the partners could play at the splashy press conference planned to unveil the merger. The need to prepare marketing materials forced the partners to settle on a name for their baby.

"CW" cropped up early on in the process as a logical amalgam of the parent companies' first initials. (Moonves would later joke with reporters that they couldn't call it "the WC," for obvious reasons.) Bibb and Goldstein pushed for the variation "CWB," arguing that the WB, no matter what its fortunes were at that moment, had the stronger brand identity and should be preserved somehow. The CBS camp nixed that idea. It had to be a fresh start.

All in all, it was an enormous undertaking to prepare for the announcement, and the clock was ticking. Warner Bros. and CBS needed to seal the deal as quickly as possible to begin the pick-and-shovel work of shoring up the affiliate base and rolling out marketing campaigns to educate viewers that UPN-plus-WB-equals-CW.

After Rosenblum looped Bibb and Goldstein in and got them working on the reel and brand, he and Maatta returned to Chicago for a week of intense dealmaking with Tribune. When they had put the finishing touches on the 10-year deal, Rosenblum and Maatta returned to the West Coast on a Saturday, and then got back on a plane the next day for New York. They were bound for what they hoped would be a stealth announcement at a press conference at the ritzy St. Regis Hotel in Manhattan. The hope was to catch the industry completely by surprise on the morning of Tuesday, January 24.

Dawn Ostroff and John Maatta met for the first time just one day before they were unveiled to the industry as the leaders behind CW. They were comfortable from the start as they shook hands in Leslie Moonves' office. Both are known for a down-to-earth, no B.S. approach to business, and their roles in the new venture were clearly defined and complementary. Maatta didn't want to be a programming executive; and Ostroff had no intention of telling Maatta how to run advertising sales and affiliate relations. Most importantly, they were peers. Ostroff and Maatta were appointed as equals who both reported to a board of executives from CBS and Warner Bros. tasked with overseeing CW.

Maatta had been enthusiastic about the prospects for the merger once he became convinced that the talks were more than just blue-sky chatter among old friends. He was unaware of his role in the new network until the negotiations were well underway in January. During the holiday break, he told his wife that he was thinking about putting a desk and bookcase in their living room so he could begin taking in legal clients. He knew there was a good chance he'd be out of work after the CW transition was completed.

The partners also easily agreed on Ostroff as the choice for heading programming. She'd earned the chance after surviving her four-year rescue mission with UPN. But it wasn't entirely a cut and dry decision for her. Ostroff felt the CW deal represented a turning point for her career. She had never taken much time off at Lifetime when she had her first child, nor when her second arrived after she joined UPN in full crisis mode. She was feeling the burn of four years of running at top speed. So when the CW job was formally offered to her, she hesitated. For about a minute.

"I did have that second thought," Ostroff says, "and then it was, 'Naah, I couldn't pass this opportunity up.' The challenge was too exciting."

By late afternoon on January 23, the day before the news conference, executives from both camps huddled in New York. There was more work to be done on the deal, but it was clear the lawyers and in-house counsel were zooming toward completion. A dozen or so of the principals, including Leslie Moonves, Dawn Ostroff, Nancy Tellem, Barry Meyer, Bruce Rosenblum, and John Maatta, decided to go to dinner to celebrate. They wound up taking over a large table at the bustling Post House steakhouse on the Upper East Side. After weeks of cloak and dagger and code words, there was a sense of giddiness about being hours away from going public with their big news. There were many toasts and much excited talk of the promise of their new venture, and the strength of their partnership. PR executives Brad Turell and Chris Ender, of CBS, arrived late after staying behind at CBS headquarters to finish writing the press release that would shock the television business when it was issued at 11 a.m. the next morning, as the news conference began.

By mid-morning on the day of the announcement, Moonves and the select group of CW planners headed from CBS to the St. Regis Hotel. Publicity executives with all of the companies involved in CW spent the morning frantically calling entertainment and business journalists to alert them to the hastily scheduled news conference. The initial bulletin about the press conference sent out to major newspapers and wire services obliquely promised it would deliver news about the creation of a broadcast network venture from "three major entertainment companies," but it did not name CBS, Warner Bros., or Tribune, or UPN and the WB. The covert operatives who pulled the CW deal together had achieved their fondest wish: the element of surprise.

No news outlet, not the *Wall Street Journal* nor the *New York Times* nor the Hollywood trades, had sniffed out the story that had been unfolding between two media giants for more than a month. The first sketchy "sources say" wire and Web site dispatches about UPN and the WB fusing into a new entity broke about 90 minutes before the news conference began. By then, it didn't matter. No media outlet and virtually none of Warner Bros.' or CBS' competitors had a clue about the deal until the partners dropped the first huge hints that Tuesday morning.

The clueless included senior executives at both networks. David Janollari officially learned that he was out of a job on the morning of the news conference. In reality, he'd been tipped off by friends a week earlier that the merger was happening. Most of UPN's staffers were just as stunned as their WB counterparts when they woke up Tuesday morning to the news as it was breaking.

The final paperwork on the CW partnership agreement was

signed at the St. Regis in the rooms where Moonves, Meyer, and various handlers waited prior to stepping before a phalanx of cameras in the hotel ballroom. Most of the people waiting backstage were preoccupied with reading over the fine print on the deal term sheet. The last I's and T's on the contract had been taken care of via phone, e-mail, and fax the night before and into the wee hours of that morning by Warner Bros.' long-serving general counsel, John Schulman, and his CBS counterpart, Louis Briskman. Briskman brought the final documents to the St. Regis for the partners to sign. Moonves and Rosenblum did the honors for their respective companies, just minutes before the scheduled start of the news conference.

As Meyer and Moonves waited backstage for their signal, the ballroom that awaited them filled with jostling reporters and cameras. Nancy Tellem and Bruce Rosenblum sat smiling in the front row. It was the kind of high-pressure situation that brings out the showman in Moonves. The CBS chieftain, then 24 days into his solo run as CEO of his own CBS Corp. empire, was confident he could sell their vision of the future to a tough, discerning crowd. And Meyer had every confidence in Moonves.

"This is an historic occasion," Moonves intoned, over the din of clicking camera shutters and other ambient sounds of a press conference. "The CW *will* be the fifth network."

As Moonves delivered one of the best performances of his executive career, outlining the vision for the network, the CBS-Warner Bros. partnership and the CW leadership team, Meyer looked around at the bank of cameras and reporters and surprisingly felt a sense of relief. Finally, they were able to speak publicly about their plans. Finally, he could gush about his enthusiasm about the potential for the merger that had hurtled to completion during the previous six weeks.

When the time for questions came, Moonves, Meyer, and Tribune's Dennis FitzSimons sat on high-perched director's chairs and batted questions from reporters and beamed. There were tough, skeptical questions lobbed but overall the veteran executives could read the reporters well enough to know that the reaction was generally positive. Or at least not overly negative. Moonves in particular was charged up and clearly enjoying the fact that they'd been able to keep the news under wraps. Meyer and FitzSimons had an unmistakable hint of relief on their faces beneath their broad smiles.

"There are moments in time," Meyer told the media horde in discussing the rationale behind the merger. "This is the moment in time."*

On the day the WB died, I happened to be in my office early. About four months before, I'd taken the plunge as an executive again, this time as president of entertainment for the female-oriented cable network Lifetime Television, where Dawn Ostroff worked before UPN.

I'd made a point of not seriously considering any executive job offers that came my way in the months after I left the WB. I needed some time to adjust, and I didn't want to wind up with the wrong business card for my second act.

My time as a "nonwriting producer," as most executives-turned-producers are known, had been enlightening. It had been a rollercoaster ride, frequently unsettling but thoroughly educational. For most of my TV career I'd worked for really big media companies. All of a sudden, I was working for me. First, I had an office on the Warner Bros.' lot and funds from the studio to buy scripts, court writers and actors, but it was not the same as working for a network. All of a sudden in the summer of 2001, I looked around and I realized I was now working for myself. The only television shows I'd be involved with were the ones that I pieced together on my own, from scratch. I wasn't going to pick pilots in the spring of 2002; I was going to have to make one and sell it.

Through the next couple of years, I had a range of interesting producing gigs, some fun, some vexing. I had the thrill of getting a

---

*   *The Hollywood Reporter*, January 25, 2006, "Network Nuptials."

comedy series picked up for NBC's fall 2002 prime-time schedule, *Hidden Hills*, and I endured the agony of watching it die after 17 episodes, or two-thirds of a season.

By the summer of 2005, I'd done some consulting work for cable networks, so when a corporate headhunter called to inquire about my interest in the vacant job as entertainment president at the cable network Lifetime, I was ready, and I was energized by the opportunity. Once I got back into executive mode, it was like riding a bicycle. I hadn't forgotten how to do it, or how to work long and hard to get things done.

On the morning of January 24, 2006, I was in my office in a corner of the Lifetime offices in a glass-box high rise in Century City, just down the street from Fox. I was there earlier than usual that day, before my assistant arrived. I almost didn't answer the call that came through on my direct line in an effort to focus on some work that I needed to finish. But because you just never know, I picked up the receiver on the fourth or fifth ring.

"Susanne?" I heard a voice ask.

"How are you?" I replied. I knew it was Garth Ancier before he'd finished saying my name.

"I want you to know what's going on. There's going to be an announcement shortly," Ancier said.

Garth took a deep breath and gently, dispassionately filled me in on the details of the UPN-WB merger talks. He didn't say anything about his own situation until I asked. He sounded resigned to the fact that management plans for the CW Network didn't include him. That was in keeping with his pragmatic nature. He was always one to talk me down from hysterics by analyzing a situation and coming up with a list of potential responses to address the problem.

As the magnitude of what Ancier was telling me sunk in, at first all I could think of was who to blame. Why would Barry Meyer give up such a meaningful brand? Why had Garth insisted on killing the frog? Why did Jamie have to leave? What if I had never left?

Over the course of the day, friends and former coworkers called to ask me what I made of the situation. The flood of calls and reconnections made during the next few weeks had the effect of reminding me of just how many people had linked arms early on to build the WB. The grief we were sharing was not for the loss of the network as it existed in 2006 but the loss of the Camelot of the WB's first five years. It was delayed sadness for something that had died a long time ago. We were sad because we would no longer have the ability to point to the WB with pride as something we'd helped create.

In time, the calls eased up, and I stopped running into WB alumni with whom I hadn't discussed it all with at least once. Finally, the real post-mortem began, and our thoughts turned to the infernal question: What went wrong? How did the WB blow a 22-point lead in the fourth quarter and wind up losing the game at the buzzer? For months after the CW announcement, debates on why our network folded were a favorite parlor game of WB alumni.

The conventional wisdom was that the game changed in 2001 after Jamie Kellner went to Atlanta. Simply put, Kellner was the soul of the WB, and when his presence was not felt on a daily basis, the enterprise lost its way. There is real truth to that theory. All of a sudden Jamie was in another time zone; I was in a producer's office on the Warner Bros.' lot and Garth was back with Jamie in Atlanta tinkering with CNN. There is also truth to the theory that letting go of *Buffy the Vampire Slayer* in that same tumultuous year was the crucial mistake that felled the WB. It was a highly public fumble that spoke volumes about where the WB was—and was not—in its growth curve as a network at the time.

There is even more tangible truth to be found in the theory, favored by business-minded types, that might be called the station factor. Or to borrow a political metaphor: it's the lack of stations, stupid. In this school of thought, Paramount's anti-WB spin at the beginning of our adventure was right on target: Time Warner would never truly commit to the WB so long as it didn't own a single WB affiliate. It's a truism of television that networks don't make money; owned-and-operated stations do. A network's owned-and-operated television stations generate cash flow 24 hours a day, which helps the parent company pay for all of that expensive prime-time programming. As successful as the WB was, our expenditures on programming and marketing grew exponentially as the audience expected more and more from us. Reverse comp didn't cut it. Without a steady income from TV stations to offset those costs, our business model was always going to be a challenge to execute successfully.

In addition, there is the irrefutable fact that the WB hit a slump starting in 2002 that extended into four straight seasons without a significant new hit. It's hard to keep a prime-time schedule vibrant after a few years without any reinforcements.

For others, the dissolution of the WB and UPN stands as an indictment of the television industry's lurch into vertical integration after the death of fin-syn and the regulatory overhaul of the mid-1990s. From the get-go, the disconnect between the WB and Warner Bros. Television, and UPN and Paramount Television stands as empirical evidence of how futile it can be to mandate creative collaboration between two distinct organizations. The WB got all of its important early hits from rivals of Warner Bros. Television. At the same time, it was World Wrestling Entertainment, not Paramount, that saved UPN from its near-death experience. The later Warner Bros.' TV-WB experience proved that vertical integration only worked if there were good vibes and good collaboration among the executives running the network and the television studio. That's not something you can mandate on a business plan.

It's also very true that the pressure-cooker environment is only heightened in situations where the parent company is on the hook for every penny of production cost on the pilot, the network license fee, and the cost of making up the potential ratings shortfalls to advertisers, if necessary. Given the chance, most writers over the age of 35 would elect to go back to the earlier era when the major studios and a fair number of sizable independent production outfits competed fiercely for creative talent and had every fiduciary incentive to pin the network down for the best possible financial deal they could wrangle.

There's a logic and an order to each of these theories, and each helps explain the complicated reasons why the WB's light went out for good on September 17, 2006. But from my vantage point there was no more important turning point than the morning of January 10, 2000, which brought the news of America Online's stock-swap merger with Time Warner. We were barely a week into the New Year. We thought we'd safely gotten past the fears of a Y2K meltdown as the new year dawned. We were wrong.

More than anything else, the AOL acquisition cost the surviving company any good will it might have with investors to float a strategic asset like the WB. The $55 billion write-down the company was forced to take following the merger, the Securities and Exchange Commission and Justice Department investigations, and the accusations of fraud and mismanagement put Time Warner's surviving corporate managers (all of them from the Time Warner side) into a cost-cutting, streamlining frenzy. With Leslie Moonves offering them a way out of the debt trench through the CW merger, how could Barry Meyer and Bruce Rosenblum say no, in all good fiduciary conscience?

Meyer and Rosenblum were duty bound to seek out alternatives for the WB because the network was first, last, and always, a business. For the people that built it brick by brick in the 1990s, however, it was always something more. It was a cause, an all-consuming passion. You wanted to work hard for Jamie Kellner to help him build the second new broadcast network of our lifetimes. We were a family. No kidding.

It was gut-wrenching, to put it mildly, for WB veterans to watch the UPN side take the reins during the CW transitional period in 2006. We respected what Dawn Ostroff and Leslie Moonves had accomplished at UPN, at long last. But the Sharks-vs.-Jets rivalry between the WB and UPN had been raging so fiercely for so long, it wasn't easy to turn it off on a dime.

In the research for this book I've talked to Jamie, Garth, John Maatta, and many other WB alums at length about what we *should* have done to keep the WB alive—whether we should have migrated it to a cable channel while we had the chance; or moved faster in getting some inexpensive unscripted programs on the air; and on and on.

In the contemporary environment of what many call personalized digital-media entertainment options, the idea of two giant media conglomerates embarking on a footrace to launch the fifth network seems quaint.

In 1995, the average American household with cable TV service received 41 channels. In 2006, it was 104, according to Nielsen Media Research. We are overrun with new channels and new screens. Every teenager with an Internet connection and a digital video camera can be the star of his or her own video-enabled blog. The notion of what a television network is to its audience is being redefined by devices and services that allow viewers to mix and match and program their own networks, on their own schedules. These are the kids who grew up on the WB as teens and young adults, and they have never known a world without Internet access, cell phones, and *South Park*.

In hindsight, it seems the WB was destined to run the course that it did. The WB and UPN emerged as a bridge between the rise of Fox and cable alternatives to the Big Three networks in the 1980s and the multichannel, multiscreen explosion of the past decade. The audience that was once dedicated to prime-time network television is splintering into ever-more discreet niches, spread among more platforms and types of entertainment than ever before.

Can it be that the timing of our arrival on the scene was spectacularly bad? Or did we help move television along to where we are today? The only thing that is certain at this juncture is that there will never be another broadcast network launch in the WB-UPN mold again. The era of a start-up network chasing after affiliate stations in markets throughout the country is over.

Dean Valentine has spent a lot of his post-UPN years thinking about these questions, too, as he's dabbled in various media ventures.

"UPN and the WB form a part of the story of media's evolution. They were [ventures] banking on the value of distribution at a time when the value of distribution was being undercut by the evolution of technology and the economics," Valentine observes.

And yet for all of the advancement we've seen, there's still something so fundamentally intimate and uniquely captivating about old-fashioned linear television at its best. It's what makes broadcast television such an attractive medium for creative people. I got a powerful reminder of that magic about three weeks before the WB signed off for the last time.

I was sitting in a red plush-velvet seat, front and center at Los Angeles' Shrine Auditorium on the night of the Primetime Emmy Awards ceremony. My husband, writer-producer Greg Daniels, and the creative team he leads as executive producer of NBC's *The Office* were nominated for best comedy series for their adaptation of the hit British series of the same name. The show hadn't been on the air very long. It was considered an extreme long shot to win. Greg and I and my parents and our eldest daughter Haley were relaxing in the "it's a thrill to be nominated" sentiment and enjoying the inventive comedy of Conan O'Brien, who is an old college friend and writing partner of Greg's.

Even after a long night of awards presentations and clever banter, it came like a bolt out of the blue to hear Bob Newhart announce *The Office* as the comedy series winner. Amid the roar of the applause, the hoots and shouts of congratulations to Greg and his staff, I watched my husband make his way up to the stage to accept his statuette.

What really got my heart pounding was seeing O'Brien throw his arms around Greg when he got up to the stage. I knew they were both thinking of how far they'd come since their salad days at Harvard, and of their time sharing a crummy little apartment in Los Angeles while both were starting out in the industry. It would have been unthinkable to imagine back then that one day Conan would be the red-hot late-night comic, hosting the Emmys and handing Greg the award for best comedy series.

For me, that one-in-a-million moment encapsulated everything I love about the television business. It's unpredictable, rollicking, and untamable one minute and conquerable the next. It's all about smoke and mirrors, and yet smarts and hard work can pay off, with a little luck. It dawned on me as Greg was making his witty acceptance speech that it was a lucky and wondrous combination of all those factors that made our WB experience so special, so unforgettable.

Jamie Kellner was right. We did good work, sometimes great work, on our best nights. I am proud to have been a part of it.

THAT'S ALL, FOLKS!

The gong was the first thing partygoers saw as they made their way up the windy landscaped steps leading to the front entrance of Garth Ancier's Beverly Hills home. Along the entryway at the top landing, a small strip of red carpet was placed in front of a seven-foot WB-logo-embossed screen backdrop, the kind of thing propped up at press conferences and premiere parties to give photo-ops the proper branding effect. It was not likely to be needed again after that Sunday night, September 17, 2006.

Eight months after the WB and UPN were rendered lame ducks with the CW merger announcement, WB's last night on the air was commemorated with the airing of the pilots of four shows that became synonymous with the frog network—*Felicity, Angel, Buffy the Vampire Slayer,* and *Dawson's Creek.* Ancier bankrolled a party on the night of the farewell for about 400 network alumni, from executive assistants to showrunners.

The weather that evening was late-summer Southern California perfect, balmy and shirtsleeves-comfortable well into the night. Jamie Kellner came in wearing khaki shorts and well-worn Topsider deck shoes. Garth was easy to spot in a sherbet-orange dress shirt and snug Levis. Wine from Ancier's considerable collection flowed freely, as did partygoers around his multi-level backyard, candle-lit and outfitted with dozens of posters and glamour photos of WB shows and stars. Television monitors showing the network's final hours on Los Angeles affiliate station KTLA-TV were sprinkled around the party areas. Beside the front door, the lightly tarnished gong that once reverberated through the WB's trailers was a bittersweet reminder of happier times.

There would be no such fanfare for UPN's departure. Dawn Ostroff and her team were preoccupied with the launch of CW on Wednesday, September 20. In most of the country, UPN's last night of programming was Friday, September 15, with two hours of World Wrestling Entertainment's *Friday Night SmackDown!* By 2006, short of Ostroff, there was no one invested enough in the network's legacy to arrange for anything more thoughtful. And she was preoccupied with stitching together the CW's patchwork quilt of shows.

Not so for the WB. Garth and a handful of staffers threw themselves into planning "A Night of Favorites and Farewells," as it was billed on the air and on Ancier's invitations. The preparatory work began with a debate among Ancier and a handful of WB staffers (and a few alumni advisers) on which shows to run. The last night happened to be a Sunday, which gave them five hours to work with, thanks to the extra 7 p.m. hour of prime time on Sundays coupled with the WB's long-standing 5–7 p.m. repeat block on the night.

Ancier and company settled quickly on the idea of running a night of maiden voyages. The WB like no other network during the previous decade had been gifted with a string of standout hour-long series pilots. These were pilots that did their jobs, establishing characters, mood, setting, tone, look, and feel in an engaging way in 42- to 44-odd minutes. The inclusion of *Buffy* in the lineup was a given, though it fell to Joss Whedon to remind Garth that the pilot was a two-parter, and thus needed a two-hour time slot. *Dawson's Creek* and *Felicity* were also no-brainers, but the fourth slot was a wildcard.

Garth wanted it to be something special, not a show that would continue on CW, i.e., *7th Heaven, Smallville,* or *Gilmore Girls,* nor a show that had just signed off the air in May, which ruled out *Charmed* and *Everwood.* So *Angel* it was, in a nod to the enduring power of the *Buffy*-verse. And it was telling for the legacy of the WB that each of those signature pilots came from a studio other than Warner Bros.:

20th Century Fox Television for *Buffy* and *Angel*; Disney's Touchstone Television in the case of *Felicity*; and Sony Pictures Television for *Dawson's Creek*. Securing the one-time rights to air the pilots from the outside studios had been trickier than Ancier expected, but he greased the wheels with the brainstorm that each studio would get a free spot to promote their DVD box set collections for each show.

Ancier and marketing staffers combed through the WB's archives of promotional photo and video shoots of the casts of its shows. The sentimental promo spots that ran on the network's last few nights were the last hurrah of the WB's marketing machine. To send off the WB in style, Bob Bibb and Lew Goldstein pulled out all the emotional stops. They assembled a number of nostalgic clip reels of WB stars at promo shoots over the years, interspersed with fade-in title cards featuring the actors' names and year they first appeared on the WB. The spots were bathed in dark primary colors and soft focus, and set to the 1999 lovesick power-pop ballad "Crawl" by Thisway, dripping with violins and hard-rock vocals.

The WB farewell party began at 5 p.m., just as the title character in *Felicity* was graduating from high school in the show's opening sequence. Bob Bibb was among the first to arrive. Leaning against the back of a large L-shaped, pillow-strewn sofa, Bob and Garth watched the first few minutes of *Felicity* on the giant-screen overhead projection TV in Garth's den next to the outdoor patio that was filling up with guests.

At the pivotal scene early on where Keri Russell flashes a twinkly smile at the camera and impetuously decides to follow her high school crush to New York City, Bob and Garth took a moment to exchange compliments—not in a backslapping way, but more as asides as their eyes stayed glued to the screen. They gave color-commentary on a well-executed pilot and marketing campaign that had made *Felicity* a pop culture sensation eight years before.

Sipping a glass of red wine, Bob wondered aloud whether *Felicity*'s premise would still work in post-September 11 America, whether New York still held the same romantic sway. Ancier pondered the thought but was soon swept away into new conversations as more guests flowed in. Like Ancier and Bibb, there were many such pauses among friends that night to acknowledge good work, good times, and great people. And it was fortunate, many observed, that some time had passed between the jolt of the shutdown news in January and the sign off in mid-September.

In the clusters that gathered in Ancier's backyard, the vibe was as much family reunion as emotional farewell. I brought my daughter Haley. Bruce Rosenblum, by this time promoted to president of the Warner Bros. Television Group, came with his 18-year-old daughter, the night before the two of them would make the drive up to northern California for her freshman year of university. She was kindergarten-age when the WB was born in 1993. I remembered attending her bat mitzvah. I caught up with many old friends, including Lew and his wife Carolyn, who were expecting their first child.

There was chatter about new jobs landed, opportunities being pursued, situations wanted, and life-changing alternatives under consideration. There was a little awkwardness between the newly unemployed and the few who made the transition to CW. But the deepest vein of resentment, even eight months later, stemmed not from the fact of their unemployment but rather from the feeling that somehow, UPN had managed to win the war even if the WB took most of the battles. CW may have been structured as a 50/50 partnership between Warner Bros. and CBS Corp., but there was no doubt from the moment Dawn Ostroff was named CW entertainment president she and Leslie Moonves were calling the key shots.

That resentment was audible in the groans let loose every so often when promotional spots and pop-up graphics for CW intruded on the screen during the WB's long good-bye. As the party wore on, the conversations grew more animated, and in some cases more contemplative about a string of what-ifs, each of them unanswerable, but nagging just the same to WB alumni.

Jamie Kellner, on the other hand, didn't look like a man whose sails were trimmed by regrets; quite the contrary. He moved around the party like a lion in autumn, warmly greeting the receiving lines that formed around him. Friends and former staffers remarked on how rested and at ease he looked, how long his hair seemed to be now that he'd been out of office for more than two years. He told them he was enjoying a slower pace of life after 35 years of hard-driving as an entertainment executive, including nearly 20 years of network bricklaying at Fox and the WB. He commented to some that there wasn't anything out there that could tempt him back into the CEO rat race. In his view, the business just wasn't fun anymore.

Five nights before the party at Ancier's house, John Maatta organized a dinner in tribute to Ancier and his contributions to the WB for about two dozen core insiders at an of-the-moment Los Angeles eatery that Maatta knew would appeal to the gourmet in Garth. Ancier arrived expecting a dinner for two. He thought it was a typically thoughtful gesture from Maatta, a nod to the time and energy they'd put in to build, and later attempt to save, the network. Ancier was floored when he walked into the private room. The turnout included Jamie, Barry Meyer, Bruce Rosenblum, Bob and Lew, Brad Turell, and most of the core WB launch team. I arrived late, but Garth saved me a seat next to him at the center of the table. That little gesture meant a lot to me.

Toasts and wine flowed all night, and all around the table, in tribute to Ancier, to Kellner, to a job well done and an exceptional team. The oratory was spurred by the wine and the moment, even among those who hadn't planned on speaking, eloquently or otherwise. Kellner impressed everyone the most with the gratitude he extended to Ancier and to "everyone at this table" for working so hard to create the WB.

"We had never heard him say [thank you] in that way before," says one who earned a seat at that table.

Noticeably absent, however, from Ancier's farewell dinner and the September 17 finale party was Jordan Levin. Levin called a number of his former WB colleagues on the day of Ancier's party to tell them he had to be out of town that night for an alumni board meeting at his University of Texas alma mater. It was no secret that relations between Levin and Ancier had been chilly since Levin's ouster from the WB two years before.

By the time the *Dawson's Creek* pilot began at 9 p.m. on the night of the finale, the crowd at Ancier's had gathered on the top landing around Ancier's rectangular pool and glass-front pool house. A wide-screen TV set was placed just outside the long sliding glass door. The din of conversation quieted as the hour advanced and more people crowded around the TV set. The volume was turned up. As I walked up the concrete steps leading to the pool area, I was ushered into the center of the crowd, directly in front of the TV. Garth announced it was almost time for the final-final farewell spot.

The crowd was quiet during the last few minutes of the *Dawson's Creek* pilot. Doe-eyed Joey was getting ready to climb out of a window in Dawson's bedroom and declare an end to their platonic innocence as best friends—forever. And that meant that plenty of people in the crowd with a special feeling for *Dawson's Creek*—myself included—were about to mist up.

And then came the go-for-broke, heart-tugging, Gen-Y button-pushing WB farewell. It was a sumptuous 60 seconds.

> *For 11 years*
> *you brought us into your homes.*
> *We made you smile*
> *and tugged at your heart,*
> *and now, we say goodbye.*
> *From all of us at the WB*
> *Thank you.*

The spot echoed the WB's opening-night segment with Bugs Bunny and Daffy Duck by featuring *Smallville* stars Tom Welling and Michael Rosenbaum sauntering through a busy Warner Bros.' soundstage exchanging banter until they bump into Michigan J. Frog. After a pause, a hop by Michigan J. gave way to a soft-focus cavalcade of stars from various eras of the WB, from Shawn and Marlon Wayans and Jamie Foxx to Stephen Collins and Treat Williams, from Sarah Michelle Gellar and David Boreanaz, to the sexy vitality of the *Dawson's Creek* kids.

There was no voice-over, only slow fade-ins and fade-outs of each line of the "For 11 years" farewell message, interspersed with the clips of the actors and set to a longer cut of the ballad "Crawl." As the slideshow faded, Michigan J. Frog hopped into the center of the screen, sporting his trademark top hat and tails. He took a last quick bow but kept his head upright and eyes fixed on the viewer as he and a "Thank you" slate faded to white.

Garth and Jamie stood side by side in the middle of the crowd as it whooped and cheered and let out a collective "awwwww" and a long round of applause at the end. The nostalgic spell was broken after about 10 seconds when a local female news anchor's head filled the screen and began chirping about highlights of the 10 o'clock news. There were groans when the elongated CW logo popped up as part of the station's logo graphic in the right-hand corner of the screen.

We were all moved by the moment. Everyone was hugging. I felt so grateful to Garth for orchestrating such a classy sign-off. Amid the huddle of well-wishes, Garth felt an arm wrap itself gently around his neck. It was Kellner, administering a bear hug. Although the network had its peculiar struggles as a business, we'd managed to achieve the kind of emotionally satisfying closure we'd given viewers in our best shows. And Kellner's legacy as a television visionary, or "television-ary" as we called him, was now 100 percent secure.

As a boss, Kellner could be infuriatingly tight-fisted, sometimes thin-skinned, mischievous, and insensitive to others. For all of his high-minded talk of creating a meritocracy where ideas are welcomed and contributions valued, he also created an atmosphere of haves and have-nots among the WB's senior executives.

Yet for all his flaws, Kellner had always been revered within the WB, and by no one more than me. Kellner was a bold and dynamic leader to a group of ambitious, competitive people who wanted to change the face of network television with the WB. Jamie was the guy who led the charge that let us do just that.

Kellner's mood that warm Sunday night in Ancier's backyard was reminiscent of our best times at the WB. Even Mr. Cool was impressed by the depth of feeling that existed among WB alums for the network they were all there to let go of. That bond was on display at

Ancier's surprise dinner, and it was palpable a few days later among the 150 or so who made it through the final minutes in the huddle beside Garth's pool.

The euphoria we all felt for what the WB had once been was so strong in the first few minutes after the sign-off that Kellner even commented on it to an outsider who was fortunate enough to be in the crowd that night.

"There are a lot of people who worked very hard here," Kellner observed, smiling broadly as he swiveled around to survey the scene. "A lot of people who really cared."

WHERE ARE THEY NOW?

Jamie Kellner—Remains the chairman and CEO of Acme Communications television station group, but otherwise retired from the media business.

Kerry McCluggage—Chairman of Los Angeles-based film, TV, and video distribution firm Allumination Filmworks.

Lucie Salhany—Partner in Echo Bridge Entertainment, a movie and TV distribution company based in Needham, Mass. Echo Bridge's employees include former UPN distribution head Kevin Tannehill.

Garth Ancier—Appointed CEO of BBC Worldwide America cable channel in February 2007.

Barry Meyer—Weathered the AOL Time Warner turbulence and remains at Warner Bros. as chairman and CEO.

Bruce Rosenblum—Promoted to president of Warner Bros. Television Group in September 2005. Remains top lieutenant and close confidant of Meyer's.

Bob Daly—resigned from Warner Bros. in July 1999; served as managing partner and CEO of the Los Angeles Dodgers from 1999 until 2004.

Jordan Levin—Co-founded Santa Monica, Calif.-based talent management and production company Generate in 2006.

Dean Valentine—Heads Symbolic Action LLC, investment fund with numerous investments "focused on the convergence of content and technology."

Tom Nunan—Partner in film and TV production company Bull's Eye Entertainment.

Bob Bibb and Lewis Goldstein—Partners in their own media and marketing consulting firm; have reunited with Susanne Daniels as marketing consultants to Lifetime Television.

Jed Petrick—Relocated to New York after leaving WB in January 2004.

Brad Turell—Appointed head of corporate communications for Hollywood talent agency Paradigm in May 2007.

Dennis FitzSimons—Named CEO of Tribune Co. in January 2003.